ESSAYS ON
THE
CLOSING
OF THE
AMERICAN
M · I · N · D

EDITED BY
ROBERT L. STONE

CHICAGO REVIEW PRESS

Library of Congress Cataloging-in-Publication Data

Essays on the closing of the American mind / edited by Robert L.
  Stone. — 1st ed.
    p. cm.
  ISBN 1-55652-052-2 : $11.95
  1. Bloom, Allan David, 1930–   .   The closing of the American
mind.   2. United States—Intellectual life—20th century.
3. Education, Higher—United States—Philosophy.   I. Stone, Robert
L.
E169.1.B6533E85   1989
973.92—dc19   89-771
                                                                 CIP

Published by Chicago Review Press, Incorporated
814 North Franklin Street
Chicago, Illinois 60610

Manufactured in the United States of America
by Banta Book System
Cover design by Jack Foster
Book design by Fran Lee
123456789

To my parents,
for inspiring
my
American mind

Contents

Introduction   xiii

ONE
Spirited Discussion Transcends the Usual Labels of Left and Right

Introduction   **3**

1. Thomas D'Evelyn, "The Schooling of American Democracy," *Christian Science Monitor* (3 July 1987).   **4**

2. Robert Pattison, "On the Finn Syndrome and the Shakespeare Paradox," *Nation* (30 May 1987): 710–19.   **7**

3. Paul Gottfried, "A Half-Open Mind," *Chronicles: A Magazine of American Culture* 11, no. 9 (September 1987): 30–33.   **12**

4. Richard Bernstein, "A 'Minute of Hatred' in Chapel Hill: Academia's Liberals Defend Their Carnival of Canons Against Bloom's 'Killer B's,'" *New York Times*, 25 September 1988: 26.   **15**

5. Robert Paul Wolff, "Book Review: *The Closing of the American Mind*," *Academe* (September–October 1987): 64–65.   **18**

6. Werner J. Dannhauser, "Allan Bloom and the Critics," *American Spectator* (October 1988): 17–20.   **22**

TWO
How Did Allan Bloom Write a Bestseller?

Introduction   **31**

7. William Goldstein, "The Story Behind the Bestseller: Allan Bloom's *The Closing of the American Mind*," *Publishers Weekly* (3 July 1987): 25–27.   **33**

8. Christopher Lehmann-Haupt, "Book Review: *The Closing of the American Mind*," *New York Times*, 23 March 1987: 13.   **37**

9. Henry Allen, "The Right Absolute Allan Bloom," *Washington Post,* 18 June 1987, Style Section: C1–C3.   **39**

10. William Kristol, "Troubled Souls: Where We Went Wrong," *Wall Street Journal,* 22 April 1987: 30.   **44**

11. Michael W. Hirschorn, "A Professor Decries Closing of the American Mind," *Chronicle of Higher Education* (6 May 1987): 3.   **47**

12. Will Morrisey, "How Bloom Did It: Rhetoric and Principle in *The Closing of the American Mind,*" *Interpretation* 16, no. 1 (Fall 1988): 145–56.   **51**

THREE
Bloom in the Classroom:
Students and Colleagues Pay Tribute to a Spellbinding Teacher

Introduction   **63**

13. John Podhoretz, "An Open Letter to Allan Bloom," *National Review* (9 October 1987): 34–37.   **64**

14. James Atlas, "Chicago's Grumpy Guru: Best-Selling Professor Allan Bloom and the Chicago Intellectuals," *New York Times Magazine* 3 January 1988: 12–31.   **68**

15. Michael P. Zuckert, "Two Cheers (At Least) for Allan Bloom" (paper presented to symposium, The Modern University—From Bologna to Bloom, held at Rhode Island University, March 1988).   **73**

FOUR
Bloom on Democracy: Is He an Elitist?

Introduction   **79**

16. Benjamin Barber, "The Philosopher Despot: Allan Bloom's Elitist Agenda," *Harper's Magazine* (January 1988): 61–65.   **81**

17. Werner J. Dannhauser, "Allan Bloom and the Critics." See #6   **89**

18. H. D. Forbes, "Opening the Open Mind," *Idler* 17 (May–June 1988): 47–52.   **90**

19. Robert N. Bellah, "Academic Fundamentalism?," *New Oxford Review* 54, no. 6 (July–August 1987): 22–24.   **91**

20. Richard Rorty, "Straussianism, Democracy, and Allan Bloom I: That Old Time Philosophy," *New Republic* (4 April 1988): 28–33.   **94**

21. H. D. Forbes, "Opening the Open Mind." See #18   **104**

22. Werner J. Dannhauser, "Allan Bloom and the Critics." See #6   **105**

23. Harvey C. Mansfield, Jr., "Straussianism, Democracy, and Allan Bloom II:

Democracy and the Great Books," *New Republic* (4 April 1988):
28–33.   **106**

24. Jeff Lyon, "America's Teacher: Mortimer J. Adler, the Nation's Self-Appointed Teacher for Most of His 85 Years, Takes On the 'Late-Bloomers' of Academe," *Chicago Tribune Magazine* 27 November 1988, sec. 10: 10–21.   **113**

25. William A. Galston, "Socratic Reason and Lockean Rights: The Place of the University in a Liberal Democracy," *Interpretation* 16, no. 1 (Fall 1988): 101–10.   **119**

FIVE

Bloom on Philosophy: Is He a Nihilist?

Introduction   **127**

26. Harry V. Jaffa, "Humanizing Certitudes and Impoverishing Doubts: A Critique of *The Closing of the American Mind*," *Interpretation* 16, no. 1 (Fall 1988): 111–38.   **129**

27. Christopher Colmo, "Allan Bloom and the American Premise."   **154**

28. Shadia B. Drury, "Allan Bloom on the Charms of Culture."   **158**

29. Thomas G. West, "Allan Bloom and America," *Claremont Review of Books* 6, no. 1 (Spring 1988): 1, 17–20.   **166**

30. Charles R. Kesler, "The Closing of Allan Bloom's Mind: An Instant Classic Reconsidered," *American Spectator* 20, no. 8 (August 1987): 14–17.   **174**

31. Eva Brann, "The Spirit Lives in the Sticks," *St. John's Review* 38, no. 1 (1988): 71–79.   **181**

SIX

The Death of Love and Decline of the Family:
Is Bloom Anti-Feminist?

Introduction   **191**

32. Allan Bloom, "Too Much Tolerance," *New Perspectives Quarterly* 4, no. 4 (Winter 1988): 6–13.   **192**

33. Betty Friedan, "Fatal Abstraction," *New Perspectives Quarterly* 4, no. 4 (Winter 1988): 14–19.   **195**

34. Martha Nussbaum, "Undemocratic Vistas," *New York Review of Books* 34, no. 17 (5 November 1987): 20–26.   **198**

35. Werner J. Dannhauser, "Allan Bloom and the Critics." See #6   **211**

36. Pamela Proietti, "American Feminists *versus* Allan Bloom?"   **213**

SEVEN
Minority Groups in the University:
Is Bloom Right About Affirmative Action?

Introduction   221

37. Werner J. Dannhauser, "Allan Bloom and the Critics." See #6   222

38. Richard L. Wright, "Book Review: *The Closing of the American Mind*," *Journal of Negro Education* 57, no. 1 (Winter 1988): 119–21.   223

39. George Anastaplo, "Allan Bloom and Race Relations in the United States" (paper presented to the Institute of Human Values, Canadian Learned Societies Conference, Windsor, Ontario, 10 June 1988).   225

EIGHT
Bloom on Rock Music

Introduction   237

40. Allan Bloom, "Too Much Tolerance." See #32   239

41. Jessica Branson, "Keeping the American Mind Shut," *U-High Midway* 63, no. 1 (16 September 1987): 2.   241

42. Scripps Howard News Service, "Like, Man, Where'd You Put the Food?," *Chicago Tribune* 8 April 1988, sec. 1: 27.   243

43. William Greider, "Bloom and Doom," *Rolling Stone* (8 October 1987): 39–40.   244

44. Frank Zappa, "On Junk Food for the Soul," *New Perspectives Quarterly* 4, no. 4 (Winter 1988): 26–29.   248

45. Steven Crockett, "Blam! Bam! Bloom! Boom!"   253

NINE
Does Bloom Exaggerate and Oversimplify?

Introduction   265

46. George Anastaplo, "In re Allan Bloom: A Respectful Dissent," *Great Ideas Today* (an Encyclopedia Britannica publication, 1988): 252–73.   267

47. John Marcham, "Universities Had No Alternative But to Make Unpopular Decisions," *Cornell Alumni News* (November 1987): 27–30.   285

48. David Rieff, "The Colonel and the Professor," *Times Literary Supplement* (4 September 1987): 950, 960.   290

49. Jean Bethke Elshtain, "Allan in Wonderland," *Cross Currents* 37, no. 4 (Winter 1987–88): 476–79.   296

50. Louis Menand, "Mr. Bloom's Planet," *New Republic* (25 May 1987): 38–41.   300

TEN

Relativism and the Decline of Public Morality:
Can Religion Cure Our Ills?

Introduction **307**

51. William R. Marty, "Athens and Jerusalem in *The Closing of the American Mind.*" **308**

ELEVEN

The University in Democratic Society:
What is Its Proper Role?

Introduction **331**

52. Timothy Fuller, "The Vocation of the University and the Uses of the Past: Reflections on Bloom and Hirsch." **333**

53. F. Russell Hittinger, "Reason and Anti-Reason in the Academy," *Intercollegiate Review* (Fall 1987): 61–64. **338**

54. John Van Doren, "Mr. Bloom, the American Mind, and Paideia," *Paideia Bulletin* 3, no. 5 (November–December 1987): 1–2. **342**

55. Tom Hayden, "Our Finest Moment," *New Perspectives Quarterly* 4, no. 4 (Winter 1988): 20–25. **344**

56. Walter Nicgorski, "Faculty Reactions to *The Closing of the American Mind,*" *Programma*, Program of Liberal Studies, Notre Dame University (1988): 8–9. **350**

57. J. M. Cameron, "Academic Problems and Cosmic Solutions" (paper presented to the Canadian Learned Societies Conference, Windsor, Ontario, June 1988). **353**

58. Gregory B. Smith, "Old Books, New Prejudices, and Perennial Questions." **359**

59. Editorials, "The Stanford Mind," *Wall Street Journal*, 22 December 1988: A12, cols. 1, 2. **362**

60. Michael Vannoy Adams, Charles Junkerman, and Allan Bloom, "Responses to 'The Stanford Mind,'" Letters to the Editor, *Wall Street Journal* 4 January 1989, 6 January 1989, 27 January 1989. **366**

61. Bill Honig, "What's Right About Bloom?," *New Perspectives Quarterly* 4, no. 4 (Winter 1988): 36–39. **370**

62. William T. Braithwaite, "Mr. Bloom and His Critics: What Could It All Mean?" **373**

Bibliography **377**

Introduction

Once each generation or so a book worth reading catches the fancy of Americans and becomes a "publishing phenomenon," one of those special books that both reflects and reinforces the state of its readers' minds. Allan Bloom's *The Closing of the American Mind* has provoked and inspired a million purchases, and sales are still going strong. More importantly, *Closing* has acted as a lightning rod attracting a spirited debate illuminated by flashes of wit and profundity and punctuated by explosions of passion. Praise and blame come from Left and Right alike, as may be seen in chapter 1 of this collection. Such a phenomenon offers an opportunity to see briefly lit, now in splendor, now in desolation, the broad and darkling plain of American politics.

Chapter 2 focuses on the favorable, early reviews that launched the Bloom phenomenon. The initial reviewers seem to have read *Closing* with a shock of recognition. Their articles, appearing in the *New York Times*, the *Washington Post*, the *Wall Street Journal*, and the *Chronicle of Higher Education* (essays 8 through 11), seem to say, "Hey, this book is about our generation, the people we know. It's true. Bloom has accurately portrayed and explained sexual love among American students and intellectual sterility among American educators. His book captures the specialists without spirit or vision and the voluptuaries without heart." "It commands one's attention and concentrates one's mind more effectively than any other book I can think of in the past five years," says Christopher Lehmann-Haupt in the *New York Times*.

What is Bloom's message? The key argument of *Closing* is simple and straightforward: people usually think and act as they have been taught. What Americans are taught today is influenced primarily by what goes on in the elite universities; the rest trickles down. The lessons taught in the elite universities are simply dreadful: truth, God, justice, and beauty are mere historical myths; therefore all morality is relative and arbitrary. So far, Bloom continues, America is living off the intellectual and moral capital stored up before the present rot set in at the top, but the political bill is coming due. Professional ethics in law and government, in medicine, and in the military have noticeably loosened in recent years. When higher education abdicates its role to teach what citizens need to make them both virtuous and competent, it has failed democracy as well as impoverished the souls of today's students. What then can be done to reverse the decline? According to Bloom, "Not much."

Exactly how it happened that the elite universities in the West came to teach harmful and false doctrines is a long and fascinating story, and Bloom tells it far better than this editor can. In short, American universities have fallen under the influence of German ideology. Immanuel Kant teaches that the existence or non-existence of God and the immortality of the soul cannot be known through reason. If so, Soren Kierkegaard seems to argue, the most important things can be known only, if at all, through religious faith. Can ethics and morality be part of reasoned political dialogue? Or can they be supported only by religious faith? If the latter is true, when that religious faith is gone, there is nothing left for man but the abyss or, for the credulous, Friedrich Nietzsche's life-affirming will to power through the "eternal return." Americans, on the other hand, traditionally believe that some truths are self-evident: that all men are created equal, that they are endowed by their Creator with certain unalienable rights, that among these are life, liberty, and the pursuit of happiness.

Collected in this book are sixty-two essays by journalists and educators responding to Bloom's message. From the pages of the *New York Times, Harper's,* and the *Wall Street Journal*—and from *Rolling Stone* and a high-school student's newspaper—the debate over *Closing* continues. Is it true, as Eva Brann argues in essay 31, that Bloom's book is the jeremiad of liberal education? Is a Jeremiah eagerly heard, a prophet honored in his own land, a prophet more than half refuted? All agree that the book, and the controversy it has inspired, is significant—a sign of our times.

The essays in chapter 3 provide first-hand accounts of Bloom's dedication to teaching and to his students, to whom he dedicated *Closing.* But some critics claim to have discovered many faults with Bloom's book. In chapter 4, several representatives of the liberal educational establishment attack Bloom's credibility. They accuse him of elitism and enmity to democracy. Harvey C. Mansfield, Jr., writing in the *New Republic* (essay 23), presents Bloom as a defender of democracy against its worst enemies and compares Bloom to Thomas Jefferson. Bloom defends conventional morality and the "natural aristocracy" only because these are necessary to support American democracy. Harry V. Jaffa, in a letter to the *New Republic* (not included here), congratulates Mansfield for the cleverness of his defense, but contends that the book he is defending is not the one Bloom wrote.

In chapter 5 a group of critics led by Jaffa, a prominent conservative, accuse Bloom of being an unAmerican nihilist, too closely allied with the Germans he criticizes. Christopher Colmo "defends" Bloom by showing the strength of Bloom's argument against Americanism. In chapter 6, prominent challengers of the conventional American family attack Bloom for being a "Neanderthal" who secretly is trying to enslave women. Betty Friedan's and Martha Nussbaum's bitter essays (33 and 34) are typical. Pamela Proietti presents a feminist defense of Bloom, arguing that families protect women instead of enslaving them. Chapter 7 then deals with the accusation that Bloom is a racist. Chapter 8 treats Bloom's attack upon rock music.

Chapter 9 collects five authors from diverse backgrounds and from different hemispheres who, although agreeing that there is some truth and some good in Bloom's book, have reservations about his passionate style and what they see as his tendency to exaggerate.

Chapter 10 is devoted entirely to an essay that addresses the paucity of overt references to religion and of concrete moral stances in *Closing*. Is this dearth a well-calculated rhetorical device, as Will Morrisey asserts in essay 12, or is it connected to the problems seen by the liberal critics in chapter 4, the conservative critics in chapter 5, and the diverse critics in chapter 9?

Chapter 11, the final chapter, addresses the larger political question raised by the phenomenal success of Bloom's book. What is the proper role of universities in a democracy? Universities, unlike most institutions in a democracy, aspire to be governed by, and to teach, reason as opposed to the will of the people. Also, higher education is selective and competitive. Thus it is inherently undemocratic. Is Bloom correct to say, then, that it is the proper purpose of America to support its universities, thereby subordinating democracy to aristocracy? Or are his critics correct to say that it is the proper purpose of aristocratic institutions such as the bar and the universities to serve democracy by moderating it?

More than three hundred reviews of Bloom's book are already in print. Ten others are printed here for the first time. (These are essays 15, 27, 28, 36, 39, 45, 51, 52, 58, and 62.) Even some excellent reviews had to be omitted. Readers are referred to the Bibliography at the end of this volume for an extensive list.

Because of limitations of space, almost all the essays in this collection had to be abbreviated. Cuts are the responsibility of the editor alone. They were made to avoid repetition in adapting the essays to a systematic examination of *Closing*. Where an essay appears promising but obviously incomplete, the reader is encouraged to consult the original publication or to write to the author for the complete, unpublished version. The headnote to each essay contains the information needed for further investigation in each case. Excised material is indicated by ellipses in the texts.

One final point: Bloom has understandably and quite properly made his reputation as a reviver of classical antiquity. No one should be misled by that fact, however. Bloom has said repeatedly in public lectures and in private conversations that we are all moderns. It is altogether fitting that his book won not the Plato or Aristotle but the Jean-Jacques Rousseau Award. This is a book about Rousseau's problem, our problem, the problem of the modern [American] soul, illumined by the glow of antiquity—not a pedantic tome evoking ghosts from the past.

ONE

Spirited Discussion Transcends the Usual Labels of Left and Right

This collection opens with Thomas D'Evelyn's warm, nonpartisan review of *The Closing of the American Mind* for the *Christian Science Monitor*. In D'Evelyn's view, Bloom's book "has the density of fiction, the sting of satire, the lucidity of philosophy;" it is a book for "authentic liberation," with "all the compact fluidity and dazzle of Emerson's essays."

Then Robert Pattison, writing in the *Nation*, praises Bloom from the Left as a "Platonic liberal" like Matthew Arnold—comparing Bloom both to Apollo, the god of music and healing, and to the Trinity (one indignant substance with three disgruntled persons: teacher, politician, and philosopher). Paul Gottfried, an editor of *The World and I*, writing in *Chronicles: A Magazine of American Culture*, attacks Bloom from the Right, arguing that Bloom cannot be a conservative because he agrees with Herbert Marcuse and Rousseau against religion and in favor of equality. Richard Bernstein, in "A 'Minute of Hatred' in Chapel Hill: Academia's Liberals Defend Their Carnival of Canons against Bloom's 'Killer B's,'" shows the fiercely defensive attitude that the liberal establishment has taken against Bloom's attack. Robert Paul Wolff, in *Academe*, mischievously surmises that "Bloom" is merely the evocative name of a fictitious character in a book, *The Closing of the American Mind*, written by Saul Bellow to satirize the shortcomings of the Committee on Social Thought where he and "Bloom" teach at the University of Chicago. The point is that Bloom's book transcends conventional partisan conflict between Left and Right, Liberal and Conservative. *The Closing of the American Mind* is a sign of the times.

Finally in this chapter, Werner J. Dannhauser, a friend of Bloom's, provides "Allan Bloom and the Critics," a critical overview of the essays that follow in this collection. Dannhauser humorously defends his friend's passion and honesty.

1

The Schooling of American Democracy

THOMAS D'EVELYN

Talking about the opening of a closed society, per *glasnost*, is one thing; talking about "the closing of the American mind," another. And yet, people are talking, and with reason. "The Closing of the American Mind" is the subject of an unlikely best seller by Allan Bloom.

This book has the density of fiction, the sting of satire, the lucidity of philosophy. It is itself part of the warp and woof of the American mind, whatever that is. Bloom's accomplishment helps define a fascinating problem, one noticed over a hundred years ago by Alexis de Tocqueville in "Democracy in America."

"In democratic communities," Tocqueville writes, "each citizen is habitually engaged in the contemplation of a very puny object: namely, himself. If he ever raises his looks higher, he perceives only the immense form of society at large or the still more imposing aspect of mankind. . . ."

To his credit, Allan Bloom—professor in the Committee of Social Thought at the University of Chicago, editor of editions of Plato and Rousseau, and author of "Shakespeare's Politics"—having contemplated his "puny self" long enough, looked away.

And when he looked away, he beheld an "immense form"—"the closing of the American mind"! His book by that title, which he calls an essay "for authentic liberation," has all the compact fluidity and dazzle of Emerson's essays. The title alone—including the subtitle, "How Higher Education Has Failed Democracy and Impoverished the Souls of Today's Students"—suggests his way of building words.

Is there such a thing as "the American mind"?

His title—a faint echo of "mind" as used by Henry Commager and Perry Miller—depends on it. As we shall see, the logical end of his analysis undermines it. In the process, though, the reader becomes aware of a set of contemporary problems very close to home, almost a modern, democratic syndrome: deregulation, commercial zeal, individualistic hedonism, pluralism.

At issue is the "closing" of the American mind. The word "closing" is loaded with philosophical (Bergson, Popper) and idiomatic (*closed society, closed minded*) dynamite. The opposite of "closed" is open (*open space, open for business, school's open!*). Bloom says that a new "openness"—a species of relativism that concludes every inquiry with "I'm OK, you're OK"—is part of the problem.

Ironically, "openness" toward truth is Bloom's norm and standard. This is

From the *Christian Science Monitor* (July 3, 1987). Reprinted with permission.

confirmed by the use of the word "soul" in the subtitle—not an evangelical soul to be saved, but Plato's "psyche," the mind open toward eternal truth.

What of Bloom's "soul"? As mirrored in this book, it's a philosophical battleground. And that's in the Platonic tradition, of which this book is a vigorous and flowering branch.

Bloom is a philosophical gladiator. An insight into this arena of thought is found in this passage from another student of Plato, Eric Voegelin: " . . .in the resistance of the philosopher to a society which destroys his soul originates the insight that the substance of a society is psyche. Society can destroy a man's soul because the disorder of society is a disease in the psyche of its members. The troubles which the philosopher experiences in his own soul are the troubles in the psyche of the surrounding society which press on him. And the diagnosis of health and disease in the soul is, therefore, at the same time a diagnosis of order and disorder in the society." (from "Plato," Louisiana University Press, 1957).

Voegelin wrote that over 30 years ago. The disorder he had experienced was that of Nazism; he had been chased out of Germany by the Gestapo. The disorder Bloom has experienced and responded to is what he sees as the invasion of the American "higher education" by German nihilism that culminated in the student protests of the '60s, and the subsequent disarray in the humanities.

Coming into the '60s, Bloom was vulnerable. He was a participant in the Great Books program at the University of Chicago; he now feels the program was naive. It counted too much on the student's capacity for spontaneous recognition of the truth.

Now Bloom knows, in Nietzsche's figure, that the bow of the mind has lost its tension from being too long unbent.

There is real anger in this book. Against what he feels were the naive expectations of the Great Books project, Bloom balances Nietzsche's emphasis on culture. "Man is pure becoming, unlike any other being in nature, and it is in culture that he becomes something that transcends nature and has no other mode of existence and no other support than a particular culture. . . . There are as many kinds of man as there are cultures, without any perspective from which man can be spoken of in the singular. . . ." Sometimes it's hard to figure out who's speaking (Bloom is paraphrasing Nietzsche). He goes on, and on: "There must be as many different kinds of mind as there are cultures. If the mind itself is not included among the things that are relative to cultures, the observations of cultural relativism are trivial and have always been accepted. Yet everyone likes cultural relativism but wants to exempt what concerns him."

Is relativistic "pluralism" the answer? We can't have it both ways, says Bloom. And yet the modern university has been restructured to accommodate cultural relativism. Each specialization has its little god, a professor with tenure.

At the center of the book is Bloom's profound piety toward the university, as it is embodied in his memory of his early days at the University of Chicago. He begins with the "pseudo-Gothic" style of the buildings, much ridiculed then and now: "It is not authentic, not an expression of what we are, so it was said. To me it was and remains an expression of what we are. One wonders whether the culture critics had as good an instinct about our spiritual needs as the vulgar rich who paid for the buildings. This nation's impulse is toward the future, and tradition seems more of a shackle to it than an inspiration. Reminiscences and warnings from the past are our only monitor as we career along our path."

"In a nation founded on reason," Bloom concludes, "the university was the temple of the regime, dedicated to the purest use of reason and evoking the kind of reverence appropriate to an association of free and equal human beings."

In contrast to Bloom's generation, students today, taught to be open to "values," are innocent of good and evil. And, pointing out the massive commercial and cultural power of rock music, Bloom argues that the omnipresence of orgiastic music has left American youth jaded, pseudo-experienced, and without spiritual appetite. His discussion of rock in light of Nietzsche's concept of music is a purple passage in the best sense of the old phrase.

Like Tocqueville, Bloom believes that equality is the soul of democracy, and democracy, he adds, is the only form of government sanctioned by the true modern philosophy. But what evil has been worked in the name of equality! Bloom tells stories about how the abstract goal of "equality" twisted the minds of suddenly active academics in the bad old '60s.

And yet: "This is the American moment in world history, the one for which we shall forever be judged," Bloom concludes. "Just as in politics the responsibility for the fate of freedom in the world has devolved upon our regime, so the fate of philosophy in the world has devolved upon our universities, and the two are related as they have never been before."

As Voegelin pointed out years ago, the philosopher experiences the disorder of his society as the disorder of his own soul. Bloom recognizes this personal integrity in Nietzsche, and with him in mind condemns those of his fellow educators who seem to be able to wrest from that disorder a guarantee of their own well-being.

Bloom does not negotiate with the *Zeitgeist*. "Men may live more truly and fully in reading Plato and Shakespeare than at any other time," he writes, "because then they are participating in essential being and are forgetting their accidental lives." So much for Marxist praxis and American practicality, so much for Nietzsche's relativism.

Bloom is properly complex about the place of the Bible in the American situation. Recognizing that in the early days, the Bible was "the only common culture," and served in many ways to keep the American mind open to the possibility of art, reason, and wisdom, today he accepts the convenience of teaching the Bible as literature, thus heading off a renewal of the religious wars. . . .

Bloom is a sublime talker. His prudence is part overreaction, part piety to old books, part genuine rediscovery of classical reason. The talk becomes most bracing when Bloom holds forth on the "theoretical experience" that frees one from the accidents of nation, birth, and wealth. With respect to the Pythagorean theorem, all men are equals.

2

On the Finn Syndrome
and the Shakespeare Paradox

ROBERT PATTISON

To use one of those word-saving tags from Shakespeare so dear to E. D. Hirsch, *The Closing of the American Mind* is to Hirsch's *Cultural Literacy* as Hyperion to a satyr. Here our mentor is Plato, not Dr. Bennett. This is the center-cannot-hold book in its traditional guise: philosophic meditation on society as idea. *The Closing of the American Mind* has already won high praise where tradition is venerated. *The New York Times* has hailed it as the most engaging intellectual performance of the past five years. The *New Criterion* has excerpted it extensively, and the *Washington Times* magazine, *Insight*, has greeted it as "the book of the year."

If nothing else, the book's success testifies to America's enduring affection for works that belittle the national intelligence. For Bloom, the center cannot hold because the ideas whose material form is American society are vicious parodies of their European originals. Even the originals as found in Hobbes, Locke, Rousseau or Weber might lead to ruin, but in their degenerate American incarnations, they have all but murdered the soul of the nation.

The Closing of the American Mind is likely to become the bible of a whole class of righteous intellectuals, so it is fitting that the spirit of Bloom emerges from its pages as a triune deity, composed of one indignant substance in three disgruntled persons—the teacher, the politician and the philosopher. Adepts will intuit the unity of this godhead, but the uninitiated must approach the divinity in its hypostases.

Bloom the teacher is an accomplished humanist who now holds various distinguished appointments at the University of Chicago, after migrating between Yale, Toronto, the Sorbonne and Cornell, where he worked in 1969, the year student protests swept across American universities. The student upheavals marked a personal and social crisis for Bloom, one from which, if *The Closing of the American Mind* can be believed, neither he nor the university is likely to recover. But through it all Bloom has expounded the great texts of the Western tradition, and his book is in part a seminar in political philosophy from Plato to Heidegger.

Hirsch might profitably attend this seminar. Here, Plato is not an advocate of the culture index but the champion of thought as the ultimate human good. Rousseau is not the father of formalism but of culture itself, as this word is

---

From the *Nation* (May 30, 1987): 710–720. Reprinted with permission.

7

understood by modern man. Bloom the teacher is always astute and scrupulously fair. Nietzsche, the great modern antagonist of Bloom's hero Socrates, at least took Socrates seriously, and Bloom pays Nietzsche and the whole philosophic tradition the same compliment.

The Closing of the American Mind is a superlative guide not only to Western political thought but to that thought as it has realized itself in the everyday relations of American society. Trotsky said that "all through history, mind limps after reality." Readers who agree with him would do well to take a Valium before reading this book. Bloom the teacher is committed to the primacy of ideas with a devotion that at moments borders on the mystical, as when he seems to suggest that Hobbes, Spinoza, Locke and Rousseau once assembled at some transcendental negotiating table to hammer out the details of contemporary civilization. But Bloom the mad professor only adds an element of psychic drama to a seminar that was already absorbing.

Bloom devotes some 150 pages to tracing the vocabulary of contemporary American society to its origins in European political philosophy. Despite the inevitable quibbles that must attend any enterprise so intangible, his connections are persuasive. We are a society that has replaced transcendent standards of good and evil with relative values. As the children of Locke, Nietzsche and Weber, we have exchanged the imperatives of religion for the suggestions of reason. In our distorted reading of these masters, we have gone the final suicidal step to "reject by the fact of our categories the rationalism that is the basis of our way of life, without having anything to substitute for it." We are all anthropologists at heart, our perverse tribute to the memory of Rousseau, and we deem ourselves no better and no worse than any other culture. Locke gave us civil rights as the reward of a disciplined secular society. Our unbridled modernism has converted those rights into amorphous openness, which devours the very liberty that gave it birth. If Nietzsche tried to recapture the exhilaration of Western man's first great age, his modern interpreters have transformed the *Übermensch* into a solipsistic gelding. Plato would have us think for the sake of our souls, but modern man has discarded his soul for what de Tocqueville called the contemplation of that "very petty object, which is himself."

Bloom is a teacher with a mission, and he becomes Bloom the politician when his seminar evolves into an apologia for the university as guardian of the intellectual tradition of Plato and the Academy. "So far I must defend Plato as to plead that this view of education and studies is in general, as it seems to me, sound enough; and fitted for all sorts and conditions of men." Bloom makes an eloquent and lengthy defense of Platonic education against the encroachments of modern barbarism—almost as eloquent and ten times as long as Matthew Arnold's when he made the same case in "Literature and Science" a hundred years ago. It is Arnold speaking above, but if we substitute stridency for charm, it might as well be Bloom.

Like Arnold's, his apologia involves a political program. Like Arnold's, his might be called Platonic liberalism, the political credo of those who, by an irony of political jargon, are now called neoconservatives. The Platonic liberal is not opposed to equality. He only insists that the masses be put on a footing with himself rather than the other way around. The Platonic liberal was born to be disillusioned. He offers the people ideal beauty; they take the Beastie Boys instead. Arnold lost his patience with democracy in 1866, when suffrage rioters trampled the flowers in Hyde Park. Bloom lost his in 1969, when the students at Cornell demanded a new curriculum at gunpoint. Both Arnold and Bloom admit that the future belongs to democracy. Both insist this future will be a nightmare unless some way is found to infuse the mob with the dispassionate love of truth, which, says Bloom, can survive only in the university. Bloom's book is a plea for defending sweetness and light against the assaults of an American democracy drunk with the wine of its philosophical fornications.

The success of this plea depends on the dialectical and rhetorical skills of Bloom the philosopher, who is given to assertions such as, "There is no real teacher who in practice does not believe in the existence of the soul." Here, Bloom is trying to strike the grand pose, as when Jean Jacques announces that all men are born free and everywhere they are in chains. Its grandeur conceded, what does Bloom's statement mean? It is meant to evoke the reasoned arguments of Plato's *Phaedrus*, but in fact there is nothing reasonable about it. It is a dictum from the age of faith. It excludes as real teachers both those with the temerity to reject the statement outright and those deluded creatures whose definition of soul differs from Bloom's. Since soul is not defined, the statement remains a dogmatic tautology. Its meaning in context is, "There is no real teacher who does not agree with Bloom," and its precise formulation is "I am that I am."

Bloom the philosopher is Torqucmada in a tunic. He poses as the disinterested lover of reason and truth, and his book, from the title on, is cast as a plea for the student to open his mind and dare to "doubt the ultimate value of what he loves." But no mind could be more firmly closed or less doubtful than Bloom's. Does this one assert that material explanations suffice to account for the mysteries of creation? Let him be anathema. Does that one deny the existence of absolutes? Let him be cast out. The stake is ready and the kindling prepared before Bloom's inquiry begins.

There are no prescriptions set down in *The Closing of the American Mind* that Bloom does not himself egregiously violate in the course of the argument. "I am not moralizing," he says, and 400 pages later pauses for breath. "I no more want to be Jeremiah than Pollyanna," he announces as he embarks on his lamentation. Pages are spent on the perils of self-centeredness. Having said so much, Bloom presents a history of Western thought that culminates in—Bloom! We are asked to believe that philosophy moved from Athens to Germany and thence to America, where it conveniently died at Cornell with Bloom in attendance. Intellectual history and Bloom's autobiography coincide. The uprising at Cornell marks not a silly and deplorable episode in the history of one university but the collapse of Western thought. In one chapter the contemporary student is berated for having no idea of evil beyond a few shallow stereotypes of Nazis. Yet 300 pages later Bloom, searching for a way to characterize the treason of Cornell's *clercs*, compares it with Heidegger's submission to Hitler.

But these contradictions are minor. More seriously, Bloom's main argument is a self-defeating paradox. Bloom the politician asks us to believe that Americans are "innocents" who rely entirely on Europe for all real thought: "There was never a native plant. We were dependent on Europe for it." Whatever America has produced is cheap and empty. But Bloom the teacher has already shown that America possesses a very distinctive culture. True, it has evolved from European originals, but its characteristic elements are precisely those native features Bloom spends his whole book excoriating: relativism, openness, self-adoration. By Bloom's own accounting, this culture chooses freedom over rights, the sacred over the religious, the present over the past. It rejects the traditional opposition of body and soul. It proceeds by a logic that has emptied the European categories of their rigorous meaning, "and now the mother-word itself—culture—has also become part of empty talk." In the New World, says Bloom, "the principle of contradiction has been repealed." There could be no more persuasive evidence of its abolition than *The Closing of the American Mind*, whose central argument is exploded by its own scholarship. Bloom sets out to prove that America has no thought of its own and demonstrates instead that it is driven by vigorous and novel beliefs that he despises. . . .

Because this is a center-cannot-hold book, Bloom feels obliged to suggest some treatment for the disease. He recommends that democracy learn to keep its mitts off the true philosophers in its midst. But at heart he doesn't believe his advice will make any difference. On his last page he exhorts lovers of truth to prepare themselves for martyrdom on the Socratic model. "Curse God and die" is, in fact, Bloom's recommendation for thinking Americans.

In one thing alone is Bloom the philosopher consistent. He repudiates compassion, the democratic man's bad-faith excuse for "elitist self-assertion." Justice, not compassion, is Bloom's ideal, and he descends on his enemies crying, "No prisoners!" The result is not quite as heroic as the author might wish. Bloom the teacher arraigns his students on a charge of ingratitude. At the beginning of his career, Bloom says, his virginal freshmen arrived at college charged with *eros*, the passionate impulse that in the *Phaedrus* drives the soul to seek the beautiful. Bloom the teacher could harness "the dark, chaotic, premonitory forces in the soul—to make them serve a higher purpose." Now jaded freshpersons present themselves, their *eros* dissipated in a phony sexual maturity or enslaved to the merely libidinous logic of rock. Bloom the teacher is a jilted suitor who has watched his beloved sneak giggling away with the strumpet relativism. He judges youth "flat-souled" and sentences it to a lifetime of reading Camus. This is spite, not justice.

Bloom the politician is no kinder to his colleagues. When he discusses the faculty at Cornell during the student riots, indictments pour out of him as from a grand jury on amphetamines. The provost was "a former natural scientist" whose "mixture of cowardice and moralism" typified the faculty as well. They were "heirs of the German university tradition . . . the greatest expression of the publicly supported and approved version of the theoretical life." At the first sign of trouble they capitulated to the mob and their own shoddy instincts: "Their collapse was merely pitiful, although their feeble attempts at self-justification frequently turned vicious." Twenty years have not withered Bloom's indignation nor staled his rage. Characteristically, Bloom ends this vindictive memoir with a denunciation of the very emotions he has indulged throughout: "Indignation may be a most noble passion and necessary for fighting wars and righting wrongs. But of all the experiences of the soul it is the most inimical to reason and hence to the university." So true. . . .

Both *Cultural Literacy* and *The Closing of the American Mind* suffer from the logical deficiency inherent in the center-cannot-hold genre. It does not follow that if the center cannot hold, mere anarchy will be loosed upon the world. There are other models of cohesion besides revolution around an axis of Platonic philosophy or shared cultural information. It does not follow that because we cannot re-create the educational glories of some imaginary past we might not invent a native American education with its own peculiar greatness.

In fact Bloom's book is an intimation of what this education can produce: not the magisterial scholarship of the German academy, but the idiosyncratic knowledge of the individual without a tradition. Not the convoluted prose of the French theorist, but the open discourse of the democrat. Not the pedantry of the doctoral candidate but the broad learning of the intellectual migrant. Bloom has it all. Tragically, the one thing missing is the essential ingredient: a sense of compassion.

3

A Half-Open Mind

PAUL GOTTFRIED

During the month of June, Allan Bloom's observations on the state of American education climbed their way dramatically toward the peak of the *New York Times* nonfiction bestseller list. Why would such a book engage a mass readership? Bloom's prose is neither light nor graceful, and his horror stories about the counterculture are certainly not fresh. These stories thematically overlap with Midge Decter's *Liberal Parents, Radical Children* (1975), in which Decter told of adolescents and young adults from permissive or experimenting homes who complicated their lives in quest of self-actualization.

The people described by Decter do correspond to types that Bloom (like myself) may have encountered as a professor, but it is hard to see why his reminiscences about burnt-out kids and their swinging parents should occasion such ecstatic approval from *The New Republic, Commentary, Insight, The Nation,* the *Washington Post,* and *National Review.*

Bloom never lets us forget that he was a student of Leo Strauss at the University of Chicago and had taken from this master a world view as well as a way of reading texts. The ancients, Plato and Aristotle, are praised for talking about virtue and truth—although it is never clear whether Bloom believes in either. He does argue that the most important contribution of classical philosophy was to have raised critical questions about the nature and ends of Man, whereas modern thought generally treats such questions as irrelevant. By a series of descents (what Straussians call "crises"), the Western world moved from classical morality through the scientific materialism of the Renaissance and Enlightenment, down to the outright nihilism of the Nazis. "Value-free" social science, existentialism, and popular culture are all seen as symptomatic of the worsening crises that have engulfed Western culture even now in rebellion against classical thought.

This Straussian picture of gloomy and progressive decadence evoked by Bloom is broken by one ray of light. Though John Locke and Jean Jacques Rousseau are classified as modernists, disciples of Leo Strauss see one or the other as a virtuous pagan. Locke is praised as the Father of the American (democratic secularist) regime, while Rousseau is admired for combining a democratic and contractual understanding of government with a civic religion of sentiment. Most Straussians, including Bloom, try to incorporate one or the other into their

Paul Gottfried is a senior editor of *The World and I* and author of *The Search for Historical Meaning.* This article is reprinted with permission from *Chronicles: A Magazine of American Culture* vol. 11, no. 9 (September 1987):30–33.

pantheon of preferred sages. Despite their materialist views of human nature, either Locke or Rousseau is held up as a proponent of democratic—and therefore good—modernity. Straussians divide between the partisans of Locke and Rousseau, but Bloom transcends this difference by speaking well of both.

To his credit, he has used arcane Straussian concepts to produce a popular work of cultural criticism. While the Straussian scaffolding creaks occasionally, the tirades against rock music, mischievous Teutons, and sensual excess give the work a lighter (even voyeuristic) quality. It has paid off. An in-depth study of Bloom in the June 19, 1987, issue of the *Washington Post* depicts him as an international celebrity. Flying to dinner with the Mayor of Jerusalem and hobnobbing with academic leaders in France, Israel, and the United States, the author of *The Closing of the American Mind* seems to be less an ivy-tower scholar than someone with connections.

One self-described right-wing populist assured me that Bloom "is agin the counterculture." I'm not sure he unequivocally is—or that his book would be selling so well if he were. For all his unhappiness with student manners, Bloom is no ally of middle-class values or of our commercial Protestant past as a nation. In a revealing attempt to explain European "revolutionaries who accepted our ideals of freedom and equality" but were (and still are) appalled by our unequal distribution of property, Bloom alludes to the efforts of our "domesticated churches in America" to preserve "the superstition of Christianity, [the] overcoming of which was perhaps the key to liberating man." He offers, by contrast, no detailed presentation of the views of the "disinherited of the *ancien regime.*" When antirevolutionary ideas are given at all, they are described as "special pleading" and linked to the genealogy of Nazism. But there is one side of the American heritage that Bloom finds congenial: "Our principles of freedom and equality and the rights based on them [that] are rational and everywhere applicable." Bloom notes approvingly that the United States fought the Second World War "as an educational project to extend them."

His view of the American past is highly selective and has no place for either Puritan oligarchs or Southern gentry. Bloom is at bottom a welfare state Whig who welcomes the spread of modern progressive ideals as the actualization of both American and European revolutionary movements. At the same time, he laments the degradation of his ideals in the form of undisciplined students, jarring popular music, and falling educational standards.

There is a paradoxical, even contradictory, tone to his argument, which moves back and forth between praising and damning democracy, skepticism, the Enlightenment, and bourgeois attitudes. Bloom wants an orderly and prosperous society that supports philosophers in their academic redoubts. Significantly, he defines philosophy as "the abandonment of all authority in favor of individual reason" and repeatedly suggests that philosophy must challenge inherited ancestral truths. Never mind, he also tells us, that "concreteness, not abstractness, is the hallmark of philosophy." Like Walt Whitman, Bloom appears to revel in contradiction: In one passage we are told, "The most important function of the university in an age of reason is to protect reason from itself, by being the model of true openness," but elsewhere are warned, "In a democracy the university protects the life of reason by opposing the emergent [sic], the changing, and the ephemeral." In the process, the university fights dogmatism. Its job, then, is to oppose "dogmatism" and support individual speculation—while resisting changing views. Through such resistance (assuming that universities can judge in advance what ideas will be ephemeral), academics uphold the "model of true openness."

One reason for such bizarre reasoning is the pervasive Teutonophobia, which is apparent in his revulsion for the social sciences and most other 19th-century German academic inventions. Bloom scorns any systematic attempt to understand social phenomena that proceeds from data and methodological criteria. He denounces Max Weber, a creator of social science, as a "dogmatic atheist" and nihilistic precursor of Nazism, without demonstrating either. Of course it was Weber and other 19th-century German professors who established professional standards of scholarship in the social sciences. They would no doubt have frowned on Bloom's concept of the university as a place where one man's speculative reason is made to exclude someone else's—in the name of openness and fighting dogmatism.

A colleague of Bloom's has observed that his true educational agenda is to replace modern scientific thinking with classical ideals. That much is true. Bloom does have reservations about scientific thinking; it is also clear that he has no intention of returning to the past, defined as the world before the 1950's. He stresses the connection between scientific materialism and liberal democracy; and while he deplores the nihilistic thrust of "absolute science," he is for democracy and the secular, demystified world to which he finds it related.

Bloom likes what he identifies with the left, rationalism, the Enlightenment, liberal (and even social) democracy. Regrettably, however, the progress of his side has led not to a high civilization but to dirty, drug-infested adolescents and to promiscuous and confused adults. Bloom must encounter these decadents even at the University of Chicago. He is properly alarmed that the new barbarians are threatening the university he once knew. Unfortunately, Bloom can never quite bring himself to recognize the close ties between his religion of democracy cum philosophical skepticism and the cultural trends he deplores. . . .

4

A "Minute of Hatred" in Chapel Hill: Academia's Liberals Defend Their Carnival of Canons Against Bloom's "Killer B's"

RICHARD BERNSTEIN

In some respects, the scene in North Carolina last weekend recalled the daily "minute of hatred" in George Orwell's "1984," when citizens are required to rise and hurl invective at pictures of a man known only as Goldstein, the Great Enemy of the state.

At a conference on the future of liberal education sponsored by Duke University and the University of North Carolina at Chapel Hill, speaker after speaker denounced what they called "the cultural conservatives" who, in the words of a Duke English professor, Stanley Fish, have mounted "dyspeptic attacks on the humanities."

There were no pictures of these "cultural conservatives" on the wall, but they were derided, scorned, laughed at—and, from time to time, taken seriously. Among the targets were William J. Bennett, the recently departed Secretary of Education, and Allan Bloom, author of the best-selling conservative lament called "The Closing of the American Mind." Including for good measure the Nobel Prize-winning novelist Saul Bellow, Prof. Mary Louise Pratt of Stanford said that at her university the three men are known as "the killer B's." Mr. Bellow wrote a foreward to Mr. Bloom's book. The enemies' list also included E. D. Hirsch Jr., whose book "Cultural Literacy" ends with a list of the concepts, ideas and events that he believes all educated Westerners should know.

What has roiled the academic calm, making uncivil libertarians of normally sedate humanities professors? With the stunning public success of the Bloom-Hirsch-Bennett school, the meeting in North Carolina was a kind of counterattack against a counterattack, a reaffirmation of the trends that were popular in the 1960's but that have been dismissed by the conservatives as cranky, muddled, guilt-ridden denials of the unique greatness of Western culture.

In the face of an announcement that Mr. Bennett and Mr. Bloom planned a foundation to promote Western classics in colleges and universities, the conference's participants denounced what they said was a narrow, outdated interpretation of the humanities and of culture itself, one based, they frequently pointed out, on works written by "dead white European males."

The message of the North Carolina conference was that American society

From the *New York Times* (September 25, 1988):26. Reprinted with permission.

has changed too much for this view to prevail any longer. Blacks, women, Latinos and homosexuals are demanding recognition for their own canons. "Projects like those of Bennett, Hirsch and Bloom all look back to the recovery of the earlier vision of American culture, as opposed to the conception of a kind of ethnic carnival or festival of cultures or ways of life or customs," Professor Fish said.

A report issued this month by the National Endowment for the Humanities was among the targets of the one minute of hate. "The Humanities in America," written by Lynne V. Cheney, the endowment's chairwoman, concluded that humanities enrollments in universities are down because so many departments have undertaken "new approaches to the humanities that treat great books as little more than the political rationalizations of dominant groups."

'Other' Cultures

Professor Fish viewed it a different way. "The thing that strikes me about the Cheney report is that it presents as something national and even universal what is in fact a particularly narrow and, finally, local sense of culture," he said. Mr. Fish acknowledged that the report says that students should also be encouraged to learn about other cultures, but he dismissed the recommendation as an afterthought. To the conservatives, he said, " 'Other' means that stuff that you can take a look at if you have time left over from the serious business."

Many of the conference's participants heralded the importance of writings from what they regard as suppressed parts of American culture, particularly the contributions of "marginalized" people—women, blacks, homosexuals and others.

The conference buzzed with code words. When the speakers talked about "the hegemonic culture," they meant undemocratic domination by white men. The scholars particularly scorned the idea that certain great works of literature have absolute value or represent some eternal truth. Just about everything, they argued, is an expression of race, class or gender.

Charges of Determinism

Of course, it could be argued that Mr. Bloom and his sympathizers never intended to dismiss other cultures as unimportant. Few universities actually leave out black or female writers from their American literature courses anymore.

But the scholars gathered in North Carolina believe that, at bottom, the conservatives do not respect the non-white contribution to American culture. At the same time, the people identified as conservatives argue that the stress on race, class and gender is too deterministic; they see it as basically a Marxist analysis that denies the capacity of great minds of whatever race or sex to transcend their circumstances and say something of universal relevance about the human condition.

"I have the conviction that great literature, no matter whom it is written by, speaks to transcendent values that we all share, no matter what our time and circumstance," Mrs. Cheney said in a telephone interview. "The real question concerns the core curriculum: What does everybody have to study? In my view, every student has to study Western culture and non-Western culture."

There is everything to be gained, she said, from studies by and about women, blacks and other elements of American culture. Still, she maintained that American history and values derive primarily from the great thinkers of Europe, and not from Asia or Africa. "On the West," she argued, "the first responsibility is to ground students in the culture that gave rise to the institutions of our democracy."

5

Book Review:
The Closing of the American Mind

ROBERT PAUL WOLFF

Afficionados of the modern American novel have learned to look to Philip Roth for complex literary constructions that play wittily with narrative voice and frame. One thinks of such Roth works as *My Life as a Man* and *The Counter Life*. Now Saul Bellow has demonstrated that among his other well-recognized literary gifts is an unsuspected bent for daring satire. What Bellow has done, quite simply, is to write an entire corruscatingly funny novel in the form of a pettish, bookish, grumpy, reactionary complaint against the last two decades. The "author" of this tirade, one of Bellow's most fully realized literary creations, is a mid-fiftyish professor at the University of Chicago, to whom Bellow gives the evocative name, "Bloom." Bellow appears in the book only as the author of an eight-page "Foreword," in which he introduces us to his principal and only character. The book is published under the name "Allan Bloom," and, as part of the fun, is even copyrighted in "Bloom's" name.

Nevertheless, Bellow is unwilling entirely to risk the possibility that readers will misconstrue his novel as a serious piece of nonfiction by a real professor, and so, in the midst of his preface, he devotes more than a page to a flatfooted explanation of his earlier novel, *Herzog*, in which, he tells us straight out, he was deliberately trying to satirize pedantry. This bit of hand waving and flag raising by Bellow detracts from the ironic consistency of the novel, but he may perhaps be forgiven, for so compellingly believable is this new academic pedant, "Bloom," that without Bellow's warnings, *The Closing of the American Mind* might have been taken as a genuine piece of academic prose.

The novel is, for all its surface accessibility, a subtly constructed palimpsest concealing what old Hyde Park hands will recognize as a devastating in-house attack by Bellow on his own stamping ground, the Committee on Social Thought. ("Bloom" is described on the jacket as a professor in the Committee on Social Thought.) The real target, indeed, is a former member of that committee, the late Leo Strauss, a brilliant, learned, utterly mad historian of political thought who spawned, nurtured, reared, and sent out into the world several generations of disciples dedicated to his paranoid theories of textual interpretation. (Strauss,

---

Robert Paul Wolff teaches philosophy at the University of Massachusetts, Amherst. His books include *In Defense of Anarchism* (1970) and *The Poverty of Liberalism* (1968). This review is reprinted with permission from *Academe* (September–October 1987):64–65.

whose hermeneutics placed special emphasis on concealment, absence, and misdirection, appears only once in the book, in an aside. Bellow leaves it to the cognoscenti to recognize the true significance of the allusion.)

As conceived by Bellow, "Bloom" is the quintessential product of the distinctive educational theories that flourished at the college of the University of Chicago during and after the heyday of Robert Maynard Hutchins. The key to those theories was the particular mid-western, upwardly mobile first-generation version of the Great Conversation that came to be known, in its promotional publishing version, as The Great Books. According to this pedagogical conception, Western civilization is a two millennia-old conversation among a brilliant galaxy of great minds, permanently encapsulated in a recognized sequence of great texts, with Aristotle's plan for the organization of human knowledge as the architectonic armature. Plato, Aristotle, Aeschylus, Thucydides, St. Augustine, St. Thomas, al Farabi, Maimonides, Erasmus, Cervantes, Bacon, Shakespeare, Descartes, Hobbes, Locke, Spinoza, Leibniz, Newton, on and on they come, reflecting on the relationship between man and the universe, chatting with one another, kibitzing their predecessors, a rich, endless, moveable feast of ideas and intellectual passions.

The list, by now, has grown enormously long, but—and this is the secret of its mesmerizing attraction to the eager young students who were drawn to Chicago—*it is finite.* However much work it may be to plow through the great books, once one has completed the task, one is *educated!* One can now join the Great Conversation, perhaps not as an active participant, but certainly as a thoughtful listener. And this is true, regardless of one's family background, upbringing, lack of private schooling, or inappropriate dress. Unlike the Ivy League, where the wrong social class marked one permanently as inferior, Chicago offered a "career open to talents."

The virtue of a Chicago education was a certain intoxication with ideas, especially philosophical ideas, that sets off graduates of the Hutchins era from everyone else in the American intellectual scene. When I taught there briefly, in the early 1960s, I was enchanted to find professors of music reading books on Kant, and biologists seriously debating the undergraduate curriculum in Aristotelian terms. The vice of that same system is a mad, hermetic conviction that larger world events are actually caused or shaped by the obscurest sub-quibbles of the Great Conversation. By a fallacy of misplaced concreteness, of the sort that the young Marx so brilliantly burlesqued in *The Holy Family,* Chicago types are prone to suppose that it is the ideas that are real, and the people in this world who are mere epiphenomena. Bellow captures this distorted mentality perfectly in "Bloom," who, as we shall see, traces the cultural ills of the past twenty years implausibly, but with a wacky interior logic, to the twisted theories of two German philosophers.

The novel (which is to say, Bellow's "Foreword") begins with what turns out to be a bitingly ironic observation. "Professor Bloom has his own way of doing things." And indeed he does! Once "Bloom" has begun his interminable complaint against modernity—for which, read everything that has taken place since

"Bloom" was a young student in the 1940s at the University of Chicago—we are treated to a hilarious discourse of the sort that only a throwback to the Hutchins era could produce.

"Bloom's" diatribe opens with some animadversions upon the culture of the young. After a few glancing blows at feminism, he quite unpredictably launches upon an extended complaint about the music that the young so favor. Bellow's image of a middle-aged professor trying to sound knowledgeable about hard rock is a miniature comic masterpiece.

Now "Bloom" arrives at his real message. The deeper cause of the desperate inadequacies of our contemporary culture, it seems, is the baleful effect upon us of Friedrich Nietzsche and Martin Heidegger! Inasmuch as only a handful of American intellectuals can spell these gentlemen's names, let alone summarize their doctrines, "Bloom's" thesis has a certain manifest implausibility. But, as Bellow well knows, true Straussians spurn the obvious, looking always in silences, ellipses, and guarded allusions for the true filiations that connect one thinker with another, or a philosophical tradition with the cultural and political world.

"Bloom's" expository style, so skillfully manipulated by Bellow, makes it extraordinarily difficult to tell what he is actually saying. Its most striking surface characteristic is an obsessive namedropping that turns every page into a roll call of the Great Conversation. Consult the book at random (my copy falls open to pages 292–93), and one finds, within a brief compass, mention of Christopher Marlowe, Machiavelli (a Straussian buzzword, this), Bacon, Descartes, Hobbes, Leibniz, Locke, Montesquieu, Voltaire, Jacques Maritain, T. S. Eliot, Rousseau, Newton, Socrates, Moses, Cyrus, Theseus, Romulus, Swift, and Aristophanes. But despite the talismanic invocation of these and many other great names, there is precious little real argumentation in "Bloom's" "book." Indeed, despite his academic style of exposition, "Bloom" rarely enunciates a thesis that he is prepared to stand behind. All is irony, allusion, exposition, and undercutting reserve. Eventually, one realizes that Bellow is deliberately, and with great skill, conjuring for us a portrait of a man of Ideas, if not of ideas, whose endless ruminations on moral and intellectual virtue conceal a fundamental absence of either.

The turning-point in "Bloom's" monologue comes late in the novel, in a chapter entitled "The Sixties." Suddenly, the mist disperses, the allusions evaporate, and we discover what is really eating away at "Bloom's" innards. It seems that, in the course of his distinguished academic career, "Bloom" taught at Cornell University during the late sixties. Two decades later, "Bloom" is so dyspeptic about the events there that he can scarcely contain himself. "Servility, vanity and lack of conviction," "pompous," "a mixture of cowardice and moralism" are among the phrases with which he characterizes his colleagues of that time. For "Bloom," at Cornell, Columbia, and elsewhere, the rebellious students were blood brothers to the Brown Shirts who supported nazism. "Whether it be Nuremberg or Woodstock, the principle is the same."

Stepping back a bit from the fretwork of the novel, we may ask ourselves what Bellow's purpose is in committing an entire book to the exhibition of "Allan Bloom." Clearly, simple good-hearted fun must have played some motivating role, as well, we may suppose, as a desire to set the record right concerning the Committee on Social Thought. But as the final portion of the book makes manifest, Bellow has a deeper aim, one that is intensely earnest and, in the fullest and most ancient sense, moral. The central message of the Greek philosophers whom "Bloom" so likes to cite is that ultimately morality is a matter of character. Plato's brilliantly rendered portraits not only of Socrates but also of Gorgias, Callicles, Thrasymachus, and the others is intended to show us how virtue is grounded in character, and right action in virtue. Merely to know what can be found in books, or indeed on clay tablets, is no guarantee of virtue. As Aristotle remarks in a celebrated ironic aside, one cannot teach ethics to young men who are not well brought up.

"Bloom," as Bellow shows us across three hundred tedious pages, is as intimate with the Great Conversation as any Chicago undergraduate could ever hope to become. And yet, at the one critical moment in his life, when he confronts inescapably the intersection between political reality and his beloved Great Books, "Bloom's" vision clouds, his capacity for intellectual sympathy deserts him, and he cries "the Nazis are coming" as he shrinks from America's most authentically democratic moment of recent times.

In the end, Bellow is telling us, the Great Conversation is not enough. One needs compassion, a sense of justice, and moral vision. Without these, the Great Books are merely dead words in dead languages. I strongly recommend *The Closing of the American Mind* to anyone who desires a fiction of the mind that takes seriously the old question of the role of reason in the formation of virtuous character.

6

Allan Bloom and the Critics

WERNER J. DANNHAUSER

1.

When discussing Allan Bloom's *The Closing of the American Mind*, I bring to my task not the dirty hands of feigned objectivity but the clean hands of a friendship generously acknowledged in the book.

Friendship does not preclude difference. Bloom loves Reason a bit more than I do, and I love Revelation a bit more than he does. However, the main difference between us is that Bloom's mind excels mine; he tells me so himself.

2.

Most books don't make waves, rather resembling pebbles that cause ripples in a vast pool of indifference. In the beginning, nobody—not the publisher, not Bloom, and not his friends—expected more than modest sales. The gloomy hoped only for a respectable reception; those of a sunny disposition, like me, dreamed of a sale of 50,000 along with a bit of a stir.

Then the book took off, selling some 500,000 copies, riding the best-seller list for nearly a year, and even now moving briskly as a paperback. Howard Cosell, Bill Buckley, and David Brinkley interviewed Bloom, whose picture kept cropping up in magazines, sometimes on the cover. "Bloomian" became an adjective and Bloom dined with the President. What happened here?

3.

Since nobody quite knows what causes books to sell, one can simply say that for once a fine book got the recognition it deserved. That happened, but requires elucidation in our vale of tears. How did this reward of virtue come about?

The book's subtitle—"How Higher Education Has Failed Democracy and Impoverished the Souls of Today's Students"—points to a huge potential audience. Education occupies a prominent place on the nation's agenda of worries, and college students together with graduates probably constitute a majority of the reading public. No doubt the book appealed to parents, college-educated or not, who knew in an inchoate way that something was wrong with higher education. They had watched their children go off to get a liberal education and come back with all sorts of substitutes or by-products: addictions, neuroses, unearned cyn-

Werner J. Dannhauser is Professor of Government at Cornell University and author of *Nietzsche's View of Socrates*. This review is excerpted with permission from the *American Spectator* (October 1988): 17–20. See excerpts from this essay following: a reply to Benjamin Barber and Richard Rorty in chapter 4; to Martha Nussbaum in chapter 6; and on the question of racism in chapter 7.

icism, a sense of emptiness. *The Closing of the American Mind* promised to tell it as it is, and delivered on its promise; it situated the troubles everybody sensed and saw in a larger context without omitting specifics, like the youngsters' predilection for rock.

The book not only captured the attention of parents concerned for their children; it also appealed to students themselves. A closing mind is not yet closed, and the young used Bloom's book to catch a glimpse of themselves. That at least is what many students have told me. Some weeks ago, on a plane, as I was looking through *The Closing of the American Mind* again in preparation for writing these words, the young man sitting next to me volunteered: "That's a *good* book." He was a graduate student of physics, an admirer of Hans Bethe, a participant in anti-nuclear demonstrations, and he was engaged to a Presbyterian clergywoman. What did he like about the book? Its passion and its honesty.

Perhaps Bloom's audience includes a whole army of "unlikely" readers, people who take to the book because of its tone, its voice. According to Saul Bellow, "Professor Bloom has his own way of doing things." Going his own way, Bloom startles one with a fresh perspective. We have pondered the crisis of our time so long and so helplessly that we welcome a new investigator on the scene, one who pays little attention to the usual suspects—TV, technology, bureaucracy—and instead casts suspicion on Machiavelli, Rousseau, Nietzsche, Heidegger. What is more, those who write about our present discontent seem above all to be tired, tired, tired. By contrast, Bloom manifests a prodigious mental energy and a flamboyance that keeps us on our toes. Unafraid to take risks by being personal, he compels admiration for his lavish expenditure of effort.

None of the above wholly explains what happened. Everybody knows, or ought to know, about the role of luck, or chance. In this case, fortune took the form of unusually favorable early reviews.

4.

Christopher Lehmann-Haupt began it all with his unstinting praise in the *New York Times* of March 23, 1987, calling *The Closing of the American Mind* a "remarkable book . . . which hits with the approximate force and effect of what electric shock-therapy must be like." Combining a deft summary of the book with an appreciation of its virtues, he also foretold the future by noting that "this book is going to make a lot of people mad." To his credit, he did not let impending controversy stop him from taking a serious book seriously.

Throughout most of May last year, a chorus of acclaim greeted the book. Roger Kimball in the *New York Times Book Review*: "*The Closing of the American Mind* is that rarest of documents, a genuinely profound book. . ." S. Frederick Starr in the *Washington Post Book World*: "Few books in recent years come close to Allan Bloom's grand tour of the American Mind either in the ambition of their reach or in the breadth of their grasp." Donald Kagan in the *Washington Times*: "This is an amazing and wonderful book that penetrates the encrusted surface of American intellectual life, reveals the confusion and emptiness that lies beneath it and explains how things got this way."

Choice words, these, especially since their authors include a college president, and a distinguished professor of classics and history. One might, of course, contend that much of this praise should be dismissed because it comes from sources right of center, but the liberal media alas proved to be rather kind. Both *Time* and *Newsweek* hedged their bets, mixing snideness and obtuseness with their wonder at the work's success, but the articles were of the kind that elicits gratitude: they publicized the book and they spelled the author's name right.

Astonishingly enough, the earliest serious review from the left turned out to be as good as an honorable man of the right (that is my description of Bloom, not his own) could expect from an honorable man of the left. Robert Pattison, in the *Nation* of May 30, 1987, attacked *The Closing of the American Mind*, but he approached it with genuine respect. He viewed Bloom as teacher, politician, and philosopher and found him a worthy adversary. For example, he graciously wrote "Bloom the teacher is always astute and scrupulously fair," scored some minor points, but consistently took the higher road of claiming Bloom lacked "a sense of compassion" as opposed to a sense of justice. One might argue that by giving Rousseau his due, Bloom had also given compassion its due, but a more fitting response to Pattison's analysis is: fair enough.

By the end of May, then, a consensus in favor of *The Closing of the American Mind* seemed to be emerging. A number of the early reviewers had warned against a coming campaign of vilification against the book, but one was now tempted to dismiss their fears.

5.

Then the fall-out began to hit the fan. The accolades kept coming in, as when George Will stated that "Bloom's best seller is a . . . sign of the high level at which many Americans can be addressed," but at the same time the reaction to the book began to descend to low levels boggling the mind, including a comparison to *Mein Kampf.* Soon I will be heaping contempt on certain specimens of this virulence, especially on those beneath contempt, but the reader may be helped by an overview. Having read almost every review of *The Closing of the American Mind*, a numbing labor, I have been able to identify the sixteen—count 'em—most frequent charges against it. Here they are, in no particular order. Bloom has been repeatedly accused of (1) idealism, (2) sexism, (3) racism, (4) elitism, (5) Straussianism, (6) esoteric writing, (7) sloppy writing, (8) absolutism, (9) making scapegoats of students, (10) ignorance of professional philosophy, (11) un-Americanism, (12) failure to understand rock music, (13) pessimism, (14) uncritical advocacy of The Great Books, (15) bad scholarship, and (16) neglect of religion. That's all.

6.

Toward the end of his life, Captain Dreyfus reportedly said about charges leveled at yet another innocent French officer, "Where there's smoke, there's fire." Confronted by the above list of accusations, one naturally wonders about which of them are true, and to what extent. . . .

7.

Having praised Bloom by damning him faintly, and having shrewdly conceded that *The Closing of the American Mind* lacks perfection, I return to an analysis of the accusations against the book. They came from both sides of the political spectrum.

The attack from the right included, sad to say, a review in these very pages by Charles Kesler (August 1987). For Kesler, Bloom is something of a Buckley-come-lately who confirms the diagnosis of *God and Man at Yale* thirty-five years later but who lacks Buckley's credentials as a conservative. The gravest of the various grave deficiencies Kesler thinks he discerns in *The Closing of the American Mind* is a failure to appreciate the grandeur of the American regime, above all of its Founding.

Now it is true that Bloom finds flaws in the founding principles—Lockeian in a decisive sense—of our country, which are decisively modern and thus partake of the problematic modern lowering of standards in order to guarantee actualization. Such an estimation, however, in no way precludes patriotism; in fact, it is a part of the self-reflective kind of patriotism a democracy like ours ought to cherish. In no way does it follow from the fact that America is not heaven that it can't be the best place on earth. Moreover, a true patriot must come to terms not only with the vulnerabilities of his country, but with the force and strength of the principles that would undermine it—hence Bloom's entirely justified insistence on giving a thinker like Rousseau his due. Ironically, at times the dismay with the book on the right seemed to stem from the same source as delight on the left; what was understood—or, rather, misunderstood—as the anti-Americanism suffusing it.

According to a kindred criticism of the author, he was far too gloomy. Almost nobody cares for a pessimist, especially if he speaks about his country's crisis or decline. Eva Brann, who cannot be called a member of the left, assured readers of the *St. John's Review,* that if Bloom had looked away from the modern university to "more or less obscure little schools" he would have discovered that "the spirit lives in the sticks." Maybe so, but with all qualified respect for St. John's, and Eva Brann's swinger prose, those of us who have dealt with its graduates find no reason for rushing into the streets to celebrate the vitality of *Geist*.

· · · ·

11.

The first really negative review came not from the Far Left but the Near Left. On May 25, 1987, Louis Menand picked on the book in the *New Republic* and thus began that journal's veritable obsession with Bloom, "a man who knows his own mind, and who thinks well of what he finds there." But what Menand found there is not what exists there, as when he declares that "the most notable feature of the book is its attack on youth. . ." The notion that Bloom makes a scapegoat of students entails a serious misreading. The book is dedicated to his students, and an easily demonstrable love of the latter suffuses its pages. It is a far cry from identifying students as the victims of higher education, which Bloom does, to blaming the victims, which he does not do.

Menand also charges Bloom with idealism. Bloom is guilty, believing as he does in "the primacy of ideas," but so what? The question is whether materialism can provide a coherent account of the world. In various books cherished and taught by Bloom, that question is debated with a profundity unreached by Menand, who thinks he has trapped Bloom by conceding that the intellect affects history but asking "What affects the intellect?" The answer, of course, is that the intellect affects not only the intellect, but a lot more.

A. J. Ayer, who brought us logical positivism, and thus the demise of philosophy departments as places in which one could profitably study philosophy, griped against Bloom in the London *Sunday Times* for ignoring, presumably because of ignorance, professional philosophers in the United States. Instead Bloom has taken seriously "the unbridled metaphysician Heidegger." That sounds right. Then Ayer listed six people to whom Heidegger "cannot hold a candle," including a world-historical figure like Roderick Chisholm. Who would have thought so?

13.

Two condemnations of Bloom must be noted for the record. As a professor, it is my happiness that neither comes from the pen of a professor.

The fulminations of David Rieff, in the *Times Literary Supplement*, easily match the vituperation anybody else has leveled against *The Closing of the American Mind*, though Rieff has stiff competition in the race to defame my friend. He compares Bloom with Ollie North, both dangerous figures of "the American Right." Bloom easily emerges as the more sinister of the two: he "takes no notice of the beauty of the American landscape" and he "has contempt for the senses." Occasionally, Rieff tries to argue seriously, as when he denies that obedience is a democratic virtue, conveniently forgetting about obedience to the law. The rest of his observations are somewhat less coherent, since he loses control on account of his "hate filled self-regarding spleen," one of his more pleasant descriptions of *The Closing of the American Mind*. His opposition honors Bloom.

No issue of higher education could possibly be discussed or resolved without comment by Fred Hechinger, the leading "expert" on the topic for the *New York Times*, who rendered judgment in its pages on October 6, 1987. By this time many of the best charges had been preempted so Hechinger had to repeat the canard about "Bloom's contempt for modern youth." He also became the 318th sage to proclaim that since *The Closing of the American Mind* was finding such a huge audience The American Mind must still be open. Moreover, he decried Bloom's reference to Margaret Mead as a "sexual adventurer." That description may be based on nothing more substantial than rumors spread by her many lovers.

.   .   .   .

17.

At the end of his review of *The Closing of the American Mind*, Bernard Rosenberg, in the spring 1988 issue of *Dissent*, finds it hard to think of a more expendable book. Near the beginning, he catches Bloom using some infelicitous prose. In between, he vents his bile not only on Bloom, but on Saul Bellow, Conor Cruise O'Brien, Bernard Lewis, Mary Ann Glendon, and Walter Berns for praising the book. He levels a whole galaxy of accusations against both Bloom and Strauss, most of which I have dealt with previously. He also perpetrates a prodigious number of errors for one review, some of which deserve mention here if only to document the depths to which the Old Left has descended.

Bernard Rosenberg asserts that David Grene called Bloom a "bloody lunatic" when, alas, he called Leo Strauss that. He contends that according to Strauss "every philosopher wrote *only* between the lines"—whose lines did he use to write between? He garbles quotations about Margaret Mead and John Dewey that he ascribes to Bloom. He claims to have read *The Closing of the American Mind* "syllable for syllable—and more than once," but when he insists that Bloom never mentions Tocqueville's conviction that the price for democracy was worth paying he must have missed some syllables on page 227. Moreover, when he says that Bloom "despises Locke," he simply doesn't know what he's talking about; in fact Bloom praises Locke on, among other places, page 293, in one of the paragraphs containing an awkward sentence Rosenberg holds up to ridicule.

One can only hope that this rant made the folks at *Dissent* feel better.

. . . . .

19.

Writing about "Allan Bloom and His Critics" I have been less than just to *The Closing of the American Mind*. I have been unable to convey a true sense of its splendors, and above all of the delights one experiences in following the author's attempts not to change the world, but to understand it. Bloom has succeeded in presenting us with what he sets out to present, a genuine "meditation on the state of our souls."

Many cynics have told me that in response to his detractors Bloom must be laughing all the way to the bank. It may be only fitting and proper to declare open season on a successful book. But slanders like racism and sexism are no laughing matter. They scar a man and they poison the wells of honest controversy. Bloom and his friends, however, can find a bit of solace in the fact that the tirades against *The Closing of the American Mind* prove something about the closing of the American mind.

TWO

How Did Allan Bloom Write a Bestseller?

Many people, including Allan Bloom himself, say that they are surprised by the phenomenal sales of *The Closing of the American Mind*. The subject is academic, the argument is complicated, and the style is dense. Simon & Schuster initially printed only 10,000, and now, two years later, nearly 1 million copies have been sold. William Goldstein in an article here from *Publishers Weekly* analyzes, from the point of view of the publisher's trade, what happened. His conclusion is that: "Whatever the reason, *The Closing of the American Mind* is, without a doubt, a bestseller made by reviews." The book "started selling really quickly on the East Coast" following the extraordinarily laudatory review by Christopher Lehmann-Haupt in the March 11, 1987, *New York Times*. Goldstein goes on to mention other early reviews that contributed to the success of the book. Henry Allen in "The Right Absolute Allan Bloom," from the *Washington Post*, says "It is also yet another jeremiad against the shallowness of the American intellect, in a tradition that goes back to Henry Adams, Henry James, H. L. Mencken, Dwight Mac-Donald and so on, a native art form founded on self-flagellating comparisons to Europe." Allen points out that it is parents, not students, who are buying most of the copies of Bloom's book. "This is what the old can never forgive in the young: a failure to have fun. And that's what this book is about: souls without the longing (the title Bloom proposed and Simon & Schuster vetoed). . . . This is what we have lost with all our liberation. . . . We're trapped in a wasteland of relativism where everything is permitted but nothing is true, the hellishness of a wasteland being not frustration but the absence of desire."

William Kristol in "Troubled Souls: Where We Went Wrong," from the *Wall Street Journal*, says: "No other recent book so brilliantly knits together such astute perceptions of the contemporary scene with such depth of scholarship and philosophical learning. No other book combines such shrewd insights into our current state with so radical and fundamental a critique of it. No other book is at once so lively and so deep, so witty and so thoughtful, so outrageous and so sensible, so amusing and so chilling." Then Michael W. Hirschorn, in the *Chronicle of Higher Education*, praises Bloom as an acute observer who eschews any narrowly political agenda and who bridges the gaps between different generations of Americans.

The summary essay in this chapter is Will Morrisey's insightful "How

Bloom Did It: Rhetoric and Principle in *The Closing of the American Mind*," which explains some of the peculiarities of the book that have distracted and irritated many of Bloom's natural allies. The peculiarities are rhetorical postures, not philosophical positions, and are well adapted to the book's intended audience: teachers. For example, Bloom mentions religion as little as possible, not because he is antireligious but because teachers tend to be easygoing atheists. Likewise, the tripartite division of the book into Students, Nihilism, and the University reflects teachers' three main concerns. Also, Bloom cleverly pits liberals' snobbery against their egalitarianism. He appeals initially to their lower instincts by suggesting slyly that another cover-up has occurred. Morrisey argues against Goldstein that the book's well-conceived rhetoric is more important in explaining its success than is the accident of a few favorable, early reviews.

The book has shown staying power that cannot be explained by the early reviews, and later reviews have been much more negative. One pattern that emerges is that the earlier reviews were written by journalists, who are in the business of taking the country's pulse. The later reviews were written by academics, who are slower to respond and have their self-interest to defend, but who take the time for a more thoughtful analysis.

7

The Story Behind the Bestseller: Allan Bloom's *The Closing of the American Mind*

WILLIAM GOLDSTEIN

No one is more surprised than the author. "Surprise is something of an understatement," admits Allan Bloom, the University of Chicago professor whose *The Closing of the American Mind* (Simon & Schuster, $18.95) is the nation's number one nonfiction bestseller, replacing, the author especially savors, *Communion*. By focusing on the state of the American university, and by extension, American society in the second half of the 20th century, *The Closing of the American Mind* addresses the problem of "the radicalization of the principle of equality" in America today, the "openness" to anything, the "tolerance," Bloom outlines, that has led to "the loss of deep significance in the choices one makes."

"It's a little as though I had made a home movie and ended up winning the Academy Award," says Bloom. There are 175,000 copies of the book in print after eight printings. For the last two months Simon & Schuster has been printing 25,000 copies a week "and we'll continue to print that number for the unforeseen future," says Charles Hayward, S & S publisher, who is sure the book will continue to sell through the summer. "And then in September, when schools are back in session," he says, "I think it will sell all the way through the end of the year."

Why is *The Closing of the American Mind* a number-one bestseller? It's an easy question with no simple answers, as the complexity of Bloom's book itself proves. And there is by definition a further difficulty that Bloom eagerly cites: "Any reasons anyone can come up with for the book's success are all *ex post facto*. They all *might* be sufficient to cause the phenomenon, but they're all invented to explain it."

Perhaps the question of why *The Closing of the American Mind* is a number-one bestseller need not even be raised. The book is a publishing anomaly, it seems on the surface, and everyone, including the author, wonders *why* the book is so successful. But as Bob Asahina, Bloom's editor at S & S, suggests, the book's popularity should probably not be wondered at, at all. "This may be the one book right now that speaks to the intelligent general reader we in publishing always talk about," Asahina says.

William Goldstein is Trade News Editor for *Publishers Weekly*. This article is reprinted by permission from *Publishers Weekly* (July 3, 1987):25–27.

Made by Reviews

Whatever the reason, *The Closing of the American Mind* is, without a doubt, a bestseller made by reviews. Charles Hayward says that the book "started selling really quickly on the East Coast" following the extraordinarily laudatory review by Christopher Lehmann-Haupt in the March 11 *New York Times*, and subsequent reviews in the Sunday *New York Times* and *Washington Post*. "If anything is to be made of it," Hayward says, "the book climbed up very rapidly in East Coast markets [with the addition of Chicago, Bloom's "hometown" territory] and slower on the West Coast."

Ann Zeman, S & S trade sales director, agrees that the book's success "is absolutely reviews-driven all the way. Reviewers thought this book was important and catapulted it onto the list." Zeman cites an early article in the *Wall Street Journal* and one in the [Chronicle of] *Higher Education* as signal reviews: "It became important for academics to read this book." As for the general public, Zeman says, "The timing is right—we are at the beginning of a new political campaign. . . . Education is a topic people are always concerned about. But it isn't always something people read about."

Zeman frankly states that "if we had expected a bestseller, we would have initially printed more than 10,000 copies. But one of the things we do best is react very quickly—the reviewers discovered the book, and we jumped on that and ran with it. We went back to press right away and started filling the pipelines."

New Advertising Campaigns

In the few weeks since *Closing* reached the 100,000-copy mark, S & S has spent $75,000 on advertising and promoting the book. There have been two waves of provocative advertising headlined "Why are so many people rushing to buy this infuriating book?" and "At last, you will know why today's young Americans are [quoting a review in *Kirkus*] *'isolated, self-centered, tolerant of everything and committed to nothing.'*" Advertising at least is one thing that went according to plan, according to Charles Hayward. "We had always planned to do *some* advertising after we saw the reviews."

In mid-April, when *The Closing of the American Mind* made its first startling appearance on the *New York Times* bestseller list at #13 (in the *Book Review* dated April 26, but prepared two weeks in advance), there were only the 10,000 copies of the book in print—and only 7000 copies had been advanced when the book was shipped the week of February 25. "That's very unusual," according to Hayward, who pinpoints "the incredible velocity of sales" as a factor in Bloom's book making it onto the *Times* list (the book also made the *Washington Post* list dated April 26). To many observers, the book was a "fluke" bestseller on a "soft" list, a theory not disproved by the few copies actually in bookstores at the time.

Hayward says "The 7000 copies were very broadly distributed—clearly, a large number of the reporting stores were reporting it as a bestseller. We don't know which stores, obviously, report to the *Times*, but I assume it is a cross-section of the chains and the major independent stores. I've never been associated before with a book that only had 10,000 copies in print when it made the list." S & S immediately went back to press. The book climbed to number 11 on the next *Times* list, then to 10, then to five, and three, and two and one on the list dated June 7.

On other bestseller lists around the country, it was the same story: #8 on the *Washington Post* list of April 26; up to seven the next week, then to six, next to five and finally to one. It made its first appearance on the *Boston Globe* list of May 17 at four, and was one on May 24. That week was its first on the *Chicago Tribune* list, at number eight; on May 31, it was still eight in Chicago; on June 7 it was one in Chicago, too. On the West Coast, *Closing* made first appearances on the *San Francisco Chronicle* and *Los Angeles Times* lists of May 10, at 11 on the former, 12 on the latter. By June 7, when it was number one everywhere else, it was three in L.A., but still only seven in San Francisco. By June 14, it was number one all over. The *PW* list (published a week before issue date), drawing on reporting from all these cities and others, tracked the book this way: number 14 on May 15; to number 11, then seven, to five, then two and one on June 19.

Ann Zeman says the book got its start in independent stores—partly a function, she says, of the fact that the initial audience was in the major cities on the East Coast. Now sales have begun to spread out around the country, she adds, and the book has moved into the top 10 at both Walden and Dalton and is number one at Ingram, as well. Simon & Schuster will publish a paperback edition of the book as part of its Touchstone line in spring 1988.

The book that has made Bloom a celebrity is first, the author says, "a book about a life I have led . . . witnessing my life as a teacher." And the lessons Bloom has learned in his lifetime make the book, as he sees it, "a book about the refined pleasures one can have if one exercises one's mind. . . . Unity is abandoned. Life becomes a matter of taste; reality will come later, young people say. But I don't think so. The basis of a fully sensual life is unity." Bloom focuses on the university in his book, as he has in his life, because, he believes, "The obvious place for that exercise in a democratic society is at the university, but they've become factories."

His book, "neither proscriptive or prescriptive," is thus also about "my sense of the impoverishment of our intellectual life. . . . Where are the refined lawyers, the refined doctors? What place is there in public life for the whole range of our capacities? I'm not urging a particular type, not even a particularly moral type. . . ." This last point is crucial.

'Are People Reading It?'

Reading it narrowly, many see Bloom's book as a neo-conservative reaction to the last 30 years of American social history. (The book was a main selection of the Conservative Book Club.) The author himself says, "The first question is, Are people reading it? The second question is, Are people reading it narrowly? . . . I suppose," he says, "that it is seen by some as neo-conservative, but I see it as a book firmly in the 'liberal tradition.' It is 'hot,' in fact, in the liberal centers—in the *New York Times*, the *Washington Post*. It belongs, obviously, to neither political party." As Charles Hayward says, "Some of the issues Bloom deals with are embraced by conservatives, but he really crosses all bounds. If it were just a book that appealed to conservatives, it wouldn't be so successful."

"The narrow view," Bloom says, "is that if I am criticizing rock music [which Bloom does at length], then I must come from the 'it comes from the Devil' school, or the 700 Club. No. I am suggesting in my argument that certainly Goethe was not less erotic than Mick Jagger. . . . If I'm criticizing divorce [which Bloom also does], I must be defending the family. Nothing could be further from the truth. I do believe that children are better off if their parents like them and stay together; I abhor the self-justification of parents who fool themselves into believing that they can do anything they want and that it doesn't affect their children."

Bloom, best known for his literal translation of Plato's *Republic* into English (published by Basic Books in 1968), says that his book probes "the mystery of the language of our souls" and adds that "in tracing the roots of the language," readers are "discovering that life is like it is in a 19th century novel. You discover that your father is a count and that you are not a servant. There is philosophic wonderment. Around us people say, 'I'm getting my act together,' 'I'm just being myself,' 'These are my values.' But there is an enormous sense of emptiness in our talking about what it means to live. We are obviously disconnected, and all this is a script written by Nietzsche." Bloom suspects that readers find "terror and relief that they might break free." What is the best way to understand our society? Bloom asks. "Understand their gods and you know everything." He is piercing our language in order to focus attention on "the problems of living in a democratic society."

'An Accurate Description'
"The book is not quite kosher to any group. I have many opinions. . . . Some may be 'conservative,' or 'liberal,' or 'neo-conservative,' but this is a strange argument, I find. It shows how narrow our political discussion is. The book is not a defense of anything; it is just a more accurate description of American life than they are getting from the popular social critics. . . . Why is someone like Christopher Lehmann-Haupt so moved? He represents the *Times*, but he is a man in his middle age with children who cares about the kind of life they lead."

Bloom believes that "the book is conservative insofar as there is obviously no freedom of mind in the Soviet Union. Aside from that, I am a corrosive force that appeals to liberals. I am conservative in that I defend the existence of the university. I support the people who are most likely to support the university. That the book has gone up the center is not an accident."

Bloom delights in the outrage and controversy that swirl around him now that he is a bestselling author (in France as well). Of course, there had been no thought of such bizarre distinction; at last one can believe the modesty of an author who claims never to have expected his book to reach so many: "The world of the bestseller is so peculiarly American," Bloom says. "There's almost no connection between that and what I was doing in this book. . . . One runs a small operation and it gets *plugged in*. There's a peculiar tone to it. But of course, the eternal intellectual dialectic"—Bloom begins to speak theoretically—"is that one has contempt for the crowd, but at the same time wants and needs it so desperately."

8

Book Review:
The Closing of the American Mind
CHRISTOPHER LEHMANN-HAUPT

Allan Bloom fools you in his remarkable new book, "The Closing of the American Mind," which hits with the approximate force and effect of what electric-shock therapy must be like. He begins by describing contemporary college students—or at least the ones he has taught and observed at such schools as Yale, Cornell, Amherst and the University of Chicago, where he now teaches—and he finds these students wanting and symptomatic of what's wrong with American society today.

They don't read the classics. They get their information from movies and drug out on rock music. They lack passion and commitment and the capacity to love. They are confused, and the universities they seek help from merely reflect their confusion. The problem, Professor Bloom asserts, is the relativity of truth in the academic mind today. "Openness—and the relativism that makes it the only plausible stance in the face of various claims to truth and various ways of life and kinds of human beings—is the great insight of our times," he writes. But this openness has had the paradoxical effect of closing the American mind.

So the reader is bound to think that this is a traditionalist speaking—after all, most of his previous books have been translations of Plato and Rousseau—and that what he is going to insist upon is a return to traditional values. Ho hum and yawn. But then, in a critique of feminist demands, he writes: "I am not arguing here that the old family arrangements were good or that we should or could go back to them. I am only insisting that we not cloud our vision to such an extent that we believe that there are viable substitutes for them just because we want or need them."

This turns out to anticipate the larger point of his book. For what he goes on to argue is not that absolute values can or should prevail over relative ones. We lost that possibility when Friedrich Nietzsche came upon the scene, "arguing with unparalleled clarity and vigor that if we take 'historical consciousness' seriously, there cannot be objectivity, that scholarship as we know it is simply a delusion, and a dangerous one, for objectivity undermines subjectivity."

Instead, Professor Bloom insists, certain values should be judged superior to others, but we can only discover them through the kind of liberal education that was dismantled in the American university during the 1960's.

Then, in the extraordinary central section of his book, called "Nihilism,

Christopher Lehmann-Haupt is a senior book reviewer for the *New York Times*. This review is reprinted with permission from the *New York Times* (March 23, 1987):13.

American Style," he analyzes how that dismantling came about through the conquest of American thought by a corrupted version of German philosophy. "This popularization of German philosophy in the United States is of peculiar interest to me," he writes, "because I have watched it occur during my own intellectual lifetime, and I feel a little like someone who knew Napoleon when he was six."

No summary would do justice to Professor Bloom's anatomy of trivialization whereby Nietzsche's description of revolutionary violence became ultimately reduced to Bobby Darin singing "Mack the Knife." Its cogency can best be suggested by the author's conclusion that the gaping void behind our current babble about morality, happiness and the way we ought to live, would instantly be revealed if only we could forbid the use of such shopworn expressions as "life-style," "values," ideology," and "charisma," all of which had their sources in serious and complex ideas.

It should be evident by now that this book is going to make a lot of people mad—feminists, scientists, black-power advocates and champions of relevance. And indeed it is probably vulnerable to charges of elitism, antiquarianism, exaggerated subjectivity and skewed generalization from the particular. I'm troubled by the author's hostility to natural science. Will it be completely beside the point of philosophy, I wonder, if particle physics arrives at a Grand Unified Theory and computer science succeeds in replicating the human brain?

Yet even to the degree that "The Closing of the American Mind" may be reactionary and cranky, it is valuable alone as a Nietzschean exercise in *becoming*, in the sense that, as the author puts it, "what is particular and emergent is all that counts historically and culturally." And what an exercise it is. By turns passionate and witty, sweetly reasoned and outraged, it commands one's attention and concentrates one's mind more effectively than any other book I can think of in the past five years.

Even its most devout enemies will learn from it. And to the extent they learn and disagree, they will have joined what the author defines as the ideal university, or "the real community of man," which "in the midst of all the self-contradictory simulacra of community, is the community of those who seek the truth, of the potential knowers, that is, in principle, of all men to the extent they desire to know.

"But in fact this includes only a few, the true friends, as Plato was to Aristotle at the very moment they were disagreeing about the nature of the good. Their common concern for the good linked them; their disagreement about it proved they needed one another to understand it. They were absolutely one soul as they looked at the problem." And so does the author of this book link himself with his readers.

The Right Absolute Allan Bloom

HENRY ALLEN

Allan Bloom, who has written a best-selling book called "The Closing of the American Mind," may be the last American man to smoke a cigarette with elegance.

In a style that vanished with ocean liners and photographs of writers in European cafés, Bloom, at 56, grasps his cigarette halfway up, lifts it from his mouth and releases a hearty and complicated cloud of smoke. Such pleasure! Such extravagance! Such flouting of latter-day aerobic taboos! It recalls a day when smoking cigarettes gave us a certain claim on life, a lost era when we valued grace over efficiency, sophistication over longevity.

Here in his apartment next to the University of Chicago, he arranges himself along his black leather couch, a pose in which his legs seem to be crossed at least three or four times. There's a gargoyle voluptuousness to him—his double-breasted Parisian suit; his magnificent ears where the light shows through and illuminates veins, the shine of his bald head, teeth that he bares now and then for emphasis, and an elaborate nose leaking smoke like a dozing dragon.

"Those people are depriving us of our *rights*, and I hate to be intimidated by *moralism!*" Bloom says, speaking of the tobacco puritans who shake their actuarial statistics in our faces. He says this in a midwestern smoker's baritone, a drawl that reminds you of Jack Benny, smug and puzzled. "There was a time when, ahhh, people, you know, used to find something *beauuutiful* in smoke, people used to love *faaactories*, the sky full of smoke, it represented energy, prosperity . . ."

He savors the curlicues of perversity here, the rejection of progressive American orthodoxy. This is pure Bloom. He smokes. He never exercises. He disdains rock music, feminism and black nationalism. He believes that the '60s were "an unmitigated disaster." He has nothing but contempt for the bedrock philosophic premise of the brightest undergraduates of the last quarter century: "Everything is relative." Now he has written a book that is at the top of best-seller lists in both America and France and has won the Prix de Genève.

"I seem to have touched a nerve," he says.

The book is subtitled "How Higher Education Has Failed Democracy and Impoverished the Souls of Today's Students," but it attacks the liberal pieties of a whole generation of educated Americans. He says we have closed our minds to 2,500 years of hard-minded thinking about truth and absolutes and replaced it with an unthinking tolerance founded on the "openness" of social science,

From the *Washington Post* (June 18, 1987, style section) C1-C3. Reprinted with permission.

relativism and our feelings. This book is making him famous. Only a few months ago he was known best among neoconservatives such as Nathan Glazer and Irving Kristol, and among students at Cornell, Yale, the University of Toronto, Tel Aviv University, the University of Paris and the University of Chicago, where he is a professor on the Committee on Social Thought.

Now he's a celebrity who gets interviewed by Howard Cosell, appears on CBS' "The Morning Program," or sits on his couch and talks while a photographer's strobe blitzes away, lighting up patches of smoke and the intellectual funk of his apartment: a samovar, walls stacked with compact discs of classical music and hung with 18th-century paintings. The windows tremble in a hot wind blowing across the campus.

"It is a source of stupefaction that this would happen. I never considered myself a writer. I'm a teacher. In a way I feel kind of . . . kind of guilty for all the people who *are* writers who hope to be on the best-seller list someday, who live for that and don't get it and it came to me as a kind of free gift, like God coming to Abraham and announcing, 'I've chosen you!'"

And he laughs and laughs. And smokes. And talks like this, strings of half-sentences: "There's this continuous need on my part to say, you know, when I'm talking, this kind of, to say let's go back, get it right, and that's a mistake, it's, I think, you know, a kind of anxiety . . ."

His book is yet another torpedo fired at the dry-rotted hull of the good ship Liberalism, but that isn't enough to explain its popularity. There have been plenty of celebrated torpedoes in the last 10 years—Thomas Sowell's "Ethnic America," George Gilder's "Wealth and Poverty," Charles Murray's "Losing Ground," Christopher Lasch's "The Culture of Narcissism"—but none has sold like this one. It is also yet another jeremiad against the shallowness of the American intellect, in a tradition that goes back to Henry Adams, Henry James, H. L. Mencken, Dwight MacDonald and so on, a native art form founded on self-flagellating comparisons to Europe. "The longing for Europe has been all but extinguished in the young," Bloom complains. But working in this tradition doesn't explain the success of the book either.

Bloom rubs his fingers together, sifting for the right word. He says: "I think people are sick and tired of the way they're talking and, ahhh, and this offers them a chance to look for common-sense language to describe themselves. This sort of I-feel-good-about-myself or I-feel-comfortable-with-such-and-such . . . The people who talk like that, those are the characters, the crazies, you know . . . it gives me the willies."

Educated Americans, being language prudes, can go into beady-eyed ecstasy at the way Bloom casts a whole list of modern vocabulary into the outer darkness. The Bloomian twist is that these are the very words that our university elite have taken for granted for decades, in their striving to become committed, concerned, value-loving personalities creating life styles of self-fulfillment and authenticity. *Committed . . . values . . . personalities* . . . Bloom loathes these words, loathes their social-science namby-pambyness, is horrified by our ignorance of their German pedigrees reaching back to Nietzsche and Max Weber, and inveighs against the way they blur moral distinctions.

For example, he writes that "when President Ronald Reagan called the Soviet Union 'the evil empire,' right-thinking persons joined in an angry chorus of protest against such provocative rhetoric. At other times Mr. Reagan has said that the United States and the Soviet Union 'have different *values*' (italics added), an assertion that those same persons greet at worst with silence and frequently with approval. I believe he thought he was saying the same thing in both instances, and the different reaction to his different words introduces us to *the* most important and most astonishing phenomenon of our time, all the more astonishing in being almost unnoticed: there is now an entirely new language of good and evil, originating in an attempt to get 'beyond good and evil' and preventing us from talking with any conviction about good and evil any-more. . . . The new language is that of *value* relativism and it constitutes a change in our view of things moral and political as great as the one that took place when Christianity replaced Greek and Roman paganism."

Strong words, big thoughts. He writes the way he smokes, one thought after another, implications and nuances fuming into the air, a sensual crankiness. The University of Chicago has tended to attract bristly types like Bloom. It has a hermetic, lonely atmosphere, medieval buildings rising from the prairie in an attempt to reconcile the American experiment and the history of western culture. The campus is surrounded by slums. It is a very serious place that takes itself very seriously, "the Harvard of the Midwest." The wind howls through the Gothic arches. . . .

At Cornell during the armed black-power upheavals of the late 1960s, he rejoiced when some of his students descended into the chaos and handed out an excerpt from Plato's "Republic."

"They really *looked down* from the classroom on the frantic activity outside, thinking they were privileged, hardly a one tempted to join the crowd," he writes. "They had learned from this old book what was going on and had gained real distance on it, had had an experience of liberation. Socrates' magic still worked."

Bloom had just turned 16 when he arrived at the university in 1946. He ended up a member of the coterie around a German political philosopher named Leo Strauss, who died in 1973, a man whom Bloom has described as living "a life in which the only real events were thoughts."

Strauss argued against relativism and for the idea of "natural right"—morals grounded in nature and the order of the universe. His students have fanned out through academia and government: Walter Berns at Georgetown University, Robert Goldwin at the American Enterprise Institute, Harvey Mansfield at Harvard, Harry Jaffa at Claremont McKenna College. A recent article in the Heritage Foundation's Policy Review listed a number of Straussians in the Reagan administration—Gary McDowell at the Justice Department, William Kristol at Education—and repeated the frequent observation that Strauss influenced columnist George Will.

Bloom got his doctorate under Strauss in 1955, with a dissertation on a Greek philosopher named Isocrates. He taught in Chicago's adult education department for a number of years before he got visiting professorships at Yale and Cornell, then tenure at Cornell. It was at Cornell that things began to go wrong.

As late as 1965 Bloom was writing that students were "extremely grateful for anything they learn. A look at this special group tends to favor a hopeful prognosis for the country's moral and intellectual health. . . ."

"I sit here in splendid isolation," he says. He has an older sister who lives in Chicago. He has never married. His building, called The Cloisters, has housed 11 or 12 Nobel Prize winners, Bloom isn't sure how many. Saul Bellow, who wrote the foreword to Bloom's book, lives in the building next door.

Bloom has not mellowed.

The word "feminism" prompts a wince of impatience. "Feminism in its extreme form condemns everything from the Bible to the erection, as you know—the history of mankind is rape, rape, rape, and it lacks nuance." Rock music, he writes, is "hymns to the joys of onanism or the killing of parents . . . a muddy stream where only monsters can swim." It was supposed to take us back to "the true source, the unconscious . . . And what have we found? Not creative devils, but show business glitz. Mick Jagger tarting it up on the stage is all that we brought back from the voyage to the underworld."

He loves attacking rock; it churns him up to a dark froth of chuckling. He says: "The way I knew I was right about something was the kids got angry, that's very important, you touch that anger. They all say, 'Yeah, but there's one group, Duran Duran, or Santana, which is different.' I had this hilarious thing three weeks ago, I was in Jerusalem and I was staying at this hotel. I had to give a lecture in two hours and I was unprepared and suddenly I heard rock music just shaking the room and I couldn't study and so I called next door and asked could they turn down the hi-fi, and they said that's not a hi-fi, Santana is playing here tonight, *right outside my room*, and they went on for eight hours, blasting out, and I said this is hell—you know, they bring to everybody his appropriate punishment. I was going to have dinner with Teddy Kollek [mayor of Jerusalem] that night and we had to leave the restaurant because it was so loud we couldn't hear, and I was being pursued in Jerusalem by what I'd attacked in the U.S. Isn't that, doesn't that seem like a parable of some kind? . . ."

He rubs his fingers, he laughs, he smokes and he talks about a world "in which, ahhh, there is no erotic imagination, no erotic longing. You know, the original title for the book was 'Souls Without Longing.' And, ahhh, the, I, impotence has never been, something, you know, see, if they were trying and not making it . . . it's that the world is full of some kind of erotic magic, and it has lost that. Nietzsche has a wonderful description of how the world looks when you're passionately in love and then when you're cooled off, the different richness of things. Eroticism is what fills the world with life.

"You see, so much of the inspiration of this book came from Rousseau—whatever he teaches, whether it's compassion or God or politics, somehow it uses that energy as the fuel . . . This powerful tension, this literal lust for knowledge was what a teacher could see in the eyes of those who flattered him by giving such evidence of their need for him. His own satisfaction was promised by having something with which to feed their hunger, an overflow to bestow on their emptiness. His joy was in hearing the ecstatic 'Oh, yes!' as he dished up Shakespeare and Hegel to minister to their need . . . The itch for what appeared to be only sexual intercourse was the material manifestation of the Delphic oracle's command, which is but a reminder of the most fundamental human desire, to "know thyself.' "

And you there, taking notes in the back row—did the earth move for you too?

"When I first read Hobbes I was 16 or 17. He says that nothing is naturally right or wrong. I liked that because it would give me all kinds of justifications. As I got older I realized that I would prefer Plato with all of his restrictions, because he's truly erotic, you know. I mean, you could say the three authors who most influenced me are Plato, Rousseau and Nietzsche, all highly erotic authors, erotic in the sense that eros is the most interesting phenomenon of man, both body and soul."

This is what we have lost with all our liberation, Bloom says. We're trapped in a wasteland of relativism where everything is permitted but nothing is true, the hellishness of a wasteland being not frustration but the absence of desire. This is what the old can never forgive in the young: a failure to have fun. And that's what this book is about: souls without longing.

Bloom is not one of them. He is a man of conspicuous appetite—as a friend says, "Ascetic? You should see Allan Bloom in a Chinese restaurant." Smoking away in his French suit, here in the ivory tower, he says, "I bless a society that tolerates and supports an eternal childhood for some, a childhood whose play-fulness can in turn be a blessing to society. . . ."

Then it's time for lunch at the faculty club. He ambles intently down the hot, bright, windy sidewalks of the campus, smoking cigarettes, talking. He sees a friend, a fellow professor. He waves. He calls to him, in his smoker's roar. He says: "I'm number one!"

10

Troubled Souls: Where We Went Wrong
WILLIAM KRISTOL

All serious revolutions are revolutions of ideas. If the Reagan Revolution turns out to be a preview of a real revolution, we may look back on three books that changed our settled views of the economic, social and intellectual universe.

At the beginning of the 1980s, George Gilder's "Wealth and Poverty" provided a critique of conventional economics' mechanistic view of economic activity and its neglect of the importance of human incentives. Four years later we had Charles Murray's "Losing Ground," a dissection of liberal social policy based on the recognition that these policies have deleterious effects on citizens' motivation and character. Having thus called attention to the central importance of character, Messrs. Gilder and Murray invited, as it were, serious and critical reflection on the state of our minds and of our souls. In "The Closing of the American Mind: How Higher Education Has Failed Democracy and Impoverished the Souls of Today's Students" (Simon & Schuster, 392 pages, $18.95), Allan Bloom, a political philosopher at the University of Chicago, has given us that.

And how he has given it to us: No other recent book so brilliantly knits together such astute perceptions of the contemporary scene with such depth of scholarship and philosophical learning. No other book combines such shrewd insights into our current state with so radical and fundamental a critique of it. No other book is at once so lively and so deep, so witty and so thoughtful, so outrageous and so sensible, so amusing and so chilling.

Mr. Bloom begins with an examination of the souls of our young people. The great virtue they have been taught explicitly and implicitly by our schools, our media and our culture, is openness. Openness—"and the relativism that makes it the only plausible stance in the face of various claims to truth and various ways of life and kinds of human beings"—is thought to be our great insight. Our students are therefore marked by an easygoing, non-judgmental, indiscriminateness of mind, and by a deep indifference of the soul.

Deprived of a serious education, lacking a real engagement with the great works of literature or the great people and events of history, our young people cheerfully enjoy various trivial pursuits, without any sense of the grandeur, the depths and the dramas they are missing. "The longing for the beyond has been

William Kristol is chief of staff/counselor to the Secretary, U.S. Department of Education, and the son of Irving Kristol, social sciences educator and editor. This article is reprinted with permission from the *Wall Street Journal* (April 22, 1987):30.

attenuated. The very models of admiration and contempt have vanished." Thus, Mr. Bloom concludes, "what is advertised as a great opening is a great closing."

Having in the first part of his book allowed us to see with new clarity and depth the state of our souls, Mr. Bloom devotes the latter two-thirds to explaining how this came to be. Part Two, "Nihilism, American Style," consists of an "explanatory dictionary of our current language," of terms like "the self" and "creativity" and "culture" and "values." All these terms, Mr. Bloom shows, are part of the language of "value relativism"; they bespeak a life of the American mind that consists of an un-self-conscious vulgarization of German philosophy, particularly of the thought of Friedrich Nietzsche. Nietzsche's high-minded, tough-minded and tragic account of modernity's movement "beyond good and evil" has become, in America, "easy-going nihilism," a mere mood of mood-iness, a vague disquiet, "nihilism without the abyss," a celebration of choice but with all choices having lost their significance, having become "no-fault choices."

Mr. Bloom's "explanatory dictionary" of our "abstract substitutes for thought" uncovers the assumptions taken for granted by our vocabulary, and shows the vast gulf between the original and serious meaning of these terms and their current easy use. As he movingly says:

"I have tried to provide the outline of an archaeology of our souls as they are. We are like ignorant shepherds living on a site where great civilizations once flourished. The shepherds play with the fragments that pop up to the surface, having no notion of the beautiful structures of which they were once a part. All that is necessary is a careful excavation to provide them with life-enhancing models. We need history, not to tell us what happened, or to explain the past, but to make the past alive so that it can explain us and make a future possible. This is our educational crisis and opportunity. Western rationalism has culminated in a rejection of reason."

Our universities, he concludes, are not places where serious thought, where a living transmission and criticism and renewal of the tradition thrive. "The University now offers no distinctive visage to the young person . . . no vision," nor a set of competing visions, of what an educated human being is. The universities fail in their fundamental task.

I hope this summary has given a sense of this remarkable book. Only a bit less remarkable has been the reaction to it by the cultural establishment. This book—a fierce and fundamental attack on the establishment and all it stands for, all that it has brought about—has so far won only praise from The New York Times, The Washington Post and the newsweeklies.

Many of the reviewers who have praised Mr. Bloom's book have not faced up to the consequences of Mr. Bloom's ideas. A college president praises Mr. Bloom's "rich and absorbing" book, with no indication that the institution over which he presides stands fundamentally indicted by it, and with no indication that he has any sense of the need for or urgency of fundamental reform. It is as if the intellectual establishment decided Mr. Bloom's book was too fresh, too invigorat-ing, too impressive to ignore or condemn, so it should be patronized, and domesticated, and defanged. But the fangs remain.

It is true that Mr. Bloom is no conventional political or social conservative; it is true that he resists signing on to any particular political or social movement, and that no such movement could substitute for the kind of serious study and thought that Mr. Bloom believes necessary. But it is also true that this thought will not occur widely without the kinds of reforms that only a broad-based political and social movement can bring about. Such a movement should take as one of its guides this extraordinary book.

11

A Professor Decries Closing of the American Mind

MICHAEL W. HIRSCHORN

Allan Bloom had an awful experience the other day.

The University of Chicago professor's book, *The Closing of the American Mind,* had been out for almost a month when a reporter from the student newspaper, the *Maroon,* dropped by.

The student had come to write a story about the controversial author of a book that argues, among other things, that the current college generation has lost its taste for reading and intellectual pursuits.

"And the youngster came over and he had never seen the book, not opened a page of it, brought the *Time* magazine review, which was a lousy review, by the way," the professor says, the words coming so fast he is almost breathless. "It never occurred to him that there's something strange about a university student beginning with *Time* magazine and ending there for deciding what to say to a professor in his own university."

"What an ethos!" he says.

Mr. Bloom is amazed by many things these days, not least by the immediate and powerful impact *American Mind* is having in academe, in the national news media, and even in France.

Put simply—which is the only way one can summarize a book that encompasses Plato's *Republic,* Mick Jagger, Woody Allen's film *Zelig,* the student riots at Cornell University in the 60's, and much more—Mr. Bloom argues that students today are dispirited, lack curiosity, and are less cultivated than any generation he has known in his long teaching career.

They are, he says, obsessed with rock music and movies and lack the intellectual tools to consider the great questions of life.

Likewise, he argues, universities are in disarray and are offering little to jolt this generation of students out of its collective lethargy.

"It is becoming all too evident," Mr. Bloom concludes, "that liberal education . . . has no content, that a certain kind of fraud is being perpetrated."

The first wave of reviews has been favorable, sometimes ecstatic. Christopher Lehmann-Haupt, writing in the New York *Times,* called the book reactionary and cranky, but added, "It commands one's attention and concentrates one's mind more effectively than any other book I can think of in the past five years."

From the *Chronicle of Higher Education* (May 6, 1987):3. Reprinted by permission.

'I'm Astonished'

S. Frederick Starr, president of Oberlin College, wrote in the Washington *Post*: "Few books in recent years come close to Allan Bloom's grand tour of the American mind in the ambition of their reach or the breadth of their grasp."

"I'm astonished by the extent of the coverage, I'm astonished by the sales, and I'm astonished by the favorableness of the response," says Mr. Bloom, happily puffing on a cigarette and clearly relishing his time in the limelight.

Mr. Bloom is unused to such fame. Known widely in academic circles for his translations of Jean Jacques Rousseau's *Emile* and Plato's *Republic*, the veteran professor in the university's Committee on Social Thought says he proceeded with *American Mind* only upon the friendly insistence of a long-time soul mate, the novelist Saul Bellow.

A Multitude of Subjects

Mr. Bloom, dressed with the traditional rumpled elegance of a veteran professor, speaks much as he writes, with energy. (Late in the book he writes, "The analogies tumble uncontrollably from my pen.") Eagerly discussing his work, his mind ranges over a multitude of subjects, leaving a guest guessing where the conversation will take him next. Often Mr. Bloom will begin a new sentence even before he has finished the previous one.

"I thought my students and my small circle would have some interest in it," he says of the book, chatting in a sun-splashed, turret-like office he shares with another professor. "Maybe that was a modesty of vanity," he adds, breaking into a gravelly laugh. "Obviously, this was the right moment."

Indeed, his *American Mind* will find resonance with the ever-increasing clamor of voices criticizing higher education and the current generation, from Secretary of Education William J. Bennett's insistence that colleges provide more intellectual bang for the buck to the New Right's charge that colleges are encouraging moral decay.

But Mr. Bloom's book is careful to avoid the facile sermonizing he says is part of the conventional right-wing critique of contemporary culture.

For instance, he says, at a recent symposium at Yale University a professor of tax law was not satisfied with his discussion in *American Mind* of how rock music has transformed life into a "nonstop, commercially prepackaged masturbational fantasy."

"He started yelling at me, Why don't you say rock is immoral? Say it!" Mr. Bloom recalls. "I don't understand this insistence that I be part of the Moral Majority."

Observing, Not Condemning

The 56-year-old Mr. Bloom does not want to appear the crusty old curmudgeon, either, and he is careful to note that he is only observing, not condemning. But, if *American Mind* conspicuously eschews a political agenda, the book makes the case that the intellectual life Mr. Bloom so loves has a relevance to every facet of modern living.

In a chapter on relationships, the professor argues that the sexual revolution has robbed sex of all mystery or eroticism.

When everything is possible, everything becomes "no big deal."

"This passionlessness is the most striking effect, or revelation, of the sexual revolution," he writes.

What bothers Mr. Bloom is not the wanton promiscuity he perceives among today's youth, but rather the paucity of intellectual prowess that is brought to bear on the basic questions of sex and love.

"The language is clichéd," he says. "Get in touch with oneself, and, I'm o.k., and, I don't feel guilty, Got to make a commitment.

"You would be amazed what serious discussion there is in Rousseau, in Nietzsche on the question of masturbation," he says. "I mean Nietzsche really thought that out."

Bridging Generations

"Whenever I raise such issues, the immediate reaction is, This is moralism. It might be a way of discussing how we can have more fun. I mean that seriously. Classic literature is supposed to address all problems that are intimate and [among students] there's an absolute confidence that it doesn't."

Mr. Bloom is making a plea for what he sees as the historical purpose of education, as posited in *The Republic*, the search for the good life, leaving the cave of ignorance for the sunshine of truth. "Literature stretches over the gaps in generations to give you models that aren't present," he says.

The contemporary mindset, he says, has impeded the academic search for higher truths by imposing on us a cultural relativism, where everything is considered to be as good as everything else. We have, he argues, denied ourselves the right to judge what our reason tells us to be the truth.

Universities, he says, do nothing to combat that failure, offering a pointless smorgasbord of academic offerings that leave students confused and without guidance.

A Great Books Approach

The top institutions, he says, don't have the wherewithal to provide a full four years' worth of liberal education.

"I'm quite convinced that Harvard could teach anything it wanted to its undergraduates," he says. Top colleges "can choose who they want and they can do with them what they want and they don't have any idea what to do with them."

To solve this problem, Mr. Bloom suggests something along the lines of the old Great Books approach to learning, though he readily agrees the approach has many drawbacks. Nonetheless, he writes, students must become acquainted "with what big questions were when there were still big questions; models, at the very least of how to go about answering them; and, perhaps most important of all, a fund of shared experiences and thought on which to ground their friendships with one another."

Yet Mr. Bloom is not yet looking for solutions. He is, instead, hoping that his book will help focus minds on what the problems are so that solutions may emerge later.

"I'd like to point people in a direction where they can find food for their hunger," he says. "Just self-consciousness is a very good thing to have."

12

How Bloom Did It:
Rhetoric and Principle in
The Closing of the American Mind
WILL MORRISEY

At least two questions arose in the early reviews of Allan Bloom's book. Given its extraordinary popularity (outstripping even the confessions of Patty Duke during the long, hot summer of 1987), how much has the "American mind" really closed? A citizenry that buys hundreds of thousands of copies of a twenty-dollar volume whose longest chapter is titled, "From Socrates' *Apology* to Heidegger's *Rektoratsrede*," deserves some credit for open-mindedness at the very least. The American bourgeoisie could have bought more copies of the new picture-album about Elvis, but no: it preferred to read "The Nietzscheanization of the Left or Vice-Versa," "Rousseau's Radicalization and the German University," and "Swift's Doubts." Does the Enlightenment really work, after all? Are Americans quite so far gone in decadence as Bloom appears to contend?

And then there is the matter of Allan Bloom's mind. Cultivated, powerful, incisive, witty—no one denies its virtues. But what does it really think? Most reviewers assumed that what they saw on the surface was what they were getting: a defense of the classics grounded firmly upon ancient Greek philosophy. But a more interesting and challenging view was urged by those who noticed the literally central place of Nietzsche's argument in the book, and decided that this, and other details, betray a nihilist's hand within a puppet-Plato. Does Bloom secretly revel in the very decadence he decries?

These questions about both minds in question, America's and Bloom's, were raised tellingly in one truly intelligent review, "The Closing of Allan Bloom's Mind: An Instant Classic Reconsidered" by Charles R. Kesler.[1] Professor Harry V. Jaffa's essay in this [book] develops many of the same points more amply, as does Professor Thomas G. West's [essay, "Allan Bloom and America"]. These critics agree that Bloom fails sufficiently to appreciate politics: he has little to say about civic, as distinguished from liberal, education; he speaks eloquently of eros but not enough of thymos; he preaches without having recourse to any discernible religion; a true son of the University of Chicago, he ignores gymnastic, and therefore exaggerates the effects of music; he fails to appreciate the statesmanship of the American founders, instead regarding them as mere practical Lockeans.

Will Morrisey is Book Reviewer for *Interpretation: A Journal of Political Philosophy.* Reprinted with permission from *Interpretation* vol. 16, no. 1 (Fall 1988):145–156.

Kesler suspects Bloom of harboring a politic nihilism; Jaffa at first raises that suspicion but ends by claiming Bloom "cannot decide" between Socrates and Nietzsche.

These substantial objections deserve careful study because there seems to be so much truth in them. Bloom does indeed avoid any thorough discussion of civic education. Far from apolitical (he introduces political considerations on almost every page), Bloom nonetheless gives few indications of how America might educate citizens, as distinguished from cultivating decent intellectuals. Bloom seems to want the rose without its protective thorn. He does not seem to appreciate the virtues of the thorn, which does a lot more than just sit around looking pretty.

As Leo Strauss taught, when competent men make glaring errors, readers should search for some underlying intention before sighing, "Homer nods." Has the translator and interpreter of Plato's *Republic* and Rousseau's *Letter to D'Alembert* suddenly forgotten what makes a political man? Has he forgotten the need for, even the nobility of, some political men, and the consequent need for civic education? Some twenty years ago, Bloom wrote:

> Today religion, philosophy, and politics play little role in the formative years. There is openness, but that very openness prepares the way for a later indifference, for the young have little experience of profound attachments to profound things; the soil is unprepared. Previously a professor had to free his students from prejudices: now he must instill prejudices in them if he wishes to give them the experience of liberation.[2]

Has Bloom now simply given up on religion and politics, leaving philosophy to live by its wits alone?

Both civility and prudence ought to give us pause, here. A book titled *The Closing of the American Mind*, with a subtitle about failing democracy and impoverishing souls, most likely has more than a pinch of rhetoric in it. But although Professor Jaffa charges Bloom with confusing politics with rhetoric, neither Bloom's critics nor his defenders have shown adequately how Bloom's rhetoric works—how a semi-obscure professor managed to galvanize the American mind with energy from his own not-simply-American mind. Only after seeing how Bloom writes can one guess why he writes that way, and what he really thinks. Only then does criticism make sense.

Judge this book by its cover, for a moment. The title appeals primarily to contemporary "liberals," secondarily to "conservatives." To assert that "the American mind" has done anything so drastic as to close, will surely distress persons who pride themselves on keeping their minds open and broad. This matter of failing democracy must also trouble and intrigue them. Could there be a new *social problem* to address? Even the colors of the dust jacket—green and grey on white—go well with the outfits worn at meetings of the National Organization of Women and similar gatherings of earnest sorts. This is just enough to overcome the contemporary liberal's repugnance to any mention of souls (as distinguished from *soul*, a concept they remember fondly from twenty years ago). "Souls" appeals rather to conservatives, who also worry about education failing democracy. "Foreword by Saul Bellow" ropes in just about everyone, too: liberals, because prominent artists must have our respect; conservatives, because Bellow is one of us, sort of. The backcover endorsements cover a similarly wide range: liberals will trust Conor Cruise O'Brien and a woman professor from Harvard; conservatives, or at least "neoconservatives," can nod happily at words of praise by Walter Berns and Harvey C. Mansfield, Jr.

Bloom dedicates the book to his students. But a dedication need not reveal a book's real audience; the preface here gives a better look at that. There Bloom speaks as a teacher, to teachers. He lets them know he is one of them ("no real teacher can doubt that his task is to assist his pupil to fulfill human nature against all the deforming forces of convention and prejudice"). He also tactfully lets them know he knows a bit more about teaching than they do (look at what makes your students angry, he advises, and—this, subtly—don't concern yourself too much with charges of "elitism"). Centrally, he suggests that the "small number" of students who "will spend their lives in an effort to be autonomous," undertaking the "solitary quest" of philosophy, are "models for the use of the noblest human faculties and hence are benefactors to all of us, more for what they are than for what they do." (When reviewers call Bloom a philosophic and not a religious man, they are simply telling us what he says of himself in his first four pages.) Though solitary, philosophers are not apolitical, paradoxically enough; Bloom concludes the argument of his Preface by observing that in modern regimes, politics and "reason in its various *uses*" (emphasis added) cohere more tightly than in traditional regimes. This raises the question of the relations among the reason that discovers theories, the reason that finds uses (abetting production, among other things), and politics—including *the* political passion, anger, to which Bloom has directed the attention of his "fellow" teachers, soon to become his students.

For years, Allan Bloom has been an untimely man. But the success of *The Closing of the American Mind* depends upon a rhetorician's good timing. The Introduction, "Our Virtue," resembles certain writings by Professor Jaffa, or perhaps the early Paul Eidelberg; its far greater popular success owes something to the second thoughts old "liberationists" now are having about liberation.

Bloom identifies moral relativism as a symptom of moral egalitarianism, and says that such relativism has replaced "the inalienable natural rights that used to be the traditional American grounds for a free society." Observing that "every educational system has a moral goal that it tries to attain," the formation of "a certain kind of human being," Bloom calls the new goal "the democratic personality," characterized by "openness." Although liberalism as such has a "tendency" toward "indiscriminate freedom," the American founders and the modern political philosophers they read, finally insisted on the natural basis of certain discriminations: e.g. the distinction between freedom and slavery, determined not by public opinion or popular sentiment but by the self-evident truth that all men are created equal by God. The Creator-God of the Declaration of Independence gets left out of Bloom's account, perhaps for philosophic reasons but surely also for rhetorical ones. Bloom is not addressing an audience for whom traditional piety counts. Whereas Jefferson and Franklin, who privately denied the divinity of Jesus, nonetheless appealed to God in the Declaration, knowing how their countrymen would conceive of God, Bloom's rhetorical problem is different. He must address secularized individuals suspicious of any mention of God, especially in political discourse.

Bloom is nonetheless firm on the moral point. Moral relativism denies the existence of the common good and (here the language turns less necessarily moral) "extinguish[es] the real motive of education, the search for the good life." "Openness" closes the mind: contemporary or relativist liberalism defeats itself. Only reason enables men to transcend the cave, which relativism merely digs deeper and wider. Reason-as-modern-science does not transcend the cave, because it cannot drive us or lure us "up." It is anerotic. The American regime in its original form does not say, simply, "Liberty!" It says, "Liberty to reason," in politics, religion, and education. "What makes its political structure possible is the use of the rational principles of natural right to found a people, thus uniting the good with one's own," the general with a particular people and place.

Bloom claims no gift of prophecy. He knows he cannot plausibly assert some ennobling, entirely new prejudice that will help to point his readers toward the truth. Instead he more prudently argues—shrewdly appealing to the remnants of generosity and to the strong will-to-gullibility in contemporary liberalism—for "respectful treatment" of "error," the myths that inculcate real virtues (and sometimes real vices) in men. Moral relativism often does rest on more than moral egalitarianism; there is a certain civility involved, however dim; Bloom will avail himself of it. By "respectful" treatment, however, he means not merely living-and-letting-live, but examining these myths as if they might be true, or contain some truth, as determined by reason—"to seek the good by using reason." Showing that moral relativism refutes itself in theory (relativism unjustifiably exempts itself from its own strictures) and in practice (fostering extremism, not toleration, "left" and "right"), Bloom aims to re-associate reason and morality in the minds of men accustomed to segregate "facts" from "values." To moralize about the Creator-God or the natural law would not work with such individuals. In order to liberate them from their unexamined assumptions or prejudices, Bloom begins with those prejudices, appealing to some features of them while dissolving others.

Bloom divides the body of his book into three parts: "Students," "Nihilism, American Style," and "The University": the taught, the teaching, the teaching institution. He does not have a section called "Teachers," preferring to measure his criticisms of his readers in small, sometimes concentrated doses. In "Students," he begins not with criticism but nostalgia. He invokes the period 1955–1965, when students were really students—and, more usefully for his purposes, when so many of today's senior faculty were students. "The old was new for these American students, and in that they were right, for every important old insight is perennially fresh." But they were also *victims*, victims of the university, which failed to give them a truly liberal education. Bloom thus begins to skillfully alternate complaints about today's wayward youth with subtle flattery and apparent sympathy for their elders.

During the course of these assessments, Bloom does indeed commit the error seen by Jaffa and Kesler: he talks books, not the Book; he almost ignores gymnastic. That is to say, he dampens spiritedness. But this is not nihilism; it is rhetoric, concededly for a philosophic not a religious purpose. Bloom is deliberately bookish because his audience is accidentally bookish. To put it another way—as Bloom does in his commentary on Plato—he "abstracts from the body," not because he has forgotten it, but because (as Socrates does) he wants his auditors to forget it. He wants to get them beyond their materialist historicism—that supreme combination of the bodily and the bookish, tending toward too much or too little thumos. Bloom uses the bookishness of historicist ideology against materialism, and thus finally against historicism itself, which tends to regard books as mere epiphenomena. Far from believing books merely artificial, as Jaffa contends, Bloom clearly regards them as written speeches, partly artificial but also originating in nature and pointing at nature. "Without books there is nothing to see" is a rhetorical exaggeration; surely no one imagines that, without Bloom's book, there would be no crisis of the university to see.

Physical eros characterizes the student generation. Bloom exploits the tendency of the middle aged and the elderly, inclined to other vices, to deplore this state of affairs, now aggravated by "liberation" ideology. He also manages to attack the eroticism of the young without making his audience feel too old-fashioned; after all, some of them grew up on Elvis.[3] This too has much to do with timing; at this stage of the game it might even become fashionable to be un-hip. Mesmerized by Bloom's discussion of eroticism, some reviewers overlook his introduction of philosophic and political themes into this account of music. He shows how music can prepare the soul for reasoning, or very nearly spoil it. He remarks that the Enlightenment believed it could do without such preparation, only to find it had removed a good defense against irrationalism by forgetting how to tame rougher passions with subtler ones—yielding bad consequences for education and politics. He even gets in a few rhetorical jabs by associating rock music with that horror, capitalism. That will make ex-counterculturites stop and think—no small achievement.

Rock music makes a solipsistic world, but one with social consequences; they are called by an oddly prim latinism, "relationships." Here Bloom observes what happens when a nation makes equality a social fact instead of a moral and political principle considered self-evidently true in a carefully defined sense. Young people are "spiritually unclad, unconnected, isolate, with no inherited or unconditional connection with anything or anyone." Again, Bloom deliberately exaggerates in a bookish way, claiming that "America is actually nothing but a great stage on which theories have been played as tragedy and comedy." Speaking to a generation of teachers for whom "concrete" and "abstract" represent respectively the apogee of praise and the nadir of blame, he shows how ideas matter even with respect to the stubborn and ever-fascinating nature of sexuality. Teacher, in your liberalism had you supposed social equality and sexual passion to be twin goods? Professor Bloom has a sobering thought for you: egalitarianism and liberation yield "passionlessness," the re-conceiving of sexual activity as "no big deal." Even compassion, the very fuel of social liberalism, gets diluted by the colorless fuel of egalitarianism. For if all are the same, why pity? And why desire? Self-protectiveness (anger and fear) replaces eros. Lacking firm natural attachments, young people attach themselves to themselves, fearful of anything much beyond that. Hectored by moralists who do not know how to educate either the reasonable or the passionate parts of the soul, students blink uncomprehendingly—not even "last men" but last persons. Because all but the youngest teachers have at least some dim memories of old eros, Bloom's rhetoric effectively appeals to their sense of superiority to their students, while carefully teaching teachers of their own longstanding errors.

The book's central part, "Nihilism, American Style," uncovers the moral and intellectual foundation of those errors: Nietzschean egalitarianism, a concept no one anticipated. Bloom clearly states that the American founders do not teach relativism or historicism. But he also says, "The great mystery is the kinship of [relativism and historicism] to American souls that were not prepared by education or experience for it." This point receives no adequate response among Bloom's critics. Professor Jaffa rightly complains, "There is not a single reference to Cooper or Hawthorne or Emerson or Whitman or Howells" in the book. But to take the central name on the list, Emerson was the man who popularized German historicism in the United States; the first American "intellectual" adumbrates nothing less (or more) than Hegelianism with the rationalism cut out. And Emerson was one of Nietzsche's intellectual heroes. This means that Americans have been somewhat vulnerable to such corruption almost from the beginning.

Bloom does offer an explanation, albeit a problematic one. He describes John Locke as an Enlightenment man who intends "to extend to all men what had been the preserve of only a few: the life according to reason." This is not theoretical reason but primarily the subspecies of useful reason that serves production, the conquest of nature. Eros and thymos do not disappear, but they are tamed, subordinated to modern natural rights—that is, to the *self*-centered. Nor is this "self" a soul in either the classical or the Christian sense; when Lockean man finds his quest for joy too joyless, he looks not to "Greek" happiness or Christian salvation, but eventually to "creativity," as anticipated by Rousseau and perfected by Nietzsche. In his central chapter (the eighth of fifteen), titled "Creativity," Bloom attacks the nihilists' exaltation of making at the expense of thinking. Democratic America shrinks from the pride of these nihilist philosophers. Rather, "there is in America a mad rush to distinguish oneself, and, as soon as something has been accepted as distinguished, to package it in such a way that everyone can feel included." Bloom deplores this egalitarianism, in part because it affords so little solid ground for statesmanlike prudence, and for politics generally. After the founding generation, genuine statesmen are rare in America, and these few do not much engage Bloom's attention here.

Hence modern political philosophy, even in its soberest forms, leaves itself vulnerable to the thrust of Nietzsche's terrible swift sword. "History" cannot replace divine providence because scientific progressivism is a lie with respect to the soul, if not with respect to the body. Insofar as the Founders partake of that philosophy—and, rhetoric aside, let's face it: Jefferson, Madison, and Franklin all did, deeply if not exclusively—their work is also vulnerable, although perhaps not in the same ways; founding a political regime is not philosophizing. In the book's central passage, Bloom summarizes Nietzsche's refutation of rationalist egalitarianism and describes Nietzsche's irrationalist elitism, his warlike will to power. Peaceful commercial republicanism stands perennially threatened by those who reject its philosophic premises. Then, in a passage publicly unnoticed by his critics, Bloom writes,

> . . . a cultural relativist must care for culture more than truth, and fight for culture while knowing it is not true. This is somehow impossible, and Nietzsche struggled with the problem throughout his career, perhaps without a satisfactory resolution.

Bloom parts company with Nietzsche precisely on the issue of the rational pursuit of truth. While conceding the force of Nietzsche's objections to Enlightenment rationalism, he concedes nothing to Nietzsche's attack on Socrates and Plato. He also insists that the Enlightenment, "whatever its failings," at least kept reason "at the center" of the soul—praising what Nietzsche condemns. . . .[4]

"Western rationalism has culminated in a rejection of reason. Is this result necessary?" The book's third part, "The University," contains the longest chapter in the book, "From Socrates' *Apology* to Heidegger's *Rektoratstrede*," suggesting a sort of history of reason as embodied in educational institutions.

But he begins with America. Citing Tocqueville on the danger of "enslavement to public opinion," Bloom echoes the sentence in the preface, on knowing oneself only by one's students. Democracy increases this danger, and modern democracy increases it still more, by making popular consent legitimate and insisting that it can be rational. "Reason transformed into prejudice is the worst sort of prejudice, because reason is the only instrument for liberation from prejudice." Then there is a sentence Bloom's critics overlook, a sentence that challenges their criticisms in two ways: "For modern men who live in a world formed by abstractions and who have themselves been transformed by abstractions, the only way to experience man again is by thinking these abstractions through with the help of thinkers who did not share them and who can lead us to experiences that are difficult or impossible to have without their help." The bookish or 'abstract' character of Bloom's argument throughout his book is, in his judgment, dictated by the character of contemporary Americans, particularly those of the 'intellectual' classes. Bloom's critics apparently do not perceive Bloom's understanding of modernity, and this prevents them from effectively challenging it, except on the issue of whether or not the American *founding* was nearly so 'abstract' as Bloom contends. The question of the effectiveness of civic as distinguished from liberal education in today's climate, necessarily depends not only on whether Bloom's rhetorical argument portrays the founders accurately, but on the extent to which he portrays today's Americans accurately.

Bloom calls "the best of the modern regimes," liberal democracy, "entirely [the] product" of Enlightenment rationalism, which he describes as "perhaps not even primarily, a scientific project but a political one." Again he does not acknowledge the Declaration's language about the Creator-God. "The authors of *The Federalist* hoped their scheme of government would result in the preponderance of reason and rational men in the United States." But this kind of reason, Bloom continues, is rudderless. Here Jaffa's critique makes sense. Put somewhat differently, if you ignore the fact that the Declaration admits no inconsistency between reason and the Creator-God, and if you therefore "bury" that God in the name of reason, it is no surprise that you find reason rudderless. In my opinion, although not professedly in Jaffa's, the founders were well aware of the distinction between reason and revelation. Their Declaration is a politic and political synthesis of the two, a synthesis that in time made America quite safe for individuals of varying religious and even irreligious hues.

However, given the nature of Bloom's audience, which ranges from religious-latitudinarian to atheistic, perhaps he must remain silent on the Creator-God of the Declaration, knowing that He will not be resurrected in such minds by Allan Bloom's rhetorical powers, formidable though these are. If intellectuals will not be brought to believe, however, perhaps they may be brought to think, to reason in a new (in fact very old) way, a way that enables them to discover the ends of human life instead of reducing those ends to the subhuman. Bloom begins by arguing that Enlightenment philosophers are not ideologues but true philosophers, men who attempt to give "the rational account of the whole." "Philosophy is not a doctrine but a way of life"—notice, here, Bloom's ultimate defense of genuine "openness"—"so the philosophers, for all the differences in their teachings, have more in common with one another than with anyone else, even their followers." Modern philosophers differ from Socrates not in their nature but in their political program. But they too know that philosophy can never be truly popular, for it inspires no awe, benefits no populace, consoles no person. Reason will never truly enlighten non-philosophers, and Enlightenment philosophers know that, even as they pretend otherwise. The modern university reflects the Enlightenment political program, whereby "the powerful are persuaded that letting the professors do what they want is good"; instead of educating aristocrats, as Socrates does, the Enlightenment educates the populace. *This pretended enlightenment is the modern version of civic education.* "The fact that popularized rationalism is, indeed, superficial is no argument against the philosophers. They knew it would be that way." Bloom takes the half-understood Enlightenment prejudices of his audience of demi-educated educators, and teaches them what those premises are, and what they logically entail. He thus imitates Enlightenment rhetoric even while showing its limitations. Speaking of ancient philosophy, Bloom observes: " . . . philosophy's response to the hostility of civil society is an educational endeavor, rather more poetic or rhetorical than philosophic, the purpose of which is to temper the passions of gentlemen's souls, softening the hard passions such as anger, and hardening the soft ones such as pity." Substitute "contemporary teachers" for "gentlemen" and you will not find a better summary of what Bloom is doing in *The Closing of the American Mind.* Like the gentleman of antiquity, the modern professor has tenure and therefore need not work too hard; he is often prey to thymotic passions, crystallized in modern rationalist fashion as ideology; a post-Christian, he makes much of compassion and *noblesse oblige.* He needs a civic education but now in true modern fashion, he is allergic to civility, to the God-given political order. His patriotism has atrophied. He is not a true aristocrat. Hence his civic education must appear to be, and may be if his abilities and temper allow it, liberal, that is, liberating. A man whose political ambitions have gone underground, or so far aboveground as to lose sight of the ground, must be brought back to political thought while remaining under the illusion that he has transcended it by the force of his intellect and the greatness of his heart. It helps if recently he has bruised his foolish head on some reality, and is ready to listen to a more sober voice. This voice asks him a question: "Does a society based on reason necessarily make unreasonable demands on reason, or does it approach more closely to reason and submit to the ministrations of the reasonable?" To prepare modern intellectuals to think about that question is a small step in the right direction. And to suggest that "perhaps," Nietzsche and Heidegger "did not take seriously enough the changes wrought by the modern rationalists and hence the possibility that the Socratic way might have avoided the modern impasse," conveys the thought of Leo Strauss in a Straussian way—namely, without bringing Strauss's name to public attention. Finally, to warn that one way to force reason and egalitarian dogma to cohabit may be seen in Soviet tyranny, and to do this so that contemporary "liberals" may find it plausible, is a public service.

In his final chapter, "The Student and the University," Bloom shows how he would reintroduce the prudent study of politics. "The apolitical character of the humanities, the habitual deformation or suppression of the political content in the classic literature, which should be part of a political education, left a void in the soul that could be filled with any politics, particularly the most vulgar, extreme and current." Here Bloom uses the snobbery of cultivated souls against their current political egalitarianism. At the same time he manages to suggest that a "coverup" has occurred, that Enlightenment has not fully enlightened certain political matters. And there is more: "Political science is more comprehensive than economics because it studies both peace and war and their relations"; it is "the only social science which looks war in the face." "Most unusual of all, political science is the only discipline in the university (with the possible exception of the philosophy department) that has a philosophic branch." Not only moderation, justice, and courage, then, but even the love of wisdom may be found among some members of the American Political Science Association, although these do not constitute the majority of the Association. Bloom would reintroduce politics, and the prudent study of stern justice and anger, by the means of flattery and curiosity—seduction, the art of eros. In Bloom's judgment, for his chosen audience, that is the only effective way to do it.

Neither Nietzsche nor any nihilist says, as Bloom does, "Philosophy is still possible." A nihilist would say, as Bloom does, "It is the hardest task of all to face the lack of cosmic support for what we care about." But this does not in itself reveal nihilism; much depends upon who "we" are. Are we beings animated first and last by love of our own—our lives, children, cities? Is death the king of terrors for us, at best to be courage overthrown? Or are "we" convinced that philosophy means "learning how to die"? Do we regard "the intense pleasure of insight" to be sufficient compensation for the knowledge that we must die? Those are the principal alternatives for the Socratic philosophers. Among their successes, the Epicureans come closest to nihilism, but are not nihilists. Nihilists find insight painful, simply. Epicureanism might be a plausible charge against Bloom, were he to leave sufficient evidence to decide the issue. He does not. Part of the antidote to mental closure is to raise questions more than one delivers answers.

It is right to regard civic education as prior to liberal education. Unfortunately, too many modern intellectuals imagine themselves liberated from civic matters, even from the obligations of civility. "Conservatives" who see the folly of this, simply are not part of the problem. They can be addressed in a different way. Students can be addressed in yet another way; even the most sophomoric among them are only junior ideologues. It isn't hard to disillusion them. Many have some of the right passions: patriotism, a desire for some sort of love beyond the universe bounded by Sesame Street and MTV. A more directly civic education may reach them. But someone has to give them that education, and there are not enough teachers who can do so. Bloom speaks to the unable majority of his profession. *Mirabile dictu,* some are listening.

---

[1] In *The American Spectator,* Vol. 20, No. 8, August 1987, pp. 14–17. For the stupidest review by an intelligent man, see Paul Gottfried: "A Half-Open Mind."

[2] Allan Bloom: "The Crisis of Liberal Education," in Robert A. Goldwin, ed.: *Higher Education and American Democracy,* Chicago: Rand McNally and Company, 1966, pp. 121–140.

[3] Professor Kesler does object to Bloom's "old-fogeyish" characterization of rock music as having "the beat of sexual intercourse." "Could this really be said . . . of the Beatles, Bob Dylan, the Four Tops?" No, but—*pace,* Professor—folksinging and Motown aren't rock, and, as for Paul McCartney's cutesy little melodic hooks—if that's rock, it's pumice. And even it induced erotic paroxysms in the girls of its day.

[4] It is true that Nietzsche wants spiritedly to defend not culture for its own sake, but culture for the sake of life. The real antagonism of truth, for Nietzsche, is not culture but life. Bloom never agrees with Nietzsche that truth, or the rational quest for it, are somehow incompatible with life. (If one denies that the quest of *unaided* reason serves truth, or life, one gets on the road not to Germany or Athens, but to Jerusalem.)

THREE

Bloom in the Classroom:

Students and Colleagues Pay Tribute to a Spellbinding Teacher

In Chapter 3 James Atlas, in "Chicago's Grumpy Guru: Best-Selling Professor Allan Bloom and the Chicago Intellectuals," confronts the Grumpy Guru in person, in his Hyde Park lair. Atlas places *The Closing* in its context as a product of the Committee of Social Thought: it is a book written in "Social Thought style." "My own theory," writes Atlas, "is that Bloom appeals to the perennial student in so many of us—that yearning, after a few years out in the busy world, to restore for a brief moment the innocence of our undergraduate days. . . . His book is about the joys of education: how to live in the world without losing one's soul. Bloom is a Socrates figure; he wants to go among his pupils debating the great ideas."

John Podhoretz and Michael P. Zuckert, two of Bloom's many outstanding students, testify in Bloom's defense as character witnesses. Whatever one may think of *The Closing,* there can be no doubt about Bloom's honesty and passion for teaching. His erotic teaching style exerts a powerful influence over the souls and lives of his faithful students. "His concern about his students *above all* is that their *eros,* or as he better puts it, their yearnings and longings, are no longer . . . capturable in the educational enterprise, but instead are finding other . . . lower outlets. . . . Desire is too readily gratified, does not reach for the heights, does not lend its energy to pursuits like education and therefore settles for so much less."

13

An Open Letter to Allan Bloom

JOHN PODHORETZ

Dear Professor Bloom:

Who would have guessed that the single most important figure in my own college education would become one of the leaders in the battle to remake American education as a whole? And yet that is what you have become, as the author of the decade's most surprising best-seller (and, along with Paul Johnson's *Modern Times,* one of the two most important conservative works of the decade). This unlikely turn of events began with the publication of an article in this magazine five years ago and culminated in the publication of *The Closing of the American Mind,* the only book in this country's history to sell over 250,000 copies in hardcover with chapter titles like "From Socrates' *Apology* to Heidegger's *Rektoratsrede*" and "Rousseau's Radicalization and the German University."

Who could have expected this? Certainly not you. The dedication of your book reads simply, "To My Students." As you are deservedly considered one of this country's outstanding teachers, the dedication is not surprising. Your students, I remember, clustered about you like acolytes, seeking to glean the mysterious truths that you seemed to have in your possession but were not entirely willing to reveal.

Finally, you've chosen to come clean, to tell your students what you've really been getting at. And what you've been getting at is them—us. Yes, *The Closing of the American Mind* is about the corrosive effect of moral and philosophical relativism on our culture. But your real concern is your students, and how relativism has changed the face of the American college campus. It is your description of life on campus—and, implicitly, the life that is led by today's college graduates once they leave campus—that makes *The Closing of the American Mind* the first book about my generation that delivers a painful shock of recognition, and does not elicit a hoot of derision on every page. Reading *The Closing of the American Mind* is a little like eavesdropping on your parents while they are talking about you. Even though what they are saying is not very flattering, it's sort of nice to be paid attention to.

The portrait you paint is a saddening one. It is of the first generation of elite Americans who have grown up without what the sociologists call the "mediating institutions"—the first generation bereft of the multi-generational family, the first to be raised almost entirely without religious instruction, the first to be more the children of Freud than the children of God.

John Podhoretz is a contributing editor of *U.S. News and World Report,* and the son of Norman Podhoretz. This essay is reprinted with permission from *National Review* (October 9, 1987):34–37.

In other words, a generation reared without absolutes, without a coherent moral or political education. Instead, we have been taught "values," and, as you make clear, "values" are the most relativistic things of all. For if "values" are nothing more than a word for any set of beliefs that someone holds valuable, then the only belief we are all obliged to respect is everyone's right to his or her own "values." This kind of cultural relativism is destructive because it "teaches the need to believe while undermining belief." So, while we live awash in moralism (see South African sanctions or the anti-smoking vendetta), we are constantly aware that our morals have no mooring.

In this world, the only immutable laws are those of science. That is why all political and social thought now must come armed to the teeth with statistics. All tangible conclusions must be proved scientifically, by actuarial, demographic, or Minnesota Multiphasic means. Otherwise any conclusion may be dismissed as merely indicative of its author's "values." (It is, by the way, part of your triumph that you refuse to use a single statistic, or any other form of independent, corroborating evidence, anywhere in the book.)

How did a healthy, happy, fervently religious, and enormously purposeful and productive America sink into this mire of relativism? You argue that American relativism—I'm-OK-you're-OK relativism—is a cheerful, mass-marketed, and thereby bizarre translation of Nietzschean nihilism as further developed in the thought of Freud, Weber, and Heidegger. . . .

A nation that lacks a binding moral philosophy cannot have a community of interests. In such a place, as you say, "there is no good reason for anything but self-indulgence."

Family bonds are weak. As you write, "The moral education that is today supposed to be the great responsibility of the family cannot exist if it cannot present to the imagination of the young a vision of a moral cosmos and of the rewards and punishments for good and evil." Children who grow up in a moral chasm need to protect themselves; selfishness is therefore "not a moral vice or a sin but a natural necessity. The 'me generation' and 'narcissism' are merely descriptions, not causes."

Now, as my generation forms itself into couples, the results are predictably parched and awful. In a college dorm, and in those (ever longer) uncommitted years after, sex is easily available, but not transforming. "They are not promiscuous or given to orgies or casual sex, as it used to be understood. In general, they have one connection at a time, but most have had several serially. They are not couples . . . They are roommates, which is what they call themselves, with sex and utilities included in the rent." Something greyer, and more somber, has taken the place of love. "Relationships, not love affairs, are what they have."

There is nothing satisfying about this "relationship" business. It is all a deal with the devil. Men struggle to reconcile their mates' responsibilities with their own, and women struggle to deal with the tug-of-war between their desire to have children and the cultural instruction to have a "career." The reason that love has now become a form of work is that the home has become a center of conflict. Sex and utilities may be included in the rent, but there is no stability and no joy.

In the last ten years, men have been under orders to change their natures.

"The souls of men—their ambitious, warlike, protective, possessive character—must be dismantled in order to liberate women from their domination." But this effort is doomed to failure. The new order can force men to change, but the change has consequences: more separation, less connection, and, ultimately, more divorce, with the spiral continuing ever downward.

"Women are pleased by their successes, their new opportunities . . ." But they also know that if they want children they may have to pursue their careers "while caring for children alone. And what they expect and plan for is likely to happen. The men have none of the current ideological advantages of the women, but they can opt out without too much cost."

The remarkable success of your book testifies to the power of your diagnosis and our yearning to escape from our plight. Yet it is just as you have us convinced you understand us that your argument, in my view, breaks down. Your prescriptions for our cure betray a misunderstanding of our country and my generation as profound as the insights of your diagnosis.

First the country. If it were true that the entire country were suffering from the crisis of the spirit that you diagnose, I think we would be finished. But to believe that, one must believe that the university's corruption is an indication of the nation's corruption. Your clear implication is that the nation has corrupted the university. You sound the old Platonic warning that the lower, "bronze" men threaten the viability and even the lives of the highest, "golden" men. Thus, you say, the university should be the home of nonconformity in the United States. "It is necessary that there be an unpopular institution in our midst that sets clarity above well-being or compassion, that resists our powerful urges and temptations, that is free of all snobbism but has standards." . . .

The American university has never been, and should not consider itself, the repository of "unpopular" wisdom in a political system hostile to ideas. "Unpopular wisdom" needs no protection in a society whose first rule is that freedom of speech shall not be abridged. Such an idea assumes that wisdom is always under siege in a democracy. But of course, the primary purpose of democracy is to allow people the freedom to propagate and support ideas and save themselves from "unpopular" wisdoms. The university is not Plato's Republic; it is a center of education. And it was doing pretty well until the elites lost their souls.

Even more troubling, I think, is your ultimate recommendation that political philosophy can save us—or, more precisely, that the study of political philosophy is the necessary first step on the way back to moral health. It seems to me that encouraging students with the particular ills you diagnose to become philosophers is to risk a cure as bad as the disease. The study of a work as profoundly unsettling as Plato's *Republic*, for instance, will only increase a student's sense of alienation and confusion, unless he is well grounded in the glorious possibilities of his civilization. Students who have been told forever that "right" and "wrong" are just terms describing value choices are not yet ready for the wisdom of a Plato.

But they are ready for the wisdom of the poets. How can a student understand what is wrong with his ideas about relationships and love unless he is touched by the beauty of a John Donne poem? If he does not understand what is so terrible about Anna Karenina leaving her husband for her lover, perhaps he is just not reading the book well enough—or, more accurately, being taught its meaning correctly. "Students," you write, "have powerful images of what a perfect body is and pursue it incessantly. But deprived of literary guidance, they no longer have any image of a perfect soul, and hence do not long to have one."

I remember one night, at 3:00 A.M., after taking that Nietzsche course, still full of your thoughts, I lay in bed reading the last few pages of *The Brothers Karamazov*, weeping as I read. Dostoyevsky's ultimate message is that untrammeled reason leads you to murder not only a shopkeeper you've never known, but your father as well, or even (in the case of the Grand Inquisitor) Jesus Christ. And at the conclusion of *The Brothers Karamazov*, Alyosha's greatness of soul becomes the inspiration for a group of children who might have been inclined to follow the Grand Inquisitor's example had they not had the great gift of knowing Alyosha.

This sort of transfiguration of experience is what we get from imaginative literature and from the Bible. From philosophy we get a sense of incompleteness, of rationality under siege. That will not serve to heal a generation whose primary flaw is that its members do not believe in love. Where can we find love? Not by the obsessive self-contemplation that philosophy engenders. Socrates may have been the greatest of all men, but he was also the most detached, the most distant, the least loving.

I think we can find love where everyone before us has: in the contemplation of others. By focusing on sex, we elite Americans have too often confused the orgasm with passion, believing that sexual fulfillment was the only way to find completion. We need a little more of Dante in us: Dante, who wrote *The Divine Comedy* for a woman he never met. . . .

Those of us who have never had a transfiguring religious experience can find out what one is like by reading Herbert. Reading Nietzsche, a young student finds only the mirror image of the nihilism with which he was raised, in which he has been trained, and from which his soul longs desperately to escape.

Is learning to love too simple a solution? I don't think so. I was delighted to note that you yourself offer one chance for recovery when you observe that this generation is "morally unpretentious." Unlike the students of the 1960s, who sought moral supremacy over their elders, today's students cheerfully and straightforwardly admit their interest in making money, getting ahead. They are, you say, "nice."

This moral unpretentiousness is a sign of health, not disease. It is an indication that they know they have little to believe in and are making do with less than they need.

They—we—are fertile ground. And you have just planted a very important seed.

Your student,
John Podhoretz

14

Chicago's Grumpy Guru:
Best-Selling Professor Allan Bloom
and the Chicago Intellectuals

JAMES ATLAS

So who was this Bloom? Before he was famous, I knew him only as a constellation in Saul Bellow's firmament, a Hyde Park crony and a fellow professor in the University of Chicago's elite graduate department, the Committee on Social Thought. Perhaps, one mischievous reviewer suggested, Bloom didn't really exist; he and his best-selling book were creations of Bellow's. What Bellow had done, wrote Robert Paul Wolff, a professor of philosophy at the University of Massachusetts, in the scholarly journal *Academe*, was "to write an entire coruscatingly funny novel in the form of a pettish, bookish, grumpy, reactionary complaint against the last two decades." The "author," Wolff slyly surmised, was a "mid-fiftyish professor at the University of Chicago, to whom Bellow gives the evocative name 'Bloom.'"

Bellow did write a foreword to "The Closing of the American Mind." The book does sound like a Bellow novel now and then, especially those highflown passages that go on about what its author calls "the big ideas." But "Bloom" was indeed Bloom, I discovered, arriving in the social science lecture hall on the Chicago campus the following afternoon. The bald figure behind the podium corresponded to the photographs that had been appearing in the national press month after month. Bloom lives.

Scattered around the wood-paneled lecture hall were perhaps 30 students, notebooks at the ready. The course title was "The Education of Democratic Man: Rousseau's 'Emile.'" Stammering, smoking, pacing, scanning the class with doleful eyes, Bloom was expounding the passage where Rousseau talks about his theory of sex education. How do we regulate this dangerous passion? Bloom paraphrased, firing up his third Marlboro of the hour. Is it good or bad? And how do we get around the prohibitions enforced by religion and society? In other words, Bloom wanted to know: "What causes a man not to do it when he can?"

Gentle, intense, benign, he guided his students through the book, pausing anxiously now and then to ascertain if they were lost. Man is by nature compassionate, he explained, but society has pitted him against himself, cor-

---

James Atlas is assistant editor of the *New York Times Magazine* and author of *The Great Pretender.* Reprinted with permission from the *New York Times Magazine* (January 3, 1988):12–31.

rupted him and spoiled his natural innocence. His efforts to preserve his property and protect himself from harm—the basis of civil society—have obscured his natural rights. And what are these rights? The enjoyment of feelings; the cultivation of one's talents; the discovery of one's true nature. "That's what an education is about," Bloom expostulated. "What's happiness?"

It was simple enough, yet Bloom's students were baffled. Suspicious. It was *too* simple. "You don't believe in the power of ideas," Bloom admonished the class. "Rousseau did." So does Bloom. Ideas matter, his book proclaims on every page; and in Bloom's own life, they clearly do. "The Closing of the American Mind" has provoked a fantastic amount of debate. Even now, 10 months after its publication, large-scale attacks continue unabated. Two essays just out—by the historian Benjamin Barber in Harper's and Alexander Nehamas, a professor of philosophy at the University of Pennsylvania, in The London Review of Books—carry forward the assault that began with David Rieff's polemic in The Times Literary Supplement of London and Martha Nussbaum's damaging assault on Bloom's classical scholarship in The New York Review of Books.

Bad reviews are one thing; the responses to Bloom's book have been charged with a hostility that transcends the usual mean-spiritedness of reviewers. "How good a philosopher, then, is Allan Bloom?" demanded Martha Nussbaum, a classics professor at Brown. "The answer is, we cannot say, and we are given no reason to think him one at all." This was mild compared to the objurgations of David Rieff, a senior editor at Farrar, Straus & Giroux. Bloom, he charged, was an academic version of Lieut. Col. Oliver L. North: vengeful, reactionary, antidemocratic. "The Closing of the American Mind," he concluded, was a book "decent people would be ashamed of having written. . . ."

This fierce polemic is hedged about with a lot of very heavy philosophizing. For Bloom, the corruption of the modern world can be variously traced to Locke, whose theory of rights prepared the way for liberalism; to Nietzsche, whose critique of bourgeois culture was appropriated by the American left; to Heidegger, who gave philosophical credence to Nazism; and to many other intellectual villains, both witting and unwitting. But as I made my way through Bloom's irascible, brilliant book, it occurred to me that his disenchantment with contemporary American life had its origin in a more recent and less abstract development, one that imperiled his own way of life: the 60s. For all its dense theoretical discourse, "The Closing of the American Mind" is an autobiography.

"When I was 15 years old I saw the University of Chicago for the first time and somehow sensed that I had discovered my life," Bloom reminisces toward the end of his book. Born in Indianapolis, the child of provincial Jewish social workers, he found out about the University of Chicago from an article in the Reader's Digest. It was 1943. "I didn't know what I wanted, but I wanted out," he told me one afternoon as we sat in his office in a corner turret of one of the university's old Gothic buildings. "I asked my parents if I could go," Bloom recalled, "but they said nonsense." Three years later, the family moved to Chicago, and Bloom's parents attended a party at the home of a psychiatrist whose son was in "the Chicago program"—a loose term for the rigorous humanities curriculum that was then in vogue on the Hyde Park campus. That did it. In 1946, Allan Bloom entered the University of Chicago.

Founded in 1891 with an initial gift of $600,000 from John D. Rockefeller, the University of Chicago was determined from the beginning to model itself upon Oxford, Cambridge and the great German universities—and to do so, noted a later president, Edward Levi, "in a most unlikely geographical place." Even Bloom can't entirely suppress his skepticism about the look of his alma mater, the "fake Gothic buildings" surrounded by slums. "But they pointed toward a road of learning that leads to the meeting place of the greats."

These aren't just words. Under the stewardship of Robert Maynard Hutchins, who began his legendary tenure as president of the university in 1929, Chicago became famous as an institution devoted to the higher learning. Mortimer Adler, recruited by Hutchins to serve as a resident intellectual guide, introduced a program devoted to the classics of Western literature, and, by the mid-1930s, what had begun as a course (General Honors 110) defined a milieu. Adler is much derided today—Bloom puts him down as a kind of equal opportunity intellectual. But for a precocious Midwestern boy like Bloom, Hyde Park was the Promised Land.

Under the tutelage of Leo Strauss, the controversial German refugee philosopher who reigned over Chicago's department of political science in the postwar years, Bloom became addicted to the classics. Strauss was a fanatical celebrant of the ancient Greeks. The subsequent history of philosophy, he argued in his many books, was no more than a distortion of the values they proposed—the quest for the true, the good, the beautiful. Many classicists view Strauss's willed reading of the classics with a good deal of skepticism. Even David Grene, Bloom's tutor in graduate school, now denounces him as "a bloody lunatic."

For Bloom, though, Strauss was the very embodiment of ideas that would surface nearly 40 years later in "The Closing of the American Mind." Philosophy was a priestly calling; modern civilization had corrupted the soul of man; egalitarianism, soft-peddled by the classical philosophers, was the enemy of excellence. It's easy to see how a student at the University of Chicago in the 1940's could imbibe such notions. The *Zeitgeist* encouraged Philosopher-Kings.

"Chicago seemed like the world to me," Bloom rhapsodizes, recalling the university in the 1940's. "There was this huge stuff in the social sciences. Someone would write down 'Eros and Thanatos' on the blackboard. It had the character of a mystic code." There was plenty going on in the real world, too. "What was exciting was being free," Bloom stresses, growing animated at the memory. Fifty-fifth Street—now a bland thoroughfare—was lined with black nightclubs and bars. Mike Nichols and Elaine May did their routines in the Compass Tavern.

As an undergraduate, Bloom lacked polish. His provincial air was a far cry from the impeccably cosmopolitan figure he's since become, striding the campus in double-breasted suits from Savile Row. But he had a strong personality, David Grene recalls. "He was frightfully enthusiastic and very dogmatic, very funny." He had no practical aim in life; he just wanted to read the classics. So he stayed on as a graduate student, writing a dissertation under Grene about the Greek rhetorician Isocrates, and in 1955 got a Ph.D. from the Committee on Social Thought.

The committee, an elite graduate department founded in 1941, had an aura of venerability from the start. Conceived and funded by the historian John U. Nef, a philanthropist and patron of the arts, it was known for intellectual rigor daunting even by University of Chicago standards. Its mandate was to encourage a few highly qualified students to range among several disciplines. Toward this end, men of great eminence whom Nef had encountered in his travels abroad were brought to Chicago—among them T. S. Eliot, Marc Chagall, Igor Stravinsky and Jacques Maritain. Permanent faculty have included Hannah Arendt, the art critic Harold Rosenberg, the Polish émigré philosopher Leszek Kolakowski, the musicologist and pianist Charles Rosen—and the two "Chicago boys" (as men who grew up in the city refer to themselves no matter how old they are), Bloom and Bellow.

Bellow, who was a student at the University of Chicago during the Depression, returned in 1963, after his novel, "The Adventures of Augie March," had put him on the map. What made him decide to come back? I ask. It's a wintry Chicago day, and we're in Bellow's cramped office on the fifth floor of the Social Science Research Building. Bellow never turns on the light, I've noticed. You sit in the dark. He illuminates in other ways. Fit and dapper in a nubby brown suit, pale green shirt, bow tie, he answers my questions by way of an anecdote about the Italian writer Niccolo Tucci. A few years ago, Bellow says, he encountered Tucci on a London street and asked him what he was doing there. "I wanted to go to a foreign country where they speak English," Tucci replied.

Bloom, meanwhile, had gone elsewhere. "A committee Ph.D. was no passport to glory," he says with a bitter laugh. He taught briefly at Yale, and finally landed a tenure-track position at Cornell. "That was the great moment in my life, when I got the job. I was an assistant professor." It was then, in his early 30's, that Bloom discovered his vocation. He was a teacher. "I had a huge success," he says. His lecturing style was famous. "He spoke with extraordinary intensity," recalls Clifford Orwin, now a professor of political science at the University of Toronto. "There were moments of tension in the seminar when he would smoke the lighted end of a cigarette. . . ."

Hyde Park reflects this tension between worldliness and unworldliness, power and the contempt for power. It's a neighborhood, notes Bellow's Herzog, of "spacious, comfortable, dowdy, apartments where liberal, benevolent people live"—a Chicago version of Weimar. Even the way people refer to their telephone numbers, citing the old "MU" (for Museum), gives off a cultural emanation.

The Committee on Social Thought is the highest expression of this mentality. The students it attracts persist in their studies of Kierkegaardian relativism or ancient Chinese texts with brave impracticality. Before they begin work on their dissertations, they must pass the Fundamentals Exam—an ordeal invariably described with horror by those who've been through it. On the appointed day, candidates are given a single page with three groups of three questions especially tailored to the list of books they've supposedly been absorbing with Talmudic zeal for the last several years. They have four days to write the examination, "with an extra day for typing." A sample question: "How satisfactory do you find Boethius' explanation of the compatibility of God's infallible knowledge and man's freedom of will?"

Once they've passed the Fundamentals, students in the program can expect to spend five or six years working for a Ph.D. "There's a Jesuit in Peru who's been working for 12," volunteered Paul Wheatley, chairman of the committee. Some never graduate and never leave—"retired students," the writer Isaac Rosenfeld called them. They work in the bookshops, attend classes, become waiters at the Cafe Medici. "It's the idea of infinite education," says Edward Rothstein, music critic of The New Republic and a former student on the committee. "The one thing Social Thought doesn't do is prepare you for reality. . . ."

But philosophy, as Bloom would be the first to admit, isn't for general consumption—especially a book as difficult as his own, written, Paul Wheatley says, in "Social Thought style." So why is "The Closing of the American Mind" so popular? Who's reading it? Educators? Parents who want to find out what's wrong with their children? Five hundred thousand people with a special interest in Heidegger?

My own theory is that Bloom appeals to the perennial student in so many of us—that yearning, after years out in the busy world, to restore for a brief moment the innocence of our undergraduate days, the long nights in the library spent struggling through "The Social Contract." His book is about the joys of education: how to live in the world without losing one's soul. Bloom is a Socrates figure; he wants to go among his pupils debating the great ideas. And Chicago is his Athens.

"I'm not a writer," Bloom confides to me one day. It's dusk, and we're heading across the quad, past the beautiful Gothic buildings with their fake leaded windows. "My life is not a theodicy. It's a series of accidents that add up to a unity." What happened was that he wrote a book "about a life I've led"—and with such ardor, such passionate intensity, that people listened. Anyway, what matters is what always matters in these stories: his 87-year-old mother is proud. "My parents were always kind of, you know, nudging me at the edges." He laughs his nervous laugh. "I think this finally satisfied her. You know, to have a son who could speak his mind."

15

Two Cheers (At Least) for Allan Bloom
MICHAEL P. ZUCKERT

. . . Bloom writes, he says, from the perspective of a teacher. That indeed captures Bloom—above all he is a teacher. And at this point I must make one bit of a personal statement of my own. At one time I was a "blossom," one of those undergraduate students taken with Bloom. I think it would be fair to say that he was the teacher who made the largest impression on me as an undergraduate. I was one of those who studied with him in what he regards as the Golden Age of the early sixties when, as Garrison Keillor used to say, "all the men were good-looking and all the children were above average"—and, Bloom believes, all (or some) of the undergraduates were remarkably receptive to genuine education. I do not entirely share either Bloom's romanticism about my generation of students, or his apocalyptic pessimism about today's student generation, but at least I can say I was there and saw something of Bloom's Golden Age at Cornell—a bit like having a witness before you to describe the Garden of Eden.

Bloom has written from the perspective of a teacher—and that above all is what he is and has been. The testy, bitter, cranky man who comes through the book in some places and has dominated it for some readers only shows us a small part of the total range of that very personal voice which emerges from *The Closing of the American Mind*. Bloom is a teacher on an older model—his teaching, his students are not a job, a career or profession, not an excuse or opportunity to do research and write books, not a vehicle for supporting a family or achieving important consulting jobs. He is a teacher. He has never married and has devoted his undivided attention and care to his students. In the years I was at Cornell he lived in a student "scholarship house" where there were no boundaries between classroom and living unit, where Bloom was with students and teaching, literally, full-time. Not teaching in the sense of lecturing (although in a lecture hall he could deliver a mean lecture), but teaching in the sense of providing an example of the animating of all one did with intelligence and learning, of considering the meaning and questioning the truth and value of the prejudices most of us take for granted. If Bloom sounds cranky on occasion, if he sounds angry at students, it is because he so loves students and so loves teaching. I do not believe any man in our time has been more fully a teacher than he has.

Bloom has been a teacher—but he has also been a scholar. And his scholarship reflects to its core the very teacherliness of the man. He has written a

Michael P. Zuckert teaches at Carleton College and was himself a student of Bloom. These remarks were presented at a symposium, "The Modern University—From Bologna to Bloom," held at Rhode Island University, March 1988. Copyright © 1988 Michael P. Zuckert.

fine book on Shakespeare and several essays on topics in political philosophy, but there is absolutely no doubt that Bloom will be remembered for two works in particular—his translations of Plato's *Republic* and Rousseau's *Emile*. The connection of those two books to each other and of both to Bloom comes to light if we think of the *Republic* in the terms in which Rousseau spoke of it, as the greatest book heretofore (i.e., up to Rousseau) on education. And Rousseau had in mind his own *Emile* as the book which would supplant the *Republic* as *the* book on education. Bloom puts it a bit less contentiously, the one is the greatest ancient book on education, the other the greatest modern book. As such they raise the great conflict between the ancient and modern understandings of things at the highest level. Neither the translations, nor the interpretive essays Bloom has attached to each book have been uncontroversial, but contrary to what some critics of Bloom have suggested, both are surely serious and scholarly works. . . .

I come now to two cheers for Allan Bloom. I propose one cheer for what Bloom has helped us understand about our students; and I propose another cheer for what Bloom has helped us understand about our universities.

Bloom's treatment of students has been widely noted by readers and potential readers—indeed I believe that much of the surprising interest in the book resulted from Bloom's almost racy discussion of topics like sex in the dorms. His discussion of students has also been among the most criticized parts of his book. But I believe that Bloom's point in his treatment of students has frequently been missed. Bloom is not attempting a general sketch of the state of students and student life (and still less of American society in general). He looks at students instead from the point of view of their educability; he concludes that the formative experiences our students undergo, at home, in school, and elsewhere in American society, are not conducive to learning. . . .

Bloom's treatment of rock music—and of student life more broadly—has been seen by some as motivated either by old-fashioned moralism or by an odd sort of salaciousness. Neither is correct. Bloom is concerned with things like rock music and the sex lives of students, because he, unlike all other writers on education one finds around today, puts what he calls eros at the center of education. Here Bloom's roots in Plato and Rousseau show up very visibly, for both thinkers, in their different ways to be sure, try to show how that restless erotic desire which forms so powerful a force in post-adolescent human beings belongs to education. In the case of Plato, *eros*, while perhaps in the first case a sexually related desire, is in fact a manifestation of a broader human desire for the eternal and the transcendent. Education, especially philosophy, is another and higher expression of that same *eros*. Or for Rousseau, *eros*, a blind force which is indeed only sexual by nature, can in human beings be sublimated and transformed; and out of it can grow beautiful, rare, and wonderful human things of which the enterprise of education is a part. . . .

His concern about students *above all* is that their *eros*, or as he better puts it, their yearnings and longings, are no longer or not so much now capturable in the educational enterprise, but instead are finding other, and he believes lower outlets. Lower—almost literally. Desire is too readily satisfied, does not reach for the heights, does not lend its energy to pursuits like education, and therefore settles for so much less. He originally wanted to title his book "Souls Without Longing," but his publishers feared that title would land the book in the religion section, next to Jim and Tammie or Jimmy Swaggart. Nonetheless, his original title better captures this aspect of his argument—education which is not just training is a going-up, a passion-driven ascent from what the philosopher Martin Heidegger calls the sphere of "average every-dayness," in which one lives on the opinions and beliefs of the society around one. Such an ascent must be driven by discontent and restlessness, and by a positive desire for "completeness," as Bloom puts it. . . .

So, my first cheer is for Allan Bloom on students—right or wrong on the details, he has surely pointed to some true truths and even more given us a way to think about students in education that is much richer than most of what we are usually served up.

My second cheer is for Bloom on the university. His treatment of this theme is even more complex than his treatment of students, and perforce I must be even more sketchy in what I say about it. He argues that the education we offer is informed by a combination of two aspirations, neither one of which alone, nor both together are really adequate. The one aspiration is to pass on the disciplines of which all of us teachers are the custodians—science for the sake of science. The other aspiration is a modern political goal which Bloom identifies as "openness," or a particular version of the moral quality of toleration. In my opinion Bloom is correct in saying these two dominate our thinking about the ends of education and I think he is also correct to raise questions about their adequacy.

At the very end of his book (a part I've noticed not even all the reviewers have read), Bloom gives a *tour de force* tour of the disciplines. Let me just state baldly some of his most striking claims: the modern university presents little sense of an ordering of the disciplines, and while there are periodic worries that merely consigning young people to one or another of these doth not an education make, yet most colleges are remarkably lacking in an ability to say what more is needed, and even more impressively, remarkably unable, or unwilling to talk about the issue. I find his claim here nearly incontestable. . . .

Let me speak of a concrete example from a discipline in the same division of the university as my own. Economics is rightly identified by Bloom as that social science which is generally conceded to be most successful. Economics has an impressive body of theory, an array of conclusions, tremendous sophistication, a good deal of prestige in the world and large numbers of majors. Moreover, it has a certain "imperialist" quality to it, attempting to export its methods and concepts to other disciplines. Or perhaps more accurately to annex for Economics territories (like politics) hitherto believed to belong to other disciplines.

But this whole, bold, impressive, arrogant edifice is constructed on premises regarding human psychology, and assumptions regarding the broader context of economic behavior which thoughtful economists, to say nothing of practitioners of other social science disciplines, admit to be problematical if not plainly fictional. Now I do not mean to say that these foundational questions mean one must or ought to reject economics as a discipline, but rather that in our practice we treat the disciplines as though they had a solidity and self-givenness which in our more thoughtful moments we know not to be a correct assessment of them. . . .

We do more or less concede Bloom's point that the disciplines are not a self-sufficient way to define education. We do in fact aspire to a moral content to our educational effort: as Bloom puts it, "our virtue" is "openness." This virtue characterizes both the university as such and its students. It provides the common ground for the enterprise within the university and much of the ground for the definition of the university's moral or political contribution to society.

Just as the title he originally wanted pointed to his first theme, so the title he ended up with points to this other theme. This "openness," which is celebrated as a virtue, has the ironic result of producing a certain sort of closed-mindedness.

Bloom opens his first chapter by saying: "There is one thing a professor can be absolutely certain of: almost every student entering the university believes or says he believes, that truth is relative." Being of an empirical bent of mind I decided to test this out. I was teaching, at the time I read this chapter, a course in American Political Thought, discussing at that moment the Declaration of Independence. The Declaration claims that certain fundamental moral and political claims about equality and natural rights are "self-evident truths." So I asked my students whether they believed that: The results: YES 7%, NO 77%, NOT VOTING 16%. When I probed beneath the surface of their votes I discovered not that my students were devoted to undemocratic ideas about human inequality but rather that they were convinced there is no such thing as "truth," self-evident or otherwise, in the sphere of claims of the sort raised in the Declaration. Although Bloom had never been to Carleton, he certainly had our number. . . .

Thus, says Bloom, openness leads to closedness. We know the answers in advance and therefore do not pursue in an open-minded way the questions. Thus most of the thought of the past is rejected, dismissed, not out of a reasoned confrontation with it, but out of a prejudicial, closed-minded commitment to openness which is itself as dogmatic as any conceivable dogmatism it fears.

FOUR

Bloom on Democracy

Is He an Elitist?

Allan Bloom argues that attention to philosophical thought and reverence for heroes would be especially efficacious for America's sickness. Quick to leap on such a prescription, Benjamin Barber, in "The Philosopher Despot," replies that such things as philosophy and heroes are necessarily undemocratic and dangerous and should be suppressed in the interest of the state. Barber sees Bloom's book as an attempt to teach Americans to become less democratic, calling *The Closing of the American Mind* "a most enticing, a most subtle, a most learned, a most dangerous tract." In the past, philosophy has supported the divine right of kings, the Inquisition, the Reign of Terror, and, in the person of Martin Heidegger, modern totalitarianism—according to Barber. "Bloom's book is as artful and painless a piece of *subversion* as we are likely to encounter from a critic of democracy." Barber is so shocked, in fact, that he proposes Americans eschew philosophy altogether and read only Emily Dickinson, Walt Whitman, Henry Adams, Emerson, James Madison, Hugo Black, John Brown, Susan B. Anthony, Martin Luther King Jr., Jefferson, Franklin, Eugene Debs, Robert Taft, Henry Hopkins, and "yes, even David Stockman." A true democracy "needs no heroes." Americans instead revere "just plain folks."

But what of the fact that Bloom claims he is defending American democracy? What about the fact that Bloom says *again and again* that he believes in liberal democracy? Never mind, says Barber. Remember that Bloom is a student of Leo Strauss, and Leo Strauss, in *Persecution and the Art of Writing*, taught that philosophers must be read with care because they tend to be foxy and sometimes lie—and therefore Bloom is lying whenever he praises American democracy and purports to defend it. Get it? Got it? Good. As Werner Dannhauser says, merely to state Barber's argument clearly is to refute it.

This demonstration is repeated by H. D. Forbes in "Opening the Open Mind," from *The Idler*, a Canadian publication that shows that Bloom's argument is favorably received in Canada and that Canadians believe that they are included in Bloom's "America." However, Robert Bellah, a professor at Berkeley and another spokesman for the academic establishment, repeats the gist of Barber's argument undaunted, accusing Bloom of "academic fundamentalism." Bellah admits that Bloom's book is "the clearest revelation of the Straussian position [he has] ever seen." But this is faint praise, because, according to Bellah's unsupported accusation, "the Straussian world is that of a fundamentalist sect, where 'the truth' cannot be risked in discussion with the unsaved. Bloom . . . appears as an urbane, immensely well-educated Jerry Falwell."

A third representative of the academic establishment, Richard Rorty in "Straussianism, Democracy, and Allan Bloom I: That Old Time Philosophy," repeats the accusation of elitism. Rorty describes himself as a historicist after John Dewey. The historicist position, says Rorty, holds that Americans should not study Plato and Aristotle because "truth" and "the nature of the good" are "obsolete." Rorty paraphrases Dewey: "Society should worry only about the freedom of the universities, and not about what is taught there." And he sums up Rawls as saying "social justice is a matter of procedure" and devoid of all "substance." It "swings free of all . . . conceptions of the good." At this point, of course, Rorty's words begin to sound like a caricature of the relativism Bloom denounces. The pith of Barber's, Bellah's, and Rorty's arguments is that Bloom personally distrusts democracy, whatever he may say to the contrary.

The elitist label is greeted with scorn by Harvey Mansfield, appearing with Rorty in *The New Republic*. Mansfield shows that morality and democracy go hand in hand. In fact, democracy is impossible without a strong public morality. Subjects of dictatorships do not need a public morality, because they are controlled by others. Citizens of a democracy are the legislators, the guardians. Mortimer Adler could not agree more. "Mortimer J. Adler, the Nation's Self-Appointed Teacher for Most of His 85 Years, Takes on the 'Late-Bloomers' of Academe" introduces us to a man who has been teaching the great books since Bloom was a baby. Adler is especially proud of his Paideia Program, which takes Sophocles and Aristotle and others into the inner-city public schools of Chicago and obtains remarkable results toward educating good citizens.

William Galston, in the summary essay of this chapter, "Socratic Reason and Lockean Rights: The Place of the University in a Liberal Democracy," agrees with Mansfield and Adler that philosophy and democracy are natural allies because both depend on the doctrine of natural right. Thus, the teachings of Nietzsche and other Existentialists must be subversive of democracy.

Therefore, for the reasons Mansfield and Galston point out, Bloom is defending democracy. The problem with America is not that democracy is bad but that the people, who rule as in all democracies, are becoming corrupted. The sickness of America is caused neither by capitalism nor by the universal franchise but rather by an intellectual failing concentrated in the universities.

16

The Philosopher Despot: Allan Bloom's Elitist Agenda

BENJAMIN BARBER

Allan Bloom's *The Closing of the American Mind* is not a book, it is a phenomenon: one of those mega-literary comets that dazzles without being clearly seen, and thus mesmerizes its critics as it speeds across America's celebrity firmament. The perplexities are staggering. How does an obscure academician known chiefly for his translations of Plato and Rousseau become a national celebrity? How can a book about the decadence of esoteric European philosophers such as Heidegger climb to the top of the best-seller list for over six months and sell nearly a half-million copies in hardback? Why are Americans so anxious to welcome a book that claims they can't read, so willing to accept a polemic that excoriates their literary intelligence? Why are liberal critics and egalitarian educators beside themselves with admiration for what can only be called a raging assault on liberal tolerance and democratic education?

From its publication last spring, *The Closing of the American Mind* took the country as much by surprise as by storm. The publisher printed only 10,000 copies of a book that at least one major publisher had turned down in a preliminary version. Bloom's beatification began mildly enough with a *New York Times* daily review calling his treatise a "remarkable" exercise in "electric-shock therapy" for complacent teachers; the Sunday *Book Review* picked up steam by lauding it as "an extraordinary meditation on the fate of liberal education in this country." Unqualified raves from many other critics followed, culminating in major spreads in weeklies such as *Newsweek*.

By late last summer, still a best-seller, the book had become a touchstone for every imaginable contemporary debate on education, as well as a totem for the neo-conservative assault on higher education, affirmative action, equal opportunity, rock music, the Sixties, the young, and sex. In September George Will paid homage to Bloom in a *Newsweek* column titled "Learning From the Giants." George Levine ran a controversial national colloquium on Bloom at Rutgers University, and *Reader's Digest* took a full-page ad in the *New York Times* to reprint their editor's version of what was called Allan Bloom's decisive "answer" to the question "What's wrong with American education?" Typical of the hyperbolic hoopla was a three-part cover story in *Insight* that referred to Bloom's argument as

---

Benjamin Barber is a professor at Rutgers University. He is the author of *Superman and Common Men: Freedom, Anarchy, and Revolution* (1971) and *Liberating Feminism* (1975). This essay is reprinted with permission from *Harper's Magazine* (January 1988):61–65.

"the most penetrating analysis of the United States to appear in many years." The book is now descending from its apogee, but its extraordinary trajectory suggests a phenomenon that has yet to be explained.

What on earth is going on here? It certainly is not the old literary love story, for the affection America seems to feel for Bloom is anything but reciprocated. It is as if the professor and the country have met on a blind date and the country, though found sorely wanting by the professor, nevertheless insists on finding the professor irresistible. He charges Americans with flat-souled philistinism, and they buy almost a half-million copies of his scathing denunciation. He claims the country has deserted the university and blames democracy for the debacle, so the country adopts him as its favorite democratic educator.

Can the mystery be unraveled? We know well enough how this peculiar land of paradox—ambivalent land of the free—can make paradoxical heroes out of freedom's severest critics. How it offers popular success to those who contemn its popular virtues; and how, to those who disdain its materialism, it offers riches. *The Other America, The Making of a Counter Culture,* and *The Greening of America* had similar receptions. Yet those books were written in the spirit of progress and reform; they saw American reality as out of tune with the promise of the American soul, and they called for progress not reaction. In *The Closing of the American Mind* we confront a different phenomenon: a most enticing, a most subtle, a most learned, a most dangerous tract. What we have here is an extraordinary and adept exercise in the Noble Lie aimed at persuading Americans that philosophy is superior to ordinary American life and philosophers superior to ordinary American citizens; and consequently this nation's higher education ought to be organized around the edification of the *few* who embody philosophy rather than the *many* who embody America.

Bloom's book is as artful and painless a piece of subversion as we are likely to encounter from a critic of democracy. For it is written by a philosopher for whom rhetoric is "a gentle art of deception," a polemicist who believes political writing in a democratic society is necessarily an act of concealment. If Americans have failed fully to understand what Bloom means, it may be because Bloom has not said exactly what he means—or does not mean exactly what he has said. In its overt hostility to all the "leading notions of modern democratic thought" such as "equality, freedom, peace, [and] cosmopolitanism," *The Closing of the American Mind* would seem to qualify as one of the most profoundly anti-democratic books ever written for a popular audience. That, however, is not how Bloom puts it. Ever the prudent educator, Bloom believes that to say exactly what you mean about liberty and equality when you live in a liberal democratic state is to court the fate of Socrates, who was tried and executed by the Athenians for thinking little of their liberty and less of their democracy. Not one of the critics raving about the nobility of Bloom's philosophical project for the reconstruction of the American soul seems to have noticed that his philosopher "loves the truth" but "he does not love to tell the truth." The leading characteristic of this ostensible paean to the virtues of open discourse is in reality a commitment to closed communication—to esoteric meaning and rhetorical ambivalence.

Bloom's celebrants have accepted his intent as stated in his preface:

This essay—a meditation on the state of our souls, particularly those of the young, and their education—is written from the perspective of a teacher. . . . [who is] dedicated to liberal education . . . Attention to the young, knowing what their hungers are and what they can digest, is the essence of the craft.

Commentators have treated his book as a racy companion volume to E. D. Hirsch's *Cultural Literacy*, with which it seems to share a yearning for a more civilized culture and an affection for the so-called Great Books. Typical of this interpretation is the *Reader's Digest* review:

[Bloom] tells us the closing of the American mind has resulted directly from "openness"—that perverse new virtue which urges us to be non-judgmental and prevents us from "talking with any conviction about good and evil." . . . Yet Americans long for something lost—the great moral truths upon which civilization rests. . . . Education is not merely about facts—it is about *truth* and the "state of our souls" . . . If there is a reassertion of moral truth rather than relativistic values, this book will be remembered as a catalyst.

The Allan Bloom honored by the critics is the philosophical moralist, doing battle with the forces of philistinism, relativism, and nihilism that beset a civilization living in the valley of the shadow of death—that is to say, in the shadow of the death of God. He appears in their encomiums as liberal humanist and concerned teacher, making war on students who fail to live up to the Socratic ideal.

With the artful and worshipful interlocutors of Socrates perching as archetypes in his imagination, Bloom can hardly be other than appalled by the average American eighteen year old, who is more than a little artless and never very reverent, particularly toward teachers. Bloom rails with indignation at the young and what the corruptions of democratic education (the Sixties) have done to them. He is repelled by their tastes, their pastimes, their sexual practices, their "niceness," their music, their reading habits, their lack of "prejudices," and their "flat-souled" lack of nobility. No wonder he complains that Harvard, Yale, and Princeton are not what they used to be—the last resorts of aristocratic sentiment within the democracy." At times Bloom's unrelenting Sixties-bashing sounds like the screeching of an aging parent wrapped in a Roman toga—ranting about the nobility of the ancients because he cannot comprehend his daughter's purple hair. When he tells us that an American university which pledges itself to serve democracy's needs is indistinguishable from a German university which dedicates itself to the service of Nazism, or that Woodstock is the American Nuremberg (flower children listening to Jimi Hendrix are to be regarded as clones of black-shirted fascists organizing a new era of genocide), we may wonder what has happened to the philosopher in search of great souls.

Yet underlying Bloom's hostility to the Sixties is a more profound anger. Like the champions of the new conservatism, Bloom is hostile not only to the moral decline of the university and its students but to much of what democrats and progressives have accomplished in the last fifty years. He does not simply oppose feminism or the abolition of the double standard in the abstract, he condemns them because they destroy the old sexual arrangements whereby a man could "think he was doing a wonderful thing for a woman, and expect to be admired for what he brought." Feminists are not merely the destroyers of the family, they are "the latest enemy of the vitality of classic texts," and since classic texts are the touchstones of a philosophical society, of civilization itself.

Bloom is aghast at modern value-relativism—that the young have neither values nor even prejudices—but he is also censorious about the values they choose to embrace. Thus, to him a concern for nuclear survival is bogus posturing; a belief in tolerance is a sign of moral flabbiness; to be "nice" and "without prejudices" merely underscores shallowness. Bloom condemns not just equality and the struggle for rights (which he believes have in any case been "won"), but the notion of rights itself, which for him means dedication to "life, liberty, and the pursuit of property and sex." The true villains are then neither Betty Friedan nor Abbie Hoffman but Erich Fromm and John Dewey—not the armed prophets of the Weather Underground but the far more dangerous un-armed prophets of therapeutic salvation and the brotherhood of man.

Bloom opposes democratic values not only as a conservative ideologue but as a philosopher wedded to reason. It is not really the last twenty or even the last fifty years that disturb Allan Bloom: it is the last two hundred years. The problems go back at least to the French Revolution and to those aspects of the philosophy of Enlightenment that led to the Revolution, since, as always for Bloom, history proceeds out of ideas rather than the other way around. In fact, nothing has been quite the same since a court composed of distrustful Athenian freemen put noble Socrates to death for the crime of being a truth-speaking philosopher in an opinion-governed society. The great divide is less between modern conservatives and modern democrats than between ancients and moderns—the central theme of Bloom's mentor and teacher, the great University of Chicago political philosopher Leo Strauss.

The German philosopher Friedrich Nietzsche signals the final eclipse of the ancient world for Bloom. Bloom's ambivalence about Nietzsche is one of the more impenetrable puzzles of *The Closing of the American Mind*, a puzzle that makes its profoundly anti-democratic argument difficult for critics to apprehend. Bloom is simultaneously full of praise for Nietzsche's analysis of modernity (he is "an unparalleled diagnostician of the ills of modernity") and full of indignation at what he considers to be the American trivialization of Nietzschean philosophy. This he regards as the primary cause of the closing of the American mind.

Nietzsche is at once hero and villain, astute cultural critic of bourgeois culture in the abstract, but nefarious corrupter of American youth in practice. Bloom's ambivalence about him is rooted in his distrust of democracy. Like Voltaire, who urges gentlemen to send their servants out of the room before debating whether God actually exists, Bloom worries not about Nietzsche's nihilistic announcement of the death of God, but about what philistine Americans may make of this unhappy news. The danger is not philosophical relativism, but pop relativism; not Nietzsche, but the "doctrinaire Woody Allen" whose way of looking at things "has immediate roots in the most profound German philosophy." If Woody Allen as a pop Nietzsche seems farfetched, Bloom himself often seems like a slightly paranoid Tocqueville who, burdened by an aristocratic background and Continental manners, finds himself inexplicably residing in the state of Illinois among barbarians he both worships and despises.

As a modern, Bloom cannot really deny that the credentials for both absolute Truth and a Supreme Being have become philosophically suspect: Nietzsche was merely the messenger for the news of their delegitimation by science and the Enlightenment. The trouble lies neither in the messenger nor in the message, but in the hungry masses that, equipped with a democratic education, beg to receive the grim tidings. These tidings only strip them of their myths and their religious comfort. Because the masses are constitutionally unfit for philosophy, the Truth leaves them defenseless and renders them dangerous. Faced with the news of God's death and Truth's uncertainty, mass man in America has simply put his soulless self in God's place, to the peril of learning, philosophy, and civilization. The demise of Authority engenders the Revolt of the Masses, whose trivialized mass culture is at war with everything noble and good. Virtue gives way to utility, reason to passion, the good to self-interest.

But how to tell such things to mass man himself? Men possessed of the idea that each of them is God must be handled carefully. To remind them of their own mortality and to tell them of the death of God may work terrible pain upon them. To avenge their suffering the messenger might be executed! The solution Bloom can only hint at (the philosopher cannot speak honestly) is certainly not to inundate the masses with books they cannot understand and are likely to misconstrue. Rather, it is to send them—like Voltaire's servants—out of the room. Bloom notes and his admirers delight in the great irony by which "openness" (which produces relativism and then nihilism) has led to the closing of the American mind. They might do well to note the still greater irony that reopening the American mind may for Bloom depend on the closing of the American university—since open minds seem to function best in highly selective, closed schools. To the educable, an education; to the rest, protection from fearsome half-truths, and a diet of noble lies such as may be required to insulate the university from mediocrity and democratic taste. Affirmative action puts into the classroom young men who can learn from Hobbes and Nietzsche only the lesson of the rightfulness of their appetites; feminism puts into the classroom young women who can learn from Dewey and Freud only the lesson of their equality with, or perhaps even their sexual superiority to, men. Philosophy is not finally to be saved by handing out Great Books to small minds, but by locking the library doors.

Bloom is remarkably candid about the nature of "the real community of man," which "is the community of those who seek the truth, of the potential knowers." To be sure, this community "in principle" includes all men "to the extent they desire to know. *But in fact this includes only a few, the true friends, as Plato was to Aristotle. . .*" (emphasis added). Bloom's rhetorical journey finally begins and ends with the ancients—with Socrates. How much misery mankind might have been spared; what revolutions, what prejudices, what myths, what armed braggarts might have vanished from the historical landscape, had the Athenians loved and followed Socrates instead of executing him.

Bloom's democratic admirers overlook his belief that democracy for the many (those not like him) and education for the few (those like him) proceed from radically incompatible premises. According to Bloom, society ought ideally to be arranged to achieve the latter even if it means undermining the former. "Never did I think," he writes, "that the university was properly ministerial to the society around it. Rather I thought and think that society is ministerial to the university . . ." Without the university thus understood, the theoretical life collapses "back into the primal slime" (presumably democratic society) from which it "cannot re-emerge."

The citizen of a democracy who understands what Bloom intends in the honor he pays Socrates will be wary in the face of Bloom's modern pedagogical claims. The citizen has every reason to mistrust the philosopher who mistrusts him. After all, it was the tyranny of "Truth" politicized that justified the divine right of kings, the Inquisition, the Reign of Terror, and such modern orthodoxies as totalitarianism.

Bloom may not be arguing that "the old [forms] were good or that we should go back to them," but he has two crucial quarrels to pick with America: the quarrel of the philosopher with democracy and equality; and the quarrel of the ambivalent cosmopolitan both with the European decadence he fears and the American philistinism he despises. The quarrel between philosophy and democracy is the quarrel between Socrates and Athens, and we have seen how deeply that struggle affects Bloom. The quarrel between America and Europe is more complex, and Bloom is torn between the two.

Champion of an innocent America corrupted by the tainting cynicism of Europe's anti-philosophies, Bloom sees himself as a loyal but knowing son of the Republic anxious to protect its less-sophisticated citizens from the Old World's newfangled nihilisms. If it is true that God has died (and there are times when Nietzsche's bad news seems also to be Bloom's bad news), don't tell the Americans! They already have a penchant for the vulgar, the novel, and the experimental, and will seize on God's withdrawal from the cosmos as a reason to try to master it themselves. In place of the tragic acceptance that characterized the ancients, the Americans will deploy ideologies of reform, growth, progress, and revolution. With their hands clasping computers and spliced genes, and their heads bursting with progressive ideologies from Marxism to welfarism, they will set out to replace their vanished Creator and improve upon his handiwork.

Nonetheless, even as Bloom cherishes America's insularity from the contagion of European cultural relativism, he cherishes Europe. As an American he may be suspicious of Europe's cynical intellectuals, but as a partisan of Europe, he is even more suspicious of America's self-righteously innocent anti-intellectuals. With innocence comes a simpleminded disdain for ideas that, as the historian Richard Hofstadter has noticed, inures us to books and debases our souls. We are finally much too practical a people for Bloom's taste: philosophy enjoins reflection, but the "hidden premise of the realm of freedom [America] is that action has primacy over thought." Bloom's aristocratic hostility to America's spirited practicality, to its optimism about change (America as the New World), to its belief in the second chance, blinds him to certain strengths of the American polity, as well as to the relationship of ordinary human beings to books.

America's true philosophers are not bookmen or academicians or theorists. They are poets such as Emily Dickinson and Walt Whitman, essayists such as

Henry Adams and Ralph Waldo Emerson, lawyers such as James Madison and Hugo Black, and moral leaders such as John Brown, Susan B. Anthony, and Martin Luther King, Jr. Bloom can argue with Dewey while Leo Strauss argues with Nietzsche, but America's true educators dwell elsewhere; their podiums are found in the open air rather than the library, the town hall rather than the seminar hall.

We continue to learn more from our doers than from our talkers, from Jefferson and Franklin, Eugene Debs and Robert Taft, Harry Hopkins, and, yes, even David Stockman. Bloom yearns for heroes and condemns us for having none worthy of the name, but what democrats aspire to is, as Brecht has written, not a country that has no heroes but a country that needs no heroes. At their best, Americans have been their own heroes, their nation a creation of anonymous settlers, cattlemen, garment workers, grade-school teachers, factory laborers, entrepreneurs, farmers, longshoremen, inventors, and just plain folks. Bloom simply gets America wrong. If Americans lack confidence in those who claim to possess Truth, it is because they are the descendants of immigrants who fled such Truth-sayers. Disguised as inquisitors, prosecutors, and king's counselors, such dogmatists impressed their Truths on the illiterate "rabble" in the form of chains. Bloom (it is almost as if he misses the chains) longs for the days in which Protestants and Catholics, hating each other, demonstrated they were "taking their beliefs seriously." Is the average American to be faulted for preferring the frivolous shallows of religious tolerance to the seriousness of the Salem witch-hunts?

The lugubrious lesson Americans may wish to draw from both Socrates and Bloom is that the philosopher's ideal of the open mind seems to flourish best in a closed society where, if philosophers do not rule, those who do rule must defer to philosophy. We ought to remember that benevolent autocrats like Frederick the Great made comfortable homes for philosophers such as Voltaire, even as those philosophers conceived rational blueprints in which there would be no room for kings. The king can at least pretend to be philosophical, whereas the self-governing common man will disdain the superior airs of both philosophers and kings. Tyrants may indeed be better friends to Truth than citizens who must learn how to live with uncertainty and difference. We citizens can understand why a philosopher of noble intentions may be aghast at a society moved by the suspicion that one man is as good as the next; but, still, we might be expected to meet the philosopher's subtle arguments with something more than a weak and self-nullifying cheer. For we are being asked implicitly to choose between the open mind and the open society, being asked to close the university to the many in order to secure it for the few, being asked to make reflection and its requisites the master of action and its requisites, being asked finally to turn the democratic culture that ought to be the university's finest product into the servant of universities that produce something called Truth. And how we answer such questions will not only affect what kind of education we will have, but whether we will remain a free and egalitarian society devoted to justice, or become a nation of deferential tutees who have been talked out of our freedom by a critic of all that has transpired since the ancient world gave way to the modern.

A great many Americans have come to sympathize with Bloom, anxious about the loss of fixed points, wishing for simpler, more orderly times. President Reagan's longing for a court filled with somber purists, his attorney general's belief in a doctrine of original intentions that turns the flexible genius of the Constitution into a Rosetta stone by which every modern conflict might be resolved, the secretary of education's campaign against the educational reforms of the Sixties, the Moral Majority's demand that the whole nation be subjected to drug testing—these are so many cries to be delivered from the twentieth century. These are the voices not of mere conservatives but of zealots, the anxious ones who see in the victories of liberty only the specter of anarchy; in equality, the victory of mediocrity; in social justice, a warrant for envy and disorder. Allan Bloom's book offers certainty to the confused and comfort to the fearful. It is a new Book of Truth for an era after God. Its only rival is democracy, which Bloom, with those he comforts, can only despise.

Nevertheless, the ideology of democracy is a sound, one might even say noble, response to the dilemmas of modernity: it permits us to live with our uncertainty, our agnosticism, our doubt, our sense of abandonment, our isolation, without murdering one another; it even promises a modicum of justice made up of equal parts of compassion and tolerance. It does not rescue us from our era, but it helps us live with its perils. The most apt response to Bloom's attempt to teach us how to be noble might be for us to teach him how to be democratic. It might even be that he would get the better of the exchange.

17

Allan Bloom and the Critics

WERNER J. DANNHAUSER

So we come to the present year of Bloom-bashing. In *Harper's Magazine* of January 1988, Benjamin Barber began with a barbed question: "Why are liberal critics and egalitarian educators beside themselves with admiration for what can only be called a raging assault on liberal tolerance and democratic education?" They aren't.

Yet, in spite of his exasperation, Barber paid some handsome tributes to *The Closing of the American Mind*, even while, or especially when, calling it "a most enticing, a most subtle, a most learned, a most dangerous tract." He found it a worthy object of opposition as "one of the most profoundly anti-democratic books ever written for a popular audience," and he advanced a complicated explanation for the fact that Bloom seemed to be defending democracy instead of attacking it. Barber's Bloom is a philosopher—something Bloom never calls himself—and a disciple of Leo Strauss.

Now in the book Bloom mentions Strauss only once and in passing, but that is, I think, due to modesty and a wish to stand on his own two feet amidst controversy. Barber is right in thinking of him as a Straussian, but his line of reasoning is too clever by half. He seems to think that because Strauss rediscovered the art of esoteric writing, Strauss himself wrote esoterically and taught Allan Bloom to do so. Thus when Bloom writes about democracy he does not mean what he says or say what he means. Get it? Got it? Good.

Barber's thesis just won't wash. Leo Strauss discussed esoteric writing, akin to writing between the lines, in *Persecution and the Art of Writing*, but there he maintains that "reading between the lines is strictly prohibited in all cases where it would be less exact than not doing so." It is a last resort, not, as in Barber's case, a first or second resort. The difficulty one has in understanding some of the books of Leo Strauss, especially his later work, is sufficiently accounted for by the fact that he is commenting on difficult texts. As for Bloom, I hope he will not be insulted when I declare that he is not all that difficult to understand.

Thus, Barber's contention that Bloom is anti-democratic goes against the grain of common sense. The two men do, to be sure, have different understandings of the true nature of democracy, with Barber favoring direct participatory democracy, as opposed to liberal, representative democracy. But that means that Barber's real quarrel is not with Bloom but with the latter's source of inspiration, Tocqueville.

The main body of this essay appears in chapter 1. See other excerpts replying to Benjamin Barber and Richard Rorty in chapter 4, to Martha Nussbaum in chapter 6, and on the question of racism in chapter 7. This material reprinted with permission from the *American Spectator.*

18

Opening the Open Mind

H. D. FORBES

Benjamin Barber, an academic notable, calls Bloom a "Philosopher Despot" and calls his book "a most enticing, a most subtle, a most learned, a most dangerous tract." Bloom is blamed for thinking that "philosophy is superior to ordinary American life" and that philosophical books like the *Republic* and *Zarathustra* are more worth reading and criticizing than the poetry of Walt Whitman or the speeches of Robert Taft. He is said to be aghast at value relativism among the young, but censorious about the values they choose—an obvious contradiction, it seems to Barber. He is like a "screeching parent wrapped in a Roman toga— ranting about the nobility of the ancients because he cannot comprehend his daughter's purple hair." He is like a shifty conspirator, quietly speaking with a forked tongue, one message for the *cognoscenti*, another for the masses.

"If it is true that God has died (and there are times when Nietzsche's bad news seems also to be Bloom's bad news), don't tell the Americans! They already have a penchant for the vulgar, the novel, and the experimental, and will seize on God's withdrawal from the cosmos as a reason to try to master it themselves. In place of the tragic acceptance that characterized the ancients, the Americans will deploy ideologies of reform, growth, progress, and revolution. With their hands clasping computers and spliced genes, and their heads bursting with progressive ideologies from Marxism to welfarism, they will set out to replace their vanished Creator and improve upon his handiwork."

So far, so good. The details come from Barber's imagination, but he has at least caught the drift of Bloom's argument.

H. D. Forbes is the author of *Nationalism, Ethnocentrism, and Personality.* This review is excerpted with permission from the *Idler,* vol. 17 (May–June 1988):47–52. Another excerpt from this review appears later in this chapter.

19

Academic Fundamentalism?

ROBERT N. BELLAH

Allan Bloom has done something rare among followers of Leo Strauss. He has given us not a translation of or commentary on a great text (as he has before with Plato, Shakespeare, and Rousseau), but an analysis of our current social, cultural, and intellectual condition—mainly, but not exclusively, in the university. The result is a book at once refreshing, dismaying, and baffling, but of such seriousness that it deserves to be widely read. Particularly those responsible for education, and that is a much larger group than university professors, should read this book. It is not a question of agreeing with Bloom. Most readers will, I believe, sharply disagree with parts of the book, as I do. But Bloom has stated many of the issues that confront us with great clarity and vigor. Those who would meet his challenge must think as hard and well as he has.

The book, already a best-seller, consists of three linked essays: one describing students at our better universities today; one on American culture since the 1930s; and one on the history of the university, particularly in the last 30 years.

The essay on students is bleak indeed. He describes their blankness with respect to literary culture upon arriving at the university (and often on leaving it as well), their compulsive absorption in rock music that deadens their response to a wide range of cultural experiences, and their self-centeredness in relation to others. Presumably Professor Bloom has students who do not fit this description, as I believe any serious teacher does, but he says little about the exceptions. Still he is on the mark much of the time. It would be interesting to teach this book.

Where I would want to argue with his description of student culture is his almost entirely negative view of the egalitarianism of students. Bloom describes a shallow reflexive egalitarianism that is only the reverse of the dominant individualism, in which persons are seen shorn of any tradition or cultural specificity, as though they were self-created personalities. These beliefs, he says, do not "result from principle, a project, an effort. They are pure feeling, a way of life. . . ." Yet his own description of the incompleteness of equality between black and white students and of the uncertain relations between the sexes suggests that deeper moral issues of equality are far from solved. Indeed the shallow egalitarianism of individual feeling may obscure the real issues of equality which would lead to clearer moral principles and stronger ethical discriminations than most students "feel comfortable with," and may hide a deep ambivalence about equality that is

Robert N. Bellah is Ford Professor of Sociology and Comparative Studies at the University of California, Berkeley, and coauthor of *Habits of the Heart* (1985) and *Varieties of Civil Religion* (1980). This review is reprinted with permission from *New Oxford Review* vol. 54, no. 6 (July–August 1987):22–24.

only partially conscious. A more sanguine view of contemporary students would find their feeling for equality a point of entry for serious reflection.

It is harder to summarize Bloom's discussion of American culture, in the second essay. Here we are treated to a sweeping discussion of the history of modern culture under what Bloom calls, in Straussian terms, the democratic regime. What is most striking here is the importance he gives to what he calls "the German connection." He detects a pervasive Nietzscheanism purveyed to us by German refugees in the 1930s and 1940s that has drastically undercut our own Anglo-Saxon heritage of early modern social thought. Weber and Freud, with their enormous influence on academic culture, and now more pervasively the general culture, have been the apostles through whom Nietzsche reached our shores. Bloom traces many of the terms that substitute for serious thought in America—self, creativity, culture, values—to a watered-down Germanism. One of his few lapses occurs in this connection where he misunderstands David Riesman's term "inner-directed," even constructing for it a false genealogy from Heidegger via Fromm. Inattention to the text is not what we expect from students of Leo Strauss. Inner-direction is not the free expression of the self as against a socially constricting other-direction, a common enough misunderstanding of the argument of Riesman's *The Lonely Crowd*. Rather inner-direction signifies the harsh superego of the old bourgeoisie introjected from external authority.

But even accepting the analysis of the baleful effects of a popularized Nietzscheanism, as I tend to do, one must not neglect the extent to which Nietzsche is himself finally grounded in the Anglo-American tradition that Bloom would defend against him. After all, it was Hobbes who said that there is no Good in itself but only the goods (desires) of individuals, and the lifelong influence of Emerson on Nietzsche is well-known. If we have succumbed to the siren song of Nietzsche and Heidegger via the more popular figures of Weber and Freud, it is surely because the ground had long since been prepared.

The third essay, on the university, is perhaps the most interesting. The opening section on the history of the university is the clearest revelation of the Straussian position I have ever seen. Historicism is indeed jettisoned, as we are shown a picture of Socrates, Plato, Aristotle, Machiavelli, Hobbes, and Locke as agreeing in essentials but differing only in the tactics with which they defend the life of the mind. Both modern democratic society and the modern university are seen as straightforward products of early modern philosophy. While the resulting picture is arresting and thought-provoking, it is surely one-sided. Bloom has respect for biblical religion as a worthy opponent of philosophy, but he has no regard for it as an influence on modern society, a mistake his teacher Tocqueville did not make. Nor does he pay the least attention to classical republicanism as an influence on the American founders, whom he treats as pure Lockians. And the picture of the university is distorted indeed when rhetoric, which dominated most of its modern history far more than philosophy, is ignored.

What follows is an ill-tempered attack on the student movement of the 1960s that scores many good points but ends up greatly exaggerating the influence of the 1960s on the current malaise in higher education. This is all the more odd since the final section, "The Student and the University," is in many ways an accurate assessment of our situation. Though he does not quite put it this way, Bloom shows that the university as an institution for the training of the functionaries of an imperial economy and an imperial state is not a very conducive place for the cultivation of the life of the mind.

What is most distressing is that Bloom seems to share in the ambivalence which for almost 400 pages he is describing with great brilliance and insight. It is finally not clear why he wrote the book or to whom it is addressed. After an appallingly accurate description of the incoherence of the best universities today, he writes, "One cannot and should not hope for a general reform. The hope is that the embers do not die out." Yet, so modest a hope is belied by the final paragraph of the book where he tells us that freedom in the world depends on the American regime, that the fate of philosophy depends on our universities, and that the defense of the two are related. Certainly fanning the embers is hardly a response to such a challenge.

Bloom writes in a vacuum. Others concerned with his problems are ignored. Neither Gadamer, Dumont, nor MacIntyre is mentioned. One begins to suspect that the Straussian world is that of a fundamentalist sect, where "the truth" cannot be risked in discussion with the unsaved. Bloom almost appears as an urbane, immensely well-educated Jerry Falwell. Yet that is unfair both to Bloom and the Straussians. We can be thankful that Bloom has condescended from the always useful task of textual commentary to give us this lively, bitter, stimulating picture of the world in which we live. Even if we do not fully understand why he has done so.

20

Straussianism, Democracy, and Allan Bloom I: That Old Time Philosophy

RICHARD RORTY

Toward the end of *The Closing of the American Mind*, Allan Bloom says:

> The real community of man, in the midst of all the self-contradictory simulacra of community, is the community of those who seek the truth, of the potential knowers, that is, in principle, of all men to the extent they desire to know. But in fact this includes only a few, the true friends, as Plato was to Aristotle at the very moment they were disagreeing about the nature of the good. . . . This, according to Plato, is the only real friendship, the only real common good. . . . The other kinds of relatedness are only imperfect reflections of this one trying to be self-subsisting, gaining their only justification from their ultimate relation to this one.

This is an admirably frank expression of doubts about democracy, doubts that are shared by lots of intellectuals—usually with a bad conscience. These doubts are about whether the many non-intellectuals will ever want the sorts of things we intellectuals want, whether a democratic community can be built on the trash and the sleaze that they apparently *do* want, whether our allegiance to the idea of democracy is more than a cynical prudential strategy: You let us have your gifted children for our universities, where we will estrange them from you and keep the best ones for ourselves. In return, we will send the second-best back to keep you supplied with technology, entertainment, and soothing presidential lies.

One advantage of the Straussian school of political theory, to which Bloom belongs, is that Straussianism gives one a good conscience about these doubts. Straussians make no bones about saying that the allegiance of the "potential knowers" with the masses is just a prudential strategy. On their view, nobody would accept the risks of being subject to the whims of an electorate dumb enough to have voted for Hitler, if there were a better alternative. But there is not, so we make the best of a bad job. Straussians reject Emerson's and Dewey's attempt to find one's moral identity in membership in a democratic community. They consider such an attempt—the attempt to pretend that a pluralistic democratic society can be more than an incoherent "simulacrum of community"—to

Richard Rorty is University Professor of Humanities at the University of Virginia and author of *Consequences of Pragmatism* (1982). This review is reprinted with permission from the *New Republic* (April 4, 1988):28–33.

be as childish as Marx's fantasy that an emancipated working class will read philosophy in the intervals of non-alienating labor.

Leo Strauss, the great émigré political philosopher who was Bloom's teacher, was relatively coy and guarded in his expression of such doubts. But his students have become increasingly open. Bloom puts in cold print a story that should only be whispered to initiates. It revolves around the "philosophers" (the Straussian name for the lovers of truth, not to be confused with the merely clever, the "intellectuals"). These philosophers have always been, of necessity, liars. In Bloom's words, "they have engaged in the gentle art of deception." Strauss spoke, still more gently, of "the need for inexactness in moral and political matters." They lie because they are not, and probably never will be, the rulers. As an interest group whose interests can never be made intelligible to non-members, they must flatter and cozen whoever does hold power. "In the days before the rise of democratic societies," Bloom says, "the philosophers allied themselves with the gentlemen, making themselves useful to them, never quite revealing themselves to them, strengthening their gentleness and openness by reforming their education."

But then the mob rose and began cutting off heads, so the philosophers had to find a way of cozening the mob. Cleverly, they "switched parties from the aristocratic to the democratic," even though they "had no illusions about democracy." They "substituted one kind of misunderstanding for another," presenting philosophy to the common man not as "his moral preceptor but as his collaborator in his fondest dreams." In other words, the mob came to believe that those nice, kind, hard-working Alphas were going to help them get the things they wanted—if not immortality, at least as prolonged a life as possible, and a life in a brave new world of ever more exciting low pleasures (public executions, Rambo films, novel quiches and jeans, and always, in the background, ever more sexually explicit forms of what Strauss liked to call "jungle music"). In exchange, the common people allowed the philosophers to live in well-funded universities—institutions they naively thought of as "serving society." "The universities," Bloom says, "flourished because they were perceived to serve society as it wants to be served."

What disgusts Bloom is that the vast majority of people in the social science and humanities departments of universities are, in his terms, intellectuals rather than philosophers. These intellectuals think that one can deal honestly with the public—if not by serving it as it wants to be served, at least by being open about how it ought to want to be served. They do not understand that the crucial function of the universities is to serve (and to replenish the supply of) philosophers.

Bloom's animus is not against the mob, but against the intellectuals—the people who, following Emerson and Dewey, assume that the success of our "democratic experiment" has made us contemporary Americans wiser than the Greeks. These are the local variety of the people whom Strauss called "historicists." Historicists believe that Plato and Aristotle are obsolete, as are Greek notions like "timeless truth" or "the nature of the good"—not to mention the philosopher/gentleman/mob way of dividing up society, and the soul/body, or reason/passion, way of dividing up human beings. Among the best examples of historicism—the clearest antitheses to Strauss—are Mill, Dewey, and Rawls. About the first two, Bloom says:

> Liberalism without natural rights, the kind that we knew from John Stuart Mill and John Dewey, taught us that the only danger confronting us is being closed to the emergent, the new, the manifestations of progress. No attention had to be paid to the fundamental principles or the moral virtues that inclined men to live according to them.

But Bloom is harshest on Rawls, whom he describes as writing

> hundreds of pages to persuade men, and proposing a scheme of government that would force them, not to despise anyone. In A *Theory of Justice*, he writes that the physicist or the poet should not look down on the man who spends his life counting blades of grass or performing any other frivolous or corrupt activity. Indeed, he should be esteemed, since esteem from others, as opposed to self-esteem, is a basic need of all men. So indiscriminateness is a moral imperative because its opposite is discrimination. This folly means that men are not permitted to seek for the natural human good and admire it when found, for such discovery is coeval with the discovery of the bad and contempt for it.

In such passages, Bloom lumps books like A *Theory of Justice* with books like *One-Dimensional Man* (which he characterizes, with some justice, as "trashy culture criticism"). He sees no difference between the know-nothing campus trashers of the '60s, with their babble about "elitism," and writers who, like Rawls and Dewey, envisage a society in which, no matter how discriminating we are in private, we do not let the institutions of society humiliate those whose tastes and habits we find contemptible. The difference that Bloom blurs is between saying, "Video games are as good as poetry," and saying, "In the interest of a pluralist democratic community that encompasses both those who read poetry and those who never will, we must make our laws and institutions as indifferent as possible to the difference between video games and poetry." Bloom has no patience with the idea that such a purported community might be more than an "incoherent simulacrum." The idea that political thinking and social institutions should swing free from a hierarchical ordering of types of human being seems, to Straussians, *the* great mistake of the modern age.

Given his view about the special kind of friendship that bound Plato to Aristotle, despite their disagreements, one would expect Bloom, somewhere in his book, to strike up conversations with theorists like Rawls, Michael Walzer, Charles Taylor, Roberto Unger, or Judith Shklar—the people who think about the same texts and problems as he does, though coming at them from different angles. But he tends to take seriously only those who share most of his own views, only those who agree that philosophers must, perforce, be liars. He has no time for historicists who think that, as Rawls says:

> What justifies a conception of justice is not its being true to an order antecedent to and given to us, but its congruence with our deeper understanding of ourselves and our aspirations, and our realization that, given our history and the traditions embedded in our public lives, it is the most reasonable doctrine for us.

For Bloom, anybody who could say that has already forfeited his candidacy for the only "real community of man"—has shown himself to be a mere "intellectual," rather than a "philosopher."

Bloom treats Dewey, who thought that notions like "the soul" and "timeless truth" belonged to the infancy of philosophy—to the period when we had not yet grown out of religious fear and awe—as himself "a big baby." Bloom is not interested in political thinkers who, unlike Machiavelli, sincerely settle for what Isaiah Berlin calls "negative liberty" (being left alone, as opposed to the "positive liberty" of being aided in achieving the good). Such thinkers believe that, as Strauss put it, "what is needed in order to establish the right social order is not so much the formation of character as the right kinds of institutions." But, Strauss thought, the latter idea will sooner or later bring one around to the claim "that the only legitimate regime is democracy"—to the mistaken idea that democracy is intellectually, not just prudentially, justifiable.

The result of this discrimination in admissions to Socratic discussion has been that Straussians have become a sort of cult. Even though this cult includes some notably learned and genuinely thoughtful people, controversy between Straussians and non-Straussians tends quickly to become rancorous, to bog down in questions about the correct exegesis either of Strauss himself, or of the texts (Plato, Aristotle, Locke, Rousseau) around which Strauss built his subtle and intricate account of our decline from antiquity into modernity.

Toward the end of a review of Rawls, Bloom said that the "greatest weakness" of Rawls's book was "the lack of education it reveals," and that the "core of the book" was constituted of "misunderstandings" of Aristotle, Hobbes, Locke, Rousseau, and Kant. Straussians typically do not countenance alternative, debatable interpretations of those writers, but rather distinguish between their own "authentic understandings" and others' "misunderstandings." In this respect they resemble the Marxists and the Catholics. The tone in which Bloom writes about Plato is the same as that in which Althusser and Fredric Jameson write about Marx, in which Maritain (and the young William Buckley) used to write about Aquinas, in which many members of what Bloom (in his best chapter) calls "the Nietzscheanized left" write about Foucault. There is no question of any of these authors having been fundamentally misguided; the only question is how to render what they wrote internally consistent.

From Bloom's point of view, however, it is misleading to suggest, as I have suggested, that there is a free, open forum in which the Straussians might argue Socratically with their opponents. For things are much worse than most people think. "We are," Bloom tells us, "like ignorant shepherds living on a site where great civilizations once flourished." The idea (widely held in Europe and Asia) that America's universities are notably free and flourishing, that they are as splendid centers of learning and forums for Socratic discussion as the world has ever known, is widely mistaken. On the contrary, the subtitle of Bloom's book tells us, "Higher education has failed democracy and impoverished the souls of today's students." Further, "The crisis of liberal education is a reflection of a crisis at the peaks of learning, an incoherence and incompatibility among the first principles with which we interpret the world, an intellectual crisis of our civilization."

The American universities, especially since the disastrous '60s, have "decomposed." In the humanities, "There is no semblance of order, no serious account of what should and should not belong, of what its disciplines are trying to accomplish and how." In America, "The philosophic language is nothing but jargon." Small wonder that the saving remnant of philosophers keeps to itself and does not mingle with the jargoneering intellectuals—all those people clever enough to manipulate abstractions, but not patient or honest enough to see the incoherence of their own historicism. Small wonder that, to these people, the Straussian remnant looks like another intolerant and self-obsessed sect.

Bloom's book raises three questions. First, is he right, over against common opinion, about the state of American higher education? Second, was Plato right, over against Dewey, in thinking that there is a permanent, ahistorical truth about the nature of human beings and of the good? Third, can one argue the first question independently of arguing the second? Or do we have to figure out whether Plato was right before we can decide whether our universities are in bad shape?

Bloom thinks that we do—that we have to start from first principles. We Deweyan historicists, on the other hand, think that "first principles" are abbreviations of, rather than justifications for, a set of beliefs about the desirability of certain concrete alternatives over others; the source of those beliefs is not "reason" or "nature," but rather the prevalence of certain institutions or modes of life in the past. So we think that the method of political theory is what Rawls calls "the attempt at reflective equilibrium." We muddle through, without any clear antecedent criterion, by juxtaposing our intuitive judgment of some recent development (a novel institution or mode of life) with some old "first principle" that seems to conflict with it, in the hope of finding a way to balance competing claims.

The historicist claim that such criterionless muddling must take the place of the Platonic appeal to immutable standards presupposes that there are lots of institutions and modes of life that Plato (and for that matter, Locke or Mill) knew nothing about. By contrast, it is essential to Bloom's position that Plato's and Aristotle's vocabulary is, for purposes of political philosophy, entirely adequate to everything that has happened since their day, that there are no alternatives of which Plato was unaware. For if history is always throwing up new material, then Plato's test of coherence could not have produced a timeless standard in morals or politics. Historicists think that we shall never have anything firmer to fall back on than our accumulated experience of the advantages and disadvantages of various concrete alternatives (judged by nothing more immutable than our common sense, the judgment of the latest, best-informed, and freest of the children of time).

Whether one is a Straussian "philosopher" or a historicist "intellectual" depends on whether one finds this lack of a timeless and unvarying standard acceptable. Strauss thought it unacceptable. He thought that "if there is no standard higher than the ideal of our society, we are utterly unable to take a critical distance from that ideal." Deweyans think this is a non sequitur. They think that we can find a critical distance just by comparing the detailed advantages and disadvantages of our institutions and modes of life with other real (historical and anthropological) or imagined (literary) alternatives—without claiming that any of these alternatives are "higher" or "closer to nature." Deweyans reject what Bernard Williams has recently called "the rationalist theory of rationality," the idea that if you cannot lay down a criterion for settling arguments in advance, then you are condemned to "irrationalism" and "relativism." For Strauss and Bloom, however, all this is incompatible with the Platonic picture of the philosopher as someone who seeks the good by nature, as opposed to simply sorting through alternative conventions.

The contrast between Dewey's stance and Bloom's comes out nicely in a passage in which Bloom harks back to Plato's myth of the cave. He says:

> A culture is a cave. He [Plato] did not suggest going around to other cultures as a solution to the limitations of the cave. Nature should be the standard by which we judge our own lives and the lives of peoples. That is why philosophy, not history or anthropology, is the most important human science.

Dewey did suggest going around to other cultures. He thought that the benefit of going around (via history and anthropology) to other cultures was the same as that offered by the arts—the enlargement of our moral imaginations. He put his faith in the arts rather than in philosophy because he did not believe that there was such a thing as "nature" to serve as "the standard." The idea of "human nature," like "the quest for certainty," was a cowardly attempt to reduce a self-creating being to one that was already finished and unchangeable.

Dewey warned that, to people still immature enough to long for certainty:

> To say frankly that philosophy can proffer nothing but hypotheses, and that these hypotheses are of value only as they render men's minds more sensitive to life about them, would seem like a negation of philosophy itself.

That is, indeed, how it seems to Straussians. Strauss organized his history of political thought around a story of decay: the story of how we have lost touch with the notion of "philosophizing" as a distinct human activity, as the activity that affords "the only true happiness," that Bloom thinks makes possible the only "real community of man." Dewey thought this change indicated maturity rather than degeneration. In his view, Plato's "spectator theory of knowledge" and his doctrine that only the "potential knowers" could form a genuine community were primitive hypotheses, whose retention, even in diluted form, will make us insensitive to the possibilities of democratic life.

What matters to us "intellectuals," as opposed to the "philosopher," is the imaginativeness and openness of discourse, not proximity to something lying beyond discourse. Both Platonists and Deweyans take Socrates as their hero. For Plato, the life of Socrates did not make sense unless there was something like the Idea of the Good at the end of the dialectical road. For Dewey, the life of Socrates made sense as a symbol of a life of openness and curiosity. It was an experimental life—the sort of life that is encouraged by, and in turn encourages, the American democratic experiment.

The Deweyan idea that society should worry only about the freedom of the universities, and not about what is taught there, is paralleled by the Rawlsian claim that social justice is a matter of procedure rather than of substance: that it swings free of alternative "conceptions of the good." When thinking about alternative social institutions, we have to substitute the Rawlsian question, "Is this institution fair to everybody, in the sense of not favoring one race, sex, IQ level, income level, or sense of the point of human existence over another?" for the question, "What is the good for man?"

Rawls's conception of justice as fairness is, for Bloom, a reductio ad absurdum of the lines of thought that have gradually, through Hobbes and Locke and Mill, led us away from the Greek question, "What sort of person should a state try to produce?" and toward the question, "How can we maximize freedom and equality?" Bloom would like the question of whether this philosophical result is absurd to be determined by "first principles." We Deweyans would like it to be determined by inspection of the merits of some concrete proposals for the reform of American institutions.

Thus one has to come back to the concrete: Is Bloom right about how things currently are with American higher education? Unfortunately, Bloom's account of what higher education should be like sounds plausible only if one already believes a lot of what Plato believed. (A more exact subtitle for Bloom's book would have been "How democracy has failed philosophy and made it difficult for students to take Plato seriously.")

Bloom gives the impression that he is doing the same sort of thing as E. D. Hirsch in *Cultural Literacy*. These books have often been reviewed and discussed together—treated as if Bloom has done for the universities what Hirsch has done for the primary and secondary schools, as if Bloom supplied the philosophical basis for Hirsch's criticism of current educational practices. But the two books could hardly be more different. Hirsch is working in the framework of a Deweyan understanding of democracy, pointing out (quite rightly) that Dewey's ideas about "skills" as opposed to "content" have worked out very badly, and that very specific reforms are needed if we are to have an electorate able to understand the issues of the day. He wants to make the students better citizens of a democracy. He wants them to recognize more allusions, and thereby be able to take part in more conversations, read more, have more sense of what those in power are up to, cast better-informed votes. Dewey would have cheered Hirsch on.

Bloom's advocacy of "the good old Great Books approach" may seem like the same sort of effort, applied to colleges as opposed to high schools. But lots of people who would favor (as I would) both Hirschian reforms in precollege education and a Great Books curriculum in the first two years of college will demur at what Bloom takes to be integral to a "Great Books approach." For Bloom is advocating not just that we make college students read "certain generally recognized classic texts," but that they be read in a particular, characteristically Straussian way, that is,

> letting them [the texts] dictate what the questions are and the method of approaching them—not forcing them into categories we make up, not treating them as historical products, but trying to read them as their authors wished them to be read.

This description of how to read may sound harmless enough, but think about it. Normally we read books with questions in mind—not questions dictated by the books, but questions we have previously, if vaguely, formulated. It is not clear how we can avoid forcing books "into categories we make up," since it is not clear how we can make our minds into blank tablets. To be sure, we need to give authors a run for their money—suspending doubt or disbelief long enough to work ourselves into an author's way of talking and thinking, trying to put ourselves in her shoes, giving her every chance to convince us. But I doubt that that sort of initial sympathetic suspension is enough for Bloom. For it is characteristic of the Straussians to think that a student who throws himself into Plato and emerges with a preference for Mill, Dewey, and Rawls has misread Plato—that his soul has already been so impoverished (by the insidious historicism that pervades contemporary intellectual life) that he is no longer capable of reading properly. If students who accept Platonism are relatively thin on the ground in the universities, so the Straussians reason, so much the worse for the universities.

When we professors start falling back on "an intellectual crisis of the greatest magnitude" or "repressive tolerance" or "the treason of the clerks" (that is, of some other professors) to explain our failure to get more students to agree with us, what is to be done? From a Deweyan angle, the only thing to do is to check out the state of academic freedom. Are the students able to read whatever they like without getting (even covertly and mildly) punished for it? Are the teachers able to say what they like and still get promoted? Do the faculties exert themselves to take in representatives of every conceivable movement—deconstructionists, Marxists, Habermasians, Catholics, Straussians? Do the government, the trustees, and the university administration keep the money coming without asking what is done with it? Is the library open late at night, and is there enough scholarship money so that the students can be found there rather than taking orders at McDonald's? Is truth being given every chance to win in a free and open encounter? By reference to such questions, American universities are in better shape than any other institutions of learning in history. But from Bloom's Platonic angle, these questions are not the only ones, nor the most important ones. Bloom thinks that we have to ask not just about institutional procedures, but about the substance of what is being taught.

About the last thing we Deweyans want is for humanities departments to have a consensus about their function and mission. When Bloom speaks of "the problem of the humanities, and therefore of the unity of knowledge," we Deweyans cannot see why knowledge should be thought of as a unity (rather than, say, as a bag of tools). The university as flea market (though not, for reasons given by Hirsch, the primary or secondary school as flea market) is fine with us. Once the defects of our high schools have been made up for by a couple of years' worth of Great Books, the students should be left free to shop around in as large and noisy a bazaar as possible.

Bloom does not offer much in the way of practical proposals. It would be nice to know how he thinks we could restructure the universities so that they would cease "impoverishing the students' souls" while still hanging on to what we have come to think of as academic freedom. (For example, can he suggest a way of getting us historicists off what he calls "the peaks of learning" without giving somebody like the secretary of education the power to fill professorial chairs?) Maybe there is a way to do this, but it is not obvious. Or maybe we can afford to lose some of our academic freedom in order to serve other goals more efficiently, but this is not obvious either. Unless Bloom follows his book up with one that gets down from first principles to the nitty-gritty (in the way that Hirsch does), it is going to be hard to evaluate the apocalyptic claim with which he ends:

> This is the American moment in world history, the one for which we shall forever be judged. Just as in politics the responsibility for the fate of freedom in the world has devolved upon our regime, so the fate of philosophy in the world has devolved upon our universities, and the two are related as they have never been before.

This suggestion that there is a close relation between the fate of philosophy and the fate of freedom amounts to the claim that unless we can recapture belief in the Greek notions that, taken together, give credence to the claim that the philosophers are the only real human community—unless we can bring ourselves, in short, to go back to Plato—we have little chance of avoiding a relapse into tyranny. Only that old-time philosophy can save us now.

The claim that resistance to tyranny depends on agreeing with Plato goes back to Strauss's idea that we can blame Hitler on false theories about man and nature and truth—on "value-relativism" and historicism. Strauss shared with many other émigrés—with Adorno, for example, his opposite number on the left—the idea that reference to what had been happening in European intellectual life helped explain the coming of fascism. Bloom takes this idea for granted when he sardonically attributes to the American disciples of Freud and Weber the view that "the trouble with Weimar was simply that the bad guys won."

On a Deweyan view, that *was* the only trouble with Weimar. The fact that, as Bloom says, "German thought had taken an anti-rational and anti-liberal turn with Nietzsche, and even more so with Heidegger," did not do much to tip the balance in favor of the bad guys, any more than the popularity of Deweyan pragmatism among American intellectuals of the '30s does much to explain why fascism did not happen here. Disagreements among intellectuals as to whether truth is timeless, whether "reason" names an ahistorical tribunal or a Habermasian free consensus, or whether the "inalienable rights" of the Declaration are "grounded" in something non-historical, or are instead admirable recent inventions (like education for women, and the transistor), are just not that important in deciding how elections go, or how much resistance fascist takeovers encounter. For Deweyans, the theoretical questions "Did Socrates answer Thrasymachus?" and "Can we answer Hitler?" get replaced by practical questions like "How can we arrange things so that people like Thrasymachus and Hitler will not come to power?"

The public rhetoric of contemporary America is an inchoate mixture of religious, Platonic, and Deweyan ideas. Words of praise and blame are constantly being used in different senses that presuppose different understandings of background notions such as "reason," "truth," and "freedom." This mixed rhetoric is just what one would expect of a pluralist society, but it makes it easy for opposing intellectual factions to find tom-toms to beat, and to secure attention for warnings that their opponents are betraying the republic. You can always raise a scare by charging "relativisim" or "irrationalism," but you can raise one equally well by charging "dogmatism" or "scholasticism." It would be easy, though cheap and dishonest, to reply to Bloom by beating my own drum and issuing my own warnings. A Deweyan response could easily go on about intellectual snobbery, failure to trust the Healthy Instincts of the People, and, of course, "elitism."

But it would be better for both sides to discuss, in a cool hour, whether our country's unease is a matter of the "deep spiritual malaise" of which we have been hearing so much lately. Perhaps this unease is just the result of running up against some unpleasant, stubborn, merely material facts. For example: that this has turned out not to be the American Century, that the "American moment in world history" may have passed, that democracy may not spread around the world, that we do not know how to mitigate the misery and hopelessness in which half of our fellow-humans (including a fifth of our fellow-citizens) live.

Deweyans suspect that we Americans are not suffering from anything deeper or more spiritual than having bitten off a lot more than we turned out to be able to chew—that is, the task of saving the world from tyranny and want. Perhaps our problem is not internal hollowness, but straightforward external failure, the shipwreck of some of the hopes on which we were raised. These hopes, like those with which Plato sailed to Syracuse, may seem naive in retrospect, but they were neither silly nor disreputable.

21

Opening the Open Mind

H. D. FORBES

In the *New Republic*, Richard Rorty, Bloom's most eminent critic, concludes a discussion of the book by admitting some discouragement. In trying to save the world from tyranny and want, we may have bitten off more than we can chew. We must live with the shipwreck of some hopes on which we were raised, but not, it seems, with revisions of the philosophical theories that encouraged those hopes. We should continue muddling along, balancing new impressions of modern life with old principles of steady progress, trying to reach a "reflective equilibrium" agreeable to our common sense. We can be confident that such views will be satisfactory, since we are "the latest, best-informed, and freest of the children of time."

The need to deal publicly with those, like Bloom, who aren't impressed by contemporary common sense, confounds Rorty. He preaches tolerance, but gets caught trying to be critical. He thinks the problem can be solved by distinguishing private from public: we can discriminate in private, but must not let the institutions of society humiliate those whose tastes and habits we happen to abhor. Rorty's language is moderate, but he is plainly willing to countenance the public treatment of Bloom as a member of an "intolerant and self-obsessed sect." Is it possible that a writer of Rorty's stature does not see the incoherence of this position?

Another excerpt from this article appears in essay 18.

22

Allan Bloom and the Critics

WERNER J. DANNHAUSER

Richard Rorty also opts for democracy, but without Benjamin Barber's genuine wit. Writing about Bloom in the *New Republic* of April 4, 1988, he has the misfortune to be rebutted conclusively by Harvey C. Mansfield, Jr. I commend their exchange to one and all, especially Mansfield's splendid defense of *The Closing of the American Mind*, which (along with H. D. Forbes's review in the *Idler*) is much the best thing written about the book. All those who carp against Bloom's elitism and conception of democracy should ponder the following statement by Mansfield which I quote because I cannot hope to match it:

> A liberal democracy such as ours is the kind of democracy that makes room for outstanding people—for a "natural aristocracy" in Jefferson's phrase. Our founding principles provide freedom for the ambitious in politics, business and culture. . . . This does not mean that ambition should live unchecked, but the general rule for business and culture has been the one stated by Madison for politics: let ambition counteract ambition. The result is the pluralism we take pride in. Elitism is a necessary feature of pluralism.

Rorty, to be sure, does not directly charge Bloom with elitism. His denigration of the latter bases itself on a Deweyan historicism and relativism. Those who want the genuine article when it comes to relativism and historicism should turn to Nietzsche, who is even better than Bloom's sensitive rendering of him.

See the main body of this essay in chapter 1.

23

Straussianism, Democracy, and Allan Bloom II: Democracy and the Great Books

HARVEY C. MANSFIELD, JR.

I do not know how to explain the paradoxical success of Allan Bloom's *The Closing of the American Mind*. Perhaps the American mind has not yet snapped shut. Perhaps it has, but has decided to punish Bloom ironically by making him rich and famous. In any case, the merits of his book—its intelligence, its range, its brilliance, its passion—were obvious enough to earn a friendly, even enthusiastic welcome from most of its first reviewers. Lately, however, the mainstream professors have been busy, and the reviews have turned sour and resentful. The *New York Times* has been compelled to change its mind: on second thought, the book that its daily reviewer said was the best in the last five years wasn't even on the annual list of the best of 1987. The *Times* listens to professors, and the professors know who Bloom is; so they know he deserves a more straightforward punishment. He's a "Straussian," a follower (in Bloom's case, a student) of Leo Strauss, an obscure professor of political philosophy at the University of Chicago who died in 1973.

Actually Strauss, though he counseled against seeking the limelight, is not obscure in the usual way, by having done nothing remarkable. He has been kept in obscurity by professors through the "silent treatment," variously applied, to discourage the reading of his books and to blight the academic prospects of his followers. Strauss and the Straussians have in general been regarded not as a challenge to be taken up, but as an embarrassment that it is a kindness to ignore if you can, like a belch at the dinner table. But with Bloom's success, impossible to ignore, fallback strategies have had to be adopted. Tendentious denigration has replaced the silent treatment, and something has had to be said directly to the naughty boy.

Richard Rorty's essay is an example of the latter. One would not know it from his confrontation of new-time Deweyans with old-time Straussians (the only distinction, apparently, that he does not consider artificial), but this is, I believe, the first extended notice that a prominent American philosophy professor has taken of Strauss. Rorty tries to pretend that Straussians invite their neglect by their

Harvey C. Mansfield Jr is Professor of Government at Harvard University and author of *The Spirit of Liberalism* (1978). This review is reprinted with permission from the *New Republic* (April 4, 1988):33–37.

clannish bad manners; but his complaint of unrequited love is malarkey. When has he ever sent flowers? In his present performance he has not one word of praise ("admirably frank" never signifies admiration) for Bloom's book. All his talk of toleration does not prompt him to any acknowledgment that he is meeting a worthy opponent.

Instead, Rorty and the other professors denounce Bloom and the Straussians as anti-democratic. They say that we (since I am a Straussian) are guilty of elitism, that we oppose democracy, and that we have a hidden agenda of conservatism (conservatism being undemocratic). These charges are answered in Bloom's book, but for those who like magazines I shall try to refute them here.

Rorty himself dismisses the charge of elitism as babble from the '60s, but it is often heard at universities and has found its way into the *New Republic*. It's elitism, in this view, for Bloom to recommend that college students read the Great Books; not enough of these books were written by women or blacks. But then Rorty, who wants a two-year Great Books requirement in college, stands guilty as well. The charge *is* babble, but it's worth a moment's consideration for the temper it reflects.

A Great Books requirement is elitism, allegedly, because it promotes an elite. But a liberal democracy such as ours is the kind of democracy that makes room for outstanding people—for a "natural aristocracy," in Jefferson's phrase. Our founding principles provide freedom for the ambitious in politics, business, and culture, as opposed to other democracies, ancient and modern, that were constituted out of dislike of the few. This does not mean that ambition should live unchecked, but the general rule for business and culture has been the one stated by Madison for politics: let ambition counteract ambition. The result is the pluralism we take pride in. Elitism is a necessary feature of pluralism. Differences are made and kept by those who have the ambition to make a difference.

Or is it that the Great Books support the wrong elite, the white male elite? To call this "elitism" implies that the right elite is closer to the people than the wrong one, hence not really an elite. It is amazing to hear intellectuals speak as if they were closer to the people than are Ronald Reagan and Lee Iacocca. Politicians and businessmen have more than ordinary ambition, but ordinary democrats, who also want power and money, can understand these desires. What they do not easily understand is people who read and write and think all the time. It is intellectuals, then, who have the most to lose in a democracy by raising the charge of elitism. That they do raise it is testimony to their hatred of the bourgeoisie (on which read Bloom), and even more, to their hatred of *defenders* of the bourgeoisie. Reagan is nothing but an actor; his intellectual defenders are class traitors. Nonetheless, his defenders, and incipient neoconservatives such as Edward Koch, have been able to turn the charge of elitism against the radicals who first used it. Let them beware. Intellectuals, the primary beneficiaries of elitism, should be the last to attack it.

Why do they attack it? Because they have lost faith in the intellect. Intellectuals no longer believe that the intellect can rise above the accidents of sex and race; so they conclude that the Great Books written by white males must reflect the interests of white males. They then feel justified in subjecting the Great

Books to a political test in order to "broaden their appeal." A radical solution would be to throw them out and start afresh with *The Color Purple*. The more usual solution is to deprive them of their privileged standing and let ignorant students choose between the Great Books and hitherto undervalued, newly interpreted works by women and blacks. A third solution has been discovered by Martha Nussbaum, Bloom's relentless critic in the *New York Review of Books*, who seems to have assigned herself the task of discrediting Bloom's scholarship. Her way is to democratize and to feminize the ancients so that they repeat her views or at least contradict his. This has the advantage of releasing the feminist scholar from the lifelong study of feminist tracts. It has the disadvantage of having to admit that white males can tell the truth if it is put in their mouths.

To insist on the Great Books is sometimes said to be elitism because it excludes non-Western civilizations. But again, the intellectuals who say this do not seriously intend to compare the merits of Western democracy with the caste system in India and the dynasties in China. They want us, instead, to be impressed with the impossibility of making such comparisons. To be convinced of this impossibility is the basis for the virtue of openness that Bloom decries and Rorty defends.

Rorty fastens on Bloom's statement that philosophic friendship, the only true human association, is the province of the few—and pronounces it anti-democratic. It would be, if philosophic friendship were a political relationship; but it isn't. It is above politics, though perhaps in some sense, as one finds in Aristotle, the ideal of politics. Philosophical friendship is neither aristocracy nor democracy, because it is critical of both. But for Rorty the historicist, the philosopher is incapable of transcending his historical, which means his political, situation. For him, the philosopher cannot be critical of his times, and any attempt on his part to do so has to be understood as a political act no less partisan for its pretense at objectivity. When Bloom expressly says in his preface that he writes from the perspective of a teacher (that is, not a politician), this can be safely disregarded because there is no such perspective. All teaching is like washing a shirt in dirty water; it is, as we say today, "socialization"—a process in which teacher and student exchange prejudices. In this view, "education" in the literal sense of being led out of one's prejudices is impossible, hence foolish to attempt.

Rorty's historicism leads to a thoroughly politicized view of the university. Since every position is in the politics of one's times, one may as well accept the inevitable and charge ahead toward the political solution of one's liking. Just this argument has been used in the debate over South African divestiture that has hounded universities in recent years. Since universities' investments are necessarily partisan, it is said, why not get on the right side? Rorty does not want a politicized university, of course; he wants a tolerant one open to all views. To get a balanced, tolerant university he has to promote his view—that of "Deweyan historicism"—because other views, especially the Straussian, tend to think they are closer to a non-historical truth than their rivals, hence tend to become intolerant. They cannot think they are closer to the truth without also wanting to impose their view, again, since thinking is never more than an effort at self-assertion.

But if a person thinks he is *not* right (non-historically), will that necessarily make him tolerant? Why could he not draw the contrary lesson just as reasonably—that as all truth is someone's truth, let's have mine? Rorty's tolerant university depends on a forbearance, or a denial of one's own will, that is not inevitable and has not occurred. Nietzsche said that men rather will nothingness than will nothing. Strauss often quoted this farseeing remark, and it is the premise of Bloom's argument that the left in our day has become Nietzschean. It explains why fascism, despite its defeats on the battlefield, has been intellectually superior to communism. Communism, in its desire to put an end to class conflict, is essentially for wimps (notice the currency of that word, by the way, as our portmanteau for everything despicable). To survive as a doctrine, communism has had to abandon its rational economics and take assertiveness training from fascism. Rorty's democratic university will do—has done—the same thing.

Besides politicizing the university, Rorty's historicism makes for bad democrats and irresponsible citizens. Good democrats think democracy can be good, and when they see it is not, they take responsibility for reforming it. Their responsibility is based on their holding democracy to the standard of good government. To do this, they must think that good government as a standard is above democracy; it is what democracy aims at, for example the ends stated in the preamble to the Constitution. They must not think that government is automatically good merely by being democratic, as this belief can make them both fanatic in their zeal for democracy and complacent as to its behavior.

The American Founders, wishing to encourage and to establish this responsibility, distinguished themselves from previous founders of republics by their attention to the vices of republics rather than merely to the enemies of republics. They saw that the vice of majority faction was a graver risk to a republic than minority faction, its enemy, because the latter is opposed by the republican form of the government and the republican genius of the people, whereas majority faction by definition looks good to the majority.

The responsible democrat, whom the Founders hoped to create, takes particular care for the things majorities ignore or neglect. Politically, he worries more about demagogues than about elitists; socially, he is less concerned about poverty than about the virtues that money cannot buy. Every regime has a partisan tendency, even democracy—despite the pretense of its defenders, encouraged by Rorty, that it includes everyone and everything. This tendency must be identified and appreciated in the light of a standard outside itself; it cannot, of course, simply be opposed. The responsible democrat needs a majority on his side, so he tries, within its limits, to bring it to understand what he understands. The responsible democrat carries in his mind a mixed picture of what majorities easily appreciate and of what they need to appreciate but tend to resist. This is a mixture of what makes a democracy democratic with what makes it work; the responsible democrat knows that these are not the same.

Rorty's democrat is altogether different. He believes he cannot know what the good is, hence cannot know whether democracy is good or not. Instead of holding democracy to a higher standard outside itself, thus dividing his loyalties, he saves all his love for democracy. The only way he can tell whether democracy works is by judging whether it is becoming more democratic. Instead of a picture of a mixed regime, he carries in his mind a picture of perfect democracy, a regime whose goal is, in Rorty's words, to "maximize freedom and equality." This is the criterion of democrats who want no criterion.

Rorty's democrat is ordinarily oblivious to the non-democratic character of many features of American democracy that make it work better, such as one-man rule in the executive, independence in the judiciary, and elections rather than lot to fill the legislature. But if these features were called to his attention, he would instinctively desire to democratize them or could think of no reason why not to. Indeed, Rorty's democrat would accuse the responsible democrat of a cynical prudence, one that justifies antidemocratic privileges, just as Rorty himself accuses Straussians of cynically adjusting to the democracy their philosophy condemns. Since for Rorty nothing can or should be shown to be good, he cannot appreciate the moral prudence of Aristotle or Burke that seeks to arbitrate between two goods, whether they are democracy and good government or good government and philosophy.

In consequence, Rorty, for all his "honesty," flatters the people and invites the intervention of extremists who are interested in maximizing but don't care about freedom and equality. Straussians such as Bloom, however, are able to tell it as it is, precisely because they insist that the simplistic goal of maximizing democracy without considering whether it is good is neither feasible nor desirable. Bloom's book is as frank as it could be, particularly on topics such as women and blacks, on which we punish frankness. Bloom's critics say nothing risky. They think it boldness to overstate, and they think it moderation to uphold our conventions.

Bloom begins his book by contrasting the democratic man (whom I have called the responsible democrat) of the American founding with the openness of the "democratic personality" that we all know too well. In doing so he relies on the scholarship of other Straussians, especially Martin Diamond, Herbert J. Storing, and Harry V. Jaffa, on the American founding. Against the flow of mainstream scholars who have come to regard the Founders as moral compromisers, guilty of using Rorty's cynical prudence, these Straussians attempt to defend the Founders' moral integrity by restoring their intellectual stature. However difficult today's historians, political scientists, and philosophers may find it to accept, Madison (for example) knew better than they what he was doing— and he was smarter, too. Once one is freed of the historicist's prejudice that diminishes every previous time and impoverishes one's own, the American founding comes to sight as a thoughtful, comprehensive deed worthy of respect and study. It does not deserve to be dismissed as cynical, and it deserves more than a patriotic salute.

Madison was wiser and more trustworthy than Dewey by far, but Rorty manages to diminish even Dewey. Rorty is not a Deweyan but a "Deweyan historicist." He has abandoned Dewey's science and therewith Dewey's naive faith in the mutual support of science and democracy. For Dewey's science Rorty substitutes John Rawls's "reflective equilibrium." It is his test of truth: Does an idea accord with "our common sense" or "what we believe and desire"? The conformism of this test does not have the dignity of conservative respect for tradition, because it lacks any sense of duty or higher calling. It looks like freedom because it is receptive to change, but how is it freedom to be a slave to fashion? Such a position is merely "with it," whatever the latest "it" happens to be. From the shifting ground of his "with it" Heideggerean Dewey, Rorty complains that Straussians are not wholehearted loyalists of democracy. But as his concluding remarks show, he is the one who has given up on America. Some Deweyan.

Rorty sees himself as the culmination of Dewey, whom he sees as the culmination of modern philosophy beginning with Bacon, Descartes, and Hobbes. He has no strong sense of the difference between culmination and corruption, because any such sense would involve him in a criterion, on the way toward the dreaded eternal. So he chooses to look on the bright side. He does not notice that the modern philosophy whose grand project was to enlighten the people now takes, in its latest version, its enlightenment from the people. His bewilderment at this reversal looks to him like greater self-confidence, as he eagerly bids us to grasp the tiller of his rudderless boat. The troubles of American democracy today come not from too much ambition but from fear of too much ambition, from doubts we do not recognize as nihilistic about the worth of the American experiment in self-government—or of any experiment in anything.

It is also said that (Rorty plays this one softly) there is a hidden conservative agenda behind the Straussians' lordly claim to be the partisans of an impossible best regime. When Bloom remarks on the alliance of the ancient philosophers with gentlemen, and then follows this up by asserting that Harvard, Yale, and Princeton are not what they used to be—well, these critics think they have really caught him with his pants down, his hidden agenda exposed. And what about all those Straussians working in Washington for the Reagan administration?

Most of the Straussians in Washington (who are neither many nor powerful) went there because they could not find jobs in universities. For some time, American universities have been increasingly politicized—and for the reason I discussed earlier, the dominant opinion shared by Bloom's critics is that universities have no way of escaping politics. In this view, the choice is only between a hidden agenda and an open one, between a facade of dishonest impartiality and an honest declaration. Of course the choice goes then to those with an open agenda. That is why Marxists and others who have learned how to be both shrewd and brazen are ever so much more respectable in our universities now than Straussians, who seem inhibited when they try to be responsible.

Speaking inhibitedly for myself alone, I will say that I do not think it a crime, legal or moral, to be a Republican. All those today who are serious about the menace of Soviet imperialism—and this includes Rorty and the editors of the *New Republic*—run the risk, as they well know, of being attacked as conservatives, or worse, neoconservatives. To become Republicans, such persons have only to consider why they choose to be attacked in this most important matter by their partisan friends. It's more sensible to arrange it that those who attack you are your enemies.

There's a big difference in this regard between political and philosophical friendship. Political friends have to suppress lesser disagreements for the sake of the greater disagreement with political enemies; philosophical friends can air all their lesser disagreements because of their greater agreement in loving truth, that is, because they are philosophers. Loving truth together is more than an abstract, formal agreement, because this love is a virtue, a habit of living. Such a virtue brings with it a host of lesser virtues, but it does not need any common interest or shared values beyond itself.

As to concrete issues in universities, Rorty will have his hands full if he wants to require two years of the Great Books in order to remedy the gross faults in primary and secondary education that have come about through the influence of his mentor John Dewey. Here too his liberal friends will give him little but grief, and he will be cheered only by the tiny band of conservatives on the faculties of American universities. His objection to putting skills over content applies to universities as well as to schools, because the academic disciplines in the social sciences and humanities have become ever more methodological, thus more hostile to the Great Books. His lament that there will not be enough Straussians in place to teach these books does not do justice to his own capacity for being persuaded by a good argument—or to his own doctrine that tells him to be impressed by a new trend.

The open agenda of Straussians is the reading of the Great Books for their own sake, not for a political purpose. Because of their elevation, the Great Books do not offer a message that is simply political. Because of their diversity, they do not contain a single political message, including that most boring of messages, relativism. Anyone who reads them in order to confirm what he already believes does not really read them. Since we all have beliefs, such reading is an effort at first; later it turns out to be the highest pleasure there is.

Bloom wrote his book about the superficial "openness" of our day that denies both the need for effort and the existence of that pleasure. Anyone who wants to follow up Bloom's book can turn to the works of Strauss, but despite what Rorty says, he will not find any Straussism there. It's no accident that people talk of Straussians but not of Straussism. Of course there are characteristic themes— the importance of founding, the centrality of politics, the presence of religion, the rhetoric of exotericism, the rivalry between poetry and philosophy, the quarrel between the ancients and the moderns, and the search for an author's intention. But these all return to the tension between politics (what is necessary for the health of society) and philosophy (what is required in thinking). To reflect on this tension is political philosophy; and political philosophy is an attempt to gain knowledge, not power.

No doubt the reading of Great Books would strengthen our democracy, but not if it is done for that purpose alone. In its best moments our democracy includes and respects what transcends it. That's how we used to understand our universities. To judge from the response to Bloom's book, the American people have a better sense of this understanding than do the universities themselves.

24

America's Teacher: Mortimer J. Adler, the Nation's Self-Appointed Teacher for Most of His 85 Years, Takes On the "Late-Bloomers" of Academe

JEFF LYON

Professor Allan Bloom
Committee on Social Thought
University of Chicago
1126 E. 59th Street
Chicago, Ill. 60637
>   *Dear Professor Bloom:*
>   *Your recently published book, 'The Closing of the American Mind,"*
> *reveals a remarkable myopia about the causes of the cultural malaise in this*
> *country. It did not originate in the 1960s. It existed in American colleges in*
> *the '30s. . . . What astounds me even more is your apparent ignorance or*
> *neglect of your predecessors at the University of Chicago—those of us . . .*
> *who broke lances in the very cause for which you have so recently become a*
> *spokesman.*
>   *To save you from the mistake of thinking that you are a lone voice on the*
> *side of the angels in the fight against the cultural barbarism of the 20th*
> *Century, in Europe as well as America, I have the temerity to recommend*
> *that you read the following items:* [There follows a concise bibliography of
> the letter writer's pertinent books, essays and lectures].

It is not that the author of the above letter disagrees with Bloom's dumbing-down hypothesis. Indeed, the writer is known far and wide for his own perfervid advocacy of classical education. It is that as someone who was fighting the same battle when Allan Bloom was still wet behind the ears—when the latter was, in fact, a student in the writer's department at the University of Chicago in the mid-1940s—he sees Bloom as an upstart who is cashing in on an idea learned at other people's feet, without giving proper credit to his mentors. Worse, fumes the author, Bloom has made a botch of regurgitating his lessons.

"The whole book is wrong, wrong, wrong." exclaimed the letter writer one recent morning, gripping the edges of his desk with two plump hands while half-

---

Reprinted with permission from the *Chicago Tribune Magazine* (November 27, 1988):10–21.

rising out of his seat. Subsiding slowing back into the chair, he grumbled, "Aside from that, it's very badly written." The sentiments were delivered in a tone of withering intellectual scorn perfected over more than half a century as America's self-appointed personal tutor. For the scornful one is none other than Mr. Great Books himself, Mortimer J. Adler.

At the age of 85, Adler, philosopher, essayist, teacher and editor, is at a stage in life when most contemporaries are ready for ear trumpets and rocking chairs. But Adler keeps up a pace that would kill a man a third his age. He still is chairman of the board of editors of the venerable Encylopaedia Britannica; oversees Britannica's "Great Books of the Western World" series; heads the Institute for Philosophical Research, a kind of Aristotelian think tank; conducts annual summer seminars at the Aspen Institute for Humanistic Studies in Colorado; was the central figure on the recent public television series, "Six Great Ideas," with Bill Moyers; lectures frequently throughout the world; and writes a book a year, with publishing contracts set through 1993. And in the midst of this already formidable schedule, he has time to do what Bloom only expounds upon—lead a genuine hands-on experiment at educational reform. The enter- prise, known as the Paideia project, intertwines classical readings with a Socratic series of seminars aimed at stimulating independent capacity for thought. The program is getting a pilot test at four Chicago schools and another 100 or so schools nationally and recently gained the imprimatur of the University of North Carolina, which took over the reins of Paideia from Adler in September.

Squaring off against this year's exponent of doomsday chic is nothing new for Adler, who, with equal disdain, has been picking fights with establishmentarians, disestablishmentarians, antidisestablishmentarians, parliamentarians, postseminarians, antiquarians and vulgarians for much of his life. At 14, he dropped out of Manhattan's De Witt Clinton High School after a run-in with the principal, who suspended him as editor of the school newspaper for refusing to fire a member of the staff. A few years later, having resurrected his education by passing a high school equivalency test, he was denied a degree from Columbia University, despite making Phi Beta Kappa, because of his stubborn refusal to fulfill the school's requirement that he attend gym class and pass a swimming proficiency test. Still later, after earning a doctorate, thus becoming perhaps the only Ph.D. in America with neither high school diploma nor bachelor's or master's degrees, he failed to obtain an appointment to Columbia's philosophy department in part because he delivered an impudent paper criticizing the views of Columbia icon John Dewey while the famous philosopher was in the au- dience. As a battler, therefore, Adler is all the more enraged that Bloom has yet to rise to his challenge. "He never even answered my letter," he says in an injured tone, as if the mark of a true philosopher is his willingness to put up his dukes.

So Adler is going to stir the pot some more. His 45th book, a collection of Adlerian essays on the subject of reforming education composed over the past half century, will feature a freshly written prologue in which he excoriates Bloom head-on. "And take a look this!" cries Adler gleefully, gesturing for his visitor to follow him into the library of his office suite. There, on a large oak conference table, are the galley proofs of the new book, which will be published next spring by Macmillan. "See that?" he exults, brandishing the title page of the proofs. The original title, "Reforming Education: The Schooling of a People and Their Education Beyond Schooling," has been crossed out with a heavy black pen. In its place is a new title—"Reforming Education: The Opening of the American Mind."

"What do you think about that?" asks Mortimer Adler, beaming slyly across the top of his bifocals. The answer seems pretty clear. Mortimer Adler is not a man who easily suffers being ignored.

It has been just four months short of 60 years since the legendary Robert Maynard Hutchins came from Yale Law School to assume the presidency of the University of Chicago at the unlikely age of 30. Shortly afterwards, he recruited his good friend, Mortimer Adler, from Columbia to come and teach the Great Books on the Midway campus. Adler had been introduced to the study of the Great Books at Columbia, where an innovative program commenced in 1921 under the auspices of John Erskine, an English professor who spent four years convincing the Columbia faculty of the value of intensive studies in what he called "the classics of Western civilization"—ranging from Homer, Thucydides, Sophocles and Aristotle down to St. Thomas Aquinas, Montaigne, Bacon and Descartes and finally Darwin, Marx, Mill, Tolstoy and Freud. Under Erskine, students were to read a classic a week during their junior and senior years, with one two-hour evening seminar each week on the book assigned. Adler unhesitatingly credits the Erskine program with setting the navigational coordinates for the rest of his life.

Some years later, in 1929, shortly after Hutchins had acceded to the helm of the U. of C., Adler and Hutchins dined together in New York at the Yale Club. An obviously distraught Hutchins confessed to Adler that he was at loose ends.

"Here I am, in charge of a great educational institution, and I know nothing about education," the worried Hutchins moaned over his supper. "I've never thought about the subject in my life. All I've been is a law-school dean."

Hutchins began picking Adler's brain, demanding to know what he recalled of his undergraduate education at Columbia. "Not much," replied Adler, with a shrug. "The only thing that really interested me was the Great Books course I took with John Erskine."

"The what?" asked Hutchins, his eyes lighting up. Eagerly, he devoured Adler's glowing description of the course and then asked Adler to name some of the books the class had read. Adler said he could do better than that and went downstairs to the checkroom for his briefcase, which happened to contain the complete list.

"I gave the list to Hutchins," Adler recalls of that night. "He gaped at it— there were 65 authors on it—and he said, 'My God, would you believe in four years at Oberlin and Yale I've only read three of those books?' "

Adler was torn between friendship and candor. Candor won out. "In that case," he informed Hutchins bluntly, "you're not truly educated." The latter looked crushed. "I know it," he cried.

With that, Hutchins took Adler's arm earnestly and said, "Look, you've got to come and teach the Great Books with me at the University of Chicago.

Because if you don't, I'll never read them, and I'll end my career an uneducated man." It was fortuitous that Hutchins knew little about education, for with few preconceptions to cloud his mind, he was able to introduce a series of radical measures at the U. of C. that would challenge the very foundations of American education. He abolished football and fraternities, championed the idea of a liberal, general education while resisting the pragmatic trend toward specialization and vocationalism that was beginning to sweep through American education and saw to it that achievement was measured by comprehensive examination rather than the accumulation of class time. The concentrated curriculum in the Great Books that was born that night in the Yale Club fit right into Hutchins' iconoclastic scheme.

Adler needed little persuading to join Hutchins, and soon he invited some cronies, including Mark Van Doren of Columbia, to come help him and Hutchins teach the Great Books, which became an integral part of Hutchins' so-called "Chicago Plan," which also included allowing promising high school sophomores to enter the university at the age of 16.

Recalls Adler: "Hutchins got the dean, Chauncey Boucher, to select 25 outstanding freshmen from the 1930 freshman class, and we proceeded to teach them a two-year course in Great Books. At the end, believing that the only good test for a Great Books course is an oral examination, we tested them orally. They passed with flying colors. A few days later we were astounded to find the same kids in Hutchins' office. They had formed a committee. 'We know we passed the exams,' they said, 'but we also know we haven't really understood these books. We think we need to read them again.' They wanted us to teach them the same course for another two years. Well, Hutchins telephoned Dean Boucher and asked him if he would authorize that. Boucher was aghast. 'You mean they want credit for taking the same course a second time? That's impossible. It violates all the academic rules. You can't pass algebra and take it again for credit.' But Hutchins persisted. He said the Great Books aren't like algebra. You can read them 10 times and get credit if you learn something new from them each time. I assure you that if Hutchins had not been a new president, he'd have never gotten that through. But it was 1932, and he was still at the crest of his wave and didn't have all the faculty opposition he was to get later. So Boucher finally said yes, and we taught the same students the same books for another two years. From that point on, the program began to gain momentum."

Adler and Hutchins were to go on to turn the Great Books into a virtual industry, aimed at lifting the intellectual horizons of the middlebrow adult market. Together, they selected 443 works by 76 authors and published them in a 54-volume, moderately priced set entitled, "Great Books of the Western World," which debuted in 1952. Not content to let the audience, rank tenderfeet and dudes, plough through these dense forests and rugged ranges unaided, Adler conceived of a unique companion volume that would serve as a ready reference to the Great Ideas contained in the Great Books.

Working seven years, he led an unprecedented mammoth team effort to cull and cross-reference 102 of those ideas so that the reader could easily locate everything that the towering minds of the past had to say on such topics as love, time, family, wisdom, democracy, beauty and so on. To this index Adler attached the name "Syntopicon," a neologism meaning "collection of topics." With the same formula in mind, Adler and Hutchins also introduced a series of Great Books seminars, attended chiefly by affluent businessmen and civic leaders and their spouses, whose crowded lives had left little room for communing with Plato, Rousseau and Descartes. These seminars were conducted once a month at the University of Chicago and became the model for an entire movement of Great Books discussion groups. But Adler's mission to bring the intellectual heritage of the West home to "Joe Dokes," as he puts it, did not end there. Upon leaving the university in 1952, Adler founded the Institute for Philosophical Research in San Francisco, where he inaugurated a literary exploration of Great Ideas in philosophy. . . .

Adler's impatience with Allan Bloom in part stems from his devotion to the ideal of a universal, early education. He considers Bloom an elitist who is only interested in educating the very bright, and he particularly objects to Bloom's emphasis on the faults of higher education. "He never mentions anything about elementary and secondary schools," says Adler. "The failure of these schools is much more important than the failure of the colleges."

Yet Adler is quick to admit that much of his quarrel with Bloom is personal. "My main objection is with his failure to give recognition," he says. "He hardly gives any background of the Great Books movement in this country. He never mentions Bob Hutchins at all. He mentions me invidiously [Adler is referred to in Bloom's book as a "business genius" who made a "roaring commercial success out of the Great Books"]. He has no understanding of the real origins of so-called relativism. This hasn't been going on just since the 1960s. It has been going on most of this century. Bloom is historically blind."

Bloom responds to these charges with an air of almost amused tolerance. "I'm prepared to take his wrath, though not without regret," he chuckles. "I really am pleased I've given a new passion to Mr. Adler this late in his career."

Bloom says he is genuinely repentant about not mentioning Hutchins in his book. "There are not many changes I'd make in the book in response to the criticisms I've received, but that's one. The University of Chicago was my inspiration, and Hutchins was the University of Chicago. I've always regarded myself as a student of Hutchins, a figure I look up to with the greatest of admiration. He was a gem, a genius of an educational administrator."

What, then, of Adler? "Well, I didn't neglect him," says Bloom. "I mentioned him and meant it good-humoredly. I think I praised him rather highly when I called him a business genius. But I would not call him a great scholar. He was definitely not part of the atmosphere of the University of Chicago that I admired most. He was an activist and a popularizer but not too much on substance. I'm all for popularization, as long as one has a profound understanding of these Great Books. But I'm not sure Mr. Adler used the books in the right way. It bothers me, the idea of a whole set of Great Books on one's shelf so people can delude themselves that in these finite volumes is all they need to know. The real problem is to get them attached to one book that speaks to them."

To Adler's specific educational criticisms, that he is elitist and ignores the needs of elementary education, Bloom defends himself by charging that Adler himself is something of an elitist. "I've never felt Mr. Adler was much of a populist in his own person. He obviously thinks he's very bright and can guide the community. As for dwelling on higher education, I was never talking about the problems of education as such. I was describing the problems in the universities. I don't know about elementary schools in the same way I know about universities. But I do know that what is done at the highest levels is ultimately going to filter down to the lower levels. Colleges are where everybody looks to for ideas, and they're also where the teachers come from."

Why didn't he answer Adler's letter?

"I thought it better not to reply," Bloom said. "It was a personal attack and angry, and I didn't think there was enough to provide for a serious dialogue. I've had so many critics you have to choose your adversaries."

25

Socratic Reason and Lockean Rights: The Place of the University in a Liberal Democracy

WILLIAM A. GALSTON

I.

Like Rousseau after the publication of the *First Discourse*, Allan Bloom awoke to find himself famous. Like Rousseau, he challenged his age at the point of its greatest and most unexamined pride. He dared to suggest that "our virtue"—untrammeled tolerance—is in fact the most destructive of vices. And what an attack! By turns passionate, ruminative, scornful, sorrowful, Bloom took on his subject in a manner utterly contemptuous of current fashion, and virtually guaranteed to enrage.

Remarkably, his book did not enrage. Instead, with rare exceptions, it was reviewed in tones ranging from respectful to rapturous in the nation's most respected newspapers and journals, and it quickly soared to the top of the best-seller lists. *The Closing of the American Mind* is more than a book, it is an event—one of those rare literary deeds that reveals the doubts, the fears, and the longings of its audience. The reception of this book deserves an inquiry of its own, as an indication of the deep foreboding just beneath the complacent surface of contemporary culture.

The Closing of the American Mind has three distinguishable, though intimately related, strands: a detailed description of modern American society, viewed through the prism of university students; an historical-analytical explanation of the ills revealed by that description; and finally, a proposed cure for those ills. These elements are linked because, as Bloom characteristically insists, "Concreteness, not abstractness, is the hallmark of philosophy. All interesting generalizations must proceed from the richest awareness of what is to be explained." (255) In this respect, and in many others, *The Closing of the American Mind* is a defense of a distinctive conception of teaching, of learning, and of modern institutional structure—the university—that shelters and sustains these activities. The book is concrete, not just objectively, so to speak, but also subjectively. It is an intensely personal and self-revealing account of one man's way of life. It is not, as some have argued, a jeremiad; it is Bloom's Apology.

William A. Galston is Scholar in Residence at Roosevelt Center, Washington, D.C., and author of *Justice and the Human Good*. This essay is reprinted with permission from *Interpretation*, vol. 16, no. 1 (Fall 1988): 101–110.

II.

On the level of description of contemporary society I will have relatively little to say in this essay, not because I am sure Bloom is right but because I do not possess the requisite evidence to say he is wrong. (In one area, though, I do have some evidence, and I feel constrained to remark that his account of the alleged lack of natural connection between fathers and their children conforms neither to my own experience nor to my observation of the men of my generation.) If there is a difficulty, it lies in the scope rather than the accuracy of Bloom's description. He states that his "sample" consists in students at the twenty or thirty best universities—the future elite. But he sometimes speaks as though what he says about these students is true of American society as a whole. Based on my own experiences, which include lengthy and systematic discussions with "ordinary Americans" across the country, I have concluded that there is much less relativism, much more respect for traditional understandings of individual rights, moral virtues, and the family than might be inferred from a sample of young elite students.

Bloom is not unaware of this difficulty, and he appears to respond to it as follows: Influential changes of opinion begin at the top and gradually filter downward. First comes dangerous philosophy, then a corruption of the intellectuals, then the students, political leaders, and finally the general public. At the end comes the ex-convict taxi driver who prattles on about Gestalt therapy.

Although this thesis is not wholly implausible, it is not the whole truth. American society today is the arena of a struggle between those who advance, and those who resist, the trends Bloom rightly deplores. During the past decade, in fact, there has been a popular revolt against the perceived moral relativism of the elites, and the gap between popular and elite beliefs is now very wide. Of course it is troubling that so many of those who are likely to be socially and politically influential do not have healthy opinions. But the public is capable of resisting what it does not like. In a democracy—for better as well as for worse—it is the people who ultimately rule.

III.

Why has the elite "American mind" deserted its founding convictions—the rights of man, the Bible—in favor of an openness that cannot make moral distinctions and eventually undermines all convictions? Bloom's official answer, which provides the plot line for much of his book, is that relativistic German philosophy gradually imposed the yoke of alien thought on what had been a sturdy Enlightenment tradition.

But this can hardly be the full answer. To begin with, the enormous success of this popularized Nietzscheanism forces us to wonder what needs it gratified and whether the unsullied American mind was really so well-ordered—to ask, that is, *why* this Continental victory occurred. Bloom suggests two seemingly contradictory but ultimately reconcilable answers. First, Nietzsche as mediated through Freud interpreted the higher in light of the lower, an approach that proved especially popular in a democracy "where there is envy of what makes special claims, and the good is supposed to be accessible to all." (232) But second, an

Americanized Nietzsche provided an essential corrective to early democratic theory, whose low but solid foundation failed to flatter democratic man sufficiently, by holding out the possibility that everyone could be creative, autonomous, a source of new values—the very definition of nobility in a transmoral, postphilosophic age (144). In short, Nietzsche as received in this country simultaneously undermined the grounds of aristocracy and offered us all the opportunity of being aristocrats.

These suggestions, in turn, make me doubt that the story can simply be the victory of foreign corruption over domestic health. It is more nearly adequate to say that vulgarized Nietzschean thought activated latent problems, and accelerated indigenous trends, already present in American life. Indeed, Bloom provides us with an impressive catalogue of such phenomena. Liberal tolerance fosters relativism when it seeks to widen its scope by placing more and more claims to superiority outside the realm of knowledge (30–31). Liberal freedom fosters relativism when it seeks to become absolute by denying all rational limits (28). Democratic egalitarianism fosters relativism by denigrating heroism and delegitimating rank-ordering among human beings (66, 90). Egoistic individualism fosters relativism by denying natural relatedness among, and duties toward, other human beings, a trend exacerbated by the liberal-contractarian view of the family (86, 112). In short, Bloom's own account suggests that modern liberal democracy is not stably well-ordered unless it is somehow mitigated by external forces (religion, traditional moral restraints, aristocracy) with which it is at war and which it tends to corrode. (See especially 251–252.)

That this is in fact the deeper stratum of his argument is suggested as well by another set of considerations. Liberal democracies are the natural home of the bourgeoisie. Bourgeois existence, says Bloom, is defined by the effort to expunge dangerous passions—for aristocratic distinction, for political power, for religious truth—in the name of tranquil and commodious living: "Neither longing nor enthusiasm belong to the bourgeois" (169). But of course these natural desires cannot be wholly eradicated, and they thus find stunted, distorted expression in democratic societies (183, 329ff). The appeal of Nietzsche, like that of Rousseau, is to the part of the soul that bourgeois existence leaves fallow, or lays waste. The gateway to the mind of America did not have to be rammed open by alien philosophy, the Enemy Without, for it was swung open to the invader by our inchoate longing for the beyond, the Enemy Within.

IV.

If relativism is the modern democratic disease, what is the cure? I can best approach this question through some personal history.

It was in the fall of 1963, during Bloom's unforgettable "Introduction to Political Philosophy," that I first encountered Leo Strauss's *Natural Right and History*. From the powerful first pages on, I sensed immediately that I was in the presence of greatness. The Introduction challenged Americans not to surrender their ancestral faith in the rights of man to German relativism, and it traced the impasse of modern thought to the seventeenth-century overthrow of classical— that is, teleological—natural science. I read on eagerly, hoping to find an account of the grounds on which the Declaration of Independence could be rationally reaffirmed and the problem posed by modern science surmounted.

But as I finished *Natural Right and History,* I was perplexed. Far from reaffirming the rights of man, Strauss argued that the philosophic ground of those rights—Hobbes' and Locke's account of the state of nature—had been decisively criticized by Rousseau, who carried the antiteleological premise of his predecessors to its logical conclusion. (My perplexity only deepened when I read, at the end of "What Is Political Philosophy?," that Nietzschean nihilism is the culmination and highest self-consciousness of modern thought, the inevitable consequence of the break with classical rationalism.) As for the problem of natural science: Strauss had made it clear at the outset that he would confine his discussion to that aspect of natural right that could be clarified within the domain of the social sciences. But at each step in his narrative, Strauss showed that the political thinkers of modernity accepted the antiteleological implication of modern science and shaped their political teachings in its light. Evidently the problem posed by science could be deferred but not indefinitely evaded. Yet as I read more and more of Strauss's writings, I could find no definitive account of this matter. In the preface to the 7th Impression of *Natural Right and History,* nearly two decades after its initial publication and only shortly before his death, Strauss explicitly reaffirmed his "inclination to prefer" the natural right teaching of classical antiquity. But to the best of my knowledge, he never cleared away what he himself had identified as the most fundamental intellectual obstacle to that reaffirmation. To summarize: while relativism is poison, neither modern nor classical natural right teachings are straightforwardly available as antidotes.

I find precisely these same difficulties at the heart of Bloom's narrative. He suggests, for example, that there is an essential conflict between the humanities—including philosophy—and modern natural science (372). At the same time, he notes that no influential modern thinker has tried to return to the preEnlightenment—teleological—understanding of nature (181). More to the point, he never recommends, or suggests the possibility, of such a return. It would seem to follow that our account of man must now be situated within the context of modern science. Yet much of Bloom's book consists in a critique of every postclassical effort to execute such a strategy (see especially 193, 301–302). There is no third path. If the problem of natural science cannot be sidestepped, it must be addressed, else the return to classical rationalism is *ex hypothesi* impossible. But Bloom refuses to accept, or make, this choice: he neither consigns natural science to irrelevance nor confronts head-on the human difficulties engendered by its antiteleological stance.

Bloom's recapitulation of Strauss's other conundrum—the status of modern natural rights—is even more fundamental to his entire enterprise. Bloom states unequivocally that the modern natural rights teaching establishes the "framework and the atmosphere for the modern university" (288), which institution it is his purpose to defend against its enemies. Modern natural right, in turn, is rooted in the state of nature (162). In particular, the American understanding of the rights of man, which undergirds the American university, rests on the state of nature as depicted by Locke (165–166). Therein lies the difficulty. Like Strauss before him,

Bloom argues that Locke's account was decisively criticized by Rousseau, who pointed out that "Locke, in his eagerness to find a simple or automatic solution to the political problem, made nature do much more than he had a right to expect a mechanical, nonteleological nature to do" (176). The modern university Bloom wishes to defend thus rests on a state of nature teaching that by his own account must be judged defective.

This chain of inference has profound implications for liberal democracy. If Rousseau is right, Locke is wrong. If Locke is wrong, then the university—indeed, America itself—is insecurely founded. Yet at this critical juncture, in a book hardly deficient in blunt speech, Bloom pulls back from the full rigor of his argument. Rousseau, he declares, "explodes the simplistic [Lockean] harmoniousness between nature and society that *seems to be* the American premise." (177; emphasis added) In this ambiguous "seems to be" lurks the deepest issue. Are the natural rights at the base of our regime, the rights to which most Americans still subscribe (166), the rights that constitute "our only principle of justice," the rights that sustain the institutions Bloom cherishes—the rights of man, so conceived—worthy of our rational devotion? That is the question. I cannot see that it receives an adequate answer in this otherwise compelling book.

VI.

I come, finally, to the question of students. Bloom maintains that, unlike the students of the 1960s, today's students are nurtured neither in the Bible nor in the tradition of the Declaration of Independence. The loss of these traditions has made today's students narrower and flatter, without the "felt need" for the kind of noble openness that only devotion to philosophic activities can gratify. There is thus less soil in which university teaching can take root, and that soil is too thin to "sustain the taller growths" (51, 61).

I have no competence to characterize today's students. But I can speak of the students of twenty years ago that Bloom evokes with such nostalgic affection, for I was one of them. It was indeed a marvelous time. But my memory of it does not fully square with Bloom's account.

I do not recall that many of us were particularly well versed in the Bible or in the doctrine of the rights of man—I know I was not. Most of us had however grown up in stable families where television was not yet a dominant force, families in which reading was encouraged and learning was respected. We reached university age in the midst of the biggest, longest economic boom in the history of the world, and we were willing to take intellectual risks because we never worried—or had to worry—about the effects of risk-taking on our future ability to earn a living. At that time, the United States was the undisputed leader of the Free World, with a virtually unblemished record of postwar diplomatic accomplishment. We trusted our government. We were not really cynical about anything. We were patriots. (We were also relativists, by the way, but Bloom cured us of that quickly enough.) The United States had the brash, open hubris of Athens before the Sicilian expedition, and we all somehow participated in it. Our willingness to learn was unqualified; our "felt need" was in large measure for a kind of aristocratic distinction that might be possible within a democratic society.

As I look across the gulf that separates today's students from those of my generation, I am struck by the importance of socioeconomic forces and political events, most of which Bloom hardly mentions: the Vietnam War, Watergate, stagflation, television, divorce, gasoline lines, American hostages in Iran. I suspect economic uncertainties have helped make today's students career-oriented, closed to speculation, afraid of taking risks; that two decades of foreign policy fiascos have undermined confidence; that repeated breaches of public trust have bred cynicism; and that television has perceptibly eroded both the capacity to concentrate and the taste for reading. I also agree with Bloom that family instability and rising divorce rates have wounded children in ways that reduce healthy openness when they reach the university.

None of this is to deny Bloom's basic thesis that if true learning is to be possible, nature needs the assistance of convention. But I believe that he unduly denigrates the independent force of political and economic circumstances in affecting the conditions for openness, in the name of a conception of modern history as produced almost entirely by the dissemination of philosophic thought. I doubt that economic stagnation and military bungling—or, for that matter, the epidemic of broken families—can be laid at the feet of Nietzsche and Heidegger.

One last thought. Bloom takes as his baseline of comparison an all-too-brief Golden Age of American higher education. It *was* a Golden Age, no doubt about it. But I am forced to wonder whether those few years were not exceptional by the standards of American history itself. For the most part, as Tocqueville stresses, the American mind is not particularly hospitable to the cultivation and exercise of noninstrumental reason. Philosophy in America will always be vulnerable to the practical disciplines: the MBA degree denounced by Bloom is but the latest link in a venerable American chain.

The problem goes deeper than the violence of the 1960s and the vacuity of the 1980s. I would suggest that Bloom has a quarrel—or at least an ambivalent relation—with bourgeois society as a whole. (Is it by chance that the emotional peak of his introductory course was the lecture on *Madame Bovary*?) Bloom cherishes the freedom that is only to be found in liberal democracy, but he despises the absence of longing in the soul of the bourgeois. He wishes to defend the university through an appeal to the principles of liberal democracy, but the thinkers to whom he appeals with the greatest frequency and effect throughout his book—Socrates, Plato, Rousseau, and Nietzsche—are all critics of liberal democracy. Locke, he suggests, is more politically salutary than Rousseau, but less psychologically profound. And besides, he insists, Rousseau was ultimately the more consistent thinker. Until the grounds for supporting liberal democracy are more firmly established than this, the status of reason—and therewith of the university—in the modern world will of necessity remain unsettled and insecure.

FIVE

Bloom on Philosophy

Is He a Nihilist?

Harry V. Jaffa, in "Humanizing Certitutes and Impoverishing Doubts," sets up an ongoing controversy about Bloom's position on the Lockean doctrines of the American founding fathers. Much of the Declaration of Independence is a paraphrase of John Locke's *Second Treatise of Government*. Leo Strauss teaches that Locke is one of the philosophers that lied. Strauss says that Locke was in favor of the reasonableness of Christianity and of natural right, but he had a secret belief (of which the American founding fathers were unaware) that Christianity and natural right are false doctrines and that what is true is hedonism, atheism, and materialism. Therefore Locke tricked the founding fathers into making a Constitution that has made America hopelessly hedonistic, atheistic, and materialistic.

It should be clear to the reader that the above argument is farfetched. Jaffa calls it "the purest nonsense." *If* Jaffa is correct that Bloom is making this nonsensical argument, then he has dealt a fatal blow to Bloom's entire project—something that those who say simply that Bloom hates democracy have been unable to accomplish. It is not democracy that is the villain of the piece but rather it is "bourgeois" democracy.

Bloom's description of the sickness of America is persuasive. Christopher Colmo, in "Allan Bloom and the American Premise," certainly agrees. But why does Bloom not argue for Lincoln and Plato the way Jaffa and Colmo do? Is it possible that the "general in the war against relativism" is a closet nihilist giving us a noble lie in order to shore up American society a little while longer in the face of the popularization of his own and Nietzsche's doctrines?

Jaffa is by no means the only critic who has gotten the impression that Bloom is a closet nihilist. Shadia B. Drury agrees with Jaffa about Bloom and agrees with Strauss that America already has an orthodoxy, what Lincoln and Aristotle call "natural right." Drury penetrates behind Bloom's rhetoric and draws forth the sinister implications of Bloom's praise of "culture."

Thomas G. West also agrees with Jaffa. West argues that the nonsensical argument about America being fatally flawed at its founding because of the secret teaching of Locke is exactly what Bloom believes, and West develops a startling metaphor to illustrate this argument. If Locke's secret teaching is correct, then America is dying of a case of political-theoretical AIDS. Any country that was

127

intended from its birth (or before) to be hedonistic, atheistic, and materialistic can have no immunity system against relativism, which will destroy it the way an invading virus destroys a human body. This is one of the most compelling metaphors in all of the reviews of Bloom—but does it prove that Bloom actually holds the nonsensical position about the secret teaching?

Charles Kesler, in "The Closing of Allan Bloom's Mind," also agrees with Jaffa that Bloom is attacking America not for becoming immoral but for becoming thoughtlessly immoral. Kesler, like Drury, argues that America's sickness is caused by departure from its founding principles, not by a bad founding working itself out.

Eva Brann, in "The Spirit Lives in the Sticks," argues that, even if Bloom is correct that bourgeois democracy is hopelessly mediocre and mindless, there are still pockets of happy and healthy people clustered around a few small liberal arts colleges, so it is still possible to lead a good life in America. Some consolation.

Michael Zuckert, in chapter 3, replies to this entire line of criticism. He argues that there is something perverse in claiming that a man who is hailed by intelligent laymen as a general in the war against relativism is a closet nihilist. What is important is the argument of Bloom's book, not his own secret opinions. Bloom's prescription for how to end America's demoralization is serious and has had a good effect on the universities and the country as a whole. To try to psychoanalyze him is both harmful and unnecessary. The public argument is more important than the private man.

26

Humanizing Certitudes and Impoverishing Doubts: A Critique of *The Closing of the American Mind*

HARRY V. JAFFA

At the end of July 1987, Mark McGwire, of Claremont, California, and the Oakland As, had hit 37 home runs, and led both major leagues. He had equaled the home run record for rookies in the American League, and was only one short of the National League record. Records, however, are for full seasons, and young Mr. McGwire still had nearly half the year's games to play. He is without question what in sports is called a "Feenom."

At about the time McGwire was taking his first turn at bat that spring, a book entitled *The Closing of the American Mind*, by Allan Bloom, was published. Its rise to the top of the nonfiction best seller list has been as explosive as young McGwire's bat. Its staying power at the top of that list—extending over many months—is no less astonishing that its swift anabasis. The demand for it is widespread—radiating outwards from Chicago, New York, Boston, and Washington (not to mention Paris, where it is said to be going like "hot crêpes")—to top most regional lists, as well as the national. It is surely as much a "Feenom," as any event in recent sports history.

Whatever the ultimate judgment may be as to the book's merits, there can be no doubt that its tremendous sales are evidence that it has touched an exposed nerve of public concern. Something, no doubt, must be conceded to the fact that its "defense" of traditional morality is accompanied by a great deal of prurient denunciation of immorality—like the famous reformer who, at the turn of the century, made highly publicized invasions of the red light districts of New York City. His church was always jammed on the ensuing Sundays, when his congregation (as well as numerous reporters) assembled to hear of his virtuous forays into these dens of iniquity. With much greater sophistication, Bloom also preaches, and does it very well.

Meanwhile [that is, in the wake of women's "liberation"] one of the strongest, oldest motives for marriage is no longer operative. Men can now easily enjoy the sex that

Harry V. Jaffa teaches at Claremont Graduate School and is the author of the important Civil War history. *The Crisis of The House Divided* (1959), and coauthor with Allan Bloom of *Shakespeare's Politics* (1964). This review is reprinted with permission from *Interpretation* vol. 16, no. 1 (Fall 1988):111–138.

previously could be had only in marriage. It is strange that the tiredest and stupidest bromide mothers and fathers preached to their daughters—"He won't respect you or marry you if you give him what he wants too easily"—turns out to be the truest and most probing analysis of the current situation (p. 132).

Reading the first part of *The Closing of the American Mind*, with its discussion—along the foregoing lines—of such topics as "Equality," "Race," "Sex," "Divorce," "Love," and "Eros," one is forcibly struck by its resemblance to the moral (as distinct from theological) aspects of the sermons of the Rev. Jerry Falwell and the homilies of the Rev. Pat Robertson. Bloom is certainly correct about relativism seducing young women—thereby saving their boyfriends that trouble. And he is also right in pointing to the other—and much greater—troubles that young men find themselves in, when in the company of their "liberated" women. If all moral choices are "values" and all are equally unsupported by reason—or by revelation, which becomes just another "opinion" or "value"—then all moral choices are equally significant, or insignificant. Thus Bloom quotes young women as saying that sex is "no big deal." Yet the truth is that sex is always a big deal, and those who think and act otherwise, leave an ever-widening trail of disaster, disease, and death in their wake.

There is, however, one surprising omission in Bloom's catalogue of the evils of relativism. He is vigorous in his portrayal of the human cost of sexual promiscuity, as the foregoing quotation indicates. Yet his observations of the aberrations of the counterculture seem frozen in "The Sixties," as the title of his most memorable chapter suggests. (Bloom left Cornell for Toronto at the end of that decade, and remained in self-imposed exile for most of the decade that followed.) His remarks about feminism, and the changing roles of men and women, for example, are dated not because they are mistaken, or irrelevant, but because in the intervening years the so-called "gay rights" movement, which Bloom hardly mentions, has emerged as the most radical and sinister challenge, not merely to sexual morality, but to all morality.

As I have argued in "Sodomy and the Academy: The Assault on the Family and Morality by 'Liberation' Ethics" (*American Conservatism and the American Founding*, Carolina Academic Press, 1984, pp. 263–78), the demand for the recognition of sodomy as both a moral and a legal right represents the most complete repudiation—theoretical as well as practical—of all objective standards of human conduct. The reason why we regard the killing of other human beings—but not the killing of cattle—as murder, is because we are members of the same species. That is to say, we share a common nature. The reason we regard the enslavement of human beings—but not of cattle—as wrong, is because we recognize an equality of rights among fellow members of the same species. This is also the reason for regarding racial or religious or even sex discrimination as wrong. Every moral distinction that can be called to mind can, I believe, be shown to have the same origin or ground, including the very idea of human rights—to which the sodomites and lesbians themselves appeal. But the word nature means generation. A species is defined by the presence in it of individuals of opposite sexes who can generate new individuals of the same species. Nature is the ground of all morality, but maleness and femaleness is the ground of nature.

The Bible, in describing man as created in the image of God, adds "male and female created he them," implying that God's own existence is grounded in the same distinction as nature's. The so-called "gay rights" movement is then the ultimate repudiation of nature, and therewith the ground of all morality. Of course, sodomy has been around for a long time—as we know from the Bible. What we are faced with here is not a demand that homosexuality be a private matter between consenting adults. We are faced with a public demand for the admission into law and morality of an equal right of homosexuality and hetero-sexuality. There has never in my experience been anything like the Gay and Lesbian Centers, now on virtually every campus—with a GLAD week (Gay and Lesbian Awareness Days) sanctioned and encouraged by the college administra-tions, and patronized by local (and even national) politicians. I have been teaching many more years than Bloom, and I have never seen students as morally confused as they are today. It is difficult enough for young people, as Bloom shows so well, to have to work out anew, with no authoritative conventions, the roles to be followed in boy/girl, man/woman relationships. But this difficulty is compounded a thousand times, when the boy/girl, man/woman relationship is itself called into question. This is as much as to say, that whether you want to belong to the human race is now a matter of personal preference. Tens of thousands—perhaps hundreds of thousands—of students across the country, who never had the least homosexual tendencies, have been seduced (and their lives ruined) by the overpowering pressure of the official patronage of the gay rights propaganda. Many young men, who do not know how to deal with "liberated" women, and many "liberated" women, who do not know how to deal with men any more (except as enemies), take refuge in sodomy and lesbianism. This has constituted the great moral crisis of the eighties on American campuses, and Bloom is almost entirely silent about it.

The chronology of the AIDS epidemic corresponds precisely with this public movement to establish sodomy and lesbianism as a recommended lifestyle. In nothing has the power of relativism—and the disgrace of American higher education—manifested itself more than in its endorsement of homosexuality. But whatever the attitude of the educational authorities, God and nature have exacted terrible retribution. This lifestyle has proved to be a deathstyle. For the first time since modern relativism has mounted its assault upon man's humanity, chastity and the monogamous family may be seen to be recovering some of their standing. Unfortunately, the new argument for the old ways is entirely based upon the argument for self-preservation. This argument will not survive the discovery of new scientific cures. Last spring I told a class of freshmen (and women) that there was a race on, between God and science, for their moral allegiance. And, I added, somewhat sententiously, that it would be very unwise for them ever to bet against God. A few years ago, this remark would have provoked gales of laughter. This time I looked out upon the most solemn faces I had ever seen! Thanks to AIDS then, we have a little breathing time to reassert the true arguments—the "enriching certitudes" (as in the *Nicomachean Ethics*), not merely Bloom's "humanizing doubts." Morality must be seen, as Aristotle sees it, as a means to implement the desire for happiness, and not merely as a restraint upon the desire for pleasure. The arguments must be made not only as to how one may avoid a bad death, but how one can pursue a good life. But one will not find those arguments in *The Closing of the American Mind.*

Notwithstanding the foregoing, Bloom speaks eloquently and even wisely of the evils of relativism. And, to the surprise and pleasure of many, it turns out that he is not just another Bible thumper. (I do not mean to suggest that these are to be despised, but only that they have no standing in our "elite" universities.) He is, rather, of all things, a professor of political philosophy, pointing to his fellow university teachers as the source of this poisonous and literally demoralizing doctrine. This surely must go a long way towards accounting for the book's apparently wide appeal to middle America. Yet those who turn to Bloom for solace and guidance are apt to find their optimism short-lived. Having eloquently portrayed the disastrous consequences of relativism he does not advocate a return to those standards of human conduct implied in its rejection and, most notably, in his own invocation and praise of the ancient "bromides" concerning chastity. Thus he writes

> It is not the immorality of relativism that I find appalling. What is astounding and degrading is the dogmatism with which we accept such relativism, and the easy going lack of concern about what that means for our lives (p. 329).

In one issue of *Insight* magazine, as well as in feature stories in *The Washington Times,* Bloom was hailed as "the general in the war against relativism." But those who thus hailed him seemed to assume that his critique of relativism implied a stand in favor of traditional morality. If so, they did not read him with sufficient care—or astuteness. Bloom does not, repeat not, find "the immorality of relativism . . . appalling." What Bloom rejects is only "easy going" relativism.

When Bloom looks at the "low" in the light of the "high," the "high" turns out to be the "extraordinary thought and philosophical greatness" of German nihilism. One might say that American relativism is comic in its blandness and indifference to the genuine significance of human choice, whereas in its German version fundamental human choices take on the agonized dignity of high tragedy. But none of Bloom's philosophical heroes—for example, Nietzsche or Heidegger—wrote tragedies. Shakespeare did. And Bloom himself once wrote extraordinarily well on *Othello.* (See *Shakespeare's Politics,* by Allan Bloom, with Harry V. Jaffa, Basic Books, 1964, Chapter 3. See especially, pp. 53ff.) Desdemona cannot imagine that a woman would betray her husband even "for the whole world." One can only surmise how students for whom sex is "no big deal" read the play. One guesses only that for them it is a black comedy about crazy people. The greatness of *Othello* is inextricably bound up with the fact—once so powerfully expounded by Bloom himself—that the covenantal act of choice of partners in marriage reproduces the covenantal act of choice of the Children of Israel by the God of Israel. Bloom wants to turn his students from their "impoverishing certitudes" to "humanizing doubts." But it seems to me that his own argument requires rather that "impoverishing certitudes" be replaced by "enriching certitudes." After all, it was a necessary condition of the tragedy in *Othello* that there be no doubt whatever in the minds of Othello and Desdemona as to the absolute significance of fidelity in marriage. "Humanizing doubt," no less than any other kind, would dissolve the tragedy into a tale of silly mistakes. It seems to me that Nietzsche's and Heidegger's theoretical teaching is far more profoundly subversive of the universe of Shakespearean tragedy, than the sitcoms of Woody Allen, which draw so much of Bloom's attention. And we must ask the same Bloom who recommended the "bromide" about chastity, whether a young woman would be more or less apt to benefit from it, if her cheap generic drugstore relativism had been replaced by the high and tragic nihilism—the parent of all relativism—of Nietzsche and Heidegger? Do we really want her to look into the abyss of nothingness and agonize over whether to have sex with her boyfriend? As Bloom must know from the literature (to borrow a familiar phrase of Leo Strauss), the outcome, in at least nine times out of ten, will be the same, whether the girl agonizes first, or just hops into bed. Thus Aristotle, in the *Nicomachean Ethics*

> Nor does goodness or badness with regard to such things [viz., passions such as spite, shamelessness, envy, and actions such as adultery, theft, murder] depend upon committing adultery with the right woman, at the right time, and in the right way, but simply to do any of them is to go wrong (1107a15ff.).

Aristotle directs the argument of his *Ethics* only to those whose characters are already formed by basic moral education. He does not suppose that liberal education should form the basis of moral choice—on the contrary, he supposes that moral education should form the basis of liberal education. Bloom, it seems to me, has got it exactly backwards.

A moving passage in *The Closing of the American Mind*, and the one that to me conveys Bloom's critique of relativism most effectively, is the following:

> My grandparents were ignorant people by our standards, and my grandfather held only lowly jobs. But their home was spiritually rich because all the things in it, not only what was specifically ritual, found their origins in the Bible's commandments, and their explanation in the Bible's stories and the commentaries on them, and had their imaginative counterparts in the deeds of the myriad of exemplary heroes. My grandparents found reasons for the existence of their family and the fulfillment of their duties in serious writings, and they interpreted their special sufferings with respect to a great and ennobling past. Their simple faith and practices linked them to great scholars and thinkers who dealt with the same material, not from outside or from an alien perspective, but believing as they did, while simply going deeper and providing guidance. There was real respect for real learning, because it had a felt connection with their lives. This is what a community and a history mean, a common experience inviting high and low into a single body of belief (p. 60).

I do not remember a more eloquent evocation of the idea of authoritative tradition, and of how it dignifies human life. Of course, Bloom is referring to the Jewish tradition—the most conservative of all traditions, beginning as it does "in the beginning." I am confident that Bloom's grandparents—like my grandparents—found a home for that tradition within the American political tradition that for them was represented by Washington, Jefferson, and Lincoln. I am sure that they felt, as did Moses Seixas, sexton of Newport's Touro Synagogue in 1790, on the occasion of Washington's visit to Newport. He hailed Washington as another Joshua who had been led by the Lord, as he himself had led the American people into the Promised Land of this new Zion of political and religious freedom. For American Jews at the time of the Revolution—and even for those today who have not become victims of a university education—have always seen this nation as also a chosen nation. From the beginning, America as the new Israel, as a light to lighten all the nations, concerning the principles of political and religious liberty, has been a theme of public discourse. And for the very reason that America could become a Zion to all the nations, it could become a Zion to the Jews themselves. George Washington's letter to the Touro Synagogue represented the first time in more than 2,000 years that Jews had been recognized as citizens of any nation. It represented the first time in human history that Jews had been recognized, as equal and fellow citizens of a non-Jewish polity. And that recognition was authoritative because it came from the one man who, as President and Head of State, and as Father of his Country, surpassed all others in moral authority. Washington's greeting to the Jews recognized them as possessing not only a technical legal equality, but as equal human participants, under the One God, in the moral and providential order which was the source of all the nation's blessings. Let me just add here, that Lincoln's greatest speeches are characterized by the combination into a peculiarly American synthesis of the moral and providential order of the Bible, and of the no less moral and no less providential order of the Declaration of Independence. In Lincoln's second inaugural address we see in absolute perfection an authoritative tradition encompassing the teachings of the Bible—both Old and New Testaments—and the teachings of the Revolution. I am confident that Bloom's grandparents understood this, in their humble—but profound—way. Why then does Bloom look only abroad, to that acid solvent of all traditions, German nihilism, for that which is already his by right of inheritance?

Here is the denouement of Bloom's genuinely poetic—and nostalgic—tribute to his grandparents.

> I do not believe that my generation, my cousins who have been educated in the American way, all of whom are M.D.'s or Ph.D.'s, have any comparable learning. When they talk about heaven and earth, the relations between men and women, parents and children, the human condition, I hear nothing but clichés, superficialities, the material of satire. I am not saying anything so trite as that life is fuller when people have myths to live by. I mean rather that a life based upon the Book is closer to the truth, that it provides the material for deeper research in and access to the real nature of things. Without the great revelations, epics, and philosophies as part of our natural vision, there is nothing to see out there, and eventually little left inside. The Bible is not the only means to furnish a mind, but without a book of similar gravity, read with the gravity of the potential believer, it will remain unfurnished (p. 60).

Bloom says that his generation—his cousins—have no "comparable learning" to that of their grandparents. But why does Bloom assume without argument that there is any learning "comparable" to the Torah and the Talmud? Bloom makes no attempt to understand his grandparents as they understood themselves, and he tacitly rejects their way of life, even as he recognizes in it something rich and wonderful that is lacking in his own.

Bloom's evocation of his grandparents is touching, but it is barren. He denies that he is saying "anything so trite as that life is fuller when people have myths to live by." What then is he saying? That "a life based on the Book is closer to the truth [and] . . . provides . . . access to the real nature of things?" But what is the source or ground of knowledge that enables Bloom to judge the Bible's proximity to the truth? According to Leo Strauss, the concept of "nature" is a discovery of philosophy, and is alien to the Old Testament. By asserting that the world is created by God, the Torah denies that there is a self-subsisting reality independent of the will of God. Of course, rabbinic Judaism, like medieval Christianity, assimilated the idea of "the laws of nature and of nature's God" within the framework of Creation. The perfect expression of this assimilation is of course in our own Declaration of Independence. Bloom's easy going judgment of the truth of the Bible is however—from the viewpoint of the Bible itself—a judgment of the high in the light of the low.

"Without the great revelations," Bloom writes, " . . . there is nothing to see out there . . ." The descent of the Bible is now explicit—to being only one of many "revelations." And such "revelations" are now lower case "books," along with "epics" and "philosophies." We need them says Bloom, "as part of our natural vision." But books are artifacts. If, however, artifacts determine the content of our vision, if without these artifacts there is nothing to see, then visual reality is in truth an artifact. "Natural vision" would then be an illusion, although not an optical illusion (since there is no optical reality)! Conversely, if there is such a thing as natural vision, then there must be natural objects of sense perception, and of knowledge. And the existence and perception of these must be independent of books. Books then would be accounts of reality, or interpretations of reality, but not themselves the ground of the reality of which they speak. To say that without books there is nothing to see, is nihilism. Yet Bloom's nihilism, manifest in these words, is, as we have seen, contradicted by his reference to both "natural vision" and "the real nature of things." This contradiction runs throughout his book from beginning to end.

Although the title of the book speaks of an "American Mind," there is in truth little or nothing American about the mind or minds that are characterized, other than Bloom's reports about his students. Bloom writes in the tradition of the great expatriates: Henry James, T. S. Eliot, Ezra Pound, and (in a somewhat different sense) Henry Adams. He reminds one of the avant-garde Parisian-Bohemians of the 1920s that included Joyce and Hemingway. He can breathe freely only in the presence of the symbols (and ruins) of Europe's aristocratic past. American democracy, as Americans themselves have understood it, is a closed book to him.

Bloom writes often about French and German philosophy and literature. Names drop upon his pages like summer flies. There are the great modern thinkers—Rousseau, Kant, Hegel, Nietzsche, and Heidegger. There are the more literary types, Ibsen, Joyce, Dostoyevsky, Proust, Kafka, Céline, Molière, Flaubert, Schiller, and of course Goethe. There is not a single reference to Cooper or Hawthorne or Emerson or Whitman or Howells. Nor any to Dreiser or Sinclair Lewis or Edith Wharton or Willa Cather. Thoreau is mentioned, but only because he represented a "side of Rousseau's thought . . ." (p. 171). Above all, there is nothing about Melville or Mark Twain! In "Tom Sawyer: Hero of Middle America," (*Interpretation*, Spring 1972, reprinted in *The Conditions of Freedom*, The Johns Hopkins University Press, 1975) I attempted to capture the art by which Mark Twain had transformed Plutarchian into Machiavellian (and

Lockean) heroism, how in *Tom Sawyer* we see the regime refounded, how we witness the coming into being of a "new order, of which Tom is a new prince [and where] the boy is father of the man, and the old are ruled by the young." Tom may be a rogue, but he is a charming one. Bloom's Tom Sawyer is Céline's Robinson, the hero of *Journey to the End of the Night*, described as an "utterly selfish liar, cheat, and murderer for pay" (p. 239).

Bloom complains loud and long that Americans do not have national books that form and represent national character, as do Frenchmen or Germans or Italians or the English. There is some justification for this complaint. But that is because the genius of America as a civilization is above all to be found in its political institutions, and its greatest writers have been its greatest political men, Jefferson and Lincoln and Washington. The American book of books, is the story of America itself, as the story of the secular redemption of mankind.

> It was not the mere matter of the separation of the colonies from the motherland [said Lincoln on his way to Washington in February of 1861] but that sentiment in the Declaration of Independence which gave liberty, not alone to the people of this country, but, I hope, to the world, for all future time. It was that which gave promise that in due time the weight would be lifted from the shoulders of all men and that all should have an equal chance. [1]

Lincoln's metaphor, of course, was that of Christian, in *Pilgrim's Progress*, with the great pack on his back—representing original sin. In the Gettysburg Address the messianic theme would be consummated in the transformation of the death on the battlefield into the rebirth of the nation. What national poetry has ever surpassed that of Lincoln? When did epic poetry and poetic tragedy ever so coincide in the actual life story of a people—a coincidence in itself no less improbable than that of philosophy and kingship—than in the movement of thought and of events from the Revolution to the Civil War?

Of course it is the themes of the Civil War that supplied the themes of America's greatest literary works. *Huckleberry Finn* confronts convention with nature, and slavery with freedom, in a uniquely American poetic transformation of the teachings of Rousseau. It is one that, I believe, equals, if it does not surpass anything that European literature of the last 200 years can show. The great white whale, like the weight that Lincoln wished to see lifted from the shoulders of men, is also a distinctively American confrontation of the problem of evil, within the framework of Biblical allegory ("Call me Ishmael"). *Moby Dick* too is a "people's book"—as much in the tradition of the *Iliad* and of the *Odyssey*—as any modern book could be. Of either of them, however, Bloom says nothing. There is irony too in the Foreword by Saul Bellow, who seems only to have this in common with Bloom: that "European observers sometimes classify me as a hybrid curiosity, neither fully American nor satisfactorily European, stuffed with references to the philosophers, the historians, and poets I had consumed higgledy-piggledy . . ." (pp. 14, 15).

Bloom writes:

> Reading Thucydides shows us that the decline of Greece was purely political, that what we call intellectual history is of little importance for understanding it. Old

regimes had traditional roots, but philosophy and science took over as rulers in modernity, and purely theoretical problems have decisive political effects. One cannot imagine modern political history without a discussion of Locke, Rousseau and Marx (p. 197).

Leaving aside the begged question of what is meant by "purely political" history, can one imagine a discussion of "modern political history" that is *only* "a discussion of Locke, Rousseau, and Marx"? Elsewhere Bloom asserts that

What was acted out in the American and French Revolutions had been thought out beforehand in the writings of Locke and Rousseau, the scenarists for the drama of modern politics (p. 162).

He adds that Hobbes had "led the way" and, as he proceeds, it becomes clear that he regards Locke as essentially Hobbes with a fig leaf covering the hedonism, atheism, and materialism that is so prominent in the former, but no less essential although concealed in the latter. We will return to this point presently. But think of it, the American and French Revolutions "scenarios" written by Locke and Rousseau! The embattled farmers who "fired the shot heard round the world" and the great protagonists in the world historical events that followed—Samuel Adams, Patrick Henry, Benjamin Franklin, John Adams, George Washington, Thomas Jefferson, Alexander Hamilton, are mere actors, following a script. Do we not have here an historical determinism equal to Hegel's? Only the "cunning of history" is replaced by the cunning of the modern philosophers. But this is the purest nonsense.

Leaving the French Revolution to others, I comment only on the American Revolution and the American Founding. The statesmen of the era, among them those just mentioned, were, if not "a graver bench than ever frowned in Greece" or Rome, certainly the equal of any (*Coriolanus*, III.i,106). And they possessed a core of conviction which—if we are to make any attempt to understand them as they understood themselves—formed the basis of everything they did. Bloom purports to write about "the American mind." But he is perfectly oblivious of the presence of this expression in one of the most famous documents of American history. In a letter to Henry Lee, May 8, 1825, Thomas Jefferson explained the sources, the purpose, and the manner of the writing of what Lincoln would call that "immortal emblem of humanity," and Calvin Coolidge (observing in 1926 the sesquicentennial of the event) called "the most important civil document in the world."

But with respect to our rights and the acts of the British government contravening those rights, there was but one opinion on this side of the water. All American whigs thought alike on these subjects. When forced therefore to resort to arms for redress, an appeal to the tribunal of the world was deemed proper for our justification. This was the object of the Declaration of Independence. Not to find out new principles, or new arguments . . . but to place before mankind the common sense of the subject; in terms so plain and firm as to command their assent . . . neither aiming at originality of principle nor yet copied from any particular and previous writing, it was intended to be an expression of the American mind, and to give to that expression the proper tone and spirit called for by the occasion. All its authority rests then on the harmonizing sentiments of the day, whether expressed in conversations, in letters, printed essays or in the elementary books of public right, as Aristotle, Cicero, Locke, Sidney, etc. . . .[2]

We must ourselves lay the greatest emphasis upon Jefferson's emphasis upon the "one opinion" on this side of the water. There really was a "public philosophy" at the time of the Revolution and the Founding. The party conflict of the 1790s exceeded in intensity anything that has come after—even that of the decade before the Civil War. Yet Jefferson, in his inaugural address in 1801, could say "We have called by different names brethren of the same principle. We are all Federalists, we are all Republicans." To speak as Jefferson did, in the letter to Lee, of the "harmonizing sentiments of the day," is to imply a consensus transcending the normal differences of opinion among a free people. Of "the elementary books of public right" mentioned by Jefferson, two are ancient, two are modern. I think it safe to assume that according to Jefferson's understanding of the American mind, that mind found harmonizing sentiments among the books of public right no less than among the conversations, letters, and printed essays. Certainly that would suggest that Americans then read John Locke's *Second Treatise* in *its* "harmonizing" sense, in which Locke quotes Hooker for authority for his doctrine, and through Hooker reaches back to Christian scholasticism, and through it to Aristotle.

Bloom not only believes that the English and American Revolutions were scenarios by Locke—he says that "the new English and American regimes founded themselves according to his [Locke's] instructions" (p. 162). According to Bloom one can save oneself all the trouble of reading political and constitutional history—like Bloom—and just read Locke. But how does Bloom read Locke?

"Perhaps the most important discovery" upon which Locke's teaching was based, according to Bloom, was that "there was no Garden of Eden . . . Man was not provided for at the beginning . . . God neither looks after him nor punishes him. Nature's indifference to justice is a terrible bereavement for man. He must [therefore] care for himself." (p. 163). The complete break with Biblical religion, as well as with classical philosophy, as represented by Aristotle and Cicero, is the necessary presupposition of Bloom's Locke.

> Once the world has been purged of ghosts or spirits, [meaning of any belief in God or immortality] it reveals to us that the critical problem is scarcity . . . What is required is not brotherly love or faith, hope, and charity, but self-interested rational labor (p. 165).

"Americans" says Bloom,

> are Lockeans: recognizing that work is necessary (no longing for a nonexistent Eden), and will produce well-being; following their natural inclinations moderately, not because they possess the virtue of moderation but because their passions are balanced and they recognize the reasonableness of that; respecting the rights of others so that theirs will be respected . . . From the point of view of God or heroes, all this is not very inspiring. But for the poor, the weak, the oppressed—the overwhelming majority of mankind—it is the promise of salvation. As Leo Strauss put it, the moderns "built on low but solid ground" (p. 167).

We need not dispute Bloom's interpretation of Locke to deny that the American mind has ever been the mind represented by that interpretation. Let us however turn here to Bloom's obiter dicta at the end of the foregoing passage. This is his only mention (or quotation) of Leo Strauss, although Strauss's words and Strauss's thoughts echo and re-echo (without attribution) throughout his book. However, as Kirk Emmert recently reminded me, the words attributed to Strauss are not Strauss's but Churchill's—albeit words Strauss himself frequently quoted. But can a regime to which a Churchill could give such unstinting devotion—a regime in whose finest hour so many would come to owe so much to so few; a regime whose glory would not be of a day, but of a thousand years—be a regime despised by God and heroes?

Bloom is the first person I have ever known to suggest that "the point of view of God" is adverse or indifferent to "the poor, the weak, the oppressed." How can a regime which Bloom himself calls the "promise of salvation" for "the overwhelming majority of mankind" be anything but a theme for the greatest heroism? Why did the Union armies march to battle singing, "As He died to make men holy, let us die to make men free . . ." Why did Churchill himself leave orders for the singing of the Battle Hymn of the Republic, in Westminster Abbey, at his funeral? Abraham Lincoln is reported as saying that God must have loved the common people—he made so many of them. But who that has ever read either the Prophets of the Old Testament, or the Sermon on the Mount in the New, could have said what Bloom says here? And may not "rational labor" be in service of faith, hope, and charity? I am sure that Bloom's grandparents thought so. Bloom's own account of the success of American Lockeanism is testimony to the proposition that this is precisely the kind of regime that the God of the Bible, who cares for the poor, the weak, and the oppressed would favor. Bloom to the contrary notwithstanding this is the kind of God most Americans have always believed in. This is what they believe when they sing "God bless America."

Let us again consult Jefferson, at his inaugural, declaring of the American mind that it is one

> enlightened by a benign religion, professed, indeed, and practiced in various forms yet all of them inculcating honesty, truth, temperance, gratitude, and the love of man; acknowledging and adoring an overruling Providence, which by all its dispensations proves that it delights in the happiness of man here and his greater happiness hereafter . . . (p. 333).

As far as I can see, everything Bloom says on the subject of the American Founding is derived from his readings of Hobbes, Locke, or Tocqueville. I have found not a word of serious interpretation—apart from his birdseed scatterings—coming from an American source: not Jefferson, Washington, Madison, Hamilton, or Lincoln. No one has maintained more persistently than I have, during the past thirty-five years, the importance in the American Founding of Locke's teachings—as they were understood and incorporated into their handiwork by the Founding Fathers. But to say that a radical atheism discovered in Locke's esoteric teaching was part of what they understood, believed, and incorporated into their regime—when every single document bearing on the question contradicts it, and there is not a shred of evidence to support it—is just plain crazy.

Bloom writes:

> It should be noted that sex is a theme hardly mentioned in the thought underlying the American Founding. There it is all preservation, not procreation, because fear is more powerful than love, and men prefer their lives to their pleasures (p. 187).

Surely no sillier remark has ever been made in a work purporting to be serious. One can only wonder what Bloom could have in mind: a treatise on the joy of sex by the Father of his country? Something to vindicate the symbolism of the Washington monument? In point of fact, Benjamin Franklin penned some of the raciest lines of the 18th century. And Jefferson's "Dialogue Between the Head and the Heart," although in no way indecorous, is nonetheless highly charged with the passions that are its subject. That moreover was written in Paris, and during Jefferson's romance with Maria Conway. I'm sure Bloom would have approved, if only he had known about it.

But Bloom writes about the thought *underlying* the Founding. And what he says can refer only to the thought of Thomas Hobbes. For it was only that old bachelor for whom self-preservation meant individual self-preservation, and who divorced preservation from procreation, the family, and civil society. What is true of the political thought of Thomas Hobbes is not however true of the American Founding. It is not even true of Locke. The centrality of property in Locke's teaching gives place as well to the family, as the object of self-preservation. Nor is it true of nature generally—notwithstanding Bloom's Hobbesian remarks about fear and love. In nature generally self-preservation is directed to the species rather than to the individual. A cock robin will attack a cat that comes too near the nest where the hen is brooding. In the case of humans, the instinct of self-preservation may be transferred from the family to the political community, as the guarantor of the family. But whatever the behavior of particular individuals, the instinct of self-preservation is almost never understood to be directed by nature to the preservation of the individual as such. Consider the following from the 43rd *Federalist*— which happens to be the central number. Madison writes, with respect to the question of the right of the Convention to scrap the Articles, rather than revise them, that it is to be

> answered at once by recurring to the absolute necessity of the case; to the great principle of self-preservation; to the transcendent law of nature and of nature's God, which declares that the safety and happiness of society are the objects at which all political institutions aim, and to which all such institutions must be sacrificed. [3]

There is no question that "the great principle of self-preservation" refers to "the safety and happiness of *society*," and not to individuals. Moreover, in using the very words of the Declaration of Independence, Madison gives us a gloss on that document as well, and on "the common sense of the subject." There is then no contradiction—as some have supposed—between the unalienable right to life, proclaimed in the second paragraph of the Declaration, and the mutual pledge of the Signers, to each other, of "our lives, our fortunes, and our sacred honor." It would have been inconceivable to them that the right to life, with which they had been endowed by their Creator, was a right to act basely, to save their skins at any cost. Moreover, the law of nature, as stated by Madison, is dedicated to the ends of safety and happiness, the alpha and omega of political life. This is in entire agreement with Aristotle's *Politics*. The teaching of the Founding, expressed in the Declaration and the Federalist, takes nature as the ground of political life in the teleological sense, not in the non-moral purposeless sense of modern science. Bloom has completely misread not only the American Founding, but all political life, since he does not read political speeches to discover the form of the consciousness of political men. He assumes that political men are mere epigones of philosophers—whether they know it or not. The political nature of man is however understood by the Founders—if one reads what they say, and not only what Hobbes or Locke or Kant say—in the light of the inequality of man and beast, as well as in the light of the inequality of man and God. This understanding corresponds very closely with the first book of the *Politics*, and as it does with the first chapter of *Genesis*. But such inequalities imply that morality and the principles of political right are grounded in a purposeful reality accessible to reason, one that corresponds as well to the teachings of biblical faith. When Madison speaks of the sacrifice of all institutions to the safety and happiness of society, he implies a fortiori that the safety and happiness of individuals may or must be sacrificed too. For the Founders, the safety or happiness of society—that is to say, of a society constructed according to the principles of legitimacy and right set forth in the Declaration of Independence—always takes precedence over the mere interests or subjective judgments of individuals. That is why Lincoln in 1861, while conceding that the citizens of the seceding States possessed the same right of revolution as their Revolutionary ancestors, denied that they ought to exercise that right for any purpose inconsistent with the purposes for which their ancestors had exercised that right. To extend slavery was inconsistent with the purposes of the Revolution. The Founding Fathers, no more than Aristotle, could conceive of a life worth living without friendship. The baseness of self-preservation at any cost—the principle of Hobbesianism—as a *moral* principle, was beyond their imagination. Hence for them there could be no interest in self-preservation separate from or independent of the survival and well-being of everything they loved. In truth, fear is not more powerful than love.

The Founding Fathers, as one of the most exceptional generations of political men who ever lived, are not to be understood as primarily Hobbesians, Lockeans, or Aristotelians. They were rather *phronimoi*, morally and politically wise men, the kind of characters from whom Aristotle himself drew his portraits of the moral and political virtues. And Aristotle understood what these virtues were, not from speculative thought as such, but from contemplating such actual examples of the virtues as came under his observation. The source of his ability to recognize these virtues, was not philosophy, but nature, the reality which was the ground of philosophy. Bloom looks to philosophy only as the source of "humanizing doubts". For him, political philosophy is nothing more nor less than the cleverly disguised question, What have you done for me lately? But men who lead revolutions, who found and preserve states, cannot be guided only by their doubts. They require convictions. And they do not look upon themselves as responsible only to those who raise doubts about those convictions. Looking only to books, politics for Bloom is a closed book. And no one can comment instructively on the relationship between political life and the philosophic life who does not know what political life is.

The vitality of classical political philosophy—why it is so close to the spirit of the statesmanship of the American Founding—is that it is grounded in the reality of political life itself. In the light of that reality one does not speak of rights divorced from right. There can be no such thing as a right to do wrong—as Lincoln said when he denied that the consent of the governed could justify the extension of slavery. And we must never forget, as Lincoln never forgot, that the rights Americans valued so highly were the rights with which they had been endowed by their Creator. Their duty to respect the rights of others did not ensue—as Bloom, following Hobbes, thinks—solely because it was to their advantage, however enlightened the self-interest which dictated that advantage. Their duty to respect the rights of others was part of their duty to God—a duty which was entirely unconditional. Hence Jefferson, in the *Notes on Virginia*,

> And can the liberties of a people be thought secure, when we have removed their only firm basis, a conviction in the minds of the people that these liberties are of the gift of God? That they are not to be violated but with his wrath?

Concerning the central event in American history—in which Abraham Lincoln found entirely plausible Jefferson's prophetic judgment concerning the wrath of God for the sin of slavery—Bloom has this to say:

> The only quarrel in our history that really involved fundamental differences was over slavery. But even the proponents of slavery hardly dared assert that some human beings are made by nature to serve other human beings, as did Aristotle; they had to deny the humanity of the blacks. Besides, that question was really already settled with the Declaration of Independence. Black slavery was an aberration that had to be extinguished, not a permanent feature of our national life. Not only slavery, but aristocracy, monarchy and theocracy were laid to rest by the Declaration and the Constitution (p. 248).

Except for Russell Kirk's allocution excommunicating the Declaration of Independence (" . . . not conspicuously American . . . not even characteristically Jeffersonian . . . not a work of political philosophy or an instrument of government") I cannot recall another place in which so few words encompassed such great errors.[4]

We note first of all Bloom's thesis: that our "differences of principles are very small compared to those over which men used to fight" (p. 248). This opinion was certified by Tocqueville (who visited here in the early 1830s and who died before the Civil War). It is therefore canonical for Bloom. It is nonetheless mistaken. I remember in 1940 trying to tutor in English a refugee Polish university professor. I finally abandoned the effort. My pupil had a German English textbook that he had brought with him from Europe, and he simply would not accept anything I told him about the English language that did not agree with his German authority!

Bloom cannot form or accept an opinion about the United States that has not come to him from a European source. Tocqueville was a great and wise writer but, as Aristotle says of the discourses of Socrates, however brilliant, original, and searching they may have been, "it is difficult to be right about everything" (*Politics* 1265a14). It hardly seems to detract from Tocqueville's greatness to say that he is not the greatest interpreter of a war he did not live to see. Bloom writes about the "fundamental differences" in the Civil War, yet there is no attempt to characterize those differences. He ignores the pronouncements of Lincoln, which represent the peak of what is American, pronouncements that belong in the company of Demosthenes, Cicero, and Burke. Leo Strauss believed the

Gettysburg Address to be a greater funeral oration than that of Pericles, just as Lincoln was clearly a greater war leader. In the Preface to the University of Chicago Press reprint of *Crisis of the House Divided* I noted that I had first encountered the Lincoln–Douglas debates in 1946 when I was reading Plato's *Republic* with Leo Strauss. I was astonished to discover that the issue between Lincoln and Douglas was identical in principle with that between Socrates and Thrasymachus. For Douglas's doctrine of popular sovereignty was simply the democratic form of the proposition that justice was the interest of the stronger.

> We in Illinois . . . tried slavery [said Douglas], kept it up for twelve years, and finding that it was not profitable, we abolished it for that reason . . . (Joint debate, Alton, Illinois, October 15, 1858. *Collected Works of Abraham Lincoln*, Vol. III, p. 297).

Whatever the people think is in their interest, said Douglas, they may vote in, and whatever they think is not in their interest, they may vote out. This is exactly what Thrasymachus thought democratic justice to be. This implies, of course, that when the tyrant does what is in his interest, he is being neither more nor less just than the people. Tyrannical justice is no less justice than democratic justice. In Douglas's version of popular sovereignty—as in the Southern version—the distinction between tyrannical and democratic justice disappears. But Lincoln thought differently. Like Socrates (and Plato and Aristotle) he thought that the principles of natural justice limited—as they ought to guide—human choice. There is a distant echo of *Crisis of the House Divided* when Bloom writes (p. 29) that "for Lincoln . . . there could be no compromise with the *principle* of equality, that it did not depend on the people's choice or election but is the condition of their having elections in the first place . . ." But Bloom secs Lincoln's argument as a demand for consistency, a demand that the people defer to the logic of the principle of their regime. But he does not inquire into the status of that principle or of the regime embodying it: is it theirs because it is right, or is it merely right for them because it is theirs? Bloom never asks. He never entertains the possibility that the foundation of this allegedly "low" regime is, as Lincoln believed it to be, "an abstract truth applicable to all men and all times" (*Ibid.*, 111, p. 376).

To the best of my knowledge, the election of 1800 in the United States was the first time in human history that a national government was replaced by its bitter political enemies on the basis of a free election. Those who lost their offices gave them up without any physical struggle. Those who gained the offices did nothing to proscribe—to execute, imprison, expropriate, or exile—those who lost. And those who lost looked forward confidently to a future in which they or others like themselves might again hold those offices. We are so accustomed to such blessings in what we are pleased to call the free world, that we fail to appreciate the uniqueness of this event, and to realize how much everything we hold dear depended upon the successful test of the principles of the Declaration of Independence in the election of 1800.

It is well to bear in mind that in the Glorious Revolution in England in 1689 the King was driven into exile just because there was no constitutional way of changing the chief executive on the basis of the elections to Parliament. Although that Revolution established the principle of Parliamentary supremacy, the King (or Queen) remained the executive head of the government until after the Reform Act of 1832. The ministers of the crown remained responsible to the unelected Crown, and not to the elected House of Commons. The Crown could not, of course, govern effectively without majorities in the Parliament, but these majorities were assembled as much by manipulation of the patronage (that is to say, by buying the votes it needed in the Commons) as by deference to the electorate. And the electors of the unreformed Parliament—with its "rotten" boroughs as well as equally "rotten" rural seats—were very far from the American standard of democratic representation in 1800. All this is, I believe, what Alexander Hamilton had in mind when he said that the British Constitution, purged of corruption, would become unworkable. The idea of a King or Queen who reigned but did not rule, and of a Prime Minister—and cabinet—that was responsible to a democratically elected legislature, had not yet been born. And so the idea of changing the executive whenever the vote of the people changed the majorities in the House of Commons, was yet unknown. The idea of a government resting upon the continuing and changing consent of the governed, registered in free elections, was a discovery of the American Founding, and was its precious gift to the world.

But the trail blazed in 1800 proved to be inconclusive. In 1860, the losing party in a national election refused to accept the results of the voting, and "seceded" to form another government. Here indeed was a supreme test of whether

> societies of men are really capable or not of establishing good government from reflection and choice, or whether they are forever destined to depend for their political constitutions on accident and force (Alexander Hamilton, *Federalist* No. 1, Modern Library edition, p. 3).

In his inauguration address, Lincoln declared that

> A majority, held in restraint by constitutional checks and limitations, and always changing easily with deliberate changes of popular opinions and sentiments is the only true sovereign of a free people (*Collected Works*, IV, p. 268).

And so it remained for the American people to demonstrate to the world

> that ballots are the rightful and peaceful successors of bullets; and that when ballots have fairly and constitutionally decided, there can be no successful appeal back to bullets . . . (*Ibid.*, p. 439).

Bloom to the contrary notwithstanding, this question of bullets versus ballots represented as fundamental a difference as any over which men have ever fought.

We noted Bloom's pronouncement above that the antebellum "proponents of slavery hardly dared assert that some human beings are made by nature to serve other human beings, as did Aristotle . . ." He has got the matter exactly backwards. The American defenders of Negro slavery did assert that that slavery was by nature just. They did so by asserting—long before Nazi theory—the biological inequality of the races. Aristotle says that someone of human birth would be servile by nature, if he differed from the generality of mankind "as widely as the soul does from the body and the human being from the lower animal" (*Politics*, 1254a16). The usefulness of such persons, by reason of the imperfection of their rational faculties, "diverges little from that of animals; bodily service for the necessities of life is forthcoming from both . . ." (*Ibid.*, 1254b25). Aristotle only calls those slaves natural who are so defective mentally as to be functionally akin to the lower animals. In the modern world, such persons are called retarded, and are usually confined to what are somewhat euphemistically called "mental" institutions. (This is supposed to distinguish them from universities.) One might however ask, how could Aristotle expect such persons to form such a social class as slaves actually formed in the ancient world? The answer is that he did not. In Book VII of the *Politics* he says that "it is advantageous that all slaves should have their freedom set before them as a reward . . ." (1330a32). But a natural slave, properly so called, *cannot* be rewarded by freedom, any more than a horse or a dog or an ox. Aristotle's discussion of natural slavery leads to the conclusion that the actual institution of slavery rested, not on nature, but on convention or law. Its sanction was force, or justice understood as the interest of the stronger (cf. 1255a19 with 1255b15). Aristotle's proposal in Book VII of the *Politics*, applied to antebellum America, would have led to the policy that Lincoln commended: that of gradual, compensated emancipation. The fact that no such policy was politically conceivable—that is to say, that no legislation to this end could be adopted by constitutional means—made the Civil War inevitable. Slavery was in fact destroyed by the only means that could have destroyed it: military necessity.

The antebellum Southern defense of Negro slavery was much harsher than Bloom recognizes. Aristotle's argument has nothing to do with "race" (as in "racism," a term of modern politics). Nothing in Aristotle's argument would justify the enslavement of an intelligent Negro by a stupid white. Bloom thinks that American slavery was an "aberration" whose place was "settled" by the Declaration of Independence. Nothing could be further from the truth. This is shown by the following excerpts from the famous "cornerstone" speech of April 1861 (before the fall of Fort Sumter) by Alexander Stephens, Vice President of the Confederacy.

> The prevailing ideas entertained by [Jefferson] and most of the leading statesmen at the time of the formation of the old Constitution, were that the enslavement of the African was in violation of the laws of nature: that it was wrong in principle, socially, morally, and politically.

Now, however, we know that

> those ideas were fundamentally wrong. They rested upon the assumption of the equality of the races. Our new government [the Confederate States of America] is founded upon exactly the opposite idea; its foundations are laid, its cornerstone rests upon the great truth that the negro is not the equal of the white man. That slavery—the subordination to the superior race, is his natural and normal condition. [5]

Stephens further asserted that the natural inferiority of the Negro—his allegedly natural aptitude for slavery—was a discovery of modern science, and he compared it to Harvey's discovery of the circulation of the blood. He identifies the idea of the social, moral, and political progress of mankind with the progress of science. The Confederacy—based upon just such an advance of science—is therefore superior to the "old" Constitution of 1787. The notorious claims made later in behalf both of national Socialism and Marxism-Leninism—that they represented political regimes grounded in the progress of scientific truth—were anticipated in principle by this most articulate spokesman for the Confederate South. Bloom's assertion that slavery "was an aberration that had to be extinguished" is itself merely the counterpart of Stephens' conviction in 1861 that opposition to Negro slavery was an aberration to be extinguished. Like all new truths, he said, it would take time for its diffusion and general recognition. With this recognition, however, would come acceptance of the justice and propriety of Negro slavery. Bloom simply dismisses—if he has not altogether forgotten—Lincoln's House Divided speech, which warned that the nation was at a crossroads, and that a decision had to be reached and taken, whether the nation was to become all free or all slave. Bloom writes as if "all slave" was never a possibility, and Lincoln an irresponsible inflammatory politician. He writes precisely as most "revisionist" American historians wrote before the publication of *Crisis of the House Divided* in 1959. In truth, however, the idea of progress can be used to vindicate either freedom or slavery. In 1861, however, no one could tell which would prevail.

The question of slavery extension went to the root of the meaning of free government, but it was the obverse of the question of whether free elections would continue to decide who would govern in a republic. By 1860 the doctrines of John C. Calhoun—which had taken the deepest root throughout the South—had completely divorced the idea of natural rights and human equality from the idea of political sovereignty, and hence from the idea of State sovereignty. It was this divorce which gave legitimacy to the idea of a constitutional right of secession. Popular sovereignty, seen in the light of the Declaration of Independence, is the collective expression of the equal right of each human person to be governed with his own consent under the rule of law. And the rule of law was itself understood to be the implementation, in accordance with the dictates of prudence, of "the laws of nature and of nature's God." These laws of nature were understood to be both moral and rational. They were understood to secure the equal rights to life, liberty, and property, and the pursuit of happiness of each human person. In severing the connection between natural rights and constitutional rights. Calhoun severed the connection between law and morality altogether. This fact was disguised to some extent because of Calhoun's typical mid-century commitment to the idea of progress—to the belief that those who were scientifically and technologically advanced were morally superior.

> The discovery of gunpowder and the use of steam as an impelling force, and their application to military purposes have *forever* settled the question of the ascendancy between civilized and barbarous communities, in favor of the former. (A *Disquisition on Government*, Cralle ed., p. 62. Emphasis added.)

Calhoun assumed—as did his contemporary Karl Marx, whose *Manifesto* was written about the same time as the *Disquisition*—that the outcome of physical conflict, whether that of proletariat and bourgeoisie, or that of white and colored races—would indicate moral no less than material superiority.

State sovereignty, in Calhoun's thought, refers then ultimately to nothing more than the force (*assumed* to be moral) at the command of the government.

In his *Disquisition* there is no abstract or rational way to distinguish—as in the Declaration of Independence—between the just and the unjust powers of government. Those who are slaves are assumed to be rightfully slaves, and those who are masters, to be rightfully masters. And if the slaves suddenly arise and enslave the masters, then each will still be rightfully what he is! This latter was not something Calhoun contemplated, but it follows the logic of his argument. It is not for nothing that Calhoun has been rightly called (by Rihard Hofstadter, in *The American Political Tradition*) "the Marx of the Master Class." This is to imply— correctly, I believe—that Calhoun anticipated, in certain fundamentals, the thought underlying the two great tyrannies of the twentieth century. If it was true, as Bloom says, that "slavery, aristocracy, monarchy, and theocracy" had been "laid to rest by the Declaration and the Constitution," then why had the thought of John C. Calhoun become so powerful? Why indeed was there ever a Civil War? (See "Defenders of the Constitution: Calhoun versus Madison," by the present writer. A Bicentennial Essay published by the Bicentennial Project of the University of Dallas.)

Next, I come to Bloom's account of "The Sixties." Bloom was forced to live through a revolutionary political event which he never really understood. It was an event in American history, the serious study of which Bloom has always regarded as superfluous. He looked upon the student radicals as Americanized versions of the Nazi youth of the 1930s, and there is some validity in this analogy. The deeper resemblance, however, is to the historicism and nihilism already present in the intellectual defense of the Confederacy—notably in the thought of both John C. Calhoun and Alexander Stephens. And there are important parallels to Calhoun in Thoreau, contemporaries who, ostensibly on opposite sides of the slavery question, were yet nearly perfect mirror images of each other. For the fact is that abolitionism and slavery, although theoretical antagonists, nonetheless collaborated in a way that, had it succeeded, would have crushed the Constitution. Their radical hostility and practical cooperation closely resembles the way in which in our century Nazis and Communists worked together to destroy the Weimar regime, which both hated worse than they hated each other. But Weimar lacked the strength of the American Founding, and Germany had no Lincoln.

The Black Power movement which brought Cornell University to its knees in 1969 (and drove Bloom into exile) was a transformation of the Civil Rights movement, in the aftermath of the victory of that movement by the enactment of the great civil rights laws of 1964 and 1965. In this transformation there was the same severance of the connection between civil and constitutional rights, on the one hand, and natural rights on the other, as had been earlier accomplished in the thought of Calhoun. Black Power became its own justification for whatever demands it could exact, just as the ownership of slaves once justified whatever the owners of slaves could exact. That the ideas animating the Black Power movement were at bottom the same as those of the leading defenders of slavery, however ironical, is nonetheless true. Bloom, however, is unconscious of this, because he is unconscious of the power and magnitude of the ideas in conflict that made the American Civil War perhaps the least avoidable great war ever.

Bloom's alienation from the American political tradition is illuminated by his pride in the fact that some of his students went among the rioters distributing a pamphlet which reprinted the passage from Plato's *Republic* (49Ic–492b) in which Socrates characterizes the *demos* itself as the greatest of sophists, the greatest of the corrupters of the young. Most radical students—and many who were not radical—would think that what it revealed most of all was Plato's antidemocratic prejudices. But the passage also lends itself easily to a Marxist interpretation—however spurious—because, according to the *Republic*, among the causes of the corruption is private property, and the leading cure for it is communism. It is difficult to imagine what effect—other than inflammatory— Bloom thought this Platonic passage might have had on the rioters.

One might reflect, however, as Bloom does not, that Socrates' characterization of democracy in the *Republic* is peculiarly inapplicable to the popular government envisaged by the American Founding Fathers. Theirs was a regime of law—in principle and aspiration, one of reason unaffected by desire. To the extent that human ingenuity could make it so, it was intended as a regime in which equal recognition was given to the requirements of wisdom and of consent. Consent was necessary however because, as Plato himself insisted, the designs of tyrants are always masked as the claims of wisdom.

Leo Strauss, in "On Classical Political Philosophy," remarks that

> "aristocracy" (rule of the best) presented itself as the natural answer of all good men to the natural question of the best political order. As Thomas Jefferson put it, "That form of government is the best, which provides the most effectually for a pure selection of [the] natural *aristoi* into the offices of government."[6]

Professor Colleen Sheehan of Villanova University has been kind enough to point out to me that in this celebrated essay, Strauss illustrates the central thesis of *classical* political philosophy—the nature of the best regime—with a quotation from a renowned letter of Jefferson to Adams. She has also pointed out that it appears to be the central passage in Strauss's essay. However one finally judges the wisdom of the Founding, there is little doubt that Strauss, like Jefferson, regarded this assimilation of aristocracy into democracy as its guiding thought. Elsewhere Strauss has written that

> Liberal education is the ladder by which we try to ascend from mass democracy to democracy as originally meant.[7]

The American Founding, insofar as it is "democracy as originally meant" is thus inadequately characterized—to say the least—as something "low." After all, why would anyone need a ladder to ascend to it?

Yet Bloom is not altogether oblivious of the higher ground. He writes,

> The students were unaware that the teachings of equality, the promise of the Declaration of Independence, the study of the Constitution, the knowledge of our history and many more things were the painstakingly earned and stored-up capital that supported them (p. 334).

Someone who can write of the American and French Revolutions as scenarios thought out beforehand by Locke and Rousseau, and who can say that "the English and American regimes [had been] founded according to [Locke's] instructions," is hardly in a position to reproach others for the lack of "the study of . . .

history." But were the students simply unaware of this history—as Bloom says here—or were they not in agreement with Bloom's own view of the Founding as "not very inspiring," and as spiritually impoverishing? Was the revolt of the sixties not at bottom a middle class revolt against the successful materialism of American life? Did not the students themselves—however misguided—believe that they were rejecting the low in favor of the high? Had not Bloom himself nurtured this revolt, even if it took forms that he did not expect or wish?

On February 21, 1861, President-elect Abraham Lincoln addressed the Senate of the State of New Jersey. He spoke of his recollection, from the earliest days of his childhood, of a small book, Weems's *Life of Washington*.

> I remember all the accounts there given of the battle fields and struggles for the liberties of the country, and none fixed themselves upon my imagination so deeply as the struggle here at Trenton . . . the crossing of the river; the contest with the Hessians; the great hardships endured at that time, all fixed on my memory more than any single Revolutionary event; and you know, for you have all been boys, how these early impressions last longer than any others. I recollect thinking, then, boy even though I was, that there must have been something more than common that those men struggled for. I am exceedingly anxious that that thing which they struggled for; that something even more than National Independence; that something that held out a great promise to all the people of the world to all time to come; I am exceedingly anxious that this Union, the Constitution, and the liberties of the people shall be perpetuated in accordance with the original idea for which that struggle was made, and I shall be most happy indeed if I shall be an humble instrument in the hands of the Almighty, and of this, his almost chosen people, for perpetuating the object of that struggle (*Collected Works*, IV, pp. 235, 236).

Leo Strauss's—and Jefferson's—"democracy as originally meant," and Lincoln's "original idea" of what the Almighty had promised "to all the people of all the world" by this "his almost chosen people," is the noble legacy—the moral no less than the intellectual foundation—that was lacking in the education of the disaffected students. Lincoln's speech at Trenton, not Socrates' denunciation of democracy, is what was needed to illuminate the folly of the rioters who, in rejecting their inheritance,

> Like the base Indian, threw a pearl away,
> Richer than all his tribe (*Othello*, v.ii).

Lincoln, who had opposed Douglas's idea of popular sovereignty on the same ground that Socrates had opposed Thrasymachus' cynical definition of justice as nothing but the interest of the stronger, could have provided a better introduction to the *Republic* than Bloom's. He could have shown the students the inner connection between the principles of classical political philosophy and those of the Declaration of Independence. Bloom could not do this because everything in his account of the American mind proves that he does not believe it to be true.

The argument of Bloom's book founders on the fact that he cannot decide between the classical rationalism that may be traced to Socrates and Socratic skepticism, and the rejection of all rationalism—and all skepticism—by Nietzsche and Heidegger. He is only certain that his "humanized" doubt is superior to any alternative, or to any decision—for example, in favor of the principles of the Declaration of Independence. Yet he concedes that the issue may yet be resolved.

Are Nietzsche and Heidegger right about Plato and Aristotle? They rightly saw that *the* question is here, and both returned obsessively to Socrates. Our rationalism is his rationalism. Perhaps they did not take seriously enough the changes wrought by modern rationalists and hence the possibility that the Socratic way might have avoided the modern impasse. But certainly all the philosophers, the proponents of reason, have something in common, and more or less directly reach back to Aristotle, Socrates' spiritual grandchild. A serious argument about what is most profoundly modern leads inevitably to the conclusion that study of the problem of Socrates is the one thing needful. It was Socrates who made Nietzsche and Heidegger look to the pre-Socratics. For the first time in four hundred years, it seems possible to begin all over again, to try to figure out what Plato was talking about, because it might be the best thing available (p. 310).

The study of the problem of Socrates was a life-long preoccupation of Leo Strauss, who was Bloom's teacher—and mine. Indeed, much of the foregoing passage might have been transcribed from Strauss's familiar conversation. In addition to his many writings on virtually all aspects of classical and modern political philosophy, Strauss wrote three books on Xenophon's Socratic writings, all of them with forewords by Bloom. In addition, he wrote *Socrates and Aristophanes*. Together, these constituted an exhaustive articulation of "the problem of Socrates," as it might be uncovered in non-Platonic (and pre-Socratic) sources. These writings of Strauss were in addition to his lengthy commentaries on the Platonic Socrates as he is presented in the *Republic*, the *Laws*, the *Statesman*, the *Apology*, the *Crito*, and yet other dialogues. Of all this Bloom makes no mention. In his overview of the history of political philosophy, "From Socrates' *Apology* to Heidegger's *Rektoratsrede*" (pp. 243–312), there is no mention of Strauss.

In our time, Bloom writes, "it was Heidegger, practically alone, for whom the study of Greek philosophy became truly central . . ." (p. 309, 310). How anyone who had studied with Strauss—or had read "What Is Political Philosophy?" or "On Classical Political Philosophy"—could have written this is almost beyond comprehension. To speak thus of Heidegger, without mentioning Strauss, is like speaking of Hitler, without mentioning Churchill. For, if the truth were known, Strauss was as surely Heidegger's nemesis as Churchill was Hitler's. One can only conclude that if Bloom says that the one thing needful is the study of the problem of Socrates, and yet makes no mention of Strauss's study of the problem of Socrates (or of Greek philosophy), then he cannot think that Strauss's study is the needful one.

Strauss moreover never reached such a lame conclusion as Bloom's, that we might now—after four hundred years—"try to figure out what Plato was talking about, because it might be the best thing available." This makes the quest for the right way of life sound like the quest for prewar whiskey during the era of prohibition! In fact, Bloom's "to figure out" is an echo of a passage from Strauss's *Preface to Spinoza's Critique of Religion*:

> For Spinoza there are no natural ends . . . He is therefore compelled to give a novel account of man's end (the life devoted to contemplation): man's end is not natural but rational, *the result of figuring it out* . . . He thus decisively prepares the modern notion of the "ideal" as a work of the human mind . . . as distinguished from an end imposed on man by nature. (*Liberalism Ancient and Modern*, p. 241. Emphasis added.)

What Bloom is looking for is a "figuring out" of Plato which is in fact not Plato at all, but a modern "ideal," ostensibly grounded in Plato, but designed like all modern ideals, to gratify a passion, rather than to subordinate passion to reason. Bloom has no intention of facing squarely the issue of philosophical realism (Socrates, Plato, and Aristotle) versus nihilism (Nietzsche and Heidegger). He has no such intention because he knows that Strauss has presented the case for the former in terms he cannot refute but will not accept. Consider the following from the end of Strauss's chapter on "The Crisis of Modern Natural Right" in *Natural Right and History.* Rousseau, according to Strauss, had a reservation against society in the name of the state of nature.

> To have a reservation against society in the name of the state of nature means to have a reservation against society without being either compelled or able to indicate the way of life or the cause or pursuit for the sake of which the reservation is made. The notion of a return to the state of nature on the level of humanity was the ideal basis for claiming a freedom from society which is not freedom for something (p. 294).

Rousseau, as interpreted here by Strauss, is the core of Bloom's soul. It is Rousseau who informs Bloom's reading of Plato's *Republic,* and who has tipped the balance within him irrevocably towards Nietzsche and Heidegger. Bloom's ideal of the university is just such a place where one can "return to the state of nature on the level of humanity." The attractiveness of this supposed return, says Strauss, is that

> It was an ideal basis for an appeal from society to something indefinite and undefinable, to an ultimate sanctity of the individual as individual, unredeemed and unjustified. This was precisely what freedom came to mean for a considerable number of men.

In the "ultimate sanctity of the individual as individual"—meaning thereby a sanctity unfettered either by God or nature—Strauss has defined the core of modern liberalism. And Bloom, a quintessential liberal, is one of that "considerable number of men." Concluding, Strauss writes that

> Every freedom which is freedom for something, every freedom which is justified by reference to something higher than the individual or than man as mere man, necessarily restricts freedom or, which is the same thing, establishes a tenable distinction between freedom and license. It makes freedom conditional on the purpose for which it is claimed.

Of course Bloom does not claim unconditional freedom for man in society—any more than did Rousseau. Nor does he attack those necessary conventions of academic life that make it comfortable and agreeable to persons like himself. But he does not admit within his own soul—nor does he teach—any idea of freedom that is conditional upon anything higher than man as man. That excludes both Athens and Jerusalem—and Leo Strauss.

Bloom to the contrary notwithstanding, we have known all along what Plato was talking about. He was talking about Justice (for example, in the *Republic*), and in the other dialogues about moderation, courage, law, and, in general, what was good and bad for man. The question about Plato is not what he was talking about, or even whether what he said appears wise or just, but whether the good and bad for man was founded in any ultimate reality, whether it existed by nature, by convention (or law), or by some unknowable divine dispensation. For Bloom the question is not, What is Justice? It is, Which book about justice do you like best? At the end of *Thoughts on Machiavelli* Strauss, rejecting Machiavelli's teaching, says "that the notion of the beneficence of nature or of the primacy of the good must be restored by being rethought through a return to the fundamental experiences from which it is derived" (p. 299). In Strauss's rejection of progress in favor of return, the books of the classical philosophers would be indispensable to us as modern men, needing emancipation from our peculiarly modern cave. But Strauss, unlike Bloom, never failed to distinguish books from the "fundamental experiences" the books were meant to articulate. The "primacy of the Good"—the upper case emphasis is Strauss's—is a primacy with respect to all books and all art, even that of Plato.

Plato's dialogues always reveal to us far more of our ignorance of each subject discussed, than knowledge of that subject. In revealing our ignorance, however, they always reveal something of our knowledge of that ignorance. And that knowledge of ignorance always reveals something—never enough to satisfy us, but something—of what it is that we wish to know. It is enough to whet our appetites, to make us wish to go on, and know more of what it is that we do not know. The life lived in accordance with the knowledge of ignorance—the truly skeptical life, the examined and examining life—is, by the light of unassisted human reason, the best life. The regime that is best adapted to the living of this life is the best regime. All other lives and regimes are to be judged in relationship to this life and this regime. The goodness of the best life and the best regime is not arbitrary. It is not to be characterized—as Bloom suggests—as merely the "best thing available." On the contrary, that goodness is "according to nature." And hence the moral and intellectual virtues which are in harmony with this goodness are not arbitrary, but also are good "according to nature."

We return to Bloom's assertion that Nietzsche and Heidegger "returned obsessively to Socrates." They did so, he says because "Our rationalism is [Socrates'] rationalism." He adds, however, "perhaps they did not take seriously enough the changes wrought by the modern rationalists and hence the possibility that the Socratic way might have avoided the modern impasse." One might encapsulate the life work of Leo Strauss in Bloom's "perhaps." For Strauss proved, I believe, that "the changes wrought by modern rationalists" had mistakenly discredited the possibility that reason might discover the right way of life and the best regime. According to Strauss, it was not true that "Our [viz., modern man's] rationalism is his [viz., Socrates'] rationalism." Modern rationalism is "scientific" rationalism, which means that it explains the world and everything in it—including whatever is regarded as good or bad for man—in terms of what Aristotle called efficient and material causes, while denying the reality of what he called formal and final causes. All formal and final causes are understood in modern science and modern philosophy as epiphenomena or by-products of efficient and material causes. They are attempts to explain the high by the low.

This is as if one would try to understand Michelangelo's David as the result of the physical force applied by the artist to the chisel on the marble, omitting from one's explanation any reference to the sculptor's brain, purpose, and skill.

Socratic rationalism assumes that Michelangelo's brain had a purpose, even before his hand attempted to give it effect, or even before Michelangelo himself had discovered what it was. Indeed, it assumes that Michelangelo could not have discovered his purpose if it had not pre-existed—through all eternity—as a potentiality of his human nature. For modern philosophy, Michelangelo's art is simply an accidental outcome of the causes that generated Michelangelo, causes utterly indifferent to his art, as they were blind to anything intelligent or intelligible. The premises of modern philosophy are the result of a doubt so radical as to eliminate all further need to doubt: hence its dogmatism. The ambition of modern rationalism was to eliminate the skepticism that had accompanied Socratic rationalism, as its shadow. By replacing skepticism with dogmatism in philosophy, it would at the same time obviate any need for faith in God. Strauss, by showing that the self-destruction of reason in modern philosophy was the self-destruction of modern rationalism alone, prepared a return to premodern rationalism. By restoring Socratic skepticism, he restored not only Socratic rationalism, but the place that that skepticism left for biblical faith.

Nietzsche and Heidegger represented the final disillusionment with—and rejection of—modern rationalism, although they seem at the same time to have rejected all rationalism. Not seeing—as did Strauss—any alternative to modern rationalism, however, they discovered: nothing. Since there is no purpose, good or evil, in any reality outside of man, all purpose in life must be willed by man. But the will has no source of guidance outside itself. What one wills as good is good. What one wills as evil, is evil. The will is its own justification, because there can be no other. Hitler's famous propaganda film "Triumph of the Will," whatever its defects as art, is an authentic manifestation of Heidegger's teaching. Here then is the core cause of modern nihilism, and of the belief that there is no ground for the existence of God, or of the noble and good things, except as useful fictions or pleasing illusions. These must be willed by man, although they are believable by *hoi polloi* only if their origin is concealed. For the true Thinker—who replaces the Philosopher—there is neither myth nor reality. The Thinker—having triumphed over the terror of the abyss—alone lives without illusions, without either hope or fear, but in an unprecedented freedom. Bloom lives with considerable discomfort in this freedom, but he has not yet figured out anything for which he would give it up.

---

[1] Lincoln, Address in Independence Hall, Feb. 22, 1861. *Collected Works*, IV, p. 240.

[2] Basic Writings of Thomas Jefferson, edited by Philip S. Foner, Halcyon House, p. 802.

[3] Modern Library Edition, p. 287.

[4] On Kirk's atrocities, see "What were the 'Original Intentions' of the Framers of the Constitution of the United States?" in *The University of Puget Sound Law Review*, Spring 1987, esp. at 380–83.

[5] The *Political History of the Great Rebellion*, Edward McPherson ed., Washington, D.C., 1865, p. 103.

[6] In *What Is Political Philosophy?* Free Press, 1959, pp. 85, 86.

[7] *Liberalism Ancient and Modern*, Basic Books, 1968, p. 5.

27

Allan Bloom and the American Premise
CHRISTOPHER COLMO

The title of Allan Bloom's book, *The Closing of the American Mind*, seems to imply that there is some important thesis that the American mind takes for granted without being able or willing to examine it. The American mind is the logical consequence of some axiom or premise of which it is not fully conscious. Bloom's spirited critique of American higher education seems to follow from his not unreasonable but surely disappointed expectation that college and university education ought to do something about the business of examining axioms and making students conscious of assumptions, especially the assumptions that make them Americans. Not content merely to point out the problem, Bloom actually sets out to remedy it. It does not take long to identify the basic belief, the limiting horizon, of American thinking or, at any rate, American political and social thinking. Beyond that, Bloom offers what one might think of as a European critique of that horizon.

First, we identify the assumption or, as Bloom calls it, "the American premise": "The simplistic harmoniousness between nature and society" (177). This only sounds confusing. Nature here means natural man, man as he would be without the protection of society. It is easy to see that such a man, or woman, would be scared. This fear—terror is a better word—actually helps us to discover what we really are, our true self. The self is the thing you are very afraid of losing "when another man holds a gun to your temple and threatens to shoot you" (174). Note, this is not your soul we are talking about, because pulling the trigger cannot really hurt that. Your self is flesh and blood, passion and longing, thinking and creating, and, above all, it is yours alone, uniquely you.

There is a harmony between the self, *my* self, and society. Americans at least seem to think so. Indeed, if their minds are closed, then they are closed most of all to the possibility of recognizing their belief in this harmony. Bloom addresses three questions: where did Americans get this collective idée fixe? Given that it is the American premise, what is wrong with the way we Americans think about our premise? And, by the way, is the premise true?

The seventeenth-century British philosopher John Locke is Bloom's principal candidate for the source of our obsession. Americans are Lockeans, we are told, and Locke's doctrine provides the basis for our national consensus (167, 175). True, as far as it goes. Indeed, some of us will even be reminded that something like this was the thesis of Louis Hartz's *The Liberal Tradition in*

Christopher Colmo is Professor, Department of Political Science, Rosary College, River Forest, Illinois.

America (1962). But Bloom presses on. Where did Locke get this idea about a harmony?

Bloom suspects that Locke was the first to use the word "self" in its modern sense (173). The self Locke would have us recognize as our own is a frail self, but fear sometimes sharpens the wits. "Man's reason can be made to see his vulnerability and to anticipate future scarcity" (167). And, of course, reason can always get a little reminder along these lines from the above mentioned gun-to-the-head. Now there is no reason why human beings who anticipate future danger and scarcity and who see clearly the true self cannot act together to avoid the danger. But there we have run head-on into the harmony we sought. Weak, fearful individuals must cooperate together in order to avoid the disasters they fear. Natural man is in natural harmony with the society that protects his most cherished possession: the self.

Bloom is willing to consider the possibility that while Locke's safety-first society might be a little vulgar, the gains in peace and security may outweigh the losses. He even accepts the possibility that Locke anticipated the shallowness of much of modern life. "The vulgarity of modern society, the object of so many complaints by intellectuals, is something the philosophers were willing to live with" (292). It is not primarily the vulgarity of the modern world that Bloom finds appalling but rather the unquestioning dogmatism with which we (Americans only?) accept such vulgarity (239). This Bloom is not, it seems, willing to live with. The same point surfaces in Bloom's account of the decade of the sixties. The Left, as Bloom remembers it, supposed a perfect harmony between "the self-development of the absolute individual and the brotherhood of all mankind." These beliefs "were inherent in our regime, they constituted its horizon. There was nothing new in it. The newness [during the sixties] was in the thoughtlessness, the utter lack of need to argue or prove. Alternative views had no existence except as scarecrows" (326). The only thing wrong then with American thinking about the American premise is the complete absence of such thinking.

At this point, I am inclined to ask whether Locke did not anticipate the thoughtlessness of the sixties as part of the above-mentioned shallowness philosophers were or would be willing to live with. Or does Bloom simply disagree with Locke about the tolerable level of vulgarity? To put it differently, is education today, though unacceptable to Bloom, pretty much what Locke would have expected? Or does Bloom sound the alarm only because things have gotten even worse than Locke imagined they could or would? Perhaps Locke never intended for a whole nation—or its "mind"—to take Lockeanism for granted. But why not? Why should not people who are not philosophers take their fundamental assumptions for granted? Bloom does not raise or answer these questions, perhaps because he himself certainly cannot take Locke for granted.

Far from taking Locke at his word, Bloom has in fact learned from Rousseau that Locke was simply wrong. "Rousseau explodes the simplistic harmoniousness between nature and society that seems to be the American premise" (177). As we have seen, nature and society here mean something like self-interest and the good of others, respectively. Now in spite of his great respect for Locke and other early modern philosophers (290–293), Bloom does not put much stock in the idea that self-interest and the good of others can be easily or even plausibly harmonized. To bring out his point, Bloom identifies being selfish with being inner-directed. If Locke can harmonize individual selfishness and the common good, then, Bloom implies, we ought to be able to see a similar harmony between being inner-directed and concern for the good of others. But these two things, as Bloom sees it, simply are not compatible. "Of course, we are told, the healthy inner-directed person will *really* care for others. To which I can only respond: If you believe that, you can believe anything. Rousseau knew much better" (178). In other words, America is built on a very potent illusion. It is never quite clear in Bloom's account whether Locke too was somehow the victim of this illusion or, alternatively, its self-conscious creator for public consumption only, thank you. In any case, one begins to have some sympathy for American educators. No wonder they do not want to start their students thinking about the foundations of American society; they are afraid of bringing the house down around their ears.

But even an idea rejected by Rousseau deserves a little consideration, especially since Rousseau at least went to the trouble of rejecting it. Is there any way to reconcile self-interest and the common good? Two decades ago, Bloom himself could write of Plato's *Republic* that it is "the *apology* of a man who benefits others because he first of all knows how to benefit himself." (Allan Bloom, ed. and trans., *The Republic of Plato* [New York: Basic Books, 1968], p. 436.) Now for all the world, it really does look as if this says that the true *apology* or defense of Socrates is that his selfish interest—which is to do philosophy—is also somehow a public good. Has Bloom changed his mind? These days Bloom tells us that "Philosophy does no such good" (273). Was Bloom, twenty years ago, pulling our leg about Socrates?

There does seem to be at least one other way to reconcile Bloom's two statements. Perhaps there is a difference between the Socratic self and the Lockean self, a difference that requires a different relationship between self and society. Locke presents the self as weak and vulnerable. Now if one follows Rousseau, as Bloom seems to do, this is surely not a promising kind of "self" to try to reconcile with society. For Rousseau, "All wickedness comes from weakness." (Jean-Jacques Rousseau, *Emile or On Education*, trans. Allan Bloom [New York: Basic Books, 1979], p. 67.) Given the weakness of the Lockean self, Rousseau may well be right to deny any "automatic harmony [of the self] with what civil society needs and demands" (168). Much depends here on accepting Locke's view of the self. As it turns out, Bloom himself suggests an alternative to the fearful Lockean self. For Bloom, "fear of death . . . cannot be the fundamental experience. It presupposes an even more fundamental one: that life is good" (169). If I understand him correctly, Bloom experiences the goodness of life not as an immediate possession but as "vague dissatisfactions" and a "longing for wholeness." He is reminded of the discussion of eros in Plato's *Symposium*. Eros is "the enticing awareness of incompleteness and the quest to overcome it. . . . Eroticism is a discomfort, but one that in itself promises relief and affirms the goodness of things." In Bloom's mind, "This longing for completeness is the longing for education, and the study of it is education" (132–133). His critique of

American higher education is that it turns out "souls without longing" (Bloom's original choice of a title for his book).

Might not the kind of "erotic" education Bloom promotes lead to the discovery or rediscovery of a self quite different from the fearful self of Locke and from the weak self that Rousseau sees as being in conflict with society? Rousseau would probably want to add that in his view it is society that makes man weak by making him dependent. Bloom is well aware that for Plato eros is not only dissatisfaction and longing. It is sometimes rewarded with moments of satisfaction, pride, even a feeling of self-sufficiency (270). If, as Rousseau says, weakness is the root of all evil, then might not a strong self be the root of some good? A strong self might render somewhat more feasible the notion of a harmony between self-interest and the good of others. Perhaps Bloom was thinking of such a strong self when he wrote twenty years ago of "a man who benefits others because he first of all knows how to benefit himself."

It is in the interest of benefitting higher education that Bloom "explodes" the simplistic harmony of the American premise. It is for this reason that Bloom's book has very much the appearance of being an attack on both the American premise and the modern notion of the self. This approach may destroy something old, but can it build something new? Can the American premise be so wrong that nothing can be salvaged? Is there not at least some partial truth in the modern notion of the self which could serve as point of departure for a fuller understanding? Is it not Platonic to assume that there is some truth in even an erroneous opinion? Moreover, may we not question the usefulness of Bloom's rhetoric? At the origin of modernity, Machiavelli did not attack the idea of virtue, he simply gave the word a new meaning. Might not Bloom's rhetoric be more effective in the long run if he did the same for the "self?" Bloom tells us that in the modern world "the study of the problem of Socrates is the one thing most needful" (310). A thorough study of the problem of Socrates would have to include Plato's *Alcibiades I*, in which Socrates seeks the self and the care of the self. Bloom directs us to Plato, and in this he is surely our benefactor and the benefactor of American higher education.

28

Allan Bloom on the Charms of Culture
SHADIA B. DRURY

Allan Bloom's *The Closing of the American Mind* is a profound and penetrating development of Leo Strauss's critique of American liberalism and the open society it engenders. It is such a powerful critique that it is bound to make us mindful of the dangers of our liberalism. But by the same token, it is a critique that contains dangers of its own. For it is an attempt to convince us that the open society that liberalism engenders is not only uncultivated and uncivilized, but in the final analysis self-destructive. If we accept this reasoning we must be prepared to exchange our open society with its freedom and diversity for a closed society embodying a single public orthodoxy. Bloom is a seductive writer who has managed to bestow the closed society with irresistible charm, and to sow in the hearts of his readers a nostalgia for a lost world of sweet solidarity. It is therefore important to beware of the dangers and limits of the closed society he recommends.

The Charms of Culture
Bloom has a very particular conception of culture. For Bloom as for Strauss, myths are the stuff of culture, and culture is the cement of society. But liberalism and openess are powerless myths and as a result, they leave America without cement. This is the meaning of Bloom's claim that America is characterized above all by the absence of culture.

Bloom understands culture as a supremely magical charm by which natural man is transformed into a citizen. Bloom believes that the secret charms of culture were known to the ancients (187ff). But they had to be rediscovered by Rousseau and Kant, because they were eclipsed in the early modern period of political philosophy. Culture is a means by which man's natural self-love is transformed into love of motherland or patriotism. Culture welds every man to his community by a bond of love. Bloom does not fully divulge the means by which this transformation of natural man into citizen is accomplished. But he does tell us that it has to do with sex (187ff). Sex is natural man's strongest passion. The object of culture is the sublimation or transfiguration of sex into love. The family is instrumental in this transformation of the natural sexual passion, hence Bloom's lament of the decline of the family. Culture extends love

---

Shadia B. Drury is Professor of Political Science at the University of Calgary and is the author of *The Political Ideas of Leo Strauss*. This essay copyright 1989 by Shadia B. Drury. The essay as it appears here is a shortened version of the original and omits some of Drury's detailed exposition of Bloom's idea of culture.

outwards from the family and attaches it to the motherland. The ingenuity of this process of sublimation is its capacity to preserve the original strength and violence of the sexual passion while attaching it to the motherland.

Culture can accomplish this glorious transformation of natural man because of her power to attract. As Bloom puts it,

> a culture is a work of art, of which the fine arts are the sublime expression. . . . Culture as art is the peak expression of man's creativity, his capacity to break out of nature's narrow bonds. . . . Culture as a form of community is the fabric of relations in which the self finds its diverse and elaborate expression. It is the house of the self. . . . (187–188)

If culture is to be seductive, she must surpass nature in beauty and grandeur. Culture must offer man something loftier and more exalted than anything he could find in nature. Man must experience culture as fulfilling a deep-felt need or yearning. Man must be made to feel incomplete in her absence. She must rescue man from his natural solitude. She must give him refuge from his alienation. She must provide him with a home and with roots.

Culture wages a war against chaos, nature, and brutishness. Culture is the triumph of order over chaos, and art over nature. Her purpose is to give man dignity by raising him above the beasts. She teaches him to despise himself and his brutishness and worship something magnificent and sublime. Culture teaches men worth and worthlessness, honor and contempt, love and hate. Culture therefore determines what a people bows before and regards as sacred. What is sacred is not determined by reason. Culture is not any more rational than it is natural. Nature and reason are universal, but culture is particular. There are a plurality of cultures, and none of them is more rational or more natural than any other. Culture must therefore be imposed, not only against nature and reason, but against other cultures. It is not enough for culture to wage war against chaos, nature, and brutishness. She must defeat other cultures if she is to triumph (202).

According to Bloom, early modern philosophers like Hobbes and Locke were ignorant of the charms of culture. Instead, they looked at man in his nakedness: untamed, self-centered, and consumed with insatiable desires. And incredible as it may seem, the early moderns set out to create a society made up of such creatures. The result was a society of atomic individualists whose natural tendencies for self-seeking and self-satisfaction were not tamed or transformed, but redirected or rechannelled into commerce. In this way, man's natural egoism assumed a form that was not destructive of social life. But by the same token, they created a society that was not elevated; it was a society in which culture, as Bloom understands it, was lacking. This was bourgeois society.

America is for Bloom the bourgeois society *par excellence*. Bloom maintains that the American Founders were the heirs of early moderns like Hobbes, and so were not privy to the sublime insights of Rousseau. American society offers man a sterile vehicle for self-preservation, self-aggrandizement, and the pursuit of wealth. Such a society cannot become the object of love and devotion. It is not possible for such a society to elicit the sort of passion that is equal to the strength and violence of the sexual passion. This is the meaning of Bloom's notorious complaint that there is no mention of sex in the American Founding (187). "Why should there be?" reviewers like Harry Jaffa have scoffed. But in light of the analysis of culture above, Bloom's apparently outrageous remark is meant to indicate the passionless nature of the American polity. America fails to provide a culture that can be embraced, loved, and appropriated by its citizens. It cannot provide its citizens with anything sublime and magnificent that they could bow before. It offers them only themselves and the opportunity to pursue the satisfaction of their brutish nature. Far from teaching them to have contempt for themselves and their brutishness, it teaches them smugness and self-satisfaction. As the Taxi driver from Atlanta said to Bloom, he was once depressed and in rough shape, but after some psychoanalysis and *Gestalt* therapy, he has found his identity and learned to like himself. Bloom comments that in a cultured society, he would have found God and learned to despise himself (147).

The crisis of Western civilization consists in the eclipse of culture and the triumph of nature and brutishness. Rationalism threatens to return man to his animal nature; it threatens to turn him into a self-satisfied brute, unable to love, honor, and worship something much greater than himself.

The Eclipse of Culture

It is legitimate to ask why Bloom, following Nietzsche and other Post-Enlightenment writers, believes that rationalism and universalism are antithetical to culture. Bloom's answer seems to be as follows. First, rationalistic culture is low and vulgar; in the final analysis it yields to the pursuit of pleasure. America has employed reason to overthrow the hardship and discipline that culture imposes. She has embraced openness as an excuse to release her from the yoke of culture. Openness parades as the equal respect for all cultures. But culture demands supremacy, not equality. The equalization of all cultures is equivalent to the demise of culture. All cultures cannot be of equal worth without becoming equally worthless. The absence of culture accounts for America's softness and laxity. And as a result, she is vulnerable to the dangers of conquest from without and atrophy from within. America is dangerously close to the scenario pictured in newsreels of Frenchmen "splashing happily in the water at the seashore, enjoying the paid annual vacations legislated by Leon Blum's Popular Front government" in 1936, the same year that Hitler "was permitted to occupy the Rhineland" (239).

Tyranny may not necessarily come from without. America's openness has turned her into a society of factions. In America, majorities have always been suspect, and American politics has therefore been dominated by minorities or factions. But Bloom fears that the irresolvable differences between these groups will break out into open hostilities. The open society will open the door to civil war. War will posit a triumphant faction. In this way, the open society will give way to a closed society dominated by a single truth. Bloom has no objections to the closed society. In his scheme of things it would be like objecting to the fact that the sun rises. What he fears is that the triumphant faction is likely to be unsavory. He is not in a position to complain that it may be evil, since good and evil are, in his analysis, products of culture.

Second, in so far as reason has a universal element it is linked by Post-Enlightenment writers to tyranny. In other words, culture cannot be universal without becoming tyrannical. As Strauss was eager to show, the "modern project" of creating a universal and homogeneous society is nothing short of a new form of tyranny. For he believed that it was impossible for man to transcend his rootedness in a particular soil, and that all attempts at universalism would end in tyranny. This was the import of his debate with Kojève and his denial of the desirability of the universal and homogeneous state, a universal state of equal and prosperous men and women. Strauss argued that the barbarism we have witnessed in our century has its roots in the same quest for universality. Universality ends in tyranny. Indeed, it is the peculiar form in which modern tyranny manifests itself.

Bloom makes the same point regarding America. He says that for all her alleged "openness" or claim that all cultures are of equal worth, she is convinced that she is the best. A closer look at American openness reveals that openness is a fraud. As Bloom puts it, American openness is a "disguised form of a new imperialism" (34). America is, in spite of herself, a closed society, for she is convinced that her own openness is superior to the closedness of other societies. To the extent that America is determined to divest every other society of closedness and make the whole world an open society modeled after herself, America is as imperialistic as Persia was in her heyday. No less than the Persians, the Americans believe that they are the best and that their way of life and thinking are the best if not the only right way.

Bloom maintains that what makes this imperialism new is not just that it is hypocritical and disguised, but that its aspirations are global. Bloom prefers the old imperialism, Persian style, because he believes that it aspired only to conquer and civilize the nations along its borders. Bloom has no objection to imperialism as such, for he believes that it is integral to the health and vitality of great nations. It is a manifestation of the natural and healthy inclination of individuals to regard their own culture as the best, and every other culture as inferior. This is the logic of culture which America denies in word, though not in deed.

Bloom's indictment of America seems to be unfair. On one hand, he believes that she is vulgar, brutish, and uncultured because she has yielded to the pursuit of pleasure. This makes her weak. But on the other hand, he believes that she displays the impulse to imperialism which Bloom obviously regards as the hallmark of culture. In other words, Bloom dislikes her strength as much as her weakness. But why? The answer is not obvious, but it is something like this. America's strength could mean that there is a chance that the universal and homogeneous society may become a reality. And if it does, that would mean the end of the diversity and multiplicity of culture. And this, from the artistic point of view, is a tragedy. Imagine a world with only a single work of art and a cheap and vulgar one at that!

It would therefore seem that Bloom's objection to America is not so much that she suffers from an absence of culture, but that her culture displays far too much strength, and this could mean that America may succeed more dramatically than any culture has ever done before. Bloom shrinks from this terrifying prospect. But why? After all, culture is a tyranny over nature; and her excellence is measured by the extent to which she succeeds in imposing her dominion. In that case, a global culture would be the culture of cultures, it would be the most successful culture of all time. But Bloom would prefer small pockets of tyranny, or what Canadians call federalism, to a global tyranny. The reason is primarily aesthetic. If the condition of political life is the domination of man by man, let us have as many diverse tyrannies as possible. This will affirm the creativity and vitality of the human spirit. The idea of a global order is repulsive to the artist, not because it will probably be unjust, but because it would make the world dull.

America's strength lies in the lowbrow character of her appeal. Her object is to create a world of comfort and prosperity, a world free of all pain and suffering. And the latter, as every artist knows, are the conditions of creativity. The universal culture, the culture to end all cultures, will return man to his animal nature. It will end the very conditions of creativity, at least for a while. Alas, the human spirit is not likely to withstand too much happiness. As Dostoyevsky wrote:

> what can one expect from man, considering he's such a strange creature? You can shower upon him all earthly blessings, drown him in happiness so that there'll be nothing to be seen but the bubbles rising to the surface of his bliss, give him such economic security that he won't have anything to do but sleep, nibble at cakes, and worry about keeping world history flowing—and even then, out of sheer spite and ingratitude, man will play a dirty trick on you. He'll even risk his cake for the most glaring stupidity, . . . just to inject into all the soundness and sense surrounding him some of his own disastrous, lethal fancies.[1]

It would seem that there is something in man that thirsts for what is hard and impossible. A world of ease and comfort is likely to be a world whose horrors are more exaggerated than those of any other world. It is in this sense that America's strength can be understood to be identical to her weakness.

Bloom's indictment of America is also an indictment of modernity. For America is the embodiment of modernity. Whether this severe indictment of modernity is justified, I will leave to others to consider. But one thing is certain: Bloom's thesis is rich and imaginative, and my primary objective has been to do it justice. Nevertheless, a few critical remarks are in order.

Critical Remarks

Bloom's analysis of culture raises a host of interesting philosophical issues. I will comment only on a few. *First*, the hypnosis of culture may be useful for the preservation of society, both against the external enemies as well as the internal winds of change. But it is also the case that the closed society, which Bloom describes in the language of culture, fills its citizens with hatred of and prejudice towards other cultures. Those who believe that their way is the only right way, and that all other ways and all other cultures are inferior, if not damnable, iniquitous, and depraved, will not hesitate to destroy others if they had the power and the opportunity to do so. Conquest of the other becomes not only a means to self-aggrandizement, but a service to those conquered. For in being vanquished they are being civilized, or liberated. Bloom would have us count among the civilized only those who are completely trapped by the spell of their own culture. In the final analysis this is bound to encourage a warmongering attitude. Strauss calls this warmongering attitude "waspishness," and praises it as a necessary component of civil society.[2]

There is a fine line between pride in one's own culture and hatred of all others. Bloom would like to tread that fine line, no doubt. But if we must err, he would have us err on the side of hatred and prejudice. For anything else smacks of openness, and that, he tells us is uncultured, impossible, and in the final analysis disastrous.

Second, is openness as politically and intellectually untenable as Bloom says it is? Bloom assumes that openness necessarily collapses into relativism. He presents us with a choice between affirming the myths and illusions of our own culture as the single embodiment of absolute reality, and renouncing all illusions. Either we cling to our culture as the only truth or we sink into the void of nihilism. Either the closed society or the spectre of barbarism. But surely there is a middle position between these two extremes that is far more reasonable than either one of them. If we reject nihilism we need not embrace the illusion that our own culture is the single representative of transcendent truth. It is more reasonable to think that the truth is too much for a single culture. Just as no man can comprehend the whole truth, so no culture can possibly represent it. This is why we must be open to the goodness embodied in other cultures. Openness is the proper posture for those who are not duped either by the nature of truth or the nature of culture. Openness so understood is the recognition of the fallibility of one's culture. It is the recognition of the impossibility of actualizing the true and the good. All this assumes of course that truth and goodness are real, or have a reality independent of culture. It presupposes that the truth is not indifferent to good and evil. It presupposes that there is a moral reality that cultures struggle to capture, but invariably fail. Some may succeed more than others, but all success is temporary. Indeed, a culture may begin to decline and degenerate as soon as it becomes sure of its success and its superiority vis-à-vis other cultures.

Openness is the recognition that there is a truth that is imperfectly embodied by a multiplicity of cultures. Openness curbs the appetite for imperialism and tyranny that are the natural components of culture. Bloom's complete rejection of openness in favor of the closed society which regards itself as the single embodiment of the truth is misguided. It is not so much openness but the natural inclinations of societies to be closed that is at the root of the horror and barbarism that Bloom earnestly hopes we will avoid.

The choice is not between affirming a single truth and a single good on one hand, or despairing in one's ability to distinguish between good and evil. Bloom follows Strauss in assuming that the good is singular, and that the search for the good is necessarily a search for a single supreme thing. However, it is more reasonable to regard the good as plural. It is more reasonable to believe that there is a plurality of goods. And if that is the case, then there must also be a plurality of good cultures. Openness is a form of pluralism that does not collapse into relativism. This is not to say that everything is equal, or that all cultures are of equal worth. Openness and pluralism are *not* the claim that there is no justice that is not someone's justice and no truth that is not someone's truth. Openness is not the claim that every war and every conquest is as justified or unjustified as every other. But the justification of war is not to civilize everyone and make them like ourselves. The justification of war is to resist iniquity and injustice. This assumes that iniquity and injustice are not relative to culture. This amounts to an assertion that there are moral standards that are not products of the charms of culture. In other words, there are principles to which all cultures can appeal in their disputes with one another. This is precisely what Bloom denies.

Bloom follows Rousseau and Nietzsche in regarding cultures as works of art, each unique and incomparable. Cultures are founded neither in nature nor in reason. As a result, they have nothing in common. They are insulated from one another by their origins in unique creativity, in a creation *ex nihilo*. So understood, cultures become solipsistic, incapable of discourse. For discourse presupposes a common ground. In its absence, the only intercourse possible between cultures is the violent quest for dominion.

Third, Bloom's nihilism is inseparable from his praise of the closed society. Bloom follows Nietzsche in thinking that culture, art and myth stand in opposition to nature, philosophy, and truth. God is myth, and myths are made by poets. Poets and artists, not philosophers, are the makers of culture. Philosophers try to deconstruct the myth and demystify culture. Their object is to replace myth and falsehood by truth. As such, they are the enemies of culture. They undermine culture in the name of freedom, reason, nature, and truth. Bloom accepts this analysis. He even thinks that Plato taught the same facts about art and culture as Nietzsche. The only difference between Plato and Nietzsche is the side they take. From the same analysis, they reach opposite conclusions. Plato sides with nature, reason, philosophy, and truth. Nietzsche sides with culture, art, illusion, and myth.

Nietzsche chooses the cave instead of the truth because he believes that the truth outside the cave is void, and nature outside the cave, the nature that is not second nature, is vulgar and boorish. Nietzsche's cave is not Plato's; it is decorated beyond recognition. Far from being dark, it is brilliant and glittering. And beyond the cave there is no sunlight, but only a night in which all cows are black. It is therefore quite understandable for Nietzsche to choose the commitment to culture, illusion, and art above the truth beyond. In view of the choice before him, it is quite plausible for Nietzsche to despise the philosophical life, the life outside the cave, because it is cold, indifferent, uncommitted and, in the final analysis, inhuman. Bloom accepts Nietzsche's analysis, but he rejects Nietzsche's choice. Bloom chooses the darkness outside the cave and the freedom that it offers. He does not deny Nietzsche's claim that the life outside the cave is inhuman. But like Strauss, he is inclined to think that it is super-human or god-like. In other words, Bloom accepts the Nietzschean analysis of culture, but he rejects the conclusions that follow from it. Yet Nietzsche's conclusions are the logical ones.

There is no reason to return to nature understood as darkness and brutishness. Indeed, Bloom himself denounces modernity because it involves a return to nature. Bloom denies that nature can be the ground of culture because he conceives of nature in Nietzschean terms. Bloom rejects modernity because it is an attempt to found culture on nature. He believes that such a culture is vulgar and brutish. But in the hands of the few, vulgarity and brutishness are magically transformed into the super-human and sublime. It is as if vulgarity were made sublime simply by becoming exclusive.

It is important to understand that Bloom does not condemn the Universities for failing to inculcate the truth. On the contrary, Bloom regards the truth as too dangerous to be spread liberally by Universities intended for mass education. His point is that the Universities, because of their commitment to openness, have failed American society on two counts. They have failed to educate either the many or the few. First, they have failed to impart to the many what Strauss calls noble lies or salutary myths and what Bloom describes as culture. The myth of openness is destructive, not salutary. It fails to cement individuals into a single whole with a single identity.

Second, the Universities have failed to provide the few with what Bloom regards as an education in the real sense: a capacity to transcend the myths of the cave and see the truth. To do this, philosophy must dismantle culture, and Bloom warns that this is a "dangerous business" (37). Philosophy breaks the spell of culture. It liberates man from the charms by which culture holds him captive. It is therefore a threat to civil society. American Universities are heirs of the modern belief that philosophy is not dangerous to political life and that it can be unleashed on the many without cost. Bloom has no intention of replacing philosophy with indoctrination into the myths of culture. But he would like to reserve it for the few. But how can this be done in Universities designed for mass education?

Bloom's solution is an education in the Great Books. The Great Books as understood by Bloom are fit to educate the many as well as the few. For they contain a dual teaching as Strauss tirelessly illustrates. In this way, philosophy, understood as the brutish return to nature, is preserved without reaking havoc on culture.

---

[1] Fyodor Dostoyevsky, *Notes From Underground*, transl. by Andrew R. MacAndrew, (New York: New American Library, 1961), p. 114.

[2] Strauss hoped to moderate waspishness. See Drury, *The Political Ideas of Leo Strauss* (St. Martin's, 1988), especially chap. 4.

29

Allan Bloom and America
THOMAS G. WEST

Allan Bloom introduced me to the study of political philosophy in three fine courses at Cornell in the mid-1960s. For that I will always be grateful. Political philosophy has been decisive for my life, just as it is for Bloom's. Yet I am about to criticize Bloom's book. I do not wish to be ungrateful. I offer my criticism in the spirit of Bloom's teacher and mine, Leo Strauss, and in the spirit of those classical political philosophers whose writings Bloom and Strauss have pointed us to throughout their careers. I mean to practice what Bloom preached.

The Closing of the American Mind is a diagnosis of the intellectual ills of our day, and, if it is not a prescription, it contains at least some suggestions for a cure. The book is most sound, I will argue, in its description of current pathologies. It is partly sound, partly unsound in its account of their origin. It is least sound in its prescription for their healing. . . .

The cause of our current malaise, in Bloom's diagnosis, is modern philosophy, which has infected us in two ways—through politics and through 19th and 20th century continental European thought. As for politics, America was founded on modern principles of liberty and equality which we got from Hobbes and Locke. Liberty turned out to mean freedom from all self-restraint, and equality turned out to mean the destruction of all differences of rank and even of nature. Our Founders may have acted, or have pretended to act, "with a firm reliance on divine providence" (Declaration of Independence), but their natural-rights philosophy came from the atheists Hobbes and Locke. (Bloom hedges on whether the Founders were self-conscious atheists or merely the dupes of clever and lying philosophers.) Bloom characterizes the Lockean doctrine of the Founders in this way:

> [In the state of nature man] is on his own. God neither looks after him nor punishes him. Nature's indifference to justice is a terrible bereavement for man. . . . [This state of nature doctrine] produced, among other wonders, the United States. (p. 163)

The practical result:

> God was slowly executed here; it took two hundred years, but local theologians tell us He is now dead. (p. 230)

Similarly, the Founders may have thought they were establishing a political order based on reason—Bloom stresses our initial claim to being the first political

---

Thomas G. West teaches in the Department of Politics at the University of Dallas and is the author of *Plato's Apology to Socrates* (1979). This article is reprinted with permission from the *Claremont Review* vol 6, no. 1 (Spring 1988): 17–20.

order so grounded—but the regime of reason turned out to be the regime where reason discovers the virtue of unleashing the passions. At first reason legitimates only the modest passions of industriousness and money-making. But having abandoned its older claim to be the rightful master of the soul, reason eventually lost its authority and became impotent against demands for self-indulgence and mindless self-expression. The story of America, according to Bloom, is a tale of the practical working out of the degradation inherent in the logic of our founding principles:

> This is a regime founded by philosophers and their students. . . . Our story is the majestic and triumphant march of the principles of freedom and equality, giving meaning to all that we have done or are doing. There are almost no accidents; everything that happens among us is a consequence of one or both of our principles. . . . [T]he problem of nature [is] always present but always repressed in the reconstruction of man demanded by freedom and equality. (p. 97)

Eventually, Bloom says, the infections occasioned by our political principles sapped the strength of religious faith and traditional morality. The relativism of today's students is, then, in Bloom's view, a perfect expression of the real soul of liberty, which from the start, in Hobbes's thought, meant that life had no intrinsic meaning. The anti-nature dogmas of women's liberation, which deny the obvious natural differences between men and women in the name of equality, are destroying the last remnants of the family, which had been the core of society through most of America's history. Likewise, the anti-nature dogmas of affirmative action—insisting that equal opportunity be suppressed until all categories of Americans come out exactly the same—deny the obvious natural differences among human beings in regard to ambition and intelligence.

Thus equality and liberty eventually produced self-satisfied relativism which sees no need to aspire to anything beyond itself—"spiritual detumescence." They also produced left-wing political movements which try to implement the "reconstruction of man demanded by freedom and equality" and which not only threaten but dominate important parts of our leading universities. Further, Hobbesian-Lockean liberty was also designed to liberate scientific technology in order to conquer nature and make life comfortable. The very idea of a conquest of nature implies disrespect for natural limits and has contributed to the decline of respect for nature's guidance in all areas of contemporary life.

The second cause of our problems today, Bloom tells us, is post-Lockean modern philosophy. The big names are Rousseau, Nietzsche, and Heidegger, but their views have been popularized (and degraded) by such men as Marx, Freud, and Max Weber. Their ideas have worked their way into our universities and our speech, giving us "The Self," "Creativity," "Culture," and "Values" (four of Bloom's chapter titles). These continental writers, more radical than Hobbes and Locke, all strongly denounced "bourgeois society," i.e., democracy American-style. From them we have learned to think of ourselves as despicably low. Yet at the same time, we have vulgarized the grand conceptions especially of Rousseau and Nietzsche and fitted them into our own democratic prejudices. Thus every nursery-school child is encouraged to be "creative."

If I may elaborate on Bloom's analysis and follow out my own medical analogy, America's founding principles, taken from Hobbes and Locke, may be compared to the AIDS virus. The body into which AIDS insinuates itself may continue to appear healthy for many years before the symptoms reveal themselves. Thus, although our founding principles were atheistic and relativistic at bottom, the body politic continued to look healthy for about 180 years before the disease began to manifest itself openly.

The AIDS virus renders the body helpless before the attack of infectious diseases. It destroys the body's ability to distinguish good from evil viruses and opens it up to the penetration of evil. AIDS is the body's relativism, the self-destructive openness of the body's mind. Similarly, an AIDS-infected American mind loses its ability to tell the difference between healthful and harmful opinions. Salutary customs and traditions, such as moral self-restraint and the habits and attitudes necessary for sustaining family life, for seriousness of purpose, and ultimately for national survival, become indistinguishable from life-destroying doctrines and beliefs, such as the hostile teachings of 19th and 20th century German philosophy. The American mind, suffering from Hobbes-Locke induced AIDS—a liberty that has no respect for nature and natural limits—therefore not only fails to resist the destructive infection of Nietzsche-Heidegger, but with its false openness the American mind mindlessly welcomes the infection, thus bringing on what may be the terminal stage of the disease.[1]

Bloom also prescribes a cure for our malady. The cure is a Great Books education in the prestige universities, taught in the spirit of opening students' minds to the charms and challenge of "the philosophic experience." Of course Bloom is not so naive as to think that reading a few good old books will transform American political and intellectual life. He means that this sort of reading might help in restoring some sort of seriousness to education and therefore to life. Bloom readily acknowledges that this is a slender hope.

*   *   *

I myself cannot subscribe to Bloom's diagnosis of the problems of American education, although I do subscribe to the general features of his account of modern relativism and its dangers.

I can sum up my main objection in this way: Far from being the source of the problem, or an important source of it, America's founding principles are for us probably the only basis for its solution; far from being the equivalent of mental AIDS, our principles *are* our immune system. Bloom is of course right when he says that Hobbes's notion of liberty cannot distinguish itself from license. He is right that there can be no principled objection, on the basis of Hobbes's doctrine, to a government-sponsored effort to make men and women the same. Indeed, as is well known, there is in Hobbes's thought no principled objection to tyranny altogether, tyranny being nothing more than monarchy misliked, and monarchy being the form of government recommended by *Leviathan*. But the American Founders were not Hobbesians, however often Bloom and his students and friends may repeat the falsehood that they were.

The Founders had a low opinion of Hobbes. James Wilson, one of the two or three most important men at the Constitutional Convention of 1787, once summed up his assessment of Hobbes by asserting that Hobbes's "narrow and hideous" theories are "totally repugnant to all human sentiment, and all human experience." Wilson says this in the context of affirming Lockean ideas about the natural rights of man. Similarly, Alexander Hamilton, in "The Farmer Refuted," attributed Hobbes's principles to the Tory Samuel Seabury.

> His [Hobbes's] opinion was, exactly, coincident with yours [Seabury's], relative to man in a state of nature. He held, as you do, that he [man] was then perfectly free from the restraint of law and government. Moral obligation, according to him, is derived from the introduction of civil society; and there is no virtue, but what is purely artificial, the mere contrivance of politicians, for the maintenance of social intercourse. But the reason he ran into this absurd and impious doctrine was that he disbelieved the existence of an intelligent superintending principle, who is the governor and will be the final judge of the universe.
> . . . To grant that there is a supreme intelligence who rules the world and has established laws to regulate the actions of his creatures; and still, to assert that man, in a state of nature, may be considered as perfectly free from all restraints of law and government, appear to a common understanding, altogether irreconcilable.
> Good and wise men, in all ages, have embraced a very dissimilar theory. They have supposed that the deity, from the relations we stand in, to himself and to each other, has constituted an eternal and immutable law, which is, indispensably, *obligatory* upon all mankind, prior to any human institution whatever.
> This is what is called the law of nature. . . . *Upon this law, depend the natural rights of mankind.* . . . (Emphasis added.)

The key point is that Hamilton, as did the other Founders, integrated Lockean language into a moral framework they had inherited from classical and medieval political philosophy and from their manly Protestantism. Nature and nature's God were the ultimate source of duty and right.

Against Hamilton, Bloom asserts, without the slightest attempt to prove it, that for Americans rights precede duties as a matter of course. He implies that Hamilton is wrong about the state of nature, that the law of nature has no moral content, and that there is in America an abandonment from the start of any idea of duty or purpose in life beyond personal whims or commitments.

> But in modern political regimes [such as America], where rights precede duties, freedom definitely has primacy over community, family, and even nature. (p. 113)

. . . The Founders were well aware of the need for public-spirited citizens. They anticipated with clarity the consequence of a loss of public virtue. They believed that a people accustomed to living however it pleased, who saw no higher purpose than, say, entertainment and having fun—a people incapable of *self-government* in the sense of controlling selfish passions and interests—would also be incapable of *self-government* in the sense of democracy, making public laws for themselves to live by. As Madison says in *The Federalist*:

> Republican government presupposes the existence of these qualities [men's capacity for virtue] in a higher degree than any other form.

But if a people ever becomes slavishly lacking in self-restraint, if their "spirit shall ever be so far debased," they "will be prepared to tolerate anything but liberty."

The students described by Bloom in the first part of his book are indeed approaching the debased character which Madison feared. But it is not true that our Founders' principles and institutions sowed what we are now reaping. It can be shown, as I have done in "The Founders' View of Education," that they in fact did everything they could to form the character of the people to make them self-assertive, self-controlled republicans. For the moment I will merely mention John Adams' educational provisions in the Massachusetts Constitution, the surprisingly strict laws regulating the public morals passed in those years by state legislatures, and the intention of the American Constitution to rectify "an almost universal prostration of morals" caused by irresponsible actions of the several state governments which had "undermined the foundations of property and credit."

. . . The first sustained attack on the founding principles was launched in the South before the Civil War by slaveholders and their apologists who wanted to get rid of natural rights so they could be free to continue to tyrannize their slaves. During the progressivist era there was a sustained denunciation of the founding, especially of the Constitution, and Woodrow Wilson among others attacked the Founders' views and institutions because, based as they were on the idea of individual rights, they stood in the way of massive state control of private life. More recently we have been subjected to constant vilifications of religion and morality in American life—Bloom mentions that nothing is less controversial in the prestige universities than such attacks—and these attacks have consistently included attacks on the idea of natural law and natural right.

But Bloom argues that the barbaric attacks on America in the 1960s were really a product of America itself, the unintended culmination of a doomed enlightenment enterprise.

> The content of this morality [viz., that of the '60s at Cornell] was derived simply from the leading notions of modern democratic thought, absolutized and radicalized. Equality, freedom, peace, cosmopolitanism were the goods, the only goods. . . . They were inherent in our regime, they constituted its horizon. (p. 326)

He makes this argument because he sees no principled distinction between liberty and equality as the Founders conceived them and liberty and equality as, say, Marx conceived them. In other words, since Bloom does not see the much more traditional character—and that means the *rational* character—of the Founders' view of liberty, he mistakes the source of the problem. Instead of debunking the founding (Bloom once rightly blamed a history teacher of his for this very thing), Bloom should be celebrating it as a fund of wisdom to be recovered for the sake of the very enterprise he wishes to foster. And instead of confusing the issue by speaking of Marxism as an extreme version of American egalitarianism, he should be vigorously denouncing Marxist hatred of political liberty, liberal education, and religion, the bulwarks of American constitutionalism.

Bloom's mistake about America proceeds, I believe, from two sources. First, he simply doesn't know much about America's origins. His own studies have been in the history of European political philosophy and European literature. And, not having studied America much himself, he has relied heavily, almost exclusively, on the facts that John Locke is America's philosopher, and that John Locke was a secret admirer and follower of Thomas Hobbes. But it is not possible to move from these facts to an account of America's founding that pays little or no attention to the actual writings and documents produced by the Founders themselves. For the question is, in what *sense* were the Founders Lockeans? Their writings show without doubt that the Founders' understanding of their own actions was entirely contrary to the deepest intention of the deeply radical Hobbes and Locke.

The history of modern political philosophy does have a logic of its own, as Leo Strauss has convincingly shown, which leads to increasingly radical statements culminating with Nietzsche in the denial of reason and philosophy itself. But intellectual history is not political history. As Charles Kesler once said, America is not just another chapter in the Strauss-Cropsey *History of Political Philosophy*.[2]

But there is a second reason for Bloom's mistake about America, and that stems from his own experience and taste. Bloom acknowledges that he never felt at home in the American midwest of his youth, that there was nothing for him in the concerns of his high school classmates (p. 244), nor in the piety of his orthodox grandfather (p. 60). But when he arrived at the University of Chicago, he says, and saw its pseudo-Gothic towers, "[he] somehow sensed that [he] had discovered [his] life" (p. 243). He implies that he knew he had discovered it before he ever met his master Leo Strauss there, and I can believe it. Bloom is describing himself as an uprooted intellectual for whom traditional religion and "bourgeois society" mean nothing. For such a man, what incentive is there to study America with any sympathy? Far from being the land of the free and the home of the brave, the American Republic was for him a dreary desert from which he longed to escape. His oasis was the university, the Republic of Letters, and there he has stayed ever since. Of course he is very interested in America as it comes to sight through the students he teaches and the university that gives him his home. But everything outside the university, Bloom implies, is philistine, bourgeois, and contemptibly vulgar. Consider the snobbishness of this typical remark of his: "The importance of these [university] years for an American cannot be overestimated. They are civilization's only chance to get to him."

Is civilization only to be found in or through universities? Considering Bloom's own relentless indictment, one wonders whether civilization is to be found at all in the "best" universities (the only exception being an isolated, often embattled, teacher here or there). Why does Bloom not look to certain less prominent but more substantial colleges, where the trends he describes have sometimes been resisted more successfully than at the better-known institutions? Or, to put it more radically, why should we respect the modern university at all? If Bloom's story of its internal decay is true, as I am inclined to believe, it seems much more likely that, if civilization is to be preserved, it will be in spite of our universities, not because of them.

Tocqueville, an authority on America whom Bloom admires, would never have suggested that universities are our access to civilization (even in 1835, when they were so much sounder than today). Indeed, Tocqueville and Bloom differ profoundly in other ways as well. To exaggerate for clarity's sake: Tocqueville never stops celebrating the virtues of small-town life in America, with its strong Protestantism, its tight moralism, its close-knit families, and its human-scale democracy, while Bloom seems to value all this only as the source of strong prejudices the liberation from which will be all the more satisfying as Bloom midwifes it. Otherwise Bloom seems ready to chime in with the Rousseauan-Nietzschean condemnation of bourgeois life. . . .

This leads to Bloom's prescription for a cure to our ills. It centers on the university. Bloom is firmly against the idea that the university should serve society. In this he opposes the Founders, particularly Washington, Adams, and Jefferson. Jefferson's conception of university education was public-spirited. The main intent is "to form the statesmen, legislators, and judges, on whom public prosperity and individual happiness are so much to depend." This is to be done by studies in "the principles and structure of government." "Political economy" is to be learned in order to promote public industry. Students are also to be enlightened with "mathematical and physical sciences, which advance the arts, and administer to the health, the subsistence, and comforts of human life." Finally, the university is to "develop their reasoning faculties" and "enlarge their minds, cultivate their morals, and instill into them the precepts of virtue and order." All of this is in order "to form them to habits of reflection and correct actions, rendering them examples of virtue to others, and of happiness within themselves."

Bloom's university, on the other hand, is to be explicitly devoted to cultivating the philosophic life, by pointing students *away* from their own countries and traditions. But in the current climate, which is already all too willing to question the value of American society and government, would this orientation not tend to ossify the prevailing prejudices?

Bloom is not indifferent to the needs of society. His final paragraph suggests that a return to the classics may also have a decisive effect on "the fate of freedom in the world." But Bloom would make the public mission of the university anti-social, or rather trans-social, any benefit to society being an accidental by-product, while Jefferson and I would make its public mission primarily political, allowing "the philosophic experience" to be cultivated without official sanction.

Is not Jefferson's university closer to what Nietzsche, Plato, and indeed anyone of common sense, would consider appropriate for the future leaders of society, not to mention future philosophers? His university would certainly accommodate the chance philosopher in one niche or other of the curriculum. But does it really make sense to attempt to go beyond this, to institutionalize an education to the philosophic life in a conventional academic structure? In the end it is who happens to be teaching and who happens to be learning that will make all the difference. Philosophers, like Caesars, can appear anywhere, and they can take care of themselves. The attempt to plan for them seems to me to betray a tendency on Bloom's part to equate, against the letter of his intention, the philosopher and the intellectual. Finally, is it really philistine to structure the university with a view to service to society, above all in attempting to educate future statesmen in the principles of republican government, but on a lesser scale training men and women to be useful to their society and to themselves? That is something that can be understood and done well by those who are far from the exalted heights of philosophy. As Rousseau, another of Bloom's authorities, reminds us, "He who will be a bad versifier or a subaltern geometer all his life would perhaps have become a great cloth maker."

The best and most accurate parts of *The Closing of the American Mind* are the beginning and end, those parts that deal directly with university life in modern America. That is what Bloom knows best because he has been immersed in it and has observed it closely since his youth. Bloom spends a lot of time with students and professors, and he has a gift for penetrating their facades and seeing what they are really like. The observations in these pages of the book, which are of course deliberately and delightfully exaggerated, reveal in the most memorable way the tendency of American young people and of university education. Particularly good are the sections on the debilitating effect of divorce on children and on their capacity to learn and love, on the sad consequences of affirmative action on black students, on the loveless love lives of so many students, and on the tremendous importance of rock and roll for young people and how it degrades their souls. . . .

Someone might ask, why are you being so hard on a book that might do a lot of good, written by the man who happens to be the one who introduced you to the study of political philosophy? To compare small things to great, Aristotle set the example in his treatment of his former teacher Plato. Truth comes before friendship, though it need not destroy friendship. It seems to me that Bloom's low view of America, and the consequent turning away from any serious political concern in his conception of American education, vitiates the good effect of his book's sound parts.

Because he feels so much at home with intellectuals, Bloom overlooks politics. He is therefore unable to appreciate that the cause of sound education in this country is much more likely to be supported by "bourgeois" politicians than by sophisticated intellectuals.

---

[1] The idea that America was AIDS-ridden from the start was suggested by Judge Robert Bork: American constitutional law seems to be "pathologically lacking in immune defenses" against "the intellectual fevers of the general society." (*Tradition and Morality in Constitutional Law* [Washington: American Enterprise Institute, 1984], quoted in Harry V. Jaffa, "Equality and the Founding," presented at the Conference on Equality and the Constitution, San Bernardino State University, April 1985.) Bork's position is even more radical than Bloom's: Bork believes that there is no theory at all inherent in our political institutions. But the result is the same: "our constitutional law [is] constantly catching cold" from the most radical intellectual opinions of the day. Bork then goes on, incoherently, to *celebrate* the fact that our Constitution has no theory of its own!

[2] Kesler is the author of the best review of Bloom's book published to date: See *The American Spectator*, August 1987, pp. 14–17. Several of the arguments in the present review are anticipated in Kesler's.

30

The Closing of Allan Bloom's Mind:
An Instant Classic Reconsidered

CHARLES R. KESLER

American conservatism has sought to reform the universities. Measured against the sweeping academic victories of twentieth-century liberalism, it has far to go. The Progressive movement quickly established its hold on American higher education, founding new departments and professional associations for the study of "scientific" political science and economics, for example, and educating thousands of young reformers who would go on to staff the agencies and commissions of the New Deal. FDR's triumph, in turn, confirmed and extended liberalism's hegemony over America's universities, which shows no imminent signs of abating. While here and there a conservative professor and perhaps even department can be found today, conservatism's influence on the academy as a whole is still negligible. William F. Buckley, Jr. diagnosed the problem thirty-five years ago in *God and Man at Yale*, and since then, in most respects, the situation has only grown worse. Just how much worse is revealed in Allan Bloom's exciting new book, *The Closing of the American Mind.*[1]

Coming from the renowned translator and exegete of Plato's *Republic* and Rousseau's *Emile*—the greatest ancient and modern works on education—a critique of the modern university is bound to be learned, provocative, witty. This book is all three, and its reviews have been so disarmingly positive that in a matter of weeks it has displaced sex and diet books at the top of the *New York Times* non-fiction best-seller list. Somewhat to the embarrassment of Bloom's thesis, which emphasizes the inability of Americans to digest serious thought, his book has become a popular hit.

The Closing of the American Mind offers, in something of the Socratic manner, an unsparing but undogmatic review of the mores prevailing in the American academy. Bloom is at his most devastating in his depiction of the typical university professoriate, most of whom are beset by secret and not so secret self-loathing because, hoodwinked by the fact-value distinction, they are unable to defend the value of their own vocation. Concerning the students he writes poetically and movingly, limning the flatness, the "niceness" that he finds in them to the exclusion of any dominating passion or conviction. Recounting the declining influence on today's undergraduates of family, religion, books, and love, and the increasing sway of feminism, divorce, rock music, and sex, Bloom invites Americans to think about what they and their children are becoming. His book

This essay is reprinted with permission from the *American Spectator* vol. 20, no. 8 (August 1987):14–17.

pleads for a return to genuine openness, to the quest for knowledge of ourselves, to the undiminished and exalting *eros* that culminates in the love of wisdom, or philosophy.

Between sharp, vivid portraits of today's students and faculty members, *The Closing of the American Mind* examines the opinions that unite them—what Bloom calls "nihilism, American style." By uncovering the philosophical roots of the language of the contemporary academy, which is filtering down into society at large—words like "values," "commitment," "self," "lifestyle," and "creativity"— he shows how our vocabulary biases our thought, illustrating the gradual "Nietzscheanization" of the American mind. Bit by bit, Americans have lost what Dante called "the good of the intellect," the ability to distinguish between good and evil and to be guided by the good. Americans like their Nietzsche watered down, however, so our relativism is easy-going and democratic—"nihilism without the abyss," in Bloom's words, and also without the Inferno. The result is both to vulgarize Nietzsche and to corrupt democracy, producing *the* moral virtue of our day, "openness." This is not the openness of inquiry but of indifference, the ho-hum acceptance of all principles and life-styles, the disposition to be "pro-choice" except when the conditions or consequences of choice are unpleasant—or when the choice is between good and evil.

But what is the character of the knowledge for which we long or ought to long? For all his talk of facing up to hard choices, Bloom never makes explicit just what is at stake educationally and politically. Consider his overall view of the present predicament. The American mind is divided between two stages of modernity: suspended between Locke and Adam Smith on the one hand, and Rousseau and Nietzsche on the other. From Locke derives the American devotion to the rights of man—life, liberty, property—and hence to the material prosperity that secures them, largely as a result of Smith's political economy. Rousseau was repelled by the self-interestedness of the Lockean scheme, which he thought destructive both of citizenship and of the genuine interests of the self, which were pre-social, pre-rational, and obscured by the "progress" Locke had unleashed. True satisfaction of the self's desires was possible only by the difficult peeling-away of the accretions of civilization, in pursuit of the sweet, natural sentiment of existence—a task that was possible only for a few solitary dreamers, not for society as a whole. Americans have, Bloom asserts, been affected by each of these strands of modern thought, so that we are schizophrenic as between self-interest and virtue, commerce and citizenship, calculation and reverie. Locke urged us to escape the state of nature; Rousseau, in his individualist mode, to rediscover and return to it.

Nietzsche took Rousseau's critique of Locke to its extreme conclusion: that man was not naturally rational (in the beginning he was pre-rational, remember) meant that nature could not provide even minimal guidance to human reason and happiness. Reason showed, on the contrary, that there was a radical separation between facts (the residue of nature) and values (the constituents of human happiness and flourishing). All values were relative, which meant that it was impossible to choose rationally between, for example, Locke and Rousseau; but it was necessary for human beings to will or create values, not for the sake of truth but for the sake of life.

What makes the American mind interesting, therefore, is precisely how its original Lockeanism has been deepened and complicated by the contradictory Rousseauean longings for social solidarity and individual happiness. As radicalized by Nietzsche, these desires are the cause of our contemporary illness; the German philosophical invasion has, like some dread virus, penetrated to the nucleus of American life and begun to take over the whole cell. Democracy has fallen victim to "alien views and alien tastes."

That, at least, is the impression given by the main contours of Bloom's argument. But when one looks closer, one discovers that Nietzscheanism is not simply an adventitious infection, exploiting a weakness (there are bound to be some) in American intellectual life; but that it so completes what was left incomplete in the American Founding as to be almost its culmination, rather than its corruption. For as Bloom describes it, the Founding was based on the "rights doctrine," deriving from Hobbes via Locke, which deduced rights from man's passions; and far from being conditional on man's obligations to God (as Madison and Jefferson had argued, for instance), it was meant to attenuate, if not to abolish entirely, man's reliance on anything higher than himself. To put it differently, the center of the American Founding was blank. Everyone had the right to pursue happiness, but the idea of happiness had no objective content; it was a matter of opinion (including religious opinion). Thus there was no way of life that could reasonably be said to fulfill man's nature or to be in accord with the divine or natural order. The story of American life—according to Bloom— consists therefore of various attempts, ever more "creative," to fill that empty center.

Thus, far from Nietzscheanism being alien to American political principles, it was the (admittedly) radical conclusion waiting to be drawn from those principles. Nietzsche, who became notorious for his declaration "God is dead," only reported His demise. In fact, God was the victim of an elaborate assassination plot and coup—masterminded by Hobbes and Locke but executed over here by their minions (or dupes), the American Founders. . . .

It is certainly a melancholy observation that the years of precipitate decline in American education—since the Second World War, but especially since the 1960s, according to Bloom—are also the years of the rise of American conservatism. This counter-revolution, along with other developments with important consequences for education and politics—e.g., the revival of Protestant evangelicism and the new prominence of country music—he passes over without comment. Of course these trends did not much affect life in the major universities, which is the focus of Bloom's inquiry. Their neglect does, however, together with the omissions already noted, indicate the real limitations of his book. It is not that concentrating on the top thirty or so universities is unreasonable. What is unreasonable is to label the vivid description of their intellectual decomposition as an account of "the American mind." Doubtless their graduates do go on to commit all sorts of mischief; one, for example, would go on to write *God and Man at Yale*. The problem is that from the point of view of the best and, in the highest sense, most characteristic American thought, the pinchbeck Nietzscheanism of the major universities, and of some parts of popular culture, deserves to be called an expression of the *un*-American mind. Bloom is not particularly interested, however, in the high-minded point of view of the Founding Fathers, Lincoln, and (in attenuated form) the majority of Americans—not because he dislikes America but because, *au fond*, he is not interested in politics. He just cannot take it seriously, except as a threat to philosophy.

That is why *The Closing of the American Mind* only resembles a Socratic inquiry. It is not really dialectical, but historical. It traces the philosophical etymology of the words used by today's undergraduates—"values," "commitment," and the like—but it does not reproduce much of the conversations in which these words occur. There is little effort to ascend from these notions to something higher; there is plenty of comparison, but little argument and definitely no "moralizing." Bloom objects to American nihilism not because it is immoral, but because it is thoughtless; and he does so without giving any account of whether a thoughtful morality exists or in what it might consist.

That this philosophical abdication is not merely temperamental is shown in Bloom's account of Socrates as, in effect, the inventor of the university or of the problem of the university. Prior to what Socrates called his "second sailing," philosophers from Thales to the young Socrates himself had inquired into nature, but had deprecated politics as the realm of convention concerning which genuine knowledge was impossible. But in Bloom's hands, Socrates becomes Thales with legal problems. According to Bloom, political philosophy, of which Socrates was traditionally regarded as the founder, means *politic* philosophy pure and simple; it is a form of public relations, a set of techniques for shielding atheistic and amoral philosophers from persecution by the many, allowing them to live peacefully among their deluded (i.e., moral) neighbors. By learning to write carefully—esoterically—and so perplexing their meaning that only a few fit souls would penetrate the orthodox surface of their works to discern the subversive teachings and forbidden pleasures underneath, philosophers could avoid Socrates' fate without abandoning his pursuits. The world could, as Bloom puts it, be made safe for philosophy.

Of course, this meant that there was not really a Socratic turn in philosophy, that Socratic and (so-called) pre-Socratic thought were not fundamentally different. Political philosophy was simply the public or pious presentation of impious, hence politically dangerous, truths, chief among them being that "Zeus is not," i.e., that the gods of the city, the guarantors of justice, do not exist. Instead of being the first philosopher to take ethics and politics seriously—to philosophize by questioning men's opinions about "What is justice?" "What is courage?" and so forth, because he saw that man is the microcosm, and that philosophy without political philosophy is largely nugatory—Socrates was a theorist who needed a good lawyer and better P.R., both of which he in effect got in Plato.

Which is not to deny that the "politic" presentation of philosophy is a vital part of political philosophy's meaning; but it was only a part, complemented by the serious philosophic study of "the human things," moral and political affairs. It was as students of such affairs that political philosophers like Plato, Aristotle, and Cicero prudently offered advice to present and future legislators.

Bloom contends, however, that political philosophers never seriously considered themselves as teachers of legislators, because the philosophic study of politics and morality did not amount to very much. Oh, he admits that "politics was a serious study to the extent that one learned about the soul from it"; but on the evidence of his own approach in this book, there is little that one can learn about the soul from politics, as opposed to erotics or culture. "Reading Thucydides," he writes, "shows us that the decline of Greece was purely political, that what we call intellectual history is of little importance for understanding it. Old regimes had traditional roots; but philosophy and science took over as rulers in modernity, and purely theoretical problems have decisive political effects. One cannot imagine modern political history without a discussion of Locke, Rousseau and Marx." But can one imagine a discussion of modern political history—of the university as part of modernity—that is nothing *but* a discussion of Locke, Rousseau, and Marx? Politics is replaced by history, and not even by genuine political history but by the history of modern political philosophy, in Bloom's account of America. . . .

Bloom's impoverished or abstract conception of political philosophy, which radically separates morality and philosophy, might seem to be balanced by his accounts of the casual amoralism of today's students and the cowardice and phony idealism of Cornell's faculty during the 1969 campus upheavals. Despite his frequent disclaimers of any intention to "moralize," it is these sections, in which he moralizes in spite of himself, that are the highlights of the book. But, to take the latter example, even his marvelously sardonic account of the Cornell uprising studiously avoids proper names. In more than twenty pages devoted to the collapse of the Cornell administration and faculty before the strident demands of the New Left, not a single participant (other than Father Daniel Berrigan) is named! I doubt that this peculiar reticence is caused by delicacy. Rather it is the way that politics looks when moral indignation, which likes to single out the innocent, the guilty, and the heroic, is proscribed as unphilosophic; and when the discrete phenomena of politics are subsumed under theoretical categories. The shameful episodes at Cornell become mere examples of Heideggerianism working itself out.

At the same time, it should be noted that Bloom does not regard the radicals' victory at Cornell and elsewhere to have resulted in the further alienation of the university from society. On the contrary, he understands it as a further subordination of the university *to* society, as part of the general relaxation of standards that he believes to be characteristically American. It was all a venture in "egalitarian self-satisfaction," with students substituting "conspicuous compassion" for their parents' "conspicuous consumption."

It was not long afterward that at least some of these parents and other members of Nixon's great "Silent Majority" saved the country from George McGovern, the kids' candidate. Given that Bloom correctly, and courageously, compares the New Left to the Fascist movements of the 1930s, one would expect him to have a few words of gratitude for the good sense of the vast majority of American voters who arrested the spread of Radicalism from the campuses to the national government.

The Closing of the American Mind scintillates, but it is not particularly conservative either in the popular or the philosophical sense of the term. Clearly Bloom's view of the American people is that they are even lower and less solid than they used to be. When it comes to handling serious German philosophy, we are "children playing with adult toys," it is all "too much for us to handle," and so on and so forth. It does no good to point out that the Germans seem to have had rather more deadly trouble with these toys than we, because at least they took their philosophy seriously, which from the strictly intellectual point of view is the thing that counts. It is at least arguable, after all, that nihilism *with* the abyss is to be preferred to "nihilism without the abyss."

In any case, the significant question is not whether the moral and intellectual tone of the American people has declined—it has, and Bloom has some harsh truths to tell us on this subject, though the decline has not always been for the reasons he presents, nor is it as bad or as comprehensive as he maintains. The truly serious question is how one ought to view this decline: in the light of America at its best, or in comparison with America at, if not its worst, then at its typical level of vulgarity. Although Bloom mentions the "race of heroes" bred out of the Declaration of Independence—men like Washington, Jefferson, and Lincoln—he dismisses them almost in the same breath. They are *passé*, simply no longer believable; "openness has driven out the local deities, leaving only the speechless, meaningless country." In adopting this point of view, however, he violates his own maxim, that "awareness of the highest is what points the lower upwards." This, in turn, is Bloom's rather restricted version of Strauss's basic hermeneutical rule, that "it is safer to try to understand the low in the light of the high than the high in light of the low. In doing the latter, one necessarily distorts the high; whereas in doing the former, one does not deprive the low of the freedom to reveal itself fully as what it is."

In fairness, the dispute is really over what constitutes "the high" in American life. In the United States, "the greatest of thoughts," Bloom remarks, "were in our political principles but were never embodied, hence not living, in a class of men. Their home in America was the universities, and the violation of that home was the crime of the sixties." True, there was never a class of priests or aristocratic censors empowered to enforce political orthodoxy in America, and that is all to the good. But there was in fact a class of men charged with embodying, with living out America's political ideals: her citizens. It was they who were charged with the duty of being Americans, of living up to the country's principles; and the pre-eminent duty of our states—defend those principles, to help to educate a properly American citizenry. There is no real consideration of this, the pre-eminent political dimension of the education of the American mind, in Bloom's book. But that is because civic education as such is not taken seriously. In nearly four hundred pages, Bloom does not mention even once the most famous of all attempts to educate the American mind—Jefferson's intricate blending of civic and philosophic education in his plan for the University of Virginia.

Is it really necessary to discuss civic education in a book on American higher education? That depends on what one believes college students, and colleges more generally, might owe to their country. In keeping with his position on the primacy of the intellectual, Bloom declares that the primary obligation is for society to minister to the universities, and not the other way 'round. If the proposition were that society ought to be ministerial to the truth, and particularly to the truth(s) that makes it free, then it might be reasonable. On the evidence brilliantly adduced in this volume, however, it is hard to see anything very good, or true, or beautiful in today's universities. Yet Bloom's position is that the university's independence from and indeed superiority to liberal society ought not to be compromised one inch. Hence his revealing treatment of McCarthyism in the 1950s: "McCarthy, those like him, and those who followed them, were clearly nonacademic and anti-academic, the barbarians at the gates."

Those "barbarians" were the nascent American conservative movement, and foremost among them was, of course, the young William F. Buckley, Jr. *God and Man at Yale*, though antedating the heyday of McCarthyism, was spiritually part of this vigorous anti-Communism; and Buckley, with L. Brent Bozell, would soon after write the most intellectually satisfying apology for McCarthy, *McCarthy and His Enemies*, which had the misfortune to be published just as the Senator was self-destructing in the Army-McCarthy hearings. That a popular reaction (even with some excesses) to the horrors of Stalinism might have been healthy, and in principle even reasonable, Bloom apparently denies. The logical absurdity of tolerating intolerance, of granting absolute freedom to Communists and others who would destroy freedom, is acknowledged by him; but it does not affect his philosophical politics, which distrusts all popular movements as potential threats to philosophy.

Yet from its earliest beginnings, American conservatism has presumed that the case for free society rested on the ability of free men and women to make precisely such difficult, and often painful, distinctions between tolerable and intolerable uses of liberty. To this extent, conservatism has insisted on viewing the low in the light of the high, has adopted the viewpoint of American citizenship at its best, has, sometimes clumsily, striven to call Americans back to their own best selves. Without always being able to articulate the principles of America, the conservative movement has presupposed that they were rationally defensible, that philosophic reason could pronounce in their favor, that politics and morality could pass muster. Allan Bloom questions the rational grounds of American moral and political principles, incisively and seductively. But in divorcing the American mind from moral and political questions as they actually present themselves to American citizens, he forces us to wonder how philosophy, and the academy, and ultimately the Republic, can be kept from becoming either frivolous or fanatical. This question, which dogs Bloom's bravura performance from beginning to end, suggests that the educational challenges facing American conservatism, from within and without, are greater than they have ever been.

31

The Spirit Lives in the Sticks

EVA BRANN

I

Here is a book which compels the question whether we should be glad of its existence. My answer is that we should be thrice glad, glad once that it was written, and glad that, having been produced, it found such favor with the public. The bulk of this review will address itself to the reservations which prompt the question in the first instance. Of the two reasons for rejoicing in its success—it is at the date of this writing in first place on the best-seller list—one is somewhat sly and the other quite straightforward. First, Mr. Bloom's book is the jeremiad of liberal education; but a Jeremiah eagerly heard, a prophet honored in his own land, is a prophet more than half refuted. As for the plain pleasure, it is simply that the book will do some concrete good.

Some good, evidenced in small incremental improvements: the ear of a foundation here, a modest program there. Mr. Bloom himself has no illusions about a great systemic reprise of liberal education (380). An indication of the practical impossibility that the requisite cohesion should ever come back, is in the concurrent success of E. D. Hirsch's book, *Cultural Literacy,* in which is advocated a return to what used to be called "general information" (now defined descriptively as acquaintance with a list of some 3800 terms), while the one solution Mr. Bloom finally offers—to be sure, with many cautionary contortions—namely the reading of Great Books (344), is disavowed in Hirsch's preface. In truth, the thought of our whole vast establishment suddenly converted to liberal learning is somehow appalling, like the image of a continent-sized wheel of fine, ripe cheese. The factor of scale seems to me serious and of the essence. Communities of liberal learning require small size and spontaneous beginnings; the unanimity which ensouls and maintains them becomes oppressive and mechanical when hugely magnified and centrally mandated.

In fact, it is strange to me that Mr. Bloom fixed on the universities as the possible loci for the learning whose loss he mourns, when surely our three thousand or so small colleges are its more likely home. The glory of the modern university has properly been not in contemplative reflection and aporetic conversation but in cumulative research and brilliant breakthroughs. And I will pit my experience in a score of more or less obscure little schools against his among a thousand university students: In these places student souls are still capable of

Eva Brann is Tutor at St. John's College, Annapolis. She is the author of *Paradoxes of Education in a Republic.* This review is reprinted by permission from the *St. John's Review* 38 (1988):71–79.

grand longings, books are read with receptive naiveté, and religion is not debased to the frisson of "the sacred." Small places are our internal educational frontier, and the spirit lives in the sticks.

With respect to the effective influence the book might exert (as opposed to the passing waves it superimposes on the roiled ocean of opinion), there is something to be regretted in Mr. Bloom's policy of presenting himself as a voice crying in a wilderness; for in fact the wilderness has quite a few cultivated clearings. He speaks namelessly of his teachers and not at all of the institutional foci of resistance to the rot he exposes. His likely motives are most reasonable: not to be set aside because of sectarian associations, and, by suppressing the names of his allies and predecessors, to win the right of keeping the targets of his contempt anonymous. Consequently this irate tract manages to preserve a certain American civility. Nonetheless, the price is that general readers will have to discover for themselves the addresses of the contemporary sources and places where effective resistance is carried on, such as St. John's College itself. [1]

One word more on the reception of the book. Quite a few people are obscurely enraged by it and express that aversion—just as Mr. Bloom indeed predicts—by means of certain schematic terms, such as racism, elitism, and nostalgia-mongering, that are currently used to impute as sin unpopular though perfectly defensible opinions. It should not be considered a sin for Mr. Bloom to observe regretfully the more than occasional self-segregation of black students in the universities.

Again, if one really wished to show him wrong, one would not angrily call him an elitist—silly term—but, by refraining, prove that democracies can indeed contain even their contraries. On "Firing Line" in May of this year Mr. Bloom respectfully but skeptically characterized the views of Midge Decter (who is, incidentally, one of his predecessors in worrying about America's young) as "serious populism." For my part, I subscribe to this sort of populism, which precisely disavows the entity called "the People" because of the conviction that people one by one have in them, besides sound sense, the roots of reflection; thus they occupy places in a continuum with the deepest philosophers and are capable of participating to some degree in a common liberal education.

This proposition is what Mr. Bloom evidently disbelieves. He thinks that philosophy, the highest pursuit, is not for everybody. I think he is wrong, democratic or undemocratic aside. (I do not want to concede either to him or to his opponents that his own opinions are truly any more incompatible with strong democratic sentiments than many other things one needs to believe along with one's civic creed. There is an argument which in its amplitude would have brought even Mr. Bloom into the democratic fold had he cared to use it: pluralism.)

To begin with, his view of aristocracy has a stylized, unreal air. He seems to think that the honor-seeking aristocratic type, the magnanimous lover of the beautiful and the useless, is dominant in real-life aristocracies, just as he must think the vain, sycophantic, utilitarian, democratic type is pervasive in democracies (250). From what I read and hear, "the beautiful" for aristocrats has usually meant—and still means—mostly horseflesh, and if Mr. Bloom were not first run through by his aristocrat's sword for impugning his stud as useless, he would soon find himself dying of boredom from the nobleman's conversation. To be sure, Squire Western is more lovable than the aesthetic snob Mr. Bloom unwittingly delineates. These aristocrats, who, Mr. Bloom himself is careful to state, are far from being philosophers, are said by him to be likely to admire philosophers for their uselessness (250). To my knowledge they used to require them to work for their places at the bottom of the table as pedagogues and secretaries. But the main point is that a careless opposition has confused the issue here. The non-utilitarian is *not* the useless but it is that which is beyond *both* the useful and the useless, and in particular it is what makes all usefulness possible. Talk of the uselessness of philosophy obscures its *universal needfulness*.

As for the actual citizens of a democracy, Mr. Bloom writes as though in this country no businessman had ever written sophisticated yet beautiful poetry or had ever composed advanced yet lovingly American music, no backwoodsman had ever achieved incomparable yet popular grandeur, no sailor had ever told an enormous moral myth which was also an account of the whaling industry. Mr. Bloom draws from his anti-populist views one simple rule for the university: It should not concern itself with providing its students with the democratic experiences they cannot escape in democratic society, but it must provide those they cannot have there (256). It should be a safe-house for aristocracy. This injunction seems to politicize and turn into paradox a true pedagogical precept, namely that colleges and universities should provide no "life-experiences" at all but should attend to book-learning and the other theoretical pursuits which are their proper business. Whatever is done in an American school cannot help but come out as a democratic experience, not least the free and direct discussion of Great Books. For it involves the democratic presumption that a cat may look at a king. Europeans tend to find this typically American and somewhat comical.

I have heard the charge of nostalgia-mongering with respect to what seems to me Mr. Bloom's very restrained rehabilitation of the fifties. To be sure, I don't quite believe his claim that these were the great days of the American universities. As I recall it, they were the very years when professors anticipated Mr. Bloom in bemoaning the apathy and lack of public commitment on the part of their students, the years whose prosperous philistinism retarded my Americanization by a decade. But his praise of the fifties is in any case only the prelude to the damning of the sixties, the anathema of the book, which Mr. Bloom hates with verve enough to energize every chapter. This autobiographical impulse is patent to everyone. Not that one would blame him. What happened at Cornell, what the faculty seems to have permitted itself by way of moral indeterminacy, might well inflict a trauma never to be forgotten. The only saving grace of the episode, which so blessedly distinguishes it from the case of the German universities under the Nazis, is that the people of this democracy never made common cause with the professors.

This is the moment to say a word about Mr. Bloom's writing. As *The Closing* is, of necessity, something of a magpie book intellectually, so in style it has a sort of mongrel eloquence: literately turned phrases suddenly develop colloquial cadences, the prose is inspissated with metaphor, and the exposition is torrential.

It aroused in me a sense of sympathetic recognition. This is a style formed under the presure of the most pervasive sort of anxiety there is. For most human misfortunes, from physical pain to miscarried love, there is local relief and the prospect of recovery, but the fear for the spirit of one's country is an incessant taint upon the enjoyment of life. Mr. Bloom's country is the America of the Universities, and the anxious patriotism which steals the serenity from his style does his sentiments honor.

II

To pass from the circumstantial to the substantive: Is this a good book?

People regularly refer to it as brilliant. So it is, but brilliance belongs to the demi-monde of intellectual virtues. It would be silly to regret the flamboyance which is winning it its audience; at the same time it would be wrong not to register, for the record, certain substantial doubts.

Let me begin this way: I would not recommend the book to students, not because it will offend their sensibilities—it can do them nothing but good to be forced to defend themselves articulately—but because it is a book not only of generational pulse-taking but also of intellectual history. I would not wish our students to get their intellectual history from this book (I shall shortly argue that it is a little too coarse-grained even of its kind)—or indeed from *any* book. To my mind, the notion that the intellect might have a history, that thought might develop a direction over the generations, should come to students as a late and suspect insight, long after each individual work of thought has been given its a-historical due.

The Closing of the American Mind is, I am implying, a *historicist* enterprise or, more fairly, next cousin to it. Since historicism, the notion that the temporal place of a text determines its significance more than does the author's conscious intention and that history through its movements is a real agent, is Mr. Bloom's *bête noir*, this is no small charge. But there is no getting around the fact that the book continually places and positions great names evaluatively from the outside in—of internal philosophical substance it contains very little. Similarly it persistently sums the spirit of the times and seeks its genealogy in intellectual movements. For example, he says that the university as we know it is the product of the Enlightenment (250), a typical historicist summation in which the tree vanishes into the forest. Indeed, some of his judgments are simply distance effects (as are most historicist conclusions), which dissolve under a close inspection. A crucial example is the claim that nowadays "*all* the students are egalitarian meritocrats" (90). If that were true, and a group held a belief without exception, one would indeed be driven, willy-nilly to the thought of a domination by a supra-individual spirit, that is, a congenital psychic infection by history. In fact it is probably false. In my experience there are always some students who are acutely if reticently proud of the advantages accruing from the right sex, religion, and social status, while those who do believe that "each individual should be allowed to develop his special and unequal talents" without reference to those factors might, I put it to Mr. Bloom, not just generationally *believe* it but also individually *think* it; it is certainly what *I* think.

The title itself is revealing. It is, to be sure, not Mr. Bloom's choice. He wanted the euphonious and accurate title "Souls Without Longing" (the French title is "*L'Ame désarmée*"). But he condoned "The Closing of the American Mind." The "Closing" part is fine: one of the most convincing chapters is the early one in which he shows how openness corrupted, which becomes the lazily tolerant path of least resistance, forecloses passionate doubting, and how the springboard of learning is vigorous prejudice. But "the American Mind" is debased Hegelianism, and a scandal. Americans do, happily, still have certain areas of consensus; nonetheless, they have more than one mind among them.

It is utterly clear to me that Mr. Bloom does not mean what his words say, but it is odd that he is willing himself to supply the example of that soul-slackening disconnection of thought from utterance that he so spiritedly attacks. In fact this permissiveness exacts its price at the end, when he makes the judgment without which the book would be pointless: "Philosophy is still possible" (307), even, presumably, in America. His philosophy of history (and the project of the book really requires one) is simply too diffuse to support this optimism after all the gloom: he has obscured the only basis upon which the possible can, according to Aristotle, ever become actual, namely prior actuality. In short, "still" is the stumbling block here.

Perhaps what is missing rather than a philosophy of intellectual history is its antithesis, a theory of *opinion-holding*, particularly an explanation of how and with what effect people say non-thoughts and become attached to terms of low thought-content. I hold to the axiom, which must seem culpably cheerful to Mr. Bloom, that shallow opinions are mostly shallowly rooted. Therefore I cannot share his passionate sadness at the deficient eros, the spiritual detumescence (136), of the American student soul. Though somewhat masked by the gormless language of the "sensitive, caring and non-possessive relationship," lustful, hurtful, exclusive love goes gloriously on.

But whether it does or no, there is something not quite consistent in this mourning over the de-compression of the soul. Mr. Bloom describes with wicked verve the fatal invasion of the limpid American mind by the dark knowledge of the German refugees. He must know what a crucial role adolescent intensity played in shaping both these Europeans and their persecutors. I think that when Americans trivialize the continental depth (157) they so eagerly absorb, they are often very sensibly—and not altogether unwittingly—counteracting their own intellectual prurience. And so, when the young cluelessly acclimatize Heideggerian *Gelassenheit* as "staying loose" (or so Mr. Bloom pretends to believe), it may not be such a tragedy: at least from staying loose there is a possible road to reason.

My doubts so far have really concerned the *nature* of generalization as practiced in this book, but my final set of complaints concerns its *quality*. The text seems to be stuffed with truth that is not the whole truth and not nothing but the truth. Of course it is very hard to hit all the small nails squarely on the head with so large a mallet, yet there are fine and there are coarse ways of epitomizing spheres of thought and trends of opinion. Mr. Bloom's often anonymous and torrential mode of presentation makes it hard to tell whether the trouble is with his accuracy or his perspective. Moreover, he sometimes seems to present an anonymous modern opinion as though it had but to come in contact with the air to self-destruct, while his great moderns, Rousseau and Nietzsche, seem somehow to merit awed admiration for setting us on the road we are condemned for following. Mr. Bloom's relation especially to Rousseau is the mystery of mysteries to me. One of the excellences of his exposition is the continual pointing to Rousseau not just as the uncannily accurate analyst but as the brilliantly effective originator of the corruption-prone side of modernity. (The book neglects to its detriment the complementary side, the reverence-producing splendor of modern science and mathematics). But then why is Mr. Bloom not on record as being at least as repelled as he is fascinated by this "inverse Socrates" (298)?

For Socrates is the pervasive hero of the book—Socrates the anomalous man, that is, not Socrates the conductor of fairly comprehensible conversations, or the contemplator of communicable truth. This curtailed Socrates comes before the American public brusquely defining the task of philosophy as learning how to die; from this picture it takes but a few steps to reach the conclusion that there is an incomposable quarrel between the philosophers and most of mankind (277–8). Mr. Bloom manages to turn Socratic philosophizing into an utter *arcanum* simply through by-passing its substance. I think that when Socrates is brought on the scene he should appear as practicing the life he thought worth living.

Indeed, the fact that actual philosophy is kept at one remove in this book, that it is a tract on the love of the love of wisdom, is responsible for a certain skewing in the analysis of contemporary ills. Let me give one of many examples I could cite.

That "the self is the modern substitute for the soul" (173) is an indispensible insight in the analysis of modernity. But in the section devoted to it Mr. Bloom simply suppresses reference to "subjectivity," the philosophical term through which are to be reached the deep and not ignoble motives for the substitution: to be utterly unfooled, to confront nature as its knower, to be freely good. Consequently contemporary talk of the self and its discovery is deprived of the respectable strain that, it seems to me, still somehow resonates in the most debased chatter. Our "three-hundred-year-long identity crisis" is, for all its latterday indignities, the unavoidable working out of a brave and compelling choice: We are essentially neither ensouled instantiations of an eternal species, nor creatures whose souls are made by God, but ungrounded spontaneous individual subjects. The function of philosophy should be not to shame us for it, but to re-dignify our dilemmas.

I want to end with the chapter on music, a chapter that is close to Mr. Bloom's heart, and that he mistakenly thinks is unregarded. In fact, young readers turn to it first and rage at it, thereby confirming his observation that rock is their love. It is, to be sure, in a book that insists that the best is for the few, somewhat inconsistent to discount the lovers of classical music because they are fewer than one in ten, but the main point, so truly observed, is that the adherence to rock is universal. (I have never heard anyone young speak against it.) I do not quite believe that rock "has one appeal only, a barbaric appeal, to sexual desire" (73). I am a sporadic watcher of MTV and know that what the visualizations pick up in the music is its weirdness, whininess, bizarrerie, meanness, and scariness—in sum, a whole vocabulary of extra-sexual excruciation, which is often ironically and even wittily exploited. The appeal is not so hard to understand; it is its universality and depth that remains a mystery.

For Mr. Bloom's explanation does not quite reach the love aroused by this, or any, music. For him, following, as he claims, Plato *and* Nietzsche, music is the "barbarous expression of the soul," the soul's primitive, pre-rational speech, pure passion. I take it as read that he knows his *Republic,* but where in it did he find this theory? His own translation corrects the impression given by earlier versions that the musical modes *express* the passions (*Rep.* 398 e 1). According to Socrates they rather *shape* them. Moreover, the music must *follow* the words, which it couldn't do if it had no close relation to reason. (Indeed it was Socrates' Pythagorean friends who propagated the great tradition of music as qualitative mathematics.) Some musical modes are more soul-relaxing than others, but these latter, the bracing ones, are the most potent instruments that the community possesses for forming the soul into grace amenable to reason. It follows that there is nothing truly primitive or pre-rational even about the most orgiastic music, and that when a sect succumbs to Wagner or a generation to rock, the explanation cannot start from raw passion, but must begin with corrupt reason. Mr. Bloom has succumbed to the prime error of those dark Germans, which is to think that the soul of a rational animal somewhere harbors a nature-preserve of pure primitive passions.

III

To conclude. *The Closing of the American Mind* is not only an opportune summation of decades of critique, but it is also among the early lappings of a turning tide. For the tide is turning, though not to float a happy and harmonious new liberal learning, but to ground us in a sad new abstinence. It has very suddenly come home to us that the world is full of dangers just where we sought our pleasures: spending, sex, substances, sound, even sunshine. We will be drawn in upon ourselves, we will have to take new thought, and in these straits liberal literacy, the attentive reading of good books, may eventually play a modest role as something of a saving grace.

Because of Mr. Bloom this thought may come a little sooner to a somewhat larger number of people. Moreover, since it comes embedded in a critique of our current condition that is wholly passionate and largely true, there will be a more immediate effect: Some readers of the *Closing of the American Mind* are bound to experience a re-opening of their minds to the all-but-foreclosed understandings behind our present. That will be its success beyond celebrity.

---

[1] Some of these fellow-fighters in the battle against the soul-unstaying piffle-terms, those relaxants of shape and significance, which are the real, or at least the most interesting, butt of the book, such as *creativity, self, culture, life-style,* and *communication,* are hearteningly easy to find. For example, there are Judith Martin's vastly popular "Miss Manners" books, which, under the guise of pronouncing on etiquette, often ironicize our linguistic mores; thus Miss Manners bids us to "make a special effort to learn to stop communicating with one another, so that we can have some conversation." Here is no inconsiderable ally!

SIX

The Death of Love and Decline of the Family

Is Bloom Anti-Feminist?

"I see the liberation of women as part and parcel of the American tradition," says Allan Bloom in the interview that opens this chapter. But Bloom also wonders, "what substitute is there for the forms of relatedness that are dismantled in the name of the new justice?" And Bloom's enemies have pounced on these doubts as evidence that he has a secret agenda. Betty Friedan here in "Fatal Abstraction," mistakenly assumes that criticism of the way things have been going since 1968 necessarily implies an attempt to turn back the clock to the family before 1968. That family consisted of one woman and one man, married for life, raising several children, with one parent earning the money, and the other parent staying home to care for the children. Any such arrangement, according to Friedan, necessarily puts the wife into a "girdle," because men are by their nature tyrannical, and raising children is not a true test of a woman's abilities.

The scholarly anti-Bloom feminist position is represented here by Martha Nussbaum in "Undemocratic Vistas." Nussbaum refers with passionate approval to Plato's discussion of women in book 5 of the *Republic*. Plato there argues that all men and women in a city should exercise together naked. And, for those above the servile classes, families should be forbidden, and the children that result from matings should be forcibly removed from their parents and raised anonymously in government-run day-care centers. Bloom suggests that, assuming that Plato is sane, all this must be some kind of satire offered tongue in cheek. Nussbaum denies this and answers that Bloom's interpretation is "bizarre" and "not accepted by any major non-Straussian interpreter."

Werner Dannhauser replies to Nussbaum's arguments with regard to the classics. But the whole purpose of Nussbaum's animus against Bloom, as Dannhauser points out, is to support arguments like Friedan's against the family. Friedan and Nussbaum believe that families, because they operate on a gender-based division of labor, are necessarily unjust; the differences between men and women are merely conventional and not natural.

On the issue of women's role in the family, the most helpful reply to Friedan and Nussbaum is provided by Pamela Proietti in "American Feminists *versus* Allan Bloom?" If Proietti is correct that families with men are good for women and provide indispensable support for love and for education of the children, then feminists will share Bloom's regret that today's family is often a troubled and unhappy one.

191

32

Too Much Tolerance

ALLAN BLOOM

NPQ: Let's look at feminism and the family. Don't you imply in your book that feminism is largely at fault for the high divorce rate because it encourages women to place their personhood above family duty?

Bloom: Not at all. I don't say feminism is the cause; I say radical individualism is the cause. I discuss the family from the point of view of the preparation of students for a liberal education.

So many kids today come from homes where the parents are divorced. The psychological effects of divorce affect the university atmosphere. There were times and places in history where the attachment to the ancestral was so great that there was no freedom for reason. Now, the situation is reversed. As a result of broken homes, there is such a quest for roots, for settling down and finding trust—there is so much insecurity—that opening students' minds to free inquiry about the nature of things is barely possible. Free inquiry is too dangerous, too unsettling.

I argue that radical egalitarianism and cultural relativism encourage the separation of individuals. As a result, kids today have no really profound connections with the world and with one another. The nuclear family is an issue because it is the only restraint against our society's moving toward what I call "social solitaries."

I wrote about women in my book with considerable care. There is no suggestion on my part about turning back the clock in any way. But there should be no illusion that liberated choices have no price. There are damages.

Who naturally cares for a child? His parents. If the parents find that out of economic necessity they can't devote attention to childrearing, others have to take their place. The fad of hysterical concern about child abuse is one aspect of the change. It comes out of the problem that so many children are taken care of by somebody else who doesn't have the motives of the parent. Parents feel guilty and frightened by their loss of supervision and therefore try desperately to make certain that those to whom they entrust their children will be reliable. But nothing can take the place of parents' motives.

NPQ: Do you think these parental problems are a matter of choice or economic necessity? It takes two wage-earners today to make ends meet.

From *New Perspectives Quarterly* vol. 4 no. 4 (Winter 1988):6–13. Excerpted with permission. See the portion of this interview about rock music in chapter 8.

Bloom: I think Americans have much more choice than they say. If they're fully conscious of the problem, men and women can make different kinds of arrangements.

The problem is deeper, though. One of the worst tendencies in America is that individuals place the highest priority on the right to "feel good about myself." That kind of "rights morality" easily becomes a cover for self-indulgence and neglect of one's duties.

NPQ: In discussing sexual liberation you seem to imply a natural order to the family that is valid across all time. You say that "Sex may be treated as a pleasure out of which men and women make what they will . . . its importance or unimportance in life is decided freely by individuals. Or, sex can be immediately constitutive of a whole law of life, to which self-interest is subordinated and in which love, marriage and child-rearing of infants is the most important business. It cannot be both."

To take one example, doesn't the technology of the birth control pill change all that? Now pleasurable sex without procreation needn't undermine the family structure.

Bloom: The pill makes it easier not to have kids, but it increases the possibility of promiscuous sex. What are the psychological effects of that? Technology does not change nature. It makes promiscuous sex safer, but it does not provide a substitute for the attachment formed by sexual fidelity. Sex is made less sacred, and the singularly deep attachment to the family, bonded by sexual pleasure, is weakened. Part of today's unattachedness comes from easy, intimate contact which, strangely, makes it harder to have profound contact. This is as true for men as for women.

Rousseau, who in my view was the real founder of the idea of sublimation, argued that the effect of eroticism was to give us the possibility of idealism and attachment. Promiscuous sex undermines eroticism by replacing its mystery with immediate gratification.

And if sexual pleasure isn't mixed with enduring relationships—"this is the only person I want to do it with"—it becomes something like what herd animals do.

I've found it much harder to teach Plato's *Symposium* recently because in the *Symposium* you're asked to justify your erotic attachments, to say what they mean about life. The beginning and the end of what most kids have to say about sex today is "I have the right to do what I want in the privacy of my own bedroom." Well, okay, but that doesn't take you very far.

Just as our age is not a good one for nuns, it is also not very good for romantic kids. I am convinced that if you don't have the language for something you pretty much end up not having it any longer. This is what is happening with the multifarious phenomena of love.

NPQ: Some women criticize you as a "speculative anti-feminist" who has no idea of the concrete realities of women's lives today.

"Women just won't fit back into the girdle," as Betty Friedan says.

Bloom: . . . Feminists have attacked me as saying that the liberation of women is not natural. That's not what I said in *The Closing of the American Mind*.

What I explicitly said was that America has two great traditions: love of nature and love of the conquest of nature. Feminism is especially related to the latter. It is very American in its love of the conquest of nature. The pill is an example of conquest over a nature which tied women to the family and dependence on males. What is difficult is to respect nature and at the same time have the passionate desire to conquer it.

So, I see the liberation of women as part and parcel of the American tradition. It's the specific ideology of contemporary feminism—of abstract equality and the notion of a very specific female essence unrelated to the male essence that I find problematic.

NPQ: Why is the "feminist ideology" problematic for the university?

Bloom: The abstract ideology of feminism is one of the great threats to the university because its partisans argue that all literature antecedent to the feminist movement is sexist, from Plato to the Bible to Huck Finn. If all literature is sexist, then of course, it can't be taken seriously. Sexism has become the absolute evil.

You hear kids today saying, "Well, you know Aristotle had this weakness of not taking women into account"—already knowing it all and judging it unworthy before knowing anything! Aristotle's very definition of a barbarian is one who treats a woman like a slave. Nature is his standard, and it was the first standard which grounded equal treatment of women. I have yet to see a better one.

33

Fatal Abstraction

BETTY FRIEDAN

. . . Bloom is wrong. Feminism was not formed as a way to be free of family responsibilities. The family had to change when women came into the family as equals, as more than family servants, as people who are entitled to their human and American birthrights of equal opportunity to move in society. But this change was for the better. Feminism has been and will continue to be necessary for the strengthening of the family because women, healthier when participating in society, and men, enriched by giving more at home, make the family a more stable institution.

Where We Went Wrong

If you go back and reread *The Feminine Mystique*, you will see that I consider child bearing and child rearing an enormously powerful part of life. This is not a mystique; it's reality. In the face of hard economics, the choice to have a child becomes a profound statement of human values, an assertion of human priorities in defiance of pressures for material success. That women were faced with an impossible either/or choice between family and career was a mistake.

When women won the right to vote in 1920, they didn't take into account how the people who gave birth to children were also going to move in society and use the political rights they had won. All their energy had been geared to proving women were equal to men, to getting the vote and the right to control their own earnings and their own property. It was hard to face the real differences between women and men, and painful to face the fact that very few women were taking advantage of their rights on paper.

In the 60s, when I entered the picture, women still needed to focus on equality because not only women's rights, but the history of women's rights, feminism, and the "career woman"—the very terms of the women's movement—were all condemned in a society still defined by men. Women were expected to stay home and give up their careers because the post-World War II feminine mystique, which was powered by Freudian psychology and the economic structure of society, told them to do this. Symbolically, the spirited heroines of the 30s, like Katherine Hepburn and Betty Davis, were replaced by dumb, dreary housewife heroines like Doris Day who lost their husbands and whose children were cursed with pneumonia when they ventured away from the home, but who repented by getting pregnant again.

Betty Friedan was the first president of NOW and wrote *The Feminine Mystique* (1963). This interview is reprinted with permission from *New Perspectives Quarterly* vol. 4, no. 4 (Winter 1988):14–19.

We were insulted by this image of the dumb housewife. We were insulted that nurses who may have taught three generations of surgeons had to stand when the doctor entered the room and were paid a tenth of a doctor's salary. We were insulted by the competent woman at home on her pedestal and the competent secretary who ran the office but who could not dream of being an executive. Women weren't supposed to apply the idea of equality to their situations. The term "sex discrimination" didn't even exist. We were angry, and we had to break out of the feminine mystique that defined us solely in terms of the child bearer.

But not to the repudiation of child bearing. That was never my message. There were some extreme, radical feminists who applied the doctrine of class war to the situation of women and men, and who chanted, "Down with men! Down with the family!" The media harped on this because it made good copy and diverted attention from the basic reality that was affecting every woman's life: we were finally taking ourselves seriously.

If the media distorted feminism's message, so does Bloom distort serious feminism when he implies that feminism repudiates the values of white Western male society. The values of freedom, equality, and human dignity originated in such a society, and have been crucial to the women's movement itself—even though today, the cutting edge of society's evolution may well come from the experience of women, and from people of cultural and religious origins who have not played a central part in our culture up to now.

I used to tell feminists long before I wrote the *Second Stage*, "If this really were a war of women against men or against the family, we would never win. Nor would we want to." There are profound biological, psychological, social, emotional, human bonds that connect men and women.

The real leaders of the feminist movement knew this all along. We always wanted more than "dressing for success." Now, in the Second Stage, we have to move beyond the male model of equality. We can't even live equality when the structures of the work world are based on men who have wives to take care of the details of life.

The economy has changed. Living in the old family form where you have the restricted-to-the-home mother and bread-winner father now means the father has to be making quite a bit of money. More and more, a family needs two incomes to survive. This is the reality of the family today.

We must restructure home and work so women can freely choose to have children, and also move freely in society. This will entail articulating life values in the public and political sphere: this time not only by women, but by men, who will have more concrete life-oriented values and not fall into the abstract trap of Bloom as they begin to share in the daily responsibilities of child rearing.

Back To The Girdle

Forget women, forget women's rights for a moment. Polarizing the family is dangerous in today's world. We have to have values of the larger human family. Polarizing the family would doom the family to a terrible economic crisis by keeping women at home or locked into low-paying jobs, divert attention from real economic problems that require new solutions, and leave men free to play win-lose games with dangerous weapons. We can't send women home again. . . .

I am not denying that there is a biological basis of human nature. But we can also choose our families, and what we choose is based on the options open to us, and on the way our perception of these options is molded by society. Attempting to define what the family should look like is an abstraction.

I would like to tell Bloom about the metaphor I use when I talk to the young girls who have grown up taking women's rights for granted. These young women of today say, "I am not a feminist, but I'm going to be an astronaut. I am not a feminist, but I am going to be a Supreme Court Justice."

I ask them, "How many of you have ever worn a girdle?" They laugh. I tell them that not long ago, every woman from the age of 12 to 92, whether she weighed 70 pounds or 270 pounds, pasted her flesh into rigid plastic sausage casing that made it hard for her to breathe and move. No woman questioned wearing one; it's what being a woman meant. . . .

But we knew. We lived through the change. We know that it is so much better being a woman when you don't have to wear that girdle, when you can be yourself and use your voice and use your eyes and let your heart feel fully and affirm your own sexuality. And I say, "You better be careful, as you struggle to move in your new high heels and super short mini skirts, that they aren't going to put you back in that girdle." Bloom is trying to put them back in that girdle.

This would be mad. With the new economic problems of today, with the serious complexities of our world, it would be dangerous to go back to the girdle. We have to go forward. We have to be able to move, and live, and raise our families and choose to have children, and if we must, help our families survive. Men and women need to share parental responsibilities as well as responsibility to the future. In this Second Stage, we need to take on, not retreat from, a complete restructuring of the nature of power.

Fatal Abstraction

Perhaps the economic earthquake of 1987 will awaken us from this age of intellectual and political somnambulism. Already, Americans are beginning to hunger for value and purpose beyond narrow material wealth.

But the hunger for purpose in life can't just be abstract, contemplative, or inner oriented. Bloom doesn't give the answer; his *Closing of the American Mind* is so abstract. Bloom's abstractions are really a trap.

We have to be careful of such abstractions. Look at the movies. Watching the new box office hit *Fatal Attraction*, I thought, "This is where I came in 25 years ago." Only this time around, the feminine mystique is much sicker. A sexually aggressive career woman seduces a wimp of a man. She represents pure evil. Meanwhile, the man's wife represents the passive housewife who is once again enshrined.

This is a dangerous movie that is playing a dangerous, regressive message. Women are going to be the scapegoat for the economic and political crisis that we are in today, and for the crisis at bay. I see a new feminine mystique developing, and not only in Allan Bloom.

34

Undemocratic Vistas

MARTHA NUSSBAUM

Asked whether women as well as men should study philosophy, the distinguished Roman Stoic philosopher Musonius Rufus, teacher of Epictetus, replied as follows:

> Women have received from the god the same rational faculty as men, the faculty that we use in communicating with one another and in reasoning about each matter, as to whether it is a good thing or a bad. Similarly, the female has the same faculties of sense perception as the male: seeing, hearing, smelling, and the rest. Similarly, they both have the same number of bodily parts, and neither has any more parts than the other. Furthermore, desire and natural orientation towards excellence belong not only to men, but also to women; for not less than men they are naturally pleased by fine and just deeds and repelled by the contrary. Since things are this way, why on earth should it be fitting for men to examine and inquire into how one should live well—which is what it is to do philosophy—and for women not?[1]

This passage states a conception of "higher education," and the place of philosophy in that education, that can be found not only in Stoic texts but in the writings of many of the greatest philosophers of the Greek and Roman world. This conception of philosophy has three elements, closely connected, and all traced by Stoics to Socrates, their model and hero:

1) Philosophical education is *practical*. It is the rational search for the best human life. Its subject is, above all, the study of moral and social conceptions, and its purpose (as Musonius later makes plain) is, through reflection, the amelioration both of the individual student's life and, through the choices of educated individuals, of the surrounding society.

2) In philosophical education the pupil is *active*. It is not the passive reception of external truths, but the following out of paths of rational and critical argument—indeed, the enlivening and developing of the pupil's rational soul. (For this reason, Musonius later stresses, it must be closely tailored, in each case, to the needs of the particular student, like the prescriptions of a good doctor.)

3) Philosophical education should be *broadly distributed*. It is appropriate to all who are by nature rational beings, that is, beings capable of practical and ethical reasoning. (Epictetus was a slave when he attended Musonius' lectures. Later he became a free man and a distinguished philosopher.)

These three elements are connected. It is because philosophy's practical

Martha Nussbaum teaches at Harvard University and is the author of *The Fragility of Goodness: Luck and Ethics in Greek Tragedy and Philosophy* (1986). This essay is reprinted with permission from the *New York Review of Books* (November 5, 1987):20–26.

content is so important for human life, both individual and communal, that making it widely available is so important—fulfills, indeed, a basic human need. And it is central to Stoicism's conception of philosophy's practical purpose and of the reasons for its broad distribution to insist that philosophical education is not abstruse contemplation but the development of each human being's capacities for active practical reasoning.

This picture of philosophy opposes itself, on the one hand, to conceptions of education that do not take philosophy seriously as a subject for human study. On the other hand, it also sets itself against all conceptions of philosophy that make of philosophy a purely theoretical and contemplative discipline and (usually for reasons closely connected with this conception of its function) limit its pursuit to a narrow favored elite. Philosophy is the critical reflection about human life; and this reflection is essential to the full health of all human beings and of society in general.

Allan Bloom, like Musonius, has written a book that defends the central role of philosophy in higher education, and defends it as essential for the health of human souls and human society. Like Musonius again, he initially presents the philosophical activity he praises as a search, through active critical argument, for the best human life; he praises as the founder of his ideal university Socrates, the paradigm of tireless rational searching to whom Stoics also appeal. But in Bloom's book the Socratic conception is in conflict with another very different idea of philosophy: the idea of a study that is open only to a chosen few specially suited by nature (and to some extent also by wealth and social position) for its pursuit; the idea of a philosophy that is concerned more with revealing fixed eternal truths than with active critical argument; of a philosophy that not only does not aim at justice and practical wisdom, individual and/or communal, but actually despises the search for social justice and beckons chosen souls away from social pursuits to a contemplative theoretical life.

To understand these contradictions, and their relation to Bloom's practical proposals for a reform of the university curriculum, we must begin with his diagnosis of contemporary American culture, for whose diseases philosophy is supposed to provide the cure. As Bloom sees it, the central problem in higher education today, and in American society more generally, is widespread rela- tivism. Both teachers and students have been taught that all conceptions of the good human life are equally valid, and that it is not possible to find an objective viewpoint from which to make rational criticisms of any tradition or any study, however apparently trivial or even base. The most any such criticism can be, according to this prevalent view, as Bloom reports it, is an expression of un- enlightened prejudice.

In education, however, so goes the prevalent view, we should refrain from such expressions of prejudice and cultivate "openness," which really means, Bloom concludes, a suspension of critical judgment and a laissez-faire attitude to all pursuits and all kinds of knowledge. The expression of relativism in the college curriculum, as Bloom sees it, is the removal of core requirements, whose absence encourages students to believe that no studies are more central to human life than others. As a result of this ethos of openness (which, Bloom argues, is really a kind of closing of the mind, incompatible with a true Socratic openness to reasoned arguments about the good), students have abandoned the idea on which the university (which Bloom traces to Socrates) was founded: the idea of a rational search for the best human life.

In support of this argument, Bloom constructs a colorful and highly rhetorical portrait of today's university students, who by his account seem to be pathetic characters indeed. Cut off from the nourishment of old religious and even secular traditions, their souls made small by the view that anything is as good as anything else, these students are rootless and enervated. Their personal relationships, devoid of lasting commitment, are further undermined, Bloom claims, by the excesses of feminism, one of his central targets, which he accuses of using "force" against "nature." Unable to pursue anything with passionate devotion, these students seem to live only for the "premature ecstasy" of rock music. Empty and selfish, "they can be anything they want to be, but they have no reason to be anything in particular."

Bloom now offers a historical argument that attempts to explain how the relativism he deplores became such a pervasive influence on American society. It is an idiosyncratic account, based almost exclusively on influences from the high intellectual tradition of nineteenth-century continental Europe. (Bloom, surprisingly, is silent about the influence of utilitarianism on American cultural and economic life—an influence that surely has a part in explaining why many Americans believe that all satisfactions are equally valid.) The account examines several key terms that the American social vocabulary has inherited from the continental tradition—terms like "the self," "culture," and "values," showing us both their original philosophical use by writers such as Nietzsche and Max Weber and how they have been democratized by American relativists. Now, he argues, this vocabulary corrupts students' perceptions of the world to such an extent that they cannot make sense of the ancient idea of a rational search for the best way of living. They speak of "my values," thinking of them as expressions of subjective preference that cannot be criticized with reference to any objective norm. They prefer the radical individualism of the term "self," with its emphasis on the subjective and idiosyncratic, to the ancient idea that human beings have a "nature" that can be objectively specified.

In order to give us a clearer idea of the ancient conception of education from which the modern university has allegedly fallen away, Bloom now offers a history of the university that traces its foundation to Socrates', and in general ancient Greek philosophy's, questioning about the best life. He then gives his own strangely un-Socratic account of the university: the university exists within democracy to call chosen "natures" away from the corrupt judgments of "the many" and teach them the superior value of the contemplative life. Bloom then tries to show us how the university, as he conceives of it, has been corrupted by contemporary democratic demands for equality, with the consequent erosion of intellectual standards. There follows a bitter account of the student movement of the Sixties, during which Bloom, lonely opponent of corruption, attempted to stop various changes that he deemed pernicious, such as the changing of curriculum requirements and even of faculty appointment procedures in response to student demands. To this time of timidity and lowering of standards he traces today's rootlessness and narcissism.

A survey of today's university departments yields, Bloom now argues, the conclusion that only the natural sciences are healthy—respected by all and flourishing in their research activities. The humanities, on the other hand, are, as he sees it, very badly off. Humanistic research lacks passion, quality, and focus; and, partly in consequence, humanities professors do not inspire respect either in their students or in society generally. Particularly weak and neglected, according to Bloom, is philosophy, which really ought to be leading the university, on account of its dedication to the deepest questions about how human beings should live. Philosophy must, he argues, be returned to its proper place as the leading force in the university. Universities should seek a remedy for their diseases in the establishment of required (and apparently uniform) core curricula based upon the Great Books of the Western tradition and principally on the central works of Western philosophy, and in particular ancient Greek philosophy, in which Bloom finds the antidote to the relativism that infects today's students.

We shall later see what he expects these curricula to accomplish, and for whom. And we can see by now some of the elements that explain his book's enormous appeal—its assault on cultural confusion and the lowering of standards, its defense of an education that will, allegedly, be a source of community and vitality, and its opposition to a narrow pre-professional specialization that cuts students off from one another and many ideas of lasting value. But in the very singleness and simplicity of Bloom's solution, so uninterested in the needs of different souls, and in the dogmatic complacency with which it is announced, so far removed from the Socratic demand for ceaseless self-questioning, we begin to sense the tension between Bloom's official allegiance to Socrates and the more dogmatic and religious conception of philosophy to which he is deeply drawn. Such simple prescriptions need careful scrutiny.

2.

. . . Now let us turn to classical philosophy. For Bloom presents himself as someone whose insights come from a lifetime spent studying the texts of the ancient Greek philosophers, in whose writings he finds a view of human nature that is the antidote to contemporary relativism about the good human life. "The substance of my being," he writes, "has been informed by the books I learned to care for. They accompany me every minute of every day of my life." His special love for these books has certainly prevented him from attending to works of literature and philosophy that lie outside the tradition they began. For he makes the remarkable claim that "only in the Western nations, i.e., those influenced by Greek philosophy, is there some willingness to doubt the identification of the good with one's own way." This statement shows a startling ignorance of the critical and rationalist tradition in classical Indian thought,[2] of the arguments of classical Chinese thinkers,[3] and, beyond this, of countless examples of philosophical and nonphilosophical self-criticism from many parts of the world. (Bloom usually forgets that nonphilosophers can also be rational.) It shows as well a most un-Socratic unwillingness to suspect one's own ignorance. I have rarely seen such a cogent, though inadvertent, argument for making the study of non-Western civilizations an important part of the university curriculum.

How does Bloom treat the books that he does read? Usually, it must be said, in a vague and offhand way. We find many statements about "the ancients." We find frequent appeals to their authority—something that is extremely odd in view of the insistence of every great ancient philosopher on the priority of rational argument to traditional authority. We find, as well, a few statements about particular writers, such as Plato, Aristotle, Cicero, and Plutarch, and, on rare occasions, a remark about a specific work. But there are almost never quotations or references to passages, and never an effort to discover the structure of an extended pattern of argument. Nor is there ever any indication that these texts are difficult to interpret, that scholars differ about their meaning. Bloom always knows what they mean, and so authoritatively that he does not need to support his statements with arguments or even precise references. In short, there is no indication that in practice Bloom accepts his own dictum that "learning must and can be both synoptic and precise."

This is all the more remarkable since in the one case, Plato's *Republic*, in which Bloom does advance a definite interpretation of a text at comparative length (which is to say, about a page and a half), he presents (following his teacher, Leo Strauss) an interpretation that is both bizarre and not accepted by any major non-Straussian interpreter of the text, beginning with Aristotle. He alleges that the *Republic* does not seriously propose the ideal city, the rule of philosophers, or the equal education of women. The *Republic*, he writes, ironically undercuts itself, and actually teaches to those in the know the impossibility of what it seems to advocate.[4] Why doesn't Bloom think it important to defend such controversial textual claims with arguments? Not to do so seems curiously lacking in respect for the text that one loves, and also for the readers with whom one is trying to converse.

Where Bloom makes authoritative claims about "the ancients" in support of his central moral and political conclusions, his argument contains extraordinary gaps and errors, of which I will mention only a few examples. In an important passage on the function of moral education, Bloom represents Aristotle's *Poetics* as saying that the fall of tragic heroes is due to "a flaw in their characters"—a mistaken Renaissance interpretation of Aristotle's concept of *hamartia* ("error," "mistake") that has been vigorously rejected by modern scholars with a remarkable degree of consensus. Aristotle, in fact, explicitly distinguishes such "mistakes" from flaws in character.

More prominent still in Bloom's central argument is his claim about ancient views of emotion. The modern feminist attempts to encourage men to be less "macho" and aggressive is criticized on the grounds that "the psychology of the ancients" shows the futility of this "nasty" attempt:

> Machismo—the polemical description of maleness or spiritedness, which was the central *natural* passion in men's souls in the psychology of the ancients, the passion of attachment and loyalty—was the villain, the source of difference between the sexes. . . . A host of Dustin Hoffman and Meryl Streep types invade the schools . . . and it is indeed possible to soften men. But to make them "care" is another thing, and the project must inevitably fail. . . . It must fail because in an age of

individualism persons of either sex cannot be forced to be public-spirited, particularly by those who are becoming less so.

Here, as so often, one senses an absence of philosophical argument. The appeal to the authority of "the ancients" is no substitute. But if in fact Plato, Aristotle, and the major Hellenistic philosophers, Epicurean, Skeptic, and Stoic (Hellenistic philosophy is explicitly included in the category "ancients" by Bloom's numerous references to Cicero and Plutarch), *had* all arrived, by agreement, at Bloom's conclusion about the moderation of "spiritedness," this would be an interesting fact, and would call for reflection.

Do they? Not in the least. All major Greek thinkers about the passions of the soul—including Plato, Aristotle, Epicureans, Stoics, and Skeptics—agree that beliefs that are learned, and are not "natural," are important elements in the formation of passions such as anger, fear, and grief. For this reason, the passions can be modified by a modification of belief. Furthermore, all hold that the grief, fear, anger (etc.) that most people feel are based, to one or another extent, on beliefs that are *false*, and that the passions, therefore, *should* be modified by a modification of belief. "Spiritedness" is Bloom's translation of Plato's words *thumos* and *to thumoeides*; these are generic words for the part of the soul that is the seat of the emotions, as opposed to the appetites—of, for example, anger, pity, grief, fear, as opposed to hunger and thirst. These words are also used to refer in particular to one of the soul's passions, the passion of anger. Plato shows in *Republic* II–III how the modification of beliefs can transform both men's and women's experience of many kinds of *thumos*—especially of fear and grief. He does allow certain members of the city (there is no reason to think them all male) to retain the capacity for anger—this is the part of Plato's view that I suppose Bloom is alluding to in his talk of "spiritedness." They retain that passion for military purposes.

All Greek thinkers after Plato, however, agree that this angry and reactive aspect of the soul (which they find in both men and women) is one of the central dangers in human life. Aristotle and his Peripatetic successors urge that it be retained but moderated, by cultivating correct beliefs about what is really an insult or damage, and what is not. They praise the virtue of "mildness of temper." The three Hellenistic schools denounce the passion far more strongly, as part of a general condemnation of the passions, treating all of them as artificial creations of corrupt society, and obsessively reflecting on devices to bring about their complete elimination.

A thinker who truly loves ancient Greek and Roman philosophy, whose "substance" has been "informed" by its greatest books, could not fail to be aware of Cicero's *Tusculan Disputations*, Philodemus' *On Anger*, Plutarch's *On Being Without Anger*, Seneca's *On Anger* and *On Mercy*, Diogenes Laertius' *Lives* of Pyrrho, Zeno, and Chrysippus, and the fragments of Chrysippus' *On the Passions*. These works argue with commitment and precision against Bloom's view of the passion of "spiritedness," denying both its naturalness and its value. Such a thinker would surely remember Seneca's *Letter* 22, in which the voice of nature herself speaks, telling the reader that she is not responsible for the passions, which she calls "plagues" infecting human life. Such a thinker would be aware that Diogenes' *Life of Pyrrho* makes explicit the connections between eliminating the passions and altering some of the ways men and women conventionally behave. The philosopher Pyrrho, in his improved and "mild" state, is praised for helping his sister with the dusting and marketing. These are not out-of-the-way texts. They are well-known and central. But Bloom, while claiming to be a lover of the ancients, simply ignores all texts that contradict his thesis.

The same question arises in connection with Bloom's more general assault on feminism as contrary to nature. Bloom tells us that feminism is "not founded on nature," and that it ends "in forgetting nature and using force to refashion human beings to secure that justice." Here again he refers to the ancient Greek tradition: not to Aristotle, who would have subscribed to his view, but whose supporting arguments about female biology are too evidently false to support a contemporary claim. Instead he appeals both to the ancient tradition in general and especially to Plato, arguing in his characteristic fashion that the explicit proposals of Socrates defending the equal education of women in the *Republic* conceal Plato's real meaning, which is actually to attack, as impossible and bad, the idea that females might "have the same education, live the same lives and do the same jobs as men."

Bloom does not mention here the evidence of Aristotle, who, after having lived and talked with Plato for twenty years, takes these proposals absolutely seriously and argues against them. He is silent about the actual lives of Spartan women, who exemplify certain of these freedoms, and are criticized by Aristotle on this account. He does not mention the well-known evidence of Oxyrynchus Papyrus 3656, which establishes firmly that Plato took the radical step (for Athens) of teaching women in his philosophical school—a fact that surely sheds light on the *Republic's* intentions.[5]

In his general discussion of "the ancients" on this topic he is entirely silent about Epicurus' support for the teaching of women; and, above all, about prominent Stoic arguments concerning women's nature, well summarized in the passage of Musonius Rufus that I have already cited. Musonius argues that nature actually *requires* that both men and women pursue philosophy, and pursue it in a way that connects it to practical and social activities. When Bloom is silent about evidence such as this, evidence that is not obscure, but is well-known and essential, what are we to think of his attitude toward his readers, and toward the books with which he claims to live? . . .

3.

But if we approach Bloom's book expecting it to be a work of Socratic philosophy, answering the Socratic demand for definitions, explanations, and rational arguments, we may be mistaking its purpose. Portions of the book, especially in its early chapters, do indeed seem to defend a conception of philosophy much like that shared by Socrates and the Stoics, according to which philosophy is each individual person's search for the good through active reasoning and critical argument. On this view of philosophy's role in human life, we would expect the claim that philosophy should be at the heart of the university in American democracy to be a claim that in this democracy each and every person ought to have both the opportunity and the incentive to engage in studies that awaken the rational search for a good life. But in the later chapters of Bloom's book, in which Bloom turns from negative argument to the statement of his own position, a very different conception emerges both of philosophy and of the university as teacher of philosophy in a democracy. This conception, which is the one Bloom seems most deeply drawn to when speaking in his own voice, is of a philosophy that is not practical, alive, and broadly distributed, but contemplative and quasi-religious, removed from ethical and social concerns, and the preserve of a narrow elite.

This shift is prepared for earlier, since from the opening of the book, Bloom presents himself to us as a profoundly religious man, who deplores the decline of revealed religion and of the Bible's authority in American society. He speaks with nostalgia of "the gripping inner life vouchsafed those who were nurtured by the Bible." He praises the life of his grandparents as a life "based on the Book"; and for him "a life based on the Book is closer to the truth" and "provides the material for deeper research in and access to the real nature of things." He approves of the old idea that the highest aspiration one might have for one's children "is for them to be wise—as priests, prophets or philosophers are wise"—not suggesting that there is any salient difference between the philosopher and the other two. For his own description of "the philosophic use of reason" he cites Maimonides:

> This then will be a key permitting one to enter places the gates to which were locked. And when these gates are opened and these places are entered into, the soul will find rest therein, the eyes will be delighted, and the bodies will be eased of their toil and of their labor.

This is a conception of philosophy quite alien to the Socrates of the *Apology* and the *Euthyphro*—and, indeed, to very many of the greatest philosophers in the Western tradition, for whom the essence of philosophy is not mystical wisdom but careful reasoning, and for whom there is no rest and no ease so long as any intellectual or moral challenge remains, as it always does for human beings, to be seriously examined.

The Socratic conception of philosophy naturally led, in the practice of the Greek Stoics, to the conclusion that each and every human being can have and ought to have the chance to have a philosophical education. For Socratic philosophizing is based on nothing more specialized than the active use of practical reason, which seems to be the common and universal possession of all humans. And if, as Socrates said, "the unexamined life is not worth living for a human being," it might seem to follow that a society dedicated to securing, for its members, the conditions of a full and worthwhile life would have a duty to make sure that they could get this higher education.

The pressure for degrees and credentials has many sources in our society. But it is this Socratic idea, I believe, that gives fundamental legitimacy to democratizing higher education in America. It is an idea deeply connected with democracy's respect for each person's rational powers. Bloom's final rejection of democracy, and of the democratization of philosophy, are connected, I believe, with his very different conception of philosophy's nature and role. Because philosophy is not the active development of each person's own practical reason, but a specialized search, carried on through esoteric books, for a contemplative theoretical wisdom, it is, according to Bloom, open only to a few specially equipped "natures," and cannot be democratized without loss of standards. And because it cannot be democratized, and because its protection is, Bloom argues, the essential function of the university, he concludes that the university, in its essential nature, is, though within democracy, an undemocratic and even anti-democratic institution.

Early in his book Bloom criticizes today's students by citing Plato's description of the democratic man from *Republic* VIII; later on, he makes Plato's attack on the democratic soul apply to modern democratic society in general. "The deepest intellectual weakness of democracy is its lack of taste or gift for the theoretical life," he writes; and he concludes that the function of the university in a democracy is to create a living alternative to democratic leveling and debasement, making it possible for "the rarest talents" to turn to the best way of life, the philosophical life (also called "the highest life"). The Bloomian university does not see itself as having any practical social aim, even the aim of educating citizens so that they will govern their own ethical lives better and more reflectively. For according to Bloom the aim of the "highest life" is to depart from the ethical and social life altogether, to find a permanent "wisdom," and to "find rest" in it.

Furthermore, Bloom derives from his idiosyncratic reading of "the ancients" the tragic moral that the relationship between the true philosopher and the "many" in a democracy must be hostile; and it must be hostile by "nature," since the "many" always fear death and therefore seek only "vulgar" satisfactions. The philosopher alone is above such fears. Being above them, he is also, says Bloom, above the moral and political life, and will seek to live apart from the people. "Changing the character of his relationship to them is impossible because the disproportion between him and them is firmly rooted in nature. Thus, he has no expectation of essential progress."

Bloom's contemplative conception of philosophy seems remarkably empty of content, since his account of philosophical activity evinces no interest in the traditional subjects of "the contemplative life," such as metaphysics, cosmology, and mathematics. Nonetheless, in the name of the contemplative, his conception teaches the would-be philosopher to look down on ethical concerns and the search for social justice. Universities, standing in the midst of corrupt and hostile democracies, must not, Bloom argues, seek to improve them—even, apparently, by training citizens to be more ethically reflective or by searching for better moral or political or economic theories. They must simply protect the nonethical life of wisdom, as Bloom understands it, making sure that the few specially chosen "natures" who are suited for this life will be able to lead it. Thus, Bloom is really proposing that the function of the entire American university system should be to perfect and then protect a few contemplative souls, whose main subject matter will, apparently, be the superiority of their own contemplative life to the moral and political life. Now we see why Bloom talked only about the elite from the beginning: because his "highest" goal has nothing to do with the good life of anyone else, and, indeed, nothing to do with morality and justice.

Bloom's proposals can be criticized on many fronts. But above all it is important to see plainly what he intends the university to be. Those who believe that the highest search for the truth does not turn away from concern for the quality of moral and social life and that the universities of America should exist for the sake of all its citizens, not only for the sake of a few, must find themselves opposed to Bloom's conception. In defending their position, they will find, contrary to Bloom's claims, strong support from the arguments of the ancient Greek thinkers, and especially of the Stoics, who spoke so eloquently of practical reason as a universal human possession, whose cultivation is a central human need.

And what of the curriculum? The Stoics saw that, in order to extend the benefits of higher education to all human beings, teaching would have to be responsive to the needs of many different types of human beings. This is why they held that a good teacher is like a good doctor, flexible and responsive to individuality. Bloom is concerned with only one narrow group of students; even in discussing this group he does not seem interested in their individuality. Thus it is easy for him to believe that a single simple solution will suffice for college teaching.

Even for the narrow group described, it is not at all obvious that the best way to induce genuine reflection is to make a list of the Great Books of the Western tradition and to require their study of all students. There are many evident problems with that approach, even apart from the special aristocratic use to which Bloom himself wishes to put it.[6] The study of great works of philosophy can indeed enliven the mind. But required lists of Great Books encourage passivity and reverence, rather than active critical reflection; they inevitably select certain texts over others of equal intrinsic worth for reasons having to do with fashion and prejudice, and then tend to tell the student that these are the really "Great" ones, and all that he or she centrally needs to know. (This is the way to Bloom's contemptuous ignorance of non-Western traditions.)

Such courses, furthermore, are likely to be taught without sufficient grounding in the historical setting and even the languages of the texts studied. (For even if one shares Bloom's opposition to relativism and historicism, as I do, one needs to know a great deal of history to know what a text of an ancient author is actually asserting.) The advantages of the Great Books approach in encouraging cohesiveness and community among students who will share knowledge of central texts—advantages which are genuine enough—may be offset by these disadvantages. Perhaps they can be overcome; but Bloom does not show us how.

But the real problem with Bloom's advice on curriculum is the problem of the book as a whole: that it is not informed by concern for the diverse needs of diverse groups of American students. If we follow, in place of Bloom's aristocratic argument, the Stoic argument I have described, we will surely require a quite different approach to teaching. Such an approach, combining a universal and nonrelative account of human needs with a refined sensitivity to students' actual social situations, can be found, I suggest, in the wise and humane book, *General Education in a Free Society*, written at Harvard in 1945 by a committee including Paul Buck, John H. Finley, Jr., I.A. Richards, George Wald, and others.[7] This book invites comparison with Bloom's because of its praise of ancient Greek models, and its rejection of an education based on narrow specialization in favor of one that is "preparation for life in the broad sense of completeness as a human being." But it is miles away from Bloom's in its evident affection for the entire country of diverse people whose education it proposes to discuss, and in the tentative subtlety with which it investigates the problem of creating a program of general education in college and university curricula for this diverse population.

The report opens with the affirmation of a statement by the then president of Harvard, James Bryant Conant: "The primary concern of American education today is not the development of the appreciation of the 'good life' in young gentlemen born to the purple. It is the infusion of the liberal and humane tradition into our entire educational system." And the authors describe their conception of education's central purpose in a way that both explicitly refers to the Socratic-Stoic tradition and links that tradition, plausibly, with the American democratic belief in the equality of citizens and in the equal need of all for rational education:

> The task of modern democracy is to preserve the ancient ideal of liberal education and to extend it as far as possible to all the members of the community. . . . To believe in the equality of human beings is to believe that the good life, and the education which trains the citizen for the good life, are equally the privilege of all. And these are the touchstones of the liberated man: first, is he free; that is to say, is he able to judge and plan for himself, so that he can truly govern himself? In order to do this, his must be a mind capable of self-criticism; he must lead that self-examined life which according to Socrates is alone worthy of a free man. Thus he will possess inner freedom, as well as social freedom. Second, is he universal in his motives and sympathies? For the civilized man is a citizen of the entire universe; he has overcome provincialism, he is objective, and is a "spectator of all time and all existence." Surely these two are the very aims of democracy itself.

But this application of the Socratic-Stoic tradition leads the authors to reject a single curricular solution, as insufficiently attentive to the needs of different groups of students. Instead, they describe several essential human capacities that education ought to develop, and the sorts of knowledge that, in general, will be suited to the development of these abilities in various parts of life. Then they sketch tentatively a variety of different ways in which curricula might, in different circumstances, approach this common task, speaking in detail only about the special case of Harvard, whose students' needs are not alleged to be either the same as or any more important than those of any other group.

An important difference between their curricular proposals and Bloom's is their insistence on the importance of history, both as a subject of study in its own right, and as a component in the study of philosophical and literary texts. Bloom gives history little place in the curriculum—apparently because he believes that it will distract students from the realization that the greatest truths are timeless. The Harvard authors plausibly insist that we cannot see how to bring timeless standards of goodness to our own society unless we have understood what possibilities historical change have made available to human beings at different times and in different places. Thus the Stoic goal of becoming a citizen of the entire universe not only does not undermine but actually promotes the claim of history to a central place in the curriculum.

There are difficulties with the Harvard report's approach; there is much vagueness. And in the authors' silence about the education of women they do not follow well the Stoic thinkers whose views about rational self-government they so eloquently invoke. But the report should be revived for our close study, as an example of genuinely democratic thought about higher education in its relationship to human diversity and human need. And its hopeful humility, in the face of the complexity of this problem, should provide a counterpoise to Bloom's stridently confident pessimism, and encouragement to those of us who do not accept Bloom's conclusion that real philosophical education must be at odds with democratic values.

According to Bloom's dark vision, the Muse who inspired the Great Books of the ancient Greek world would be horrified at the chaos of contemporary America. She would surely flee for comfort, if she could, behind the walls of a privileged elite university, there to talk about hidden truths with a few chosen souls. Walt Whitman, a different sort of admirer of ancient Greek traditions, imagined the ancient Greek muse actually choosing America as her home, on account of its active vitality and its commitment to the worth of each human being's self-development. In his poem "Song of the Exposition," he imagines this Muse migrating and settling down, not deterred from her inspirational role by the presence of rough conditions, creating, like this democracy, in the midst of labor and alongside laboring men and women.

We see her

> *vigorously clearing a path for herself, striding through*
> the confusion,
> *By thud of machinery and shrill steam-whistle undismay'd,*
> *Bluff'd not a bit by drain-pipe, gasometers, artificial fertilizers,*
> *Smiling and pleas'd with palpable intent to stay.*

This is democratic romanticism. That does not make it either false or impossible. It expresses a noble wish for a country in which the souls of all citizens would flourish, each in its own setting, and find respect. We might consider it, as an antidote to Bloom's apocalypse, and as the opening to a genuinely democratic discussion of democratic education.

---

[1] Musonius Rufus, *Should Women Too Do Philosophy?*, Teubner edition by O. Hense (Leipzig: 1905); see also C.E. Lutz, *Yale Classical Studies* (1947), p. 3ff.

[2] See Martha Nussbaum and Amartya K. Sen, "Internal Criticism and Indian Rationalist Traditions," a Working Paper of the World Institute for Development Economics Research, Helsinki, and to be published in *Relativism*, ed. M. Krausz (Notre Dame University Press, 1988); also Bimal K. Matilal, *Perception* (Oxford University Press, 1985).

[3] See especially Benjamin Schwartz, *The World of Thought in Ancient China* (Harvard University Press, 1985).

[4] The same view is asserted in Bloom's notes to his translation of the *Republic* (Basic Books, 1968), without any more satisfactory argument than what is presented here.

[5] For this and other related evidence, and a discussion, see Mary R. Lefkowitz, *Women in Greek Myth* (Johns Hopkins University Press, 1986), p. 144.

[6] A different and genuinely democratic approach to core requirements (at the level of elementary and

secondary, not university, education) is carefully argued for in E.D. Hirsch, Jr., *Cultural Literacy: What Every American Needs to Know* (Houghton Mifflin, 1987).

[7] See reference above, note 2. The committee that prepared the report was chaired by Paul H. Buck; John H. Finley, Jr., was vice-chairman. Its members were: Raphael Demos, Leigh Hoadley, Byron S. Hollinshead, Wilbur K. Jordan, I.A. Richards, Phillip J. Rulon, Arthur M. Schlesinger, Robert Ulich, George Wald, and Benjamin F. Wright.

35

Allan Bloom and the Critics

WERNER J. DANNHAUSER

Everyone I know predicted that the *New York Review of Books* would trash *The Closing of the American Mind*, but who would do the trashing? The assignment fell to Martha Nussbaum, a classical scholar. If she failed in writing the world's most devastating put-down it was not for lack of trying, but because, as my unscientific survey reveals, so many people had difficulty coping with her tiresome prose.

Professor Nussbaum's review (November 15, 1987) bore the title "Undemocratic Vistas," and Bloom was denounced not as un-American, but as undemocratic simply, an opponent to rule of the many, an elitist. That labeling, however, was done more effectively a bit later by critics like Benjamin Barber. Her strangest characterizations of Bloom refer to his "religious conception of philosophy" and his presenting himself "as a profoundly religious man." In this respect, she might enter into a fruitful dialogue with Robert Bellah and Kenneth Minogue; may the best person win.

More nearly novel is Professor Nussbaum's depiction of Bloom as a sexist; she provides the scholarly background for Betty Friedan's remark that Bloom wants to put women back in their girdles. Leaving foundation garments aside, I take Professor Nussbaum's argument to run as follows. According to the Stoics, who were correct, philosophical education should be practical, active, and "*broadly distributed*" (emphasis hers), which is to say that both men and women can "do" philosophy. Feminism is one of Bloom's "central targets," and Bloom also alleges that Plato is not serious about the equal education of women in *The Republic*. How this chain hangs together beats me, for why shouldn't somebody who detests excessive feminism and who doubts Socrates' seriousness in Book V of *The Republic* nevertheless preach and practice the equal education of women in today's world, as Bloom does? But one must assume this line of reasoning if one is to account for Nussbaum's beginning with a long quotation from Musonius Rufus, "the distinguished Roman Stoic philosopher." Why couldn't she come up with a similar quotation from Epictetus and/or Cicero? Why does she have to rely on "the well-known evidence of Oxyrynchus Papyrus 3656"?

As can be seen from these samples, Professor Nussbaum's learning is nothing if not ostentatious, and she places it in the service of her primary mission, the discrediting of Bloom's scholarship; a task for which she arms herself with six hefty footnotes. Some of these are simply ridiculous, as when she illustrates Bloom's "startling ignorance" of the critical and rationalist tradition of

---

See the main body of this essay in chapter 1, and additional excerpts in chapter 4 and chapter 7.

Classical Indian Thought, by referring to a piece of work Bloom could not have read because it has not yet been published—a work co-authored by Martha Nussbaum. Another one is surpassingly odd and raises the crux of her case against Bloom.

Having tartly noted Bloom's general failure to provide "precise references" for his interpretations of classical philosophy, Nussbaum makes an imprecise exception for a definite interpretation Bloom presents at the length of "about a page and a half," in which he "alleges that *The Republic* does not seriously propose the ideal city, the rule of philosophers, or the equal education of women. *The Republic*, he writes, ironically undercuts itself and actually teaches to those in the know the impossibility of what it seems to advocate." Now Bloom does hold this view, but no such passage exists in *The Closing of the American Mind*. The footnote asserts that the same view is asserted in Bloom's notes to his translation of *The Republic*. Wrong again: it is asserted in the interpretive essay accompanying the translation, which, by the way, all by itself attests to Bloom's competence to deal with classical texts.

Much is at stake here. Nussbaum introduces an issue Bloom raises *elsewhere* in order to find him and "his teacher, Leo Strauss" incompetent as interpreters of classical philosophy. She is far too certain of her ground when she maintains quite erroneously that Bloom's and Strauss's view is "bizarre and not accepted by any major non-Straussian interpreter" of *The Republic*. Before the nineteenth century, and even later if one counts Nietzsche, that view was held by thinkers of the stature of Cicero, Thomas More, Rousseau, and Pascal. Let a quotation from Pascal suffice to make my point, because unlike Nussbaum, he does not differentiate at all in this respect between Plato and Aristotle:

> If they [Plato and Aristotle] wrote on politics, it was as if laying down rules for a lunatic asylum; and if they presented the appearance of speaking of a great matter, it was because they knew that the madmen, to whom they spoke, thought they were kings and emperors. They entered into their principles in order to make their madness as little harmful as possible.

36

American Feminists *versus* Allan Bloom

PAMELA PROIETTI

Betty Friedan, in the previous essay, asserts that Bloom is an ally of those male reactionaries who want "to put [women] back in that girdle." The "girdle," which both distorted and weakened the bodies of otherwise healthy women, becomes a symbol for Friedan of the way in which patriarchy distorted the souls of women. She views his commentary on feminism and modern family life as some sort of rationale for the narrow conservative goal of returning women to thralldom in the patriarchal family of our past.

American women owe a debt of gratitude to Friedan and the many other feminist writers and activists who have helped to make our lives more fully human. Over the course of more than a century, feminist political agitators have won for American women the right to vote and the federal courts' belated recognition of a woman's right to the "equal protection of the laws," and thus have given countless numbers of women access to those public professions which allow women more fully to develop their human potential. Most of these vast changes in women's lives are today accepted by an overwhelming majority of Americans as both just and socially advantageous. Bloom himself acknowledges the irreversibility of these reforms, although many of his feminist critics seem to ignore this aspect of Bloom's arguments.

Clearly no professional woman today can decently fail to acknowledge the debt she owes to the American feminist movement. Yet feminist writers truly have not made the major contributions to scholarship that they credit themselves with. The vast majority of self-professed feminist scholars have found it impossible to read the major works of Western philosophy with the openness required to understand the atonishing originality of these great minds. (One may take as an example what has come to be regarded as a "classic" work of feminist scholarship, Susan Moller Okin's commentary on Aristotle in *Women in Western Political Thought*. Okin persistently assumes what she wishes, but fails, to prove: that Aristotle is a simple elitist and misogynist. Her reading of Plato portrays a somewhat more complicated misogyny.) Feminist commentators, Betty Friedan among them, have read Bloom in the same manner, that is they were predisposed to think of Bloom as the Enemy.

Perhaps it is inevitable that a movement leading to so many important changes in law and society would subordinate the somewhat idle pursuit of knowledge to more pressing political goals. The partisan animus that has led to such poor scholarship has also allowed for the dissemination of those simplistic

---

Pamela Proietti teaches at the University of Dallas. This essay © 1988 by Pamela Proietti.

teachings that are so useful to democratic reform movements. A more balanced account of the tradition would probably lead to political inaction, as an inevitable consequence of the confusion it would engender in the minds of the intended audience. My radical feminist friends have often reminded me of this political truism.

Yet feminist critics are mistaken in their assumption that Bloom has some sort of political agenda in mind as he writes these criticisms of the world we Americans now inhabit. Perhaps most feminists make this mistake because they themselves have a political agenda in mind whenever they write anything. If Bloom does have a "political" agenda, it seems to be confined to the politics of the university. He doesn't appear to be much interested in what is going on outside of the university, except insofar as it restricts the possibilities for the pursuit of wisdom within the university. His forceful attack on the feminist attempts to refashion the university curriculum stems from his justifiable fears that good books will no longer be read with the necessary seriousness and openness in the American university of the near future. Once radical feminists have banished serious reading of great Western philosophers from undergraduate education, they will also have unwittingly destroyed the moral and philosophical foundation of feminism itself.

Bloom does not make much effort to disguise his true beliefs, as had Aristotle and other philosophic critics of their own societies. In fact, he does very little to disguise the fact that the patriotic introductory chapter of his book contradicts the core teachings of the book, which are not truly democratic and not exactly supportive of the ideas of natural rights and natural equality upon which he initially lavishes so much praise. Given Bloom's transparency, the feminist misinterpretations of his arguments seem to be the result of sheer paranoia, whereas the feminist misreadings of a thinker such as Aristotle could plausibly be viewed as honest mistakes. Feminist readers of Bloom have ignored such statements as the following: "I am not arguing here that the old family arrangements were good or that we should or could go back to them. I am only insisting that we not cloud our vision to such an extent that we believe that there are viable substitutes for them just because we want or need them" (p. 130).

The feminists' criticism of Bloom assumes that anyone who finds serious defects in the newly emerging family must be advocating some sort of return to patriarchy. But we are never told why we should interpret doubts about the health of the modern family as a veiled endorsement of patriarchy. Many readers will be impressed by the accuracy of Bloom's description of our present predicament. The discussion of love and of *eros* at the end of Part I is remarkable for its insight and clarity. The entire first section of the book is a *tour de force* as an analysis of modern American culture. It reminds this reader of de Tocqueville's study of American democracy, and many critics have noted that the first part of the book is the most powerful of the book's three sections. Most of my colleagues were unable to stop reading the book, whether or not they agreed with Bloom's arguments, until they had finished Part I.

Bloom describes his own approach to questions of love and erotic desire when he asserts that his virtue consists in "knowing that I do not know" (p. 134).

Feminist readers could learn much by taking this Socratic disclaimer seriously, but they are as unlikely to do so as were the democratic citizens of ancient Athens. Bloom takes, on the whole, a rather distressing view of the American feminist movement and of recent changes in the American family. He is not giving a partisan opinion of the gains made by the American feminist movement, which he correctly regards as an inevitable political consequence of the radical individualism of modern political thought. Bloom is most eager to describe some of the consequences of the movement of women toward ever greater liberty and legal equality with men. What perhaps is so irksome to a feminist reader is that Bloom dwells upon all the negative and mostly unintended consequences of women's liberation from the private prison of the household.

True, it *may* be impossible for Bloom or any man (or, for that matter, any young woman today) to imagine what life in that "prison" was like, but that is not the issue here. What should be at issue is the accuracy and logical plausibility of Bloom's observations. Betty Friedan's critique studiously avoids directly confronting any of Bloom's arguments, and with good reason. Bloom is persuasive in his assessment of the underlying causes of the weakness of modern marriage and family relationships. The consequences of radical individualism and sexual liberation for marriage and family have been for many years painfully obvious. Liberal feminists (Friedan among them) are afraid that, if they acknowledge the existence of these problems, most Americans will see the feminists as the major cause of their problems and will blame the feminist political movement for having undermined the force of love and familial duty in the modern American family.

Much of what Bloom says of contemporary love and marriage was anticipated by previous thinkers, most notably Locke and Rousseau. When Bloom describes the uncertainty of modern marriage, he is echoing Paragraph #82 in Locke's *Second Treatise of Government*, with the notable difference that Bloom now speaks openly about a problem that Locke could only hint at in his times: "Neither men nor women have any idea what they are getting into any more, or, rather, they have reason to fear the worst. There are two equal wills, and no mediating principle to link them and no tribunal of last resort" (Bloom, pp. 126–127). Marriage today consists of two individuals who have both been taught that self-fulfillment is the goal of life and have also been taught that they need not sacrifice personal desire for the sake of higher duties. They feel themselves to be autonomous; they do not feel bound by any contractual duties beyond the time when that contract ceases to be pleasant.

Bloom reminds the reader that the subjection of women ensured that at least one partner was expected to sacrifice complete personal fulfillment for the sake of duty to children (p. 130). In reality, of course, both parents did this to a large extent. The jobs that most men were leaving the household for were not all that fulfilling either, as women were soon to learn. Although both partners could find reasons for dissatisfaction, husbands and wives were bound in duty to their children and to one another. In his brief study of the history of the American marriage, Bloom is more concerned with understanding the causes of the attenuation of that sense of duty that he is with either extolling or condemning the feminist movement. Bloom is interested in analyzing some of the obvious data on the breakdown of the American family. And he does a much better job of thinking through these problems than do his feminist critics, most of whom rely upon some facile suggestions about needing time to "reeducate" men toward new and better ideas and to convince government to establish a national day-care program for children. No one today, apart from the most rigidly doctrinaire feminist, believes in such simplistic "solutions" to our contemporary social ills.

Bloom, unlike his feminist critics, is eager to reflect upon the deeper significance of certain unpleasant facts: women, for the most part, remain attached to and supportive of their children, while an alarming number of men today appear to be much less interested in the welfare of their children (if we can deduce anything from the statistics regarding child custody suits and the widespread failure of fathers to pay court-mandated child-support payments). In the course of a thoughtful analysis of the modern family, Bloom demonstrates the plausibility of his premise that the patriarchal family must have provided a stronger bond between men and their families than is present in today's arrangements. His book provides an extended meditation on these important questions, and his arguments are convincing.

As women have become more independent and have developed their own lives outside of the home, men can no longer feel that they are needed by their wives and children, at least not in the same compelling and absolute way. These men are also no longer allowed to think of their wives and families as belonging to them in any sense, either noble or base. Wives are now independent "persons," and younger wives demand to be treated as such. The two careers of these two equal "persons" will not easily be harmonized one with the other. Each time one of the two faces a career move or advancement, the impact upon the other has to be discussed. When men had the only career outside of the home, this source of conflict was not present. Women themselves also no longer feel that they cannot get along in the world without a man. In fact mothers, who are concerned with the welfare of their children above all else, teach their daughters that men are unreliable today, that a women must have a career suitable for the support of herself and her children.

The real social and moral problem that American families face today is not that bogeyman of the feminists, the reestablishment of the traditional patriarchal family. Bloom is quite right when he exclaims that all of that has now "disintegrated" (p. 126). Patriarchy finally crumbled because the flawed foundation of patriarchal society could not endure against the onslaught of the moral challenges to its fundamental injustices (pp 127–131).

Patriarchy is clearly becoming an historical anachronism in modern Western societies. Locke was the first of many philosophers in modern times who have, with increasing boldness, openly challenged patriarchy. Bloom, three hundred years after Locke, is merely pointing out that we have found nothing satisfactory to take its place. If one judges from the point of view of children as well as the common good, one could argue that patriarchy was better than the moral vacuum that has replaced it. For all of its injustices to women, the patriarchal system was more beneficial to society's children than is the current state of psychological and (all too often) physical neediness that characterizes the majority of our children's lives. Surely feminists ought to care enough about our children to seriously consider Bloom's arguments.

Bloom's point is that this demise of patriarchy has placed more stress upon the family, due to the greater demands made upon men by women and the lessened moral or, to use an old-fashioned word, "spiritual" satisfaction that men are able to derive from the relationship. At the same time that marriage has become more stressful and less satisfying to men, other forces at work in Western society have encouraged both men and women to view natural selfishness as a legitimate basis for human choice. More powerful forces have drowned out the message of our churches that self-absorption is an evil to be overcome for the sake of the higher good of duty to others.

The feminist assault upon Bloom's book is misdirected, because the feminists deny the strongest and most irrefutable parts of Bloom's arguments, while they also misjudge the underlying intentions of the author. For this reason they are unable to grasp both the gist of Bloom's arguments and any of the *real* weaknesses of the book, weaknesses that might be apparent to less partisan readers.

It could be argued that the demise of patriarchy would not have had the disastrous effects which Bloom describes if it had not been accompanied by a lessening of the force of religious belief in the lives of most Americans. When a husband ceased to think of his wife and family as his property, might he have found a still stronger basis for family love in the Biblical portrayal of married love as an incarnation of divine love? But this was no longer as accessible to twentieth century man as it had been in past centuries.

The movement of modern philosophy, from Hobbes and Descartes to Rousseau and the Nietszche, led to a simultaneous decline in the status of religion and the status of reason. And the "dogmatic atheism" of modern sociology devalues the rational in man and in our tradition, and thus "culminates in the paradoxical conclusion that religion is the only thing that counts" (p. 211). Bloom articulates our modern philosophic and moral dilemma with exquisite clarity and forcefulness. But the reader is confused by Bloom's various and seemingly inconsistent representations of religion and reason. At one moment, Bloom celebrates the "spiritually rich" home of his Bible-educated and pious grandparents and suggests that they were "closer to the truth" than their American-educated grandchildren, who seem unable to think about the most fundamental human questions (p. 60). At other times, Bloom appears to endorse the understanding of Nietzsche and of our modern scientists that God is dead (pp. 180–207). Bloom even *appears* to believe that Plato's views on religion and on poetry closely parallel the views of Nietszche (p. 207). Thus we are led to wonder about Bloom's understanding of Plato's teaching on reason and the ground of reason. Does Bloom truly believe that Socrates and Plato provide a real alternative to modern nihilism, as he has occasionally implied (pp. 179, 269–274, 308)?

Bloom's prose style, ever enchanting, even seductive, is never more so than in the numerous passages in which he celebrates *eros* or laments its demise. He is so seductive that we may not be fully aware of what he is saying, or implying, when he so frequently links the "sexual" drive and the lust for wisdom. We ought to seek out the nature of this being, about whom Bloom asks: "Are we lovers anymore?" (p. 133).

The nature of man to which our traditional religious leaders speak is not the same nature of man which Bloom celebrates in his book, in which *eros*, as distinguished from "love," is central. (In the first part of the book, Bloom ends with a two-part discussion of love and *eros* [pp. 122–137]; yet it is solely the latter that becomes the central theme of the book. Here again Bloom is apparently following his teacher Rousseau.)

For this reader, Bloom's celebration of "*eros*" had an eerie and empty quality, and in this he may have a great deal in common with those contemporary feminist intellectuals whom he rightly condemns in his discussion of the modern university. Neither Bloom nor these feminists can adequately account for any *ground* of "self-fulfillment" or erotic longing. Bloom calls Nietzsche a "cultural relativist" whose attack on relativism and nihilism only served to worsen the problem Nietzsche was confronting (Bloom, pp. 198–202). Surely, however, Bloom's celebration of *eros* has the same unsettling effect that Nietzsche's supposed answer to nihilism has on his readers, Bloom among them. Bloom's celebration of erotic longing, in which *eros* is an end-in-itself, thus needing no teleological foundation, bears some lamentable resemblance to Nietzsche's celebration of the creativity of life-affirming values by the Superman.

Whether or not Bloom offers any real solutions to our present spiritual crisis, his description of this crisis is a thoughtful and compelling one. We should not ignore his timely reminder that what happens in American education will affect the political future of our nation and of the world. Many of Bloom's readers will be as concerned about the future of the United States as Bloom is about the future of philosophy. Bloom reminds us that these two goals, that of protecting philosophy and that of protecting the freedom of the United States and her Western allies, "are related as they have never been before" (p. 382). Liberal feminists are in truth undermining the cause of freedom and justice when they so thoughtlessly rail against Bloom's thoughtful analysis of the modern family and the modern university.

SEVEN

Minority Groups in the University

Is Bloom Right About Affirmative Action?

Charges of racism cling tenaciously to Bloom's book, arising for the most part from some brief, benevolently intended remarks about affirmative action. In fact, since these comments were not necessary for his larger thesis, they may have been imprudent precisely because they exposed him to charges of racism. The most damaging of these charges appeared in *The Chronicle of Higher Education* on January 20, 1988, in the text of a speech by Clifton R. Wharton, Jr., former chancellor of the State University of New York, who said that Bloom's views made "ordinary garden variety racism seem almost benign."

Werner J. Dannhauser here bemoans Wharton's "irresponsibility," and regrets that once the damage had been done it was difficult to repair. "Today the charges of racism and sexism are easy enough to refute but next to impossible to remove."

In fact, there has not been much fuel for this controversy from the black press. Reprinted here is an early review by Richard L. Wright of Howard University which appeared in *The Journal of Negro Education*. Wright does not mention Bloom's remarks about affirmative action at all. Instead he praises the book and says: "Such a critique of the university is bound to be disquieting to those historically disadvantaged populations who have been oriented to believe that their status and that of their children can be enhanced through the quality of education the university uniquely provides."

However, in the long essay in this chapter, George Anastaplo does challenge Bloom's comments on affirmative action. Bloom suggests that affirmative action (or "reverse discrimination" or "quotas") for minorities does not help them much in the short run and actually harms them in the long run because they feel inferior and segregate themselves defensively in the universities and in the larger society. Anastaplo gently takes Bloom to task for this view, arguing that affirmative action is politically useful because it makes minorities feel less forsaken. If properly understood and used carefully, it is harmless to professional standards and to the principle of equality before the law.

221

37

Allan Bloom and the Critics

WERNER J. DANNHAUSER

. . . *The Closing of the American Mind* contains not one shred of evidence for the charge of racism, a term with only one viable definition: the evil of inflicting injustice on other people for the sole reason of race. Bloom's "offense" has been to note, with sadness and regret, that relations between the races in the universities have deteriorated. He does severely criticize the idea of Black Power and affirmative action for their part in bringing about this lamentable state of affairs, but if one is unable to do that without incurring the ugliest of epithets, "racist"—and it begins to look like that—public discourse should close up shop.

Today the charges of racism and sexism are easy enough to refute but next to impossible to erase, having become the most obvious tools with which scoundrels can bludgeon those who see through them. As a result the universities, where these terms are bandied about recklessly, have become far less free than the surrounding society. . . .

See the main body of this essay in chapter 1.

38

Book Review:
The Closing of the American Mind
RICHARD L. WRIGHT

The text, *The Closing of the American Mind*, by Professor Allan Bloom, presents a devastating critique of American institutional life in general and of university life in particular. Bloom's pivotal thesis, as formulated in his own words, is that "higher education has failed democracy and impoverished the souls of today's students." There is not a single, significant dimension of American personal, interpersonal, social, institutional, philosophical, and intellectual life that remains unaddressed in a manner that can be characterized as no less than scathing. The sensitive and concerned reader leaves this book with the disturbing image of American society as a polluter of spirits, as a defiler of character, as intellectually bankrupt, and as unwilling or unable to recognize its essentially decadent and pathological state. Even the rock music industry is portrayed as "robber barons, who mine gold out of rock" and whose loud musical products not only make "conversation impossible," but are punctuated with "grunt formulas" constituting in essence a "gutter phenomenon" for American youth.

The university is the principal target of this penetrating assault, which addresses insightful attention to the 1960s, that period of student unrest, protest, and resulting professorial capitulation. A major tenet of the exposition is that the sixties challenged the university to reveal its character and substance, which it failed to do for lack of same. Accordingly, the university as an intellectual desert has not yet come to recognize that the students who enter come "uncivilized" and that the university has failed in its responsibility to civilize them. Such a critique of the university is bound to be disquieting to those historically disadvantaged American populations who have been oriented to believe that their status and that of their children can be enhanced through the quality of education that the university uniquely provides.

The text is certainly worth reading. It will make one angry, but not before it makes one think. As a seasoned and accomplished university professor, Bloom is qualified to view his topic from close range, citing numerous personal and illustrative experiences as support. His diversified array of material, both historical and contemporary, gives breadth and depth to his caustic analysis and disturbing conclusions. At times, the author falls into tedious diatribes which detract only minimally from his essential argument. Overall, his presentational format, his

---

Richard L. Wright is a professor in the School of Communications, Howard University. This review is reprinted with permission from the *Negro Journal of Education* vol 57, no. 1 (Winter 1988):119–121.

graphic and captivating manipulation of metaphor, and his experiential, historical, and referential support collectively make for a powerful statement—which may prove irritating but which cannot be ignored!

The university community, the book's primary audience, must digest and seriously reflect upon the challenge inherent in Bloom's denunciation of university life, which should not be viewed as the work of the enemy from within the ranks, but more productively as the candid yet caring thoughts of a sensitive, competent, and knowledgeable scholar who has lost faith in the mission of the university as it is presently constituted. This reflection is necessary in order for the university to recover its essential educational function. As Bloom concludes, essential questions do not always seek answers; their greatest merit is their ability to sustain continuing and permanent dialogue.

This text may provide the one great opportunity of this century, as we prepare for the next, for the university to accept the challenge to reflect critically and caringly upon itself. Bloom has provided the framework out of which such reflection might proceed.

39

Allan Bloom and Race Relations in the United States

GEORGE ANASTAPLO

Liberal education, which consists in the constant intercourse with the greatest minds, is a training in the highest form of modesty, not to say of humility. It is at the same time a training in boldness: it demands from us the complete break with the noise, the rush, the thoughtlessness, the cheapness of the Vanity Fair of the intellectuals as well as of their enemies. It demands from us the boldness implied in the resolve to regard the accepted views as mere opinions, or to regard the average opinions as extreme opinions which are at least as likely to be wrong as the most strange or the least popular opinions. Liberal education is liberation from vulgarity. The Greeks had a beautiful word for "vulgarity"; they called it apeirokalia, *lack of experience in things beautiful. Liberal education supplies us with experience in things beautiful.*
—Leo Strauss

I.

It is curious that Allan Bloom's learned jeremiad against contemporary higher education, *The Closing of the American Mind*, should have aroused the considerable interst that it evidently has in Canada. Not that Canadian educators do not confront, or at least see themselves as beginning to confront, conditions and problems similar to those faced by educators in the United States.

What makes the substantial Canadian interest curious is that many of the political, intellectual and social developments that Professor Bloom points to as critical to the subversion of education in the United States have not yet been as much a part of the Canadian experience. Thus, for example, the Sixties academic experiences in the United States, which seem so critical to Mr. Bloom's account, have had few or no counterparts in English-speaking Canada. Mr. Bloom, who taught at the University of Toronto for several years, is no doubt aware of this.

Of course, Canadian universities and education have been affected by developments in the United States. But, perhaps much more important, all of Western civilization has been radically transformed by modern science and by the technology made possible, if not even dictated, by that science. Surprisingly little

George Anastaplo is Professor of Law, Loyola University of Chicago; and Lecturer in the Liberal Arts, the University of Chicago. This paper was presented at the Canadian Learned Societies Conference, Windsor, Ontario, June 10, 1988. Copyright 1988 by George Anastaplo.

is made by Mr. Bloom of this profound transformation, which has been dramatized by the effects of automobiles and movies after the First World War and of
aviation, medicine, and television after the Second World War. Among the side
effects of modern science have been a sustained challenge to the ancients, a
supposedly informed replacement of the classics by more "relevant" works, and a
radical revision of the sense of community, not least with respect to religious
affiliations. Programs in general enlightenment and in education on an unprecedented scale have both contributed to and drawn upon these effects of modern
science.

II.

Canadians can find in Mr. Bloom's book not only concerns similar to theirs about
education but other enduring concerns as well. One such concern takes the form
of the question, "What country have I?"

Mr. Bloom is seen by some as too "European," that is, Continental. He has
for decades now seemed more at home in France than in the United States,
especially the United States in its more puritanical mode. He can also be
recognized as not sufficiently grounded in the American regime to be able to
minister to it reliably. Some even suspect he enjoys "America-bashing," as he
looks down on unsophisticated countrymen who do not appreciate as he does
either the accomplishments or the dangers of the German metaphysicians.

Canadians, too, can wonder about what defines their country. They, too,
can look abroad for guidance—but to Great Britain much more than to the
Continent. (Quebec has a peculiar relation with France, more with Eighteenth-
Century than with Twentieth-Century France in critical respects.) When English-
speaking Canadians look abroad for guidance, they can find in Britain a healthier
political tradition than that available on the Continent, a tradition not altogether
unlike that found in the United States as well.

III.

Mr. Bloom is perhaps at his most appreciative of his country in what he says about
its ability to assimilate immigrants. The principle of equality is deeply rooted in
the United States and is pervasive in its influence. (See *Closing*, e.g., p. 89.)

Thus, Mr. Bloom testifies to what Jews have been able to become and to do
in the United States (*Closing*, p. 53):

> Frenchness is defined by participation in [the French] language, its literature and the
> entire range of effects it produces. Somehow the legalistic arguments about rights
> [in France] do not touch the privilege conveyed by participation in it. In America
> there are in principle no real outsiders, while in France persons who, although
> citizens, are marginal to this tradition, for example, Jews, have always had to think
> hard about what it is they belong to. In France, the Jew's relation to what is
> constitutionally French is a great and complex literary theme. The response to the
> issue is not universal and causes the development of an interesting spectrum of
> human types. A Jew in America, by contrast, is as American as anyone; and if he is
> singled out or treated differently, unconditional outrage is the appropriate response.

This state of affairs is compared by Mr. Bloom with race relations in the
United States. He, in his portrait of university students in his country, opens the

half-dozen pages he devotes to the topic, "Race," with these remarks (*Closing*, p. 91):

> The one eccentric element in this portrait, the one failure—a particularly grave one inasmuch as it was the part most fraught with hope—is the relation between blacks and whites. White and black students do not in general become real friends with one another. Here the gulf of difference has proved unbridgeable. The forgetting of race in the university, which was predicted and comfortably expected [Predicted and expected by whom? one might well ask Mr. Bloom] when the barriers were let down, has not occurred. There is now a large black presence in major universities, frequently equivalent to their proportion in the general population. But they have, by and large, proved indigestible. Most keep to themselves. . . . The programmatic brotherhood of the Sixties did not culminate in integration but veered off toward black separation. White students feel uncomfortable about this and do not like to talk about it. This is not the way things are supposed to be.

It is salutary to explore here what Mr. Bloom says in his subsection on "Race," using this as my point of departure in glancing at critical aspects of his general discussion of education. (I have had occasion to develop a systematic critique of *Closing* in the 1988 volume of *The Great Ideas Today*, an Encyclopedia Britannica publication.) I will try to present my remarks on this occasion in a way appropriate for a Canadian audience.

IV.

Mr. Bloom, as he surveys race relations in the United States, seems to suggest that whites (not only students but their teachers and perhaps their parents as well) have done almost all they can reasonably be expected to do to secure racial justice. Consider, for example, this passage (*Closing*, p. 92):

> I do not believe this somber situation is the fault of the white students, who are rather straightforward in such matters and frequently embarrassingly eager to prove their liberal credentials in the one area where Americans are especially sensitive to a history of past injustice. These students have made the adjustment, without missing a beat, to a variety of religions and nationalities, the integration of Orientals and the change in women's aspirations and roles. It would require a great deal of proof to persuade me that they remain subtly racist. Although preferential treatment of blacks goes against a deep-seated conviction that equal rights belong to individuals and are color-blind, white students have been willing by and large to talk themselves into accepting affirmative action as a temporary measure on the way to equality. . . . So the tendency among white students is to suppress the whole question, act as though it were not there, and associate with the minority of blacks who want to be associated with and forget the rest. They cannot befriend blacks as blacks, and the heady days of a common purpose are gone. The discriminatory laws are ancient history, and there are large numbers of blacks in the universities. There is nothing more that white students can do to make great changes in their relations to black students.

I note in passing that the fundamental issue here is not whether anyone is "racist," subtly or otherwise. Certainly, Mr. Bloom himself should not be accused, or even suspected of "racism." Rather, he is to be commended for his instructive frankness about a troublesome subject.

Mr. Bloom's account of the Sixties, and particularly of the troubles at Cornell in which he ineffectually participated, again and again touches upon the race-relations issue. He observes, for example (*Closing*, pp. 334–335),

Under pressure from students the Founding was understood to be racist, and the very instrument that condemned slavery and racism was broken. The races in the Northern universities have grown more separate since the Sixties. After the theory of the rights of man was no longer studied or really believed, its practice also suffered. The American university provided the intellectual inspiration for decent political deeds. It is very doubtful whether there is a teaching about justice within it now that could again generate anything like the movement toward racial equality. The very thing the Sixties students prided themselves on was one of their premier victims.

We have noticed that Mr. Bloom has said (*Closing*, p. 92), "There is nothing more that white students can do to make great changes in their relations to black students." It can seem to the typical reader of Mr. Bloom's book that what he says here about white students is believed by him to apply also to universities at large, if not also to the United States generally—that there is nothing, or at least little, more that can be done to improve race relations. Those of you familiar with long-standing differences here in Canada between the dominant English-speaking elements and the aggrieved French-speaking elements may recall the repeated heartfelt insistence in our own time by the English-speaking that there was nothing more they could do to improve relations, that it really was up to the French-speaking to take advantage of the great opportunities offered in Canada to everyone who was willing to throw off outmoded and crippling allegiances and to work hard in an ever-growing economy.

Again I quote from Mr. Bloom, this time a passage that young people tell me they find particularly offensive (*Closing*, p. 93):

Blacks are not sharing a special positive intellectual or moral experience; they partake fully in the common culture, with the same goals and tastes as everyone else, but they are doing it by themselves. They continue to have the inward sentiments of separateness caused by exclusion when it no longer effectively exists. The heat is under the pot, but they do not melt as have *all* other groups.

In short, "they" do not know what is good for them?

V.

The Quebec parallels are instructive in examining race relations in the United States. Consider, on the one hand, English-speaking concerns over the years about the special privileges, subsidies, and services provided to Quebec; consider, on the other hand, the continuing French-speaking concerns about the danger of being exploited and submerged by the English-speaking, especially with the United States so near and so powerful in its cultural and economic influences.

The French-speaking position, with its awareness of race relations in the United States, was dramatically presented in Pierre Vallierès's protest, *Nègres blancs d'Amérique* (Montreal: Editions Parti pris, 1969). The separatism advocated by French-speaking radicals came to be regarded, at least for the time being, as folly. It was not unrelated to the Black Power movement in the United States, which has always had, however, even less of a political base to build upon. The continuing, however transformed, concerns of French-speaking Canadiens may be seen in a report on M. Vallières in this morning's paper: "Twenty years on, FLQs's fiery ideologue sees gentler vision of revolution." (Bertrand Marotte, *Toronto Globe and Mail*, June 10, 1988, p. A2) In another article this morning

Quebec Premier Robert Bourassa is reported to have said that "the English-speaking minority in Quebec is not really in trouble and does not need Government help as urgently as do Francophones outside the province. . . . Mr. Bourassa is careful in his dealings with the potentially troublesome issue of language in Quebec. He has to persuade Francophones, who tend to distrust him on the matter, that he is a dedicated defender of their language and culture, while preventing the Anglophones in the province, and the rest of the country, from criticizing him for being as harshly nationalist as his Parti Quebecois predecessors." (Benoit Aubin, "Linguistic protection a duty, PM says," *Toronto Globe and Mail*, June 10, 1988, p. A4)

One advantage the United States seems to have over Canada in such matters is that the founding principles of the community are much more evident in the United States. (A valuable study here is George Grant's book, *Lament for a Nation: The Defeat of Canadian Nationalism* [Princeton: D. Van Nostrand Co., 1965].) Even so, if one can judge reliably from one's occasional vists to Montreal, things do seem better in Quebec these days than they did two decades ago. This may be partly because Quebec did secure more control over its life, partly because the rest of Canada has been sensible, partly because economic conditions have improved throughout the country, and partly because all could see that a decent Canada is indeed special and very much worth preserving in its uniquely tolerant complexity. Responsible conduct, by both Provincial and National leaders, has contributed to an overall improvement.

It remains to be seen, of course, what political effects severe economic and social distress will have once the generation that was radicalized in Quebec high schools, universities and law schools two decades ago takes over substantial control of Quebec life. Much will depend, then, on the political teachings that all Canadians have come to share.

VI.

It is salutary in such matters to put forward one's best foot. It is here that I have a serious difficulty with Mr. Bloom. However good his intentions may be in what he has to say about race relations in his country, he sometimes caters to the worst elements on both sides of the color barrier. One may even suspect that catering to the worst, more than reaching for the best, can sometimes contribute to success in the volatile mass market where *apeirokalia* often seems the order (or disorder) of the day.

Bearing upon this is Mr. Bloom's disturbing account of his Cornell experiences in the late Sixties. Far too much is made by him of that matter: it was not representative of what was generally happening in the academic world at that time; and it probably did not happen even at Cornell quite the way Mr. Bloom remembers it. It is part of the charm of Mr. Bloom, and contributes to his considerable success as a teacher, that he dramatizes everything that touches his life. He again and again over reacts to the crises, and supposed crises, that confront him, something which has been true of him at least since I first came to like him as a fellow graduate student three decades ago.

The students at Cornell were somewhat better than he paints them. The faculty and administration were rather inept—as well as trapped by bad luck and by their zeal in having recruited as many academically-vulnerable minority students as they did. We can be reminded of the folly which decent and intelligent men can stumble into when we recall that so sophisticated a Canadian Unionist as Pierre Trudeau could invoke the War Measures Act in 1970, perhaps contributing thereby to the radicalization of the "French Power" movement in Quebec. The "Black Power" movement in the United States has been similarly served by its opponents.

VII.

It should be evident from what I have said that it seems to me that Mr. Bloom treats the subject of race relations rather cavalierly. He does not seem to appreciate either how complicated the race issue is or how limited his own grasp of it may be. Indeed, it seems to me that there is something perversely impolitic about Mr. Bloom's approach to such subjects. One gathers that he is somewhat surprised and rather troubled by the hostility aroused, especially on college campuses, because of what he has had to say in *Closing* about such topics as race relations and feminism.

His surprise is itself a reflection of his occasional naivete about politics. It cannot suffice in such situations for one to be, as Mr. Bloom's friends do know him to be, a decent, generous man who means well. In any event, it is to be hoped that Mr. Bloom and his sympathizers can contribute as much to academic reform as Mr. Trudeau contributed, despite his missteps, to the preservation, perhaps even the deepening, of Canadian unity.

VIII.

We can now return, however briefly, to the problem dramatized by Mr. Bloom of the self-segregation of certain minority students on campuses. This sort of social development was anticipated by what James Baldwin said forty years ago about the relations between Negroes and Jews in the United States, the very Jews Mr. Bloom can now recognize as having become remarkably Americanized. Mr. Baldwin could speak, as in his February 1948 article for *Commentary,* of "the Negro's ambivalent relation to the Jew." (*Notes of a Native Son* [Boston: The Beacon Press, 1955], p. 66) On the one hand, Jewish history provides a model for Negroes seeking their own escape from Egypt. On the other hand, there is this reservation (*ibid.*, pp. 67–68):

> But if the Negro has bought his salvation with pain and the New Testament is used to prove, as it were, the validity of the transformation, it is the Old Testament which is clung to and most frequently preached from, which provides the emotional fire and anatomizes the path of bondage; and which promises vengeance and assures the chosen of their place in Zion. . . .
> This same identification, which Negroes, since slavery, have accepted with their mothers' milk, serves, in contemporary actuality, to implement an involved and specific bitterness. Jews in Harlem are small tradesmen, rent collectors, real estate agents, and pawnbrokers; they operate in accordance with the American business tradition of exploiting Negroes, and they are therefore identified with oppression and are hated for it. I remember meeting no Negro in the years of my growing up, in my family or out of it, who would really ever trust a Jew, and few who did not, indeed, exhibit for them the blackest contempt. On the other hand,

this did not prevent their working for Jews, being utterly civil and pleasant to them, and, in most cases, contriving to delude their employers into believing that, far from harboring any dislike for Jews, they would rather work for a Jew than for anyone else. It is part of the price the Negro pays for his position in this society that, as Richard Wright points out, he is almost always acting. A Negro learns to gauge precisely what reaction the alien person facing him desires, and he produces it with disarming artlessness. The friends I had, growing up and going to work, grew more bitter every day; and, conversely, they learned to hide this bitterness and to fit into the pattern Gentile and Jew alike had fixed for them.

I suspect that the typical French-speaking Canadians have said similar things about the English-speaking whom they have had to deal with routinely. Be that as it may, we can detect here the roots of the ugly anti-Semitism which erupts from time to time in American Negro "ghettos."

Mr. Baldwin added, in his 1948 *Commentary* article (*Notes of a Native Son*, p. 69),

At the same time, there is a subterranean assumption that the Jew should "know better," that he has suffered enough himself to know what suffering means. An understanding is expected of the Jew such as none but the most naive and visionary Negro has ever expected of the American Gentile. The Jew, by the nature of his own precarious position, has failed to vindicate this faith.

So precarious is this position, as Jews still see it, that they tend to come down hard against affirmative-action programs—and this, too, has contributed to the eruptions of anti-Semitism to which I have referred. Consider how Mr. Bloom responds, almost instinctively, to affirmative-action programs in universities (*Closing*, p. 96):

Affirmative action now institutionalizes the worst aspects of separation. The fact is that the average black student's achievements do not equal those of the average white student in the good universities, and everybody knows it.

He concludes the subsection on "Race" in *Closing* with these comments (*ibid.*, pp. 96–97):

[D]emocratic society cannot accept any principle of achievement other than merit. White students, as I have said, do not really believe in the justice of affirmative action, do not wish to deal with the facts, and turn without mentioning it to their all-white—or, rather, because there are now so many Orientals, non-black—society. Affirmative action (quotas), at least in universities, is the source of what I fear is a long-term deterioration of the relations between the races in America.

(It is easy, considering the general tone of Mr. Bloom's discussion of these matters, to overlook his qualification here: "at least in universities.")

IX.

Mr. Bloom tends to see the self-segregation of minority students in universities more as a cause than as a symptom. Again and again he observes that whites have done all they can to remedy matters.

But such self-segregation is not limited to campuses. It is evident in most of our social life even where the races come together in now-integrated facilities. Mr. Bloom does not recognize this. Nor does he recognize either the extent to which racial incidents have infected campuses in recent years or the ways in which other groups than Negroes segregate themselves. Even the Jews whom he sees as thoroughly accepted still segregate themselves to a considerable extent, partly out of habit, partly for the sake of "comfort," and partly as a defense. Is there not something natural about this? (The Asian-American students that Mr. Bloom sees as integrated on campuses are far more separated from the mainstream than he recognizes. The fewer there are of a minority on a campus, the more likely are they to be integrated into the life of the general community.)

The way Mr. Bloom discusses these matters conceals from view the appalling obstacles—in part due to long disturbed Negro family relations, in part due to lingering community resistance—that the typical Negro student faces. This is apparent to anyone who inquires into the personal backgrounds of Negro students. Even those whose family circumstances are stable can succumb to the bitterness James Baldwin draws upon in concluding his 1948 *Commentary* article (*Notes of a Native Son*, pp. 71–72):

> It is this bitterness—felt alike by the inarticulate, hungry population of Harlem, by the wealthy on Sugar Hill, and by the brilliant exceptions ensconced in universities—which has defeated and promises to continue to defeat all efforts at interracial understanding. I am not one of the people who believe that oppression imbues a people with wisdom or insight or sweet charity, though the survival of the Negro in this country would simply not have been possible if this bitterness had been all he felt. In America, though, life seems to move faster than anywhere else on the globe and each generation is promised more than it will get: which creates, in each generation, a furious, bewildered rage, the rage of people who cannot find solid ground beneath their feet. Just as a mountain of sociological investigations, committee reports, and plans for recreational centers have failed to change the face of Harlem or prevent Negro boys and girls from growing up and facing, individually and alone, the unendurable frustration of being always, everywhere, inferior—until finally the cancer attacks the mind and warps it—so there seems no hope for better Negro-Jewish relations without a change in the American pattern.
>
> Both the Negro and the Jew are helpless; the pressure of living is too immediate and incessant to allow time for understanding. I can conceive of no Negro native to this country who has not, by the age of puberty, been irreparably scarred by the conditions of his life. All over Harlem, Negro boys and girls are growing into stunted maturity, trying desperately to find a place to stand; and the wonder is not that so many are ruined but that so many survive. The Negro's outlets are desperately constricted. In his dilemma he turns first upon himself and then upon whatever most represents to him his own emasculation. Here the Jew is caught in the American crossfire. The Negro, facing a Jew, hates, at bottom, not his Jewishness but the color of his skin. It is not the Jewish tradition by which he has been betrayed but the tradition of his native land. But just as a society must have a scapegoat, so hatred must have a symbol. Georgia has the Negro and Harlem has the Jew.

It would be silly, as well as dangerous, to deny the great improvements in race relations made in the United States since 1948. But it must also be recognized that much remains to be done, that the crippling effects of centuries of slavery, sustained racial discrimination, and a grinding poverty may require generations of constructive efforts to remedy. (This is something that Moses, for one, recognized. Many of the same considerations bear as well upon the status and future of American Indians on this Continent.)

X.

What I have had to say about Mr. Bloom on race relations is directed at serious defects in his book as a sociological report. But these defects depend upon, if they do not contribute to, even more serious defects in his understanding of academic life.

One such defect is Mr. Bloom's "clean slate" approach to college education. At times, of course, he recognizes that it is better for students to come to college with a sound secondary-school education. But his despair about the fate of most students rests, in part, upon his assumption that "everything" depends on what is provided at the university. Thus, he can say (*Closing*, p. 336), "The importance of these years for an American cannot be overestimated. They are civilization's only chance to get to him."

This surely cannot be true. The community at large, the family, and various religious and other social associations, to say nothing of the mass media, shape most of us profoundly. If the "slate" is not properly prepared, the great books that liberal education depends upon are not likely to be made meaningful. For one thing, students require acceptance, from their youth, of the moral interests and standards that the greatest books appeal to and undertake to refine.

XI.

Another defect in Mr. Bloom's general account of education can be traced back to his assumptions about the insularity and autonomy of universities. He can be grateful to any society "that tolerates and supports [that] eternal childhood" which he believes university life to provide for its faculty members. (*Closing*, p. 245) This does not seem to me, however, a felicitous way of describing academic life, echoing as it inadvertently does Callicles' criticism, in Plato's *Gorgias*, of the life of Socrates as an irritating instance of arrested development.

We have noticed Mr. Bloom's observation (*Closing*, p. 335), "The American university provided the intellectual inspiration [in the Civil Rights Movement?] for decent political deeds." But in such matters, the university is apt to be primarily a conduit. The highest "intellectual inspiration" has always come, in the United States, much more from great political and religious teachers than from the universities.

To this defect in Mr. Bloom's account can be traced perhaps his failure, in his diagnosis of student misconduct in the Sixties, to pay sufficient attention to the effects of the Viet Nam War and the Civil Rights Movement on academic life in the United States. He does not seem to appreciate the extent to which universities and other institutions, including established religions, usually depend upon, even more than they contribute to, a sound political order.

XII.

Mr. Bloom's inadequate political sense may be seen, I have suggested, in *the way* he talks about race relations, however instructive and hence useful his frankness may be. Particularly challenging are such comments as, "There is nothing more that white students can do to make great changes in their relations to black students." (*Closing*, p. 92) Critical here may be his sympathy for those white students who "do not really believe in the justice of affirmative action." (*Ibid.*, p. 96)

Would white students continue to believe there is "nothing more [they] can do to make great changes in their relations to black students"—would they continue to believe this if they had been taught by Mr. Bloom and those of like mind that affirmative action may justly be used by a sensible community? When and how affirmative action should be used, and how it should be explained, very much depends on prudence—that is, on proper training, however acquired.

XIII.

In the training of Americans in these matters, the British and Canadians can be most helpful, if only because they do not yet have the supposed constitutional barriers, grounded for Americans in misreadings of the Fourteenth Amendment, to experimenting with affirmative-action and other remedies for deep-seated racial prejudices and its long-term consequences. Flexibility is called for here, *including a willingness to discard attempted remedies that do not work as they should*, something that can be hard to do. The appropriate ends here for the community at large are justice and domestic tranquility. It is the common good, even more then the rights of minorities or the ugliness of racism, that the prudent community should contemplate in attempting to deal with race relations.

Thus, it is natural right and political philosophy that we should look to for primary guidance in these matters. Allan Bloom, who has graced us with a most helpful translation of Plato's *Republic*, can be here very much our benefactor.*

---

*The epigraph for this paper is taken from Leo Strauss, *Liberalism Ancient and Modern* (New York: Basic Books, 1968), p. 8.

I have, in the following publications, discussed at greater length various of the matters touched upon in this paper:

1) "Canada and Quebec Separatism," in Anastaplo, *Human Being and Citizen: Essays on Virtue, Freedom, and the Common Good* (Chicago/Athens, Ohio: Swallow Press/Ohio University Press, 1975), p. 139;

2) "Race, Law, and Civilization," in Anastaplo, *Human Being and Citizen*, p. 175;

3) "American Constitutionalism and the Virtue of Prudence: Philadelphia, Paris, Washington, Gettysburg," in Leo Paul S. de Alvarez, ed., *Abraham Lincoln, The Gettysburg Address, and American Constitutionalism* (Irving, Texas: University of Dallas Press, 1976), p. 77;

4) "What Is a Classic?" in Anastaplo, *The Artist as Thinker: From Shakespeare to Joyce* (Athens, Ohio: Swallow Press/Ohio University Press, 1983), p. 284 (see, also, *ibid.*, p. 255);

5) "Abraham Lincoln's Emancipation Proclamation," in Ronald K. L. Collins, ed., *Constitutional Government in America* (Durham, N.C.: Carolina Academic Press, 1980), p. 421;

6) "Slavery and the Constitution: Explorations," in *Texas Tech Law Review* (forthcoming);

7) *The Constitution of 1787: A Commentary* (Baltimore, Maryland: Johns Hopkins University Press) (forthcoming).

EIGHT

Bloom on Rock Music

One of the most controversial sections of *The Closing of the American Mind* is the chapter entitled "Music," which describes rock music as "junk food for the soul." Bloom is a very keen observer of the souls of his students. He sees that his students of twenty-five years ago, who were raised on classical music, were passionately interested in higher learning about truth, justice, beauty, friendship, etc. But students of the present generation, who are raised on rock music, have shown themselves to be interested only in commerce, to love less, and to be less happily married. Bloom agrees with Plato that there is a connection between the kind of music to which one listens and one's character. Classical music is essentially harmonic; rock music is essentially rhythmic. Harmonic music makes its listeners more contemplative; rhythmic music makes its listeners more passionate. (Military marches are much more rhythmic than other kinds of music.) Then, when rhythm is combined with electrical amplification and mechanical reproduction, the effect of prolonged exposure on the brain is like that of drugs. The most frequently quoted passage in *The Closing of the American Mind* is as follows:

> Picture a thirteen-year old boy sitting in the living room of his family home doing his math assignment while wearing his Walkman headphones or watching MTV. He enjoys the liberties hard won over centuries by the alliance of philosophic genius and political heroism, consecrated by the blood of martyrs; he is provided with comfort and leisure by the most productive economy ever known to mankind; science has penetrated the secrets of nature in order to provide him with the marvelous, lifelike electronic sound and image reproduction he is enjoying. And in what does progress culminate? A pubescent child whose body throbs with orgasmic rhythms; whose feelings are made articulate in hymns to the joys of onanism or the killing of parents; whose ambition is to win fame and wealth in imitating the drag-queen who makes the music. In short, life is made into a nonstop, commercially prepackaged masturbational fantasy.

Jessica Branson, a high-school girl who listens to rock music, testifies in a newspaper story here that she found Bloom's racy description of students' vices (above) to be more shocking than the lyrics of rock music. However, a news item distributed by Scripps Howard News Service finds scientific support for Bloom's thesis. According to this item, exposure to rock music causes abnormal neuron structures in the region of the brain associated with learning and memory.

William Greider in "Bloom and Doom" from the *Rolling Stone* is an energetic Bloom-basher. He starts out amused at Bloom's description of rock music: "As I read through the book, Professor Bloom actually made me feel young

237

again. This is exactly what our parents warned us about in the Fifties." But he soon becomes hostile, accusing Bloom of a "nasty reactionary attack on the values of young people."

A more laconic Frank Zappa, in an interview reprinted here, admits that rock music as we know it is very bad, but he says that this is caused by the greedy capitalists who sell it to children, not by the pure artists like himself who make it. Therefore, children, not parents, should control what music the family purchases.

The final essay in this chapter is by Steven Crockett, the only participant in the debate who is knowledgable about both political theory and rock music. Crockett argues that Bloom's thesis, as it stands, must be either false or exaggerated because, properly understood, it is an argument against all music. And Bloom not only admits but relies upon the self-evident fact that there is an important difference between good music and bad music. If it is rhythm that makes music bad (which Crockett does not admit), then classical music too is bad, because some classical music has more rhythm than does some rock music. Also, if one examines the words of rock songs, one finds that some are harmful but many are benign. At the least, it seems that Crockett has shown that Bloom has not yet proved his thesis.

40

Too Much Tolerance

ALLAN BLOOM

NPQ: What about rock music? You dismiss rock n' roll as "junk food for the soul" which gives vent to the unmediated, barbarous expression of the "rawest passions" and against which there is no intellectual resistance. You say it may well be that a society's greatest madness appears as normal to itself, and that rock offers "nothing noble, sublime, profound, delicate, tasteful or decent. It is only intense, changing, crude and immediate"—confirming Tocqueville's fears about the baseness of democratic art.

Bloom: I've simply pointed out how terribly important rock music is to the lives of kids today.

I think the chapter on rock music is one of the best interpretations of the passages on music in Plato, which argues that music expresses the dark, chaotic forces of the soul and that the kind of music on which people are raised determines the balance of their souls.

The influence of rock music on kids today reasserts a central role of music that had fallen into disuse for almost a hundred years. Once we recognize this new centrality, however, we have to discuss which passions are aroused, how they are expressed, and the role this plays in the life of society. That kind of critique has never taken place.

NPQ: In general, you avoid blaming consumer capitalism as a major force in the "degradation" of culture, especially concerning rock n' roll.

You also suggest that rock musicians release the dark forces in the soul without taming them through form and beauty as did Bach or Beethoven. Frank Zappa argues that the problem is not in the musicians, but in the middle-aged recording executives who are pandering to the base tastes of the public in order to boost sales.

Bloom: I do say that the spread of rock music is a result of the mixture of infantile taste and business exploitation of it. I didn't say for a moment that consumer society isn't a problem; it brings with it a huge amount of vulgarity. The nature of consumer society is to exploit the passions. But rock music is particularly crafted to suit its targets.

However, I'm not an economic determinist. A Marxist description is obviously very powerful, but it is a cheap criticism which avoids taking responsibility for one's own life. Parents, after all, can still influence kids' taste. They should not be deprived of the right to direct their children's education. The

---

See the portion of this interview pertaining to Feminism in chapter 6.

ubiquity of rock n' roll exposes the poverty of the home. There is a hidden message in rock that young people grasp immediately: they have inviolable rights to the expression of their uneducated sentiments. The electronic devices, the hi-fi and TV, are a common highway passing through all the houses in America, and there is no resistance to it. Privacy, which means the possibility of having a different life from what is most popular, disappears.

41

Keeping the American Mind Shut

JESSICA BRANSON

The summer's suprise best-seller, "The Closing of the American Mind" by University of Chicago professor Allan Bloom has been on the New York Times best-selling-book list nearly two dozen weeks, spending much of that time at the top.

Because the book focuses on the failure of American universities to teach and the failure of their students to learn, professor Bloom originally expected mostly educators to buy it. But evidently, education has become a major concern for a lot of people and the book, surprisingly, rose to the top.

High schoolers might find the chapter entitled "Music" most interesting. Professor Bloom feels rock music jeopardizes students' futures because they listen to it to escape reality. Professor Bloom says young people "live for rock music" because "it gives them on a silver platter, with all the public authority of the entertainment industry, everything their parents used to tell them they had to wait for until they grew up . . ."

To illustrate his point, Professor Bloom links together a worn-out phrase: Sex, drugs and rock and roll. He writes, "Young people know that rock has the beat of sexual intercourse."

He describes a young person who listens to rock music as "A pubescent child whose body throbs with orgasmic rhythms, whose feelings are made articulate in hymns to the joys of onanism and the killing of parents, whose ambition is to win fame and wealth in imitating the drag queen who makes the music. In short, life is a nonstop, commercially prepackaged masturbational fantasy."

But to this teenaged rock listener, professor Bloom's arguments are just too extreme. He writes as if rock corrupts every child in America. His ideas about how rock relates to sex are more vulgar than any video on MTV he criticizes.

Though he's a professor teaching in the '80s he can't seem to accept differences in people's sexual preferences. He says, "In Mick Jagger's stage routine he was male and female, heterosexual and homosexual . . ." To me that's reality, not vulgarity, because there are homosexuals in the world.

Rather than criticizing rock music, professor Bloom should realize that its themes are only derived from real life and the music shouldn't be blamed for what it describes.

Throughout history, one sees the same types of criticism for every significant musical innovation. People criticized jazz in its early stages for the same reasons.

Jessica Branson is a high school student at the Laboratory Schools of the University of Chicago. This review is reprinted with permission from *U-High Midway* (September 16, 1987):2.

If Americans listened to these attacks, they would have been cheated out of an entire art form.

It's ironic professor Bloom writes that students should take off their Walkmen and face reality and entitle his book "The Closing of the American Mind," when it is he who is attempting to close the minds of Americans. Just like his.

42

Like, Man, Where'd You Put the Food?

From University of Chicago philosopher Allan Bloom to parents of teen-agers, Americans offended by rock music now have new ammunition.

A physicist and a neurobiologist recently conducted an experiment to test the effects of various background sounds on laboratory mice. The results were fascinating.

Harvey Bird of Fairleigh Dickinson University in Rutherford, N.J., and Gervasia Schreckenberg of Georgian Court College in Lakewood, N.J., had one group of mice spend eight weeks exposed to the discordant drumbeats of rock.

When placed in a maze, says Schreckenberg, these mice "took much longer to find the food than the others. They were wandering off with no sense of direction."

When dissected, their brain tissue revealed abnormal neuron structures in the region associated with learning and memory.

The mice who had spent the eight weeks listening to Johann Strauss waltzes performed normally.

This is an editorial reprinted with permission from Scripps Howard News Service, April 8, 1988.

43

Bloom and Doom

WILLIAM GREIDER

Allan Bloom blames the waywardness of the young on, among other things, rock & roll and Mick Jagger, the lowlife satyr of dirty dancing. "Rock music," Bloom writes, "has one appeal only, a barbaric appeal, to sexual desire—not love, not *eros*, but sexual desire undeveloped and untutored."

Rock & roll, according to Bloom, has only three themes: "sex, hate and a smarmy, hypocritical version of brotherly love." Bloom's antirock diatribe hits full stride when he likens pop music to a "pubescent child whose body throbs with orgiastic rhythms; whose feelings are made articulate in hymns to the joys of onanism or the killing of parents; whose ambition is to win fame and wealth in imitating the drag-queen who makes the music. In short, life is made into a nonstop, commercial prepackaged masturbational fantasy."

As I read through the book, Professor Bloom actually made me feel young again. This is exactly what *our* parents and teachers warned us about in the Fifties when we first started listening to Elvis Presley and Bill Haley and tuning in black stations on the car radio. Rock & roll, they said, will rot your brain. Jungle music unleashes dangerous impulses that will lead to the Big Mistake.

I read on, and my nostalgia deepened. According to Bloom, American youth in the Eighties—even the best and the brightest at the leading universities, where he has taught for thirty years—are "spiritually unclad, unconnected, isolated, with no inherited or unconditional connection with anything or any-one." That's a fair summary of what was said about us—children who came of age in the Eisenhower era. We too were spiritless, ill educated, self-centered, timid and utterly without serious purpose. Our parents had given us everything they had lacked growing up in the Depression. In return, we frittered away our lives on sex, TV and cars. We did not read the great books that our parents claimed to have read. Or listen to opera. Or study the Bible. Now Bloom comes along and enshrines my generation for poring over Plato and questing endlessly for the Good, the True and the Beautiful.

The professor is correct about one important distinction between kids of the Fifties and Eighties. In my youth we talked endlessly about sex. Today young people actually do it. And it seems to drive the fifty-six-year-old Bloom crazy, and no doubt rankles many others from his generation and mine. Underneath an ostensibly moral concern, many parents feel a strong current of jealousy as they observe their children exploring realms forbidden to them in their younger years. (Surprisingly this seems especially true of mothers and daughters.) Life is unfair.

This essay is reprinted with permission from *Rolling Stone* (October 8, 1987):39–40.

Even Bloom, an old bachelor himself, sounds a bit envious. He denounces Mick Jagger with such relish that one may wonder if the professor himself is turned on by Mick's pouty lips and wagging butt.

Bloom's other complaints—about television, movies, women and feminism, psychiatry, left-wing professors and Sixties political movements—seem silly and dated. It's as though someone had dug up an old right-wing screed from the Nixon-Agnew era and published it twenty years late. Except for this: *The Closing of the American Mind* is probably the hottest best seller of 1987 and certainly the most surprising. With 350,000 copies in print, Bloom's book has reigned atop the non-fiction-best-seller list of *The New York Times* more than four months, outselling all the fitness and diet books and the get-rich-quick manuals. Clearly the professor has touched a nerve, but of what sort?

Robert Asahina, Bloom's editor at Simon and Schuster, was as surprised as anyone by the book's commercial success. Trying to explain the phenomenon, Asahina pointed first to the literate, impassioned quality of Bloom's prose. The professor's rhetoric is laced with high-blown discourses on his great-books heroes (Plato, Socrates, Descartes, John Locke and the Founding Fathers) and his enemies list, those villains whose twisted thinking he claims brought us to our present predicament (Freud, Max Weber, Nietzsche, Heidegger and Sartre, as well as Americans like John Dewey and Charles Beard). The average reader is undoubtedly flattered by Bloom's intellectual name-dropping; it's always fun to be high-minded about someone else's ignorance.

The second reason for the book's success is that by lucky timing, according to Asahina, the book's appearance coincides with a surge of national concern about the disappearance of traditional education. Another current best seller, *Cultural Literacy*, by E.D. Hirsch Jr., also taps the same anxieties. "There is a sense, even among young people . . . that there is something wrong with their education," Asahina said.

Perhaps, but I don't think that's what the Bloom craze is all about. Bloom's jeremiad is ostensibly about the quality of education, a fervent plea for restoring to their rightful place the masterworks of literature, music and art. This is an inoffensive program that, at least in the abstract, sounds wholesomely intellectual.

But Bloom's real agenda is much darker—to launch a nasty, reactionary attack on the values of young people and everyone else under forty. His multi-count indictment is a laundry list of cheap slanders made to sound vaguely authoritative, because, after all, Bloom is a teacher who supposedly hangs out with students. In fact, Bloom sounds bewildered by young people—and strangely out of touch with them.

Bloom's ignorance is starkly revealed by his vicious comments on the children of divorced parents. They are, he claims, "less eager to look into the meaning of their lives or risk shaking their received opinions. . . . They tend to have rigid frameworks about what is right and wrong and how they ought to live." Anyone who knows the children of divorce realizes that most of them are the opposite. They are constantly searching and testing every proposition about life.

They are absorbed, sometimes obsessively, by the very questions Bloom claims they cannot face.

After a lifetime as a teacher, Bloom apparently detests the young. A lot of other "grown-up" Americans seem to feel the same way. But Bloom's lament is cleverly constructed so that it often conveys malign opinions he does not want to state explicitly. Young people today, he says, are universally "nice"—tolerant and open, free of old prejudices based on race, sex, religion, class. Compared with past generations, this is probably accurate, but less so than Bloom thinks. (Where has he been for the past two years when so many campuses erupted in ugly conflicts over race and sex, including a gay-baiting scandal at his own University of Chicago?) Bloom, in any case, does not intend *tolerant* as a compliment. It's meant as a put-down.

The decline of prejudice, he says, is nothing but evidence of "nihilism, American style." Today's students don't hate simply because they're too vacant to believe in anything. "It was not necessarily the best of times in America when Catholics and Protestants were suspicious of and hated one another," he writes, "but at least they were taking their beliefs seriously."

What exactly is that supposed to mean? That Bloom longs for the "good old days" when people were up front about religious prejudice? He slides over the ugly implications of his argument with abstractions: "Prejudices, strong prejudices, are visions about the way things are. They are divinations of the order of the whole of things, and hence the road to a knowledge of that whole is by way of erroneous opinions about it." Does Bloom mean to suggest that anti-Semitism is really just a way to appreciate Judaism, that membership in the Ku Klux Klan is a prerequisite for racial understanding? This is mean-spirited sophistry. Part of Bloom's disillusionment may be that few of his students are willing to buy his line.

Bloom's portrait of his students is bigoted itself. Nobody reads Shakespeare or Plato or Homer anymore. He sees people on campus mostly watching videos on MTV (in which Bloom detects a whiff of Hitler, but not to worry: these kids are too lazy to mount a fascist movement). His students do not care about foreign places, and the few who do are interested only in the third world, not the great European cultures. The only classical music known to the young is Ravel's *Bolero*, because it has a strong, sexual beat. They are self-centered, whiny little brats who show no gratitude for the blessings that civilization—and their parents—have generously bestowed on them. They have no heroes, no ideas, no curiosity.

In my experience, this is rubbish. Every generation has an abundance of airheads and a minority of serious students. But my impression is that the kids coming of age in the Eighties are actually much better educated than my generation was. Bloom and a lot of others have forgotten what the good old days were really like.

The smart young people I know today have a brainy hipness that people like Bloom can't handle. I know a young woman from Yale who manages to read Hegel while simultaneously watching *Wheel of Fortune*; a junior at Princeton who is absorbed by the Old Testament but also hooked on Oprah Winfrey; and a recent Ivy League graduate who reads the Greek philosophers in Greek and the

Germans in German but who is also fascinated by African language and culture (and who really wants to play guitar in a rock band).

If I suggested to these young people that they were searching for the Good, the True and the Beautiful, they would laugh. They study philosophy, they would say, only because it is a challenging mind game. If Plato nourishes the soul, so does Vanna White.

Professor Bloom doesn't get the joke. People like him never do. When young people refuse to genuflect before the same icons their forebears held sacred, earnest priests of tradition always rush forward to denounce them. Bloom's true sympathies are with parents. And I suspect that's the most important reason this book is a best seller. He panders to disappointed parents, people who resent their children, who can't forgive them for doing with their lives other than what Mom and Dad had in mind. These poor parents "spend all they have providing for the kids." And what, according to Bloom, do they get in return? A bunch of zonked-out zombies, lost in masturbatory fantasies and in thrall to Jagger, Michael Jackson and Prince.

Bloom's explanation of this social decay is less interesting, because it is so standard. Black-power activists traumatized him by flashing guns at Cornell in 1969, and like many neo-conservative professors, he saw them as the forerunners of fascism in America. Sigmund Freud gets blamed for spawning psycho-babble. Lefty colleagues in the academy are accused of subverting the classics, the Bible and the Constitution. Even Woody Allen slyly corrupts the impressionable young.

Bloom's biggest complaint, though, is with women. The American family is crumbling because women abandoned it, lured away by the false doctrines of feminism and presumptions of equality. With a straight face, Bloom repeats all of the hoariest clichés about sex and marriage: "Of necessity . . . it was understood to be the woman's job to get and hold the man by her charms and wiles because, by nature, nothing else would induce him to give up his freedom in favor of the heavy duties of family." In other words, once women started giving it away without matrimony, the family was doomed. Since men have no natural affinity for children and family, once free sex came on the scene, men had no incentive to accept the bondage of marriage.

But where have we heard all this before? Doesn't Bloom sound an awful lot like Jerry Falwell and the other right-wing televangelists? Running down Bloom's diagnosis of our social ills, I realized it is a perfect fit with the standard born-again sermon, covering the same ground from the Good Book to rock & roll. Maybe this, too, explains Bloom's popularity—he is peddling fundamentalism for high-brows. It is the same bilious blend of prejudice, regret and resentment, the same simplistic appeal to the "golden days" of memory, and it bashes the same targets.

44

On Junk Food for the Soul

FRANK ZAPPA

The Nature of Music

Music is the soul's primitive and primary speech . . . without articulate speech or reason. It is not only not reasonable, it is hostile to reason. . . . Civilization . . . is the taming or domestication of the soul's raw passions. . . . Rock music has one appeal only, a barbaric appeal, to sexual desire—not love, not eros, but sexual desire undeveloped and untutored—A. Bloom

This is a puff pastry version of the belief that music is the work of the Devil: that the nasty ol' Devil plays his fiddle and people dance around and we don't want to see them twitching like that. In fact, if one wants to be a real artist in the United States today and comment on our culture, one would be very far off the track if one did something delicate or sublime. This is not a noble, delicate, sublime country. This is a mess run by criminals. Performers who are doing the crude, vulgar, repulsive things Bloom doesn't enjoy are only commenting on that fact.

In general, anti-rock propositions began when rock n' roll began, and most of these were racially motivated. In the 50s, petitions were circulated which said, "Don't allow your children to buy Negro records." The petitions referred to the "raw unbridled passion" of screaming people with dark skin who were going to drive our children wild. Some things never go out of fashion in certain ideological camps. They are like tenets of the faith.

Music's real effect on people is a new field of science called psycho-acoustics—the way an organism deals with wiggling air molecules. Our ears decode the wiggling air molecules, and that gives us the information of a particular musical sound. Our brain says, "This is music, this is a structure," and we deal with it based on certain tools we have acquired.

I personally make music because I want to ask a question, and I want to get an answer. If that question and answer amuse me, then statistically, there are a certain number of other people out there who have the same amusement factor. If I present my work to them, they will be amused by it, and we will all have a good time.

I need to be amused because I get bored easily and being amused entertains me. If I could be easily amused, like many people who like beer and football, I would never do anything because everything that would be beautiful for my life would already be provided by American television.

Frank Zappa and the Mothers of Invention were an important influence in rock music of the sixties. Lately Zappa has publicly defended rock against attacks from cultural conservatives. This interview is reprinted with permission from *New Perspectives Quarterly* vol. 4, no. 4 (Winter 1988):26–29.

But beer and television bore me, so what am I going to do? I am going to be alive for X number of years. I have to do something with my time besides sleep and eat. So, I devise little things to amuse myself. If I can amuse somebody else, great. And if I can amuse somebody else and earn a living while doing it, that is a true miracle in the 20th Century!

Music and the Dark Forces of the Soul

To Plato and Nietzsche, the history of music is a series of attempts to give form and beauty to the dark, chaotic, premonitory forces in the soul—to make them serve a higher purpose, an ideal, to give man's duties a fullness.—A. Bloom

This is a man who has fallen for rock's fabricated image of itself. This is the worst kind of ivory tower intellectualism. Anybody who talks about dark forces is right on the fringe of mumbo jumbo. Dark forces? What is this, another product from Lucasfilm? The passions! When was the last time you saw an American exhibit any form of passion other than the desire to shoot a guy on the freeway? Those are the forces of evil as far as I am concerned.

If there are dark forces hovering in the vicinity of the music business, they are mercantile forces. We meet the darkness when we meet the orchestra committees, when we get in touch with funding organizations, when we deal with people who give grants and when we get into the world of commerce that greets us when we arrive with our piece of art. Whether it's a rock n' roll record or a symphony, it's the same machinery lurking out there.

The reason a person writes a piece of music has got nothing to do with dark forces. I certainly don't have dark forces lurking around me when I'm writing. If someone is going to write a piece of music, in fact they are preoccupied with the boring labor and very hard work involved. That's what's really going on.

What Makes Music Classical

Rock music . . . has risen to its current heights in the education of the young on the ashes of classical music, and in an atmosphere in which there is no intellectual resistance to attempts to tap the rawest passions. . . . Cultivation of the soul uses the passions and satisfies them while sublimating them and giving them an artistic unity. . . . Bach's religious intentions and Beethoven's revolutionary and humane ones are clear enough examples.—A. Bloom

This is such nonsense. All the people recognized as great classical composers are recognized at this point for two reasons:

One, during the time these composers were alive and writing they had patrons who liked what they did and who therefore paid them money or gave them a place to live so that the composers could stay alive by writing dots on pieces of paper. If any of the compositions these men wrote had not been pleasing to a church, a duke, or a king, they would have been out of work and their music would not have survived.

There is a book called *Grove's Dictionary of Music and Musicians*, with thousands of names in it. You have never heard of most of the people in that book, nor have you heard their music. That doesn't mean they wrote awful music, it means they didn't have hits.

So basically, the people who are recognized as the geniuses of classical music had hits. And the person who determined whether or not it was a hit was a king, a duke, or the church or whoever paid the bill. The desire to get a sandwich or something to drink had a lot to do with it. And the content of what they wrote was to a degree determined by the musical predilections of the guy who was paying the bill.

Today, we have a similar situation in rock n' roll. We have kings, dukes, and popes: the A&R guy who spots a group or screens the tape when it comes in; the business affairs guy who writes the contract; the radio station programers who choose what records get air play.

The other reason the classical greats survived is their works are played over and over again by orchestras. The reasons they are played over and over again are: 1) all the musicians in the orchestra know how to play them because they learned them in the conservatory; 2) the orchestra management programs these pieces because the musicians already know them and it costs less to rehearse them; 3) the composers are dead so the orchestras pay no royalties for the use of the music.

Today, survivability is based on the number of specimens in the market place—the sheer numbers of plastic objects. Many other compositions from this era will vanish, but Michael Jackson's *Thriller* album will survive because there are 30 million odd pieces of plastic out there. No matter what we may think of the content, a future generation may pick up that piece of plastic and say, "Oh, they were like this."

I suppose somewhere in the future there will be other men like Bloom certifying that the very narrow spectrum of rock n' roll which survives composes the great works of the later half of the 20th Century.

The Difference Between Classical Music and Rock n' Roll

Rock music provides premature ecstasy and, in this respect, is like the drugs with which it is allied. . . . These are the three great lyrical themes: sex, hate and a smarmy, hypocritical version of brotherly love. . . . Nothing noble, sublime, profound, delicate, tasteful or even decent can find a place in such tableaux.—A. Bloom

Again, Bloom is not looking at what is really going on here. The ugliness in this society is not a product of unrefined art, but of unrefined commerce, wild superstition and religious fanaticism.

The real difference between the classics and rock n' roll is mostly a matter of form. In order to say we have written a symphony, the design we put on a piece of paper has to conform to certain specifications. We have an exposition that lasts a certain amount of time, then modulation, development and recapitulation. It's like a box, like an egg carton. We must fill all the little spaces in the egg carton with the right forms. If we do, we can call it a symphony because it conforms to the spaces in that box.

Compare that creative process to rock n' roll. If we want to have an AM hit record, we have another egg carton to fill. We have an intro, a couple of verses, a bridge, another verse, and then a fade out. All of which requires a "hook." That's a very rigid form. If we wander away from that form, our song's not going to go on the radio because it doesn't sound like it fits into their format.

Now, whether the person writing the song graduated from a conservatory or whether they came out of a garage, they know that in order to finish a piece they have to do certain things to make it fit into a certain form. In the classical period the sonata or a concerto or symphony had to be that certain size and shape or else the king was not going to like it. One could die. These were literally matters of life and death, but not in the way Bloom defines them.

The Rock Business

The family spiritual void has left the field open to rock music. . . . The result is nothing less than parents' loss of control over their children's moral education at a time when no one else is seriously concerned with it. This has been achieved by an alliance between the strange young males who have the gift of divining the mob's emergent wishes—our versions of Thrasymachus, Socrates' rhetorical adversary— and the record-company executives, the new robber barons, who mine gold out of rock.—A. Bloom

There is some truth to that, but how did we get to this point and what do we do about it?

We got here because teenagers are the most sought after consumers. The whole idea of merchandising the pre-pubescent masturbational fantasy is not necessarily the work of the songwriter or the singer, but the work of the merchandiser who has elevated rock n' roll to the commercial enterprise it is.

In the beginning, rock n' roll was young kids singing to other kids about their girlfriends. That's all there was. The guys who made those records came from Manual Arts High School. They went into a recording studio, were given some wine, $25 and a bunch of records when their song came out as a single—which made them heroes at school. That was their career, not, "Well, we're not going to sing until we get a $125 thousand advance."

Today, rock n' roll is about getting a contract with a major company, and pretty much doing what the company tells you to do. The company promotes the image of rock n' roll as being wild and fun when in fact it's just a dismal business.

Record companies have people who claim to be experts on what the public really wants to hear. And they inflict their taste on the people who actually make the music. To be a big success, you need a really big company behind you because really big companies can make really big distribution deals.

Even people who are waiting to go into the business know it's a business. They spend a great deal of time planning what they will look like and getting a good publicity photo before they walk in the door with their tape. And the record companies tend to take the attitude that it doesn't make too much difference what the tape sounds like as long as the artists look right, because they can always hire a producer who will fix up the sound and make it the way they want it—so long as the people wear the right clothes and have the right hair.

Retaining Classical Music

Classical music is dead among the young. . . . Rock music is as unquestioned and unproblematic as the air the students breathe, and very few have any acquaintance at all with classical music. . . . Classical music is now a special taste, like Greek language or pre-Columbian archeology, not a common culture of reciprocal communication and psychological shorthand.—A. Bloom

On this point, Bloom and I can agree, but how can a child be blamed for consuming only that which is presented to him? Most kids have never been in contact with anything other than this highly merchandised stuff.

When I testified in front of the Senate, I pointed out that if they don't like the idea of young people buying certain kinds of music, why don't they stick a few dollars back into the school system to have music appreciation? There are kids today who have never heard a string quartet; they have never heard a symphony orchestra. I argued that the money for music appreciation courses, in terms of social good and other benefits such as improved behavior or uplifting the spirit, is far less than the cost of another set of uniforms for the football team. But I frankly don't see people waving banners in the streets saying more music appreciation in schools.

When I was in school, we could go into a room and they had records there. I could hear anything I wanted by going in there and putting on a record. I won't say I enjoyed everything that was played for me, but I was curious, and if I had never heard any of that music I wouldn't know about it.

Once we're out of school, the time we can spend doing that type of research is limited because most of us are out looking for a job flipping hamburgers in the great tradition of the Reagan economic miracle. When all is said and done, that's the real source of America's barren and arid lives.

45

Blam! Bam! Bloom! Boom!

STEVEN CROCKETT

Hear the pounding, throbbing, ecstatic song of Bloom:

> *Nothing* is more *singular* about this generation than its *addiction* to music. (68)
> . . . [A] very large proportion of young people . . . *live* for music. (68)
> . . . [T]hey cannot take seriously *anything* alien to music. (68)
> Classical music is *dead* among the young. (69)
> It is Plato's teaching that music . . . encompasses *all* that is today *most* resistant to philosophy. (71)
> It is not only not reasonable, it is *hostile* to reason. (71)
> Music provides an *unquestionable* justification . . . for the activities it accompanies. (72)
> . . . [M]usic is at the *center* of education. . . . (72)
> . . . [R]ock music has *one* appeal *only* . . . to sexual desire. . . . (73)
> . . . [It] has a much more powerful effect than does *pornography* on youngsters. . . . (74)
> . . . [N]*othing* noble, sublime, profound, delicate, tasteful, or even decent can find a place [on MTV]. (74)
> . . . [Our] society's *best* young and their *best* energies [are] so occupied. (75)
> . . . [It is] as *incomprehensible* as . . . the *caste* system, *witch-burning, harems, cannibalism,* and *gladitorial combats.* (75)
> . . . [T]he family spiritual *void* has left the field open to rock music. . . . (76)
> The result is *nothing* less than parents' loss of control over their children's moral education at a time when *no* one else is seriously concerned with it. (76)
> The rock business is *perfect* capitalism. . . . (76)
> It has all the moral dignity of *drug-trafficking.* . . . (76)
> . . . [R]ock music encourages passions and provides models that have *no* relation to *any* life the young people who go to universities can *possibly* lead. (80)
> . . . [A]s long as they have the Walkman on, they *cannot* hear what the great tradition has to say. (81)
> . . . [W]hen they take it off, . . . they are *deaf.* (81) [emphasis added]

In my conversations with people who praise Bloom's book, they commonly excuse his untempered speech on the grounds that he is merely calling attention to a difficulty and trying to begin a discussion on it, that his intemperance is a matter only of style. But if there is any substance in this ejaculation of "no's," "nothing's," "all's," "in-'s," "un-'s, and extreme comparisons, it is that style matters. In Bloom's book, the "style" from which "some," "sometimes," "usually," "perhaps," and the like are banished becomes a matter of logic, so much so, that if his opinions were to come to dominate liberal education, liberal education would become, as I shall argue later, politicized beyond anything Bloom criticizes. His

---

Steven Crockett is Attorney at Law, U.S. Nuclear Regulatory Commission, Washington, D.C. and a graduate of St. John's College, Annapolis. This essay copyright 1989 by Steven Crockett.

pages on music contain only the worst examples of this new syllogistic, in which the only quantifiers are "all" and "none."

But more of this strange new logic later. For now, simply see that the self-indulgent outbursts of the section on music demonstrate that Bloom is not merely calling attention to the importance of rock music. He does not have to condemn capitalism, parents, all music, and the best of a generation to tell us what we already know: that rock seems to be everywhere, that much of it is no good, that too few young people listen to good music, that too many violate the simplest rules of civil behavior by playing rock at all times, places, and volumes, that parents and teachers are not always adequate to dealing with such behavior, that adulation of rock heroes distracts, and that rock showcases sex too much.

. . . Nor is his section on music just another ill-informed and thoughtless attack on rock. Rock is only the occasion for Bloom to attack all music. But even more: Bloom believes that rock marks an epoch, a recovery of the Dionysian at precisely the moment when it stands to do the most harm. His pages on music constitute at once an emulation of Nietzsche's *The Birth of Tragedy From the Art of Music* and an answer to it. As Nietzsche saw Luther, Bach, Mozart, Beethoven, and Wagner as glorious Dionysian Harbingers of the recovery of all things German and of the decline of Socratic culture, so Bloom sees Mick Jagger, Michael Jackson, and Prince as the cause of the Deafening of the American Ear, the rendering it closed to Socrates.

Thus, Bloom's pages on music are neither merely a caution, nor merely an invitation to dialogue, nor merely another diatribe on rock. Those pages are instead a booming indictment which states that music now, in the "American Moment in world history," when "the fate of freedom" and "the fate of philosophy" are at stake (382), steals the best energies from the best young.

Clearly, there is no point in trying to engage Bloom in discussion of his all-or-nothing propositions. But it may not be too late to rescue a few from being swept away by this tidal wave of Bloomboom.

I begin simply by asking whether the two fundamental propositions of the chapter on music are true. These propositions are that "rock music has one appeal only . . . to sexual desire" (73), and, more important, that music "is not only not reasonable, it is hostile to reason" (71).

What, then, is the argument that "rock music has one appeal only"? Bloom rightly sees that the argument cannot escape being technical. That is, one must look to see how the music is constructed. This is Socrates's approach in the *Republic*, where he invites the musical Glaucon to tell him which modes and rhythms have the desired effects (399a).

And to what element in the structure of rock does Bloom point? The "beat." Not melody, not harmony, not even rhythm. Just, the "beat." "Young people know that rock has the beat of sexual intercourse" (73).

Of course, this bold comparison has some plausibility to it. The performers' costumes are erotic, their gyrations are erotic, many (though far fewer than Bloom lets on) of their lyrics are erotic: for instance, the Beatles' "Why don't we do it in the road" (how can Bloom write all those pages on rock and not mention the Beatles?), and the songs in which the word "rock" is a euphemism for another four-letter word ending in "-ck."

But Bloom is claiming more: "Rock music provides premature ecstasy. . . . I suspect that rock has an effect similar to that of drugs" (80).

So let us consider the proposition that "rock has the beat of sexual intercourse."

Bloom helps a little here by claiming, what will surprise many teachers, that "Ravel's *Bolero* is the one piece of classical music that is commonly known and liked" by young people (73). The "beat" of *Bolero* shares with the beat of rock two characteristics: regularity and volume. *Bolero* also rises to a "climax," and surely Bloom would delight in attributing a sexual significance to this aspect of the piece. But the attribution won't help his argument much, since few rock songs have climactic forms, but a great many works of the European tradition do. One of the most glorious of these works is the *Agnus Dei* from the *Missa L'Homme armé* by the late fifteenth century composer Ockeghem. I hesitate to say that this music "provides premature ecstasy."

Of course, there is more to the rock beat than regularity and volume; there is also the universal emphasis (I confess I do know of one exception) in rock music on the off beat, on beats 2 and 4 of a 4-beat measure, or on 7 of an 8-beat measure, and so on. This emphasis on the off beat is, strictly conceived, more a matter of rhythm than of beat, but it is so prominent a mark of rock that I shall assume that Bloom has it too in mind when he rails about the "beat" of rock. These three—regularity, volume, and emphasis on the off beat—are the main marks of the beat of rock. Beyond these, the "beats" of any two pieces of rock music have little in common. Now, where is the "premature ecstasy?"

Please overlook my indiscretion if I express a fear that the rock beat is too regular for sexual intercourse. If it is not, then nearly all music mimics sexual intercourse, for nearly all music includes its own measure in the form of a regular beat and would fail to make sense without that measure. Indeed, Nietzsche says that "a regular beat like that of waves lapping the shore," is "a plastic rhythm expressly developed for the portrayal of Apollonian conditions" (Golffing trans., 27). He locates the Dionysian element, the ecstatic, not in rhythm, but instead in melody and harmony. The regularity of rock is, in fact, much closer to the regular motion of the heavenly bodies, to Ptolemy's circles and epicycles, the study of which, Ptolemy says, would "prepare understanding persons with respect to nobleness of actions and character by means of the sameness, good order, due proportion, and simple directness contemplated in divine things, making its followers lovers of that divine beauty, and making habitual in them, and as it were natural, a like condition of the soul."

Volume is no better an inducer of sexual ecstasy, unless all marches are really erotic rather than spirited.

What then of the pervasive, invasive, off beat? Surely here there lurks something sexual. Alas, the facts are, as always, not to be characterized on the run. I don't have to look far for counterexamples. Here at hand is the last recording I bought, entitled simply *Diane Reeves*. It's got jazz, rock, and pop on it, every piece emphasizing the off beats—and the loud, and the regular. They should serve as a good test of the notion that—either severally or jointly—volume, regularity, and off beats are the "beat of sexual intercourse."

Consider the lyrics of the two songs which got frequent airings on Washington, D.C., radio stations. First, some lines from "Sky Islands":

> *Deep inside yourself*
> *There's a treasure island*
> *Full of wealth untold*
> *Waiting for discovery.*

> *There has got to be something more than living day to day.*

> *Being all you can be is your destiny.*
> *Spread your golden wings and fly with me.*

Where's the sex? Not unless it lurks deep somewhere in "wealth," or "fly," or maybe "inside." Great thoughts? Likely not, but taken as a whole, it's no lightweight piece. The melody, for instance, is cast in what the medieval theorists called the hypodorian mode and exploits well the resources of that mode.

Take another example from the same album: "Better Days." Just when the music really "gets down," in the first chorus, Ms. Reeves sings:

> *How can I be sure what is right or wrong?*
> *And why does what I want always take so long?*
> *Please tell me where does God live and why won't he come to me?*

> *I want to know the answers before I fall off to sleep.*

And to whom is she singing? She is remembering what, when she was 3 or 4, she would ask her grandmother!

Well for heaven's sake, there must be something sexy on this album besides the cover. (Ms. Reeves is a handsome woman.) Ah, here is a song by Herbie Hancock, the "teacher" on the PBS series called "Rock School." ("A contradiction in terms!" snarls Bloom.) Here, if anywhere, we'll find premature ecstasy. Oh, but shoot! The first one is by Hancock and his wife. Nothing premature here. And besides, the first line is, "Sometimes I wonder if everything's under a plan for us all." And as the dactyls of the words suggest, the rhythm of the music is close to a waltz (with an empahsis on an off beat—beat 2—of course).

Examples abound of the disconnection between sexual ecstasy and rhythm which emphasizes the off beats in a measure. Not only, as I've just shown, do songs which emphasize the off beats often have nothing to do with sex, often songs which are sexual do not emphasize the off beats. A fine example is Michael Jackson's "Human Nature," which is all about a one-night stand. (What Bloom must think of using that title for those lyrics!) But the rhythm emphasizes beats 1 and 3.

Comparing the beat of rock to the "beat" of sexual intercourse is about as grounded an undertaking as comparing what musicians call the "deceptive cadence" to coitus interruptus. (Listen to the solo section for harpsichord in the first movement of Bach's *Brandenburg Concerto No. 5,* and then ask yourself if the deceptive cadence in measures 213–214 interrupts your sexually ecstatic state.)

So much for the first of Bloom's two key propositions about music. Rock is music, not sex. Rock stars are musicians, not performers in pornographic films. Herbie Hancock was raised on European art music, became one of the best jazz pianists of his generation, and writes songs with the blind Homer of Motown, Stevie Wonder. Rock and jazz guitarist Alan Holdsworth revels in the harmonies which were centuries in the making. One young man famous for his performances of Bloom's beloved Mozart is also a rock musician.

If rock is music, then what is music? Bloom's second key proposition is that music is "irrational":

> It is Plato's teaching that music, by its nature, encompasses all that is today most resistant to philosophy. . . .
> Plato's teaching about music is, put simply, that rhythm and melody, accompanied by dance, are the barbarous expression of the soul. . . . Music is the soul's primitive and primary speech and it is *alogon*, without articulate speech or reason. It is not only not reasonable, it is hostile to reason. (71)

And he claims that Socrates' archenemy Nietzsche, who said that Dionysian "music is the true idea of the cosmos" (130), agrees with Plato! Bloom apparently is thinking that the Dionysian realm is the realm of the many-headed beast in Socrates's image of the soul, but this comparison has about as much of the ring of truth to it as a claim that Freud and Plato both divided the soul into parts in the same way. The similarities are superficial and the differences deep.

But the notion that rock is Dionysus risen is at least superficially attractive. (A book without superficially attractive ideas does not sell well.) In fact, some rock musicians would seem to agree, and perhaps whatever mortal combatants agree on must be true. Here are the lyrics of the title song from *Off the Wall*, the album which marked the start of the final stage of Michael Jackson's ascent to the top:

When the world is on your shoulder
Gotta straighten up your act and boogie down
If you can't hang with the feelin'
Then there ain't no room for you this part of town
Cause we're the party people night and day
Livin' crazy that's the only way

So tonight gotta leave that nine to five upon the shelf
And just enjoy yourself
Groove, let the madness in the music get to you
Life ain't so bad at all
If you live it off the wall

. . . . . .
Do what you want to do
There ain't no rules it's up to you

. . . . . .
Gotta hide your inhibitions
Gotta let that fool loose deep inside your soul
. . . . . .

And if this first album did not make it clear enough that Nietzsche wrote the lyrics, the second album, *Thriller*, has a picture of reclining, ringleted Jackson— an operation or two closer to the ideal Greek bisexual beauty—with a tiger cub on his knee, thus instantly calling to mind the mozaic in the Pella Museum in Greece of ringleted Dionysus almost reclining on the back of a leaping panther.

Here, too, the lyrics are Nietzsche's, as Vincent Price intones in the title song (speaking to Pentheus?): "And whosoever shall be found/Without the soul for getting down/Must stand and face the hounds of hell/And rot inside a corpse's shell." What divinity of malevolent humor decreed that the medieval melodic mode in which both of these songs are set should be called "Dorian," the same name by which the quite diffcrent—and to Socrates morally acceptable—mode in the Republic should be called? The theme of Jackson as the Dionysian revivifier continues in his most recent album Bad, and in Walt Disney's short film, Captain E.O., where Jackson repeats, on a grander scale, Papageno's trick in the Magic Flute of turning an old hag into a beautiful woman. But then, instead of marrying her, as Papageno did, Captain E.O. dances out the door, singing "You're just another part of me!"

Jackson clearly does better as Dionysus than as Harry Reems. But the proposition that music is hostile to reason is even less supportable than the proposition that rock induces sexual ecstasy. Where in Plato is there warrant for such nonsense? As usual, Bloom doesn't bother to quote or cite. But in fact, in Book VI of the Republic, Socrates make "harmonics," the study of motion heard (which is parallel to astronomy as the study of motion seen) the capstone of the liberal arts. And in the Timaeus, Timaeus tells the "likely" story that the cosmos was constructed using the ratios embodied in what we would call the Phrygian scale, and that the cosmos rings whenever truth is spoken, the way unstruck and undampened strings on the piano sympathetically vibrate in response to a struck string. Even today, the doctrine of a musical cosmos is alive and well in "superstring" theories of "everything," which pursue, by means of mathematical group theory, the unification of the four (now five?) fundamental forces. In these theories, the zoo of subatomic particles is reduced to a few strings vibrating in different ways! But, I'm sure Bloom isn't interested in such things, since, as he says in his inimitable "style," "All that is human, all that is of concern to us, lies outside of natural science." (356) (emphases added)

Apparently, by calling music alogon, ("without speech" or "irrational"), Bloom feels that he is recovering, through this Greek word, a precious insight about music, and he may indeed be recovering an insight, but very likely not the one he had in mind. The classic use of the word is in Euclid's Elements, Book X, Def. 3, where any straight line which is incommensurable with a given straight line is said to be alogos. Thus, the diagonal of a square is alogos because it is incommensurable with the side of the square. That is, there is no length of line which measures both of them a "whole" (as we say now) number of times. The diagonal is "without speech," because there is no number which can be spoken to characterize how long the diagonal is in relation to the side. Calling the diagonal some multiple of $\sqrt{2}$ only obscures the difficulty, which is fundamental to both ancient and modern methematics.

However, the diagonal of the square is not therefore "hostile to reason." Indeed, the great theme of Euclid's Elements is the spelling out of the ancient approach of reason to this unspeakable object. This same "irrationality" is so important in the history of Western music that that history could be written around the "unspeakable ratio" between the diagonal and side of the square.

Here, as in mathematics, the difference between ancient and modern lies in their respective approaches to this ratio, the moderns reveling in it and using it as the foundation of the system of tonal relations called "tonality."

Far from condemning music as *alogos*, in one dialogue Plato implicitly says that the proper object of the philosopher's search is *alogos*. In the *Meno*, Socrates, trying to overcome Meno's sophistical reluctance to join in the search for virtue, resorts to a mathematical example. He sets Meno's servant the task of telling him how long the side of a square twice the size of a square with a side of 2 would be. Meno's servant tries sides of 4 and then 3, but each makes a square more than twice the size of a square with a side of two. He is now speechless, unlike Meno after his failures to come up with an acceptable account of virtue. Socrates nonetheless tells the servant to try again to say from what line the double square is made. "Try to tell us exactly. And if you do not wish to count, show from what kind" (83E–84B). Of course, the servant could not possibly count out the answer, since the side of the double square is the diagonal of the original square, and the diagonal is *alogos*. But he could show by simple geometry that the square on the diagonal is twice the original square. This dialogue within a dialogue suggests that virtue cannot be wholly captured in speech, but that it nonetheless can be demonstrated to reason. It may be *alogos*, but it is not unknowable.

But we do not need Plato to show us that music is not hostile to reason. The musical experiences of listeners concretely show that music is the occasion for the exercise of reason in at least three ways.

The first way is through measurement. There is no music without measure, either of the lengths of notes, or of the height of tones, or of the intervals between them. There is pause for philosophy here: How does the soul convert the frequency of vibrations into the "height" of tones? How does the soul recognize intervals? Could it ever use anything so complicated as Euclid's method of determining sameness of ratio? How does the soul determine that two lengths of time have the same length? How does it determine the beat in any piece of music? Whatever its method, it is more wondrous than the mathematical operation of finding the greatest common measure of a series of lengths. To feel this wonder, and to feel the magnitude of the effort required to find and keep the beat, Bloom might try to tap out the beat in Ms. Reeve's "Sky Islands," which hides the beat in a welter of emphasized off beats and conflicting rhythms. Yet find the beat the soul does, or else the rest of the music fails.

Second, music requires reason to distinguish parts and bind them into wholes which have beginnings, middles, and ends. Ordinarily, music seems to come already divided into parts and bound into wholes, as if the music itself did the analysis and synthesis, without any intervention on our parts. But the appearances are misleading. Those of us who have studied twentieth century European art music a good deal have frequently felt, on encountering a piece of such music for the first time, that it seemed to make no sense, or was featureless and all the same. But then on hearing it again some hours or days later, we cannot imagine how we could have failed to discern its sense. I was thirteen or fourteen years old when I first had this experience, with Paul Hindemith's beautiful *Three Sonatas for Organ*. The first time I heard a recording of them, I listened closely, but they seemed to be mere piles of notes (though I believe I dimly heard a beat). But a few weeks later I, by chance, heard the same recording under much the same conditions, and now the *Sonatas* had melodies and rhythms, phrases and cadences, harmonies and progressions—in a word, every note had meaning. Somehow, during those few weeks, the music had acquired a shape. But how could that be? The recording was the same. I, literally speaking, "heard" no more the second time than I had the first. Therefore, only I had changed. But how had I changed?

I believe that, without conscious effort, I had compared the *Sonatas* and had discovered that they differed from each other and that each had parts which in turn differed from each other. But what was crucial was that I had learned to interpret all the parts, small and large, in terms of the whole. Individual tones I interpreted as belonging in phrases; individual phrases I interpreted as belonging in sections; and so forth up the hierarchy from foreground to background.

The "world" of the *Sonatas* seemed to have acquired gravitational fields in which the tones displayed natural tendencies. Or better, the tones in the "world" of the *Sonatas* had become more than material, for, besides having matter and form, they seemed to have purpose too, as if they were moral agents.

Whenever a listener catches his soul in these acts of analysis and synthesis, as I did for the first time in my youth, he is a little like Copernicus, for just as this great seeker of the shape of the whole discovered that the motions we attribute to the planets are in part our own, so too did I, only a modest seeker, discover that the motions I seemed to "hear" in the music were not matters of sense at all, but were the reflections of the actions of my own soul. (How could St. Augustine regard the pleasures of music as gratification of the senses?)

How the soul accomplishes this analysis and synthesis I understand even less than I do how the soul measures, but this "sense" of part and whole is arguably the distinguishing mark of the "musical" soul, broadly conceived. As Socrates says in the *Republic*, "the man properly reared on rhythm and harmony would have the sharpest sense for what's been left out and what isn't a fine product of craft or what isn't a fine product of nature" (401e). And Glaucon proves his point.

The third way in which music is the occasion for the exercise of reason is even harder to capture and describe, but again, as were the soul's measuring and actions on parts and wholes, this third way is revealed when the listener encounters some difficulty. The difficulty in this case is the listener's occasional "emotional" inertness in "response" to music he loves, or someone else's inertness in response to music we love. As a cultivated Hindu woman is reported to have said upon hearing Mozart's music for the first time: "Very good music, but very shallow." And each of us has felt, at one time or another, as this woman did. We measure a piece of music; we construe its syntax; we, being musical, pronounce it well made. But we are not "moved" by it. Yet, we may be again at a later time.

. . . Socrates was only partly right about the usefulness of music in education. He recognized that not every kind of music is suitable for every purpose. But he, and others in his wake, including Bloom, talk as if the music is active and the listener is passive. Socrates knows that teaching is not the imposition of form on a passive object. Then why does he think that music makes the man? The aim of education is not to instill, but to call forth, to provide occasions. The best music provides the occasion for the listener to "hear" his soul's own activity reflected back to him as great beauty, a divine singer telling a wordless story, the cosmos ringing with the truth. The listener in large part reaps what he sows, and the rational and the "irrational" are related, as Aristotle speculates, as the convex is related to the concave (*Nichomachean Ethics*, 1102a).

. . . Bloom's principal propositions about music are demonstrably false. Why then does he attack music with a vehemence unparalled elsewhere in the book? Is this vehemence his "soul's defense against a wound of doubt about its own"?

NINE

Does Bloom Exaggerate and Oversimplify?

George Anastaplo's "In re Allan Bloom: A Respectful Dissent," from *The Great Ideas Today* (Encyclopedia Britannica, 1988), warns the reader not to accept any of Bloom's statements uncritically. According to Anastaplo, Bloom exaggerates and distorts somewhat almost every topic he discusses: race, students, music, Plato, Rousseau, sex, and what happened in America during the sixties. Bloom plays fast and loose with his subjects because his book was intended to be "highly provocative." Says Anastaplo: "A people shaped by television insists upon spectaculars as well as upon instant gratification—in sports, in politics, and in intellectual experiences—and it is these tastes that *The Closing of the American Mind*, with its cascades of pronouncements on scores of books and authors, caters to." Anastaplo then offers avuncular advice to Bloom on how to spend his winnings from the sale of his book.

An example of the kind of problem Anastaplo is talking about can be found in the first essay here, by John Marcham, Cornell's director of university relations from 1964 to 1967. Marcham presents factual support for his claim that Bloom oversimplifies and exaggerates the events at Cornell in 1969 that affected him so profoundly. And William A. Galston, one of Bloom's defenders, says that Bloom exaggerates the decline of American universities by taking as his baseline the University of Chicago during the fifties.

A broader, more negative attack on Bloom's book is made in "The Colonel and the Professor," by David Rieff. Rieff compares Bloom to Colonel Oliver North and takes him to task for being too negative. "The odd thing is that Bloom doesn't seem actually to *like* America. Indeed, when it comes time for him to describe anything about the place, he speaks only in what might be called that new grammatical mood invented by neo-conservatives: the denunciative. Bloom hates American mores, decries American families, despises American teenagers, and takes no notice of the beauty of American landscape. . . . The real glories of American culture. . . , whether Bloom likes it or not, are Hollywood and pop music. . . . Level-headed, realistic humanity is the essential quality that is as absent from *The Closing of the American Mind* as it is from Colonel North's plans for Nicaragua's future." "Allan in Wonderland," by Jean Bethke Elshtain, argues that Bloom's attitude is patronizing and agrees with Rieff that condemning everything is unproductive. "Mr. Bloom's Planet," by Louis Menand, in the *New Republic*, also agrees with Rieff. Even if Bloom is correct in his diagnosis, it is not teacherly to gratify our wish to think ill of our own culture and to make young people the scapegoats.

46

In re Allan Bloom:
A Respectful Dissent

GEORGE ANASTAPLO

Aronson sent up a cry of rapture when he won the million dollar prize in a lottery.
Levi asked him, "What made you pick a number like 52, anyway?"
"It came to me in a dream," replied Aronson. "I dreamed I was in a theater,
and on the stage there were six columns of dancers with eight dancers in each
column. So I chose 52."
"But six times eight is 48, not 52!" said Levi.
Aronson chortled, "So O.K., *you* be the mathematician!"

—Anon.[1]

Prologue

If it had been at all anticipated that a million copies of Allan Bloom's *The Closing
of the American Mind* would eventually be sold, many things in it would no
doubt have been written much more carefully than they were—but if that had
been done, the book would have sold nowhere near as well as it has.[2]

Professor Bloom's widely acclaimed book provides shorthand reminders of
what is wrong in higher education today. Everywhere one goes this year on
campuses, one encounters people interested in the Bloom phenomenon, just as
last year one encountered people interested in the Bork phenomenon. Since I am
known to have been in school with both Robert Bork and Allan Bloom at the
University of Chicago (in the Law School and the Committee on Social
Thought, respectively), I have been asked many times about these celebrities who
share the not altogether happy capacity of saying plausible, even sensible, things
in a highly provocative manner.[3]

We are all in Mr. Bloom's debt for the dozens of fine students in political
philosophy he has helped train and for several fine things he has published.[4]
Particularly instructive have been his studies of Shakespeare,[5] his translation of
Plato's *Republic*,[6] and his translation of Rousseau's *Émile*.[7] We would be even
further in his debt if he could now transform some of his phenomenal winnings
from the best-seller lottery into the leisure needed to prepare for publication his
brilliant doctoral dissertation on Isocrates.[8]

Mr. Bloom is one of many who are privileged to recognize Leo Strauss as a
teacher.[9] He, however, has had a publishing success inconceivable for his master.
In fact, I estimate that more copies of *Closing* have been sold than of all the books
published by Mr. Strauss and his other students combined.[10] For better *and* for

George Anastaplo is Professor of Law, Loyola University of Chicago, and Lecturer in the Liberal Arts, the
University of Chicago. This essay is reprinted with permission from *The Great Ideas Today*, an
Encyclopedia Britannica publication, 1988:252–273.

worse, the form, tone, and substance of *Closing* will represent to many, for a long time to come, what the Straussian persuasion means.[11]

The Closing of the American Mind has become an "event," making it difficult for us to assess the book in itself. Since there is in its overall argument relatively little that is both new and sound, it would not warrant much attention if it were merely still another academic title. But the astonishing reception of the book places it outside the normal range of scholarly interest. One can be reminded of what the citizens of Thebes faced when they discovered the remarkably unnatural creature they had in Oedipus. We can see great success turn into an appalling curse in Sophocles' *Oedipus Tyrannos*.

In any event, the unnatural is hard to talk about because the usual points of reference are not available. In Mr. Bloom's circumstances, moreover, a clear grasp of the situation is hard to secure by those who cannot help but be jealous of, as well as appalled by, what has chanced to happen.

I.

The unnatural was once readily associated with the impious. Something of the impious may be detected in Mr. Bloom's book, which is rather odd considering that it stands for a return to an older way of education.

One form impiety can take is neglect of one's origins and teachers. Leo Strauss, Allan Bloom's principal teacher, is ignored, even though there are in his book dozens, if not hundreds, of echoes of that teacher's work.[12] Nor can one easily gather from this book that most of the things Mr. Bloom has to say about the current failings of higher education in this country are things already long bruited about at the University of Chicago and elsewhere when he first arrived on the academic scene in the 1940s.[13]

To be sure, Mr. Bloom is prepared, in private conversations and in public interviews, to acknowledge both Mr. Strauss and the University of Chicago.[14] But the stance taken throughout his book is that of the pioneer staking out new ground rather than that of the laborer cultivating soil already cleared by others. This desperate self-assertiveness, which is less generous than Mr. Bloom is naturally inclined to be, is intimately linked, I suspect, to his decision to dramatize the 1960s as somehow the point of departure in the United States for the crisis he is announcing.[15]

Is it not misleading to permit a grounding in the classics to seem so self-centered that one can neglect what is due to one's teachers and to one's community?[16] This is the questionable side of what is often condemned as "elitism." Certainly, it is not healthy to leave the impression that those upon whom one has depended, and from whom one has learned much, have not been duly appreciated. This is an instructive aspect of that extreme form of impiety found in an obvious repudiation of the divine.

II.

Something of the determination to enlist everything in the service of his thesis may be seen in the way Mr. Bloom deals with the texts of the great writers he draws upon. One can easily get the impression, if this book were all one had to go by, that he never truly studies such books but merely uses them. I am reminded of a comment I once heard from Mr. Strauss about Nietzsche: he always found Nietzsche interesting in his masterful generalizations, but he often found him simply wrong in the details which he could check out for himself.[17]

One observation after another in *Closing* is questionable: Socrates is presented more in opposition to Achilles than Plato indicates;[18] Aristotle is presented as saying that sexual intercourse, rather than moral virtue, is one of man's two peaks;[19] enterprising moderns such as Hobbes and Locke are presented as if they wanted to uproot ambition;[20] Maimonides is presented as if he identified theology with philosophy;[21] Goethe is presented in a way that seems to leave a useful discussion dependent upon errors in translation of a key passage in *Faust*;[22] Schiller is presented in a way that makes him seem far less sophisticated than he is about Homer;[23] and Rousseau, Kant, Hegel, and Nietzsche are presented as "thinkers of the very highest order," even though they are fundamentally wrong in critical respects.[24] One can easily conclude that there is in the abundance of *Closing*, which is much more biographical and sociological than philosophical, hardly a statement about any of the great authors or their books that can be confidently relied upon.[25]

It may even make one wonder what good the kind of education advocated in *Closing* is if it should exhibit, if not depend upon, such unreliable scholarship. There is a warning here for all of us who have been liberated by Mr. Strauss, who was himself the model of care and restraint in his broad-ranging scholarship, however daring and unconventional he was willing to appear in his conclusions. A proper education should make one cautious in one's uses of sources, moderate in the tone of one's political and social advocacy, and anything but overbearing in one's assessment of the less enlightened, keeping in mind that it is usually easier to attack than to defend. Related to these concerns is the perennial question of how influential the traditional education can be if its advocates display themselves, both in public and in private, as decidedly self-indulgent.

Someone may protest that it is not fair to assess *Closing* as a scholarly work. Still, all reports indicate that it was originally prepared as a book that would appeal only to a limited academic audience. It is common knowledge that the publisher had a lot to say about how the text should be rearranged. What governed the arrangement of the material was not the author's ideas but the publisher's commercial instincts, with the "packaging" of the book taking precedence over its substance. Cannot we see reflected in such deference to consumerism one major cause of the deterioration of American education rightly decried by Mr. Bloom?

It is difficult to take seriously any book whose author has acquiesced in a comprehensive rearrangement of what he had thought fit to say. Mr. Strauss, on the other hand, was legendary in his insistence upon the integrity of those scholarly texts he had carefully prepared.[26] He would have found congenial the injunction issued by another fastidious author[27] to his publisher: "I write; you print."

III.

The deficiencies all too evident in Mr. Bloom's use of books and authors in the great Western tradition may be seen as well in his handling of American things, not least with respect to the origins and principles of the regime. He has too low a view of the Founders, virtually taking them to have been primarily Hobbesians. He does not seem to appreciate what Mr. Strauss said about the elevated character of what the Founders said and did.[28] But then, Mr. Bloom himself is so much more interested in intellectual accomplishments than in the moral virtues that he can easily be taken to be a nihilist.[29] Be that as it may, his approach, which runs the risk of mere crankiness if not even of sterility, raises serious questions about any effort to guide citizens properly.

However dubious Mr. Bloom's view of the American founding is, even more so is his view of the lamentable re-founding he in effect sees as having taken place here after the Second World War. Much is made of "the German connection," with Nietzsche, Heidegger, and the like presented as principally responsible for the relativism and the moral and intellectual decline which this country has suffered.[30] The dramatics Mr. Bloom relies upon here and elsewhere are critical to his success both as the author of *Closing* and as a teacher. This is not to deny, however, that he can have a salutary effect upon bright students, in large part because he can and does point them back to the powerful, yet sober and sobering, works of Leo Strauss.

Long before Mr. Bloom first came to the University of Chicago as a college student in the middle 1940s, vigorous criticism could be heard there and elsewhere of the rise of relativism and a related decline in higher education. The developments criticized did not depend upon the European scholars Mr. Bloom makes so much of, who had fled from the Nazis a decade before. When Chief Justice Vinson informed us, in his 1951 opinion affirming the Communist Party leaders' Smith Act convictions, that "nothing is more certain in modern society than the principle that there are no absolutes," he, his colleagues, and their teachers had not been shaped primarily by Nietzsche and the like.[31] And when Justice Holmes, two generations before, ridiculed any notion of the common law as "a brooding omnipresence in the sky," he drew upon a legal realism movement that went back into the nineteenth century.[32]

Much more influential in this country than German thinkers, who continue to find it difficult to make headway against American common sense, has been modern science, especially in physics, astronomy, and biology, subjects about which Mr. Bloom does not pretend to know much.[33] These developments have affected the religious opinions of the American people, just as they have those of others around the world. They have also induced a deep uncertainty in secular thought about man's place in the universe. Nietzsche and Heidegger, among others, have been shaken by the same developments, which go back to Machiavelli, Hobbes, and Locke, but have responded to them in ways that the typical American thinker still finds uncongenial.

One obvious consequence of modern science is the remarkable technology harnessed to it. This has led to a steady escalation in the standard of living, an unprecedented personal and social mobility, and the development of all kinds of devices (including birth-control aids) which promote self-gratification and undermine a sense of community. What automobiles and movies began to do to the American community after the First World War, aviation, medicine and television have continued to do in an even more intensive and pervasive form since the Second World War. Indeed, it is an astonishing feature of *Closing* that so little is said in it about the disastrous effects of television upon American education and upon community life here as in other parts of the world.[34] Do not we all know what it has done to the capacity of students to read, to concentrate, and to work? They are much more apt now than they were two generations ago to expect their teachers to entertain them.

A people shaped by television insists upon spectaculars as well as upon instant gratification—in sports, in politics, and in intellectual experiences—and it is these debased tastes that *Closing*, with its cascades of pronouncements on scores of books and authors, caters to. The middle-class book buyers who have been drawn to Mr. Bloom's learned jeremiad find it more congenial to believe that the chronic problems of their children are due to the drugs, music, and sexuality that outsiders have foisted upon them than to blame the television and other such innovations that those parents have been themselves too caught up with to deny to their children. Too much is made of the effects of the universities, and not enough of science and technology (which are fairly independent of the influences of academic life), in the shaping of the American people.

IV.

Whatever the principal influences upon us—whether modern science, or technology, or thinkers ranging from Machiavelli and Hobbes to Rousseau, Nietzsche, and Heidegger—they all contribute to one result, a serious questioning of the status of nature among us. Mr. Bloom is too good a student of Leo Strauss not to be aware of how critical the problem of nature is in any effort to understand the modern development.

The merits of *The Closing of the American Mind* are evident here. Consider how one critic has put his recognition of what the book can surely teach us:

> Mr. Bloom reminds us that the present defect of schooling at all levels is basically intellectual. The jumble of "subjects" into which the curriculum has fallen is part of the problem, as is the reduction of learning to psychological adjustment and job skills, rather than the struggle for truth and an underlying understanding of things. And this reduction has not been at odds with what the universities teach, but in line with it, reflecting the chaos of learning which has overtaken them and the low view of human nature which, at least in the social sciences, they have adopted.
>
> Mr. Bloom recalls this for us in trenchant terms that could have been used half a century ago by Robert M. Hutchins, then president of the university at which Mr. Bloom teaches. For the complaint as to higher education in this country is at least as old as that, though Mr. Bloom does not go very far toward acknowledging the fact, and though few writers on the subject have been as eloquent as he in making the case.[35]

Mr. Bloom, who has been very much (I believe too much) influenced by Rousseau and Nietzsche, is probably most eloquent in depicting the confusion in students' souls and in the souls of many of his colleagues. And there is something commendable in his willingness to speak the truth as he sees it.

Thus the book has become, and is likely to remain for a decade, a convenient symbol of what is wrong in American higher education. It is less likely to be useful as a guide to what can be done about our problems. Even though

Closing is not easy to read—with relatively few readers getting past the sensational exposés, in the opening chapters, of the vagaries of student life—it may nevertheless help impressionable people begin to respect the study of good books as at least fashionable.

It does contribute to the dramatic character of Mr. Bloom's assault upon established educational prejudices that he should seem much more original, far less derivative, than he is. The soundness of Leo Strauss's thought is testified to, however, in that it can assert itself despite Mr. Bloom's many mistakes, if not wrongheadedness. It has been somewhat sad, nevertheless, to see how bitterly Mr. Strauss has been attacked in some quarters because of this book. I can only hope that some of Mr. Strauss's critics and their readers can be encouraged to go look at "the real thing" rather than settle for the caricature of the Straussian approach to political philosophy that has been conjured up by some reviewers.

In any event, the thoughtful reader who is aware of Mr. Strauss's virtues can better appreciate, as he watches some Straussians carry on, how various of Socrates' naturally ambitious or temperamentally difficult students could be mistaken as products of his teaching. In any event, Mr. Bloom may have sensed that he could "let himself go" as he has in *Closing* only if he kept Mr. Strauss "literally" out of sight. His mentor here would be Alcibiades.

V.

One consequence of Mr. Bloom's putting an emphasis upon developments in postwar America is that he can make as much as he does of various sensational episodes in the Sixties, not least the much-publicized disturbances at Cornell University in which he happened to be involved as a member of its government department.

It is odd that so much can be made of student unrest in the Sixties without saying much more than is said in *Closing* about the effect upon the young of the misconceived, self-destructive, and perhaps unconstitutional American involvement in the war in Indochina. It is silly to neglect a conflict that has had so unfortunate an effect in this country upon the level of patriotism, upon faith in government, and upon respect for a defensible worldwide strategy.[36]

Also silly is any suggestion that mere self-interest moved students to oppose the draft. This approach fails to appreciate how much the most celebrated instances of resistance to improper governmental actions in Anglo-American constitutional history have taken the form of opposition to demands upon citizens.[37] Who knows what would have happened to American resistance in the 1770s if the British government had given in to the American colonists' "self-centered" demand that they be subjected to no taxation without representation? Be that as it may, it is hardly fitting to hear those without military experience of their own berating the young for their reluctance to fight in what seemed to them, and may well have been for us, an unjust war.

Even the "war" that Mr. Bloom does happen to know something about personally—the Cornell struggle of 1969—seems to have been considerably more complex than he makes it out to have been. There is no indication, in Mr.

Bloom's account of the Cornell troubles, of the experiences, fears, and concerns of the people, whether students or faculty, who were ranged against the position he passionately supports. It is not appreciated, for example, that some of the more aggressive minority students may have actually believed they were defending themselves. [38] Nor is it appreciated how much more dangerous military service could be at that time than life during even the most troubled days on the Cornell campus—and yet Mr. Bloom is much more sympathetic toward intimidated faculty members than he is toward students disturbed at the prospect of being shipped off to Vietnam. [39]

All this is not to deny that there was something traumatic for Mr. Bloom in his Cornell experience, so much so that he must be fierce in the way he deals with it two decades later. His account of Cornell, which some consider the best thing in *Closing*, is the most obviously flawed part of the book. *Closing* would be far better without its final seventy pages. It is unfortunate when mistreatment, whether in one's childhood or early in one's career, cannot be risen above, if not even made good use of, in one's maturity. Mr. Bloom may be in critical respects a soul with too much, or rather the wrong kind of, longing. [40]

I had occasion to watch close up student sit-ins and the like on several campuses in the Sixties. I found rebellious students usually far more thoughtful, and far more restrained, than Mr. Bloom remembers them. And I could be struck by the unwillingness or inability of many faculty members, even on the University of Chicago campus, to talk with them seriously during one crisis after another. I recall one occasion in Chicago, after the administration and faculty had "broken" a student sit-in, informing the dean of the college, during a chance encounter at a reception in a faculty home, how his students had understood the issues. They have been beaten, I added, and they are at this moment meeting to assess what has happened. I then presumed to advise him that it would be an act of magnanimity, and not without use in reestablishing a proper trust between faculty and students on the campus, if their dean would go to them and treat them in their defeat as an honorable enemy. He would go, he told me, if I would accompany him. We at once left the reception for the student center. But after we entered the building, and just as we got to the door of the meeting hall, I was astonished to watch him fade away without either explanation or apology. It was a most remarkable disappearing act—and ever after made me skeptical about faculty who proclaimed that they, but not the students, were open to rational discourse. [41]

Of course, the students at Cornell may have been different, but I suspect not. I have talked at length with those in a position to know what happened there. If, however, Cornell was as special as Mr. Bloom remembers it, one may well wonder whether it is instructive about what was (or was not) happening elsewhere in this country. In any event, it is difficult to see, even if one accepts Mr. Bloom's no doubt sincere account as completely reliable, that what happened there says much one way or another about modes of education. To see it all, as Mr. Bloom seems to do, as the beginning of what happened to the universities under the Nazis can only be characterized as a perverse kind of wishful thinking. [42]

VI.

It is also odd that so much can be made of student unrest in the Sixties without saying much more than is said in *Closing* about the effect upon the young of the civil rights movement. This too bears upon what really went on at Cornell and how students there understood the issues.

Something of Mr. Bloom's limitations in assessing those students may be seen in what he says about what is happening these days to minority students on campuses. He comments adversely on their self-segregation and their failure to take advantage of the opportunities offered them. He does not seem to appreciate how deep-rooted the problems of race relations still are in this country, problems that are bound to be mirrored in campus life.[43]

Related to his limitations here is his depreciation again and again of feminist efforts. One can see that unfortunate attitudes about minorities and about women are as intermingled in Mr. Bloom as some ideologues believe them generally to be. Here, as elsewhere, it seems that Mr. Bloom cannot help himself, which *is* an odd state of affairs in one so gifted. This is not to deny that women are finding that the feminist cause is more complicated than they had taken it to be, perhaps even that natural differences between women and men are more critical than some had been led to believe.

Also related to all this is what Mr. Bloom has to say about rock music, which, along with what he has to say about students' sexual relations, has aroused the greatest public interest in the book.[44] I am persuaded, after discussing Mr. Bloom's account of music with a number of people versed in rock music, including some who do not personally care for it, that he is probably wrong in what he says about what that music is generally like, and what it does to those who listen to it. The redeeming feature of his discussion is, however, that it emphatically reminds us of ancient teachings about the significance of music, and of art generally, in forming the human soul.[45]

I do not challenge the observation that students are much more caught up by overt sensuality than they were in my college generation or in the generation before. But, I suspect, this is not because of special influences upon the young— such as the music they listen to—but rather because of that general relaxation of restraints which goes back to the Second World War and because of the general intensification of appeals to the sensual seen in the mass media catering to the adult world. What I as a teenager saw among my young Air Corps comrades during the war has made subsequent student eroticism seem child's play by comparison. All this is complicated by the now fashionable reading of the First Amendment which extends its protection to obscenity and other kinds of expression not anticipated by the framers of the Bill of Rights.

Various of the matters I have touched upon here are also important for raising the question of what nature means in ordering human relations. It is easy if not even mandatory these days for intellectuals to deny the guidance of nature, especially if one overreacts (in the name either of justice or of compassion) to long-standing mistreatment by the community of racial minorities, of women, and of homosexuals. Some conservative critics of *Closing* believe it does not go far enough, in that it does not extend to the claims of homosexuals the strictures it lays down against the claims of feminists and of racial militants. But I would prefer to see Mr. Bloom become as relaxed about racial minorities and about uppity women as he commendably is about the aggressive homosexuals among us. All three groups will need, for decades to come, respectful sympathy and informed guidance from the people who dominate public opinion, including those who control higher education.[46]

VII.

Mr. Bloom's limitations as a reporter of political movements, including of what did happen at Cornell, are suggested by his dismissal of the McCarthy Period as not having had a significant effect in the universities of this country. And yet there is abundant testimony to the contrary, so much so that one must wonder where he was while all that was going on.[47]

The interesting question here is not what was going on—for that is clear enough—but rather why Mr. Bloom should have so misapprehended things. It seems to have something to do with his urge to make as much as he does both of his Cornell experience and of "the German connection." One need not deny that the Sixties were important: after all, we are all talking about gender, civil rights, war, and sexual relations in somewhat the way the Sixties taught us to—and that has healthy aspects as well as unhealthy. But the McCarthy Period has also had a lasting effect, partly because the passions it pandered to and the thoughtlessness it encouraged did contribute to American involvement in Vietnam—and that, in turn, helped make some intellectuals and all too many of the young become irresponsible as citizens.

Student opinion about their teachers in the Sixties was influenced by what was remembered about how faculties had caved in to loyalty forays against the universities a decade before. Faculties, by and large, did stand up to rampaging students in the Sixties much better than they had to governmental intimidation in the Fifties, even though the students had a better cause than did the government inquisitors. But, then, it was considerably more dangerous for professors to resist the inquisitors.[48]

One contribution that the Reagan administration has inadvertently made to a sounder polity is to teach the country that patriotism is not enough, that common sense and a respect for constitutional processes are still needed if government is to conduct itself properly. (The 1987 Iran-*Contra* revelations were particularly instructive here, especially when it became known that the covert actions resorted to had included supplying arms to the very people in Iran who were partly responsible for killing our Marines in their Beirut barracks.) Perhaps the legacy of the McCarthy Period may finally be working itself out of our system.

It is odd that Mr. Bloom sees Justice Holmes's "clear and present danger" test as exemplifying a "gradual movement away from rights to openness." That is, he does not seem to appreciate that the worst abuses during the McCarthy Period were ratified by judicial recourse to the "clear and present danger" test, not curtailed by it.[49] This is further testimony to Mr. Bloom's limitations in his efforts to describe and assess the practices as well as the principles of the American regime both at this time and at its founding.[50]

Epilogue

Various chance factors have combined to make *The Closing of the American Mind* soar as it has. The immediate ground from which it took off was prepared by the Reagan administration before the shameful Iran-*Contra* revelations sapped its vitality. The book appeals in large part to those who "know" that there is something really wrong with the young, with racial minorities, with homosexuals, with feminists, and with the unpatriotic (especially among intellectuals). It also appeals, and properly so, to those who have been told repeatedly, for several generations now, about the shortcomings of American higher education.

There *was* a golden age in American higher education when Allan Bloom, as a fifteen-year-old, first came to the University of Chicago—but that was principally due to the presence on campuses of large numbers of older men who had served several years in a proper war and who were serious about an education. Perhaps, indeed, nothing would contribute more to the seriousness of higher education today than the general requirement of a few years of high-minded national service immediately after high school.

Be that as it may, American students in the best universities may still be better, in that they are more open to radical intellectual challenge, than their European counterparts. It should at once be added that the universities in this country, if they are to continue to enjoy the massive public support they need to survive, have to provide many programs in addition to the finest training in the liberal arts that relatively few students can make much use of. The best prospects for liberal education remain in the small colleges of this country, whether standing alone or as more or less autonomous parts of universities.

Although chance has been critical in making Mr. Bloom a wealthy celebrity, it is a fate he is as much entitled to as any scholar of our generation. He, like the great Protagoras, does work at his calling and he is known as an eloquent champion of those privileged to study with him. I still recall the considerable pleasure he had, and that his friends shared, when he got his contract to translate the *Republic*.[51] Indeed, I know no one among the academics with whom I have been associated for four decades now who would enjoy spending the fortune he is making as much as Mr. Bloom is likely to, and who would be less corrupted in the process.

It would give Allan Bloom's friends considerable pleasure if he could now take his loot, invest it conservatively, and live quite comfortably ever after while taking care of his health better than he ever has, curtailing sharply his oppressively lucrative lecture schedule, and returning to a serious study, with the help of Leo Strauss, of the Bible and the Greek texts which lie at the roots of all that he properly stands for.[52]

---

[1] This story is adapted from Leo Rosten, *The Joys of Yiddish* (New York: McGraw-Hill, 1968), p. 173. *See*, for a eulogy of the spiritual prototype for the hero of this story, Anastaplo, *The Artist as Thinker: From Shakespeare to Joyce* (Athens, Ohio: Swallow Press/Ohio University Press, 1983), pp. 270–71. *See also* note 45 below. *See*, on the Establishment-minded kibitzer in this story, note 48 below.

The reader is urged, as with my other publications, to begin by reading the text of this review without reference to its notes.

[2] We have here a variation upon an ancient Cretan paradox.

The full title of Mr. Bloom's book is *The Closing of the American Mind: How Higher Education Has Failed Democracy and Impoverished the Souls of Today's Students* (New York: Simon and Schuster, 1987). The book is described in this fashion by the *New Yorker* (July 6, 1987, p. 82):

> This essay, whose author is a political philosopher at the University of Chicago, argues that American universities have yielded intellectual and moral authority to the point where their students are not taught values, and are not even allowed to discover them. Because the traditional curriculum has been eroded, undergraduates have little chance to understand the ideas that shaped the past, and the result is that they do not learn to think coherently about the present. This process may be described, at least in part, as good intentions gone awry: post-Second World War faculties, attempting inclusiveness, taught tolerance, drifted into a pervasive relativism, and left themselves without any intellectual foundation for moral judgment. At present, the author finds the university compartmentalized: science departments are enclaves of self-importance; the humanities faculties "do not believe in themselves or what they do"; and political science is "a haphazard bazaar." He allows his readers to decide whether the disarray of our learned institutions represents or misrepresents the condition of the wider society.

[3] *See*, for what can be said on behalf of Judge Bork, Anastaplo, "On the Judging of Judges: The Bork Case," *University of Chicago Maroon*, Oct. 6, 1987, p. 21.

[4] Among the fine publications by Mr. Bloom's former students have been meticulous translations of Greek texts: Plato's *Laws*, by Thomas L. Pangle (Free Press); Aristotle's *Politics*, by Carnes Lord (University of Chicago Press); Plato's *Euthyphro, Apology,* and *Crito,* and Aristophanes' *Clouds,* by Thomas G. West (Cornell University Press). The Pangle translation of the *Laws* is dedicated to Mr. Bloom.

Various of Mr. Bloom's former students like *Closing* because it reads the way they fondly remember him in his lecture courses.

[5] *See* Allan Bloom (with Harry V. Jaffa), *Shakespeare's Politics* (New York: Basic Books, 1964). This book is dedicated by Mr. Bloom and Mr. Jaffa "To Leo Strauss, Our Teacher." See *Commentary*, July 1987, p. 14.

[6] *See* Allan Bloom, trans., Plato, *The Republic* (New York: Basic Books, 1968). *See* note 9 below. This translation is dedicated by Mr. Bloom to his mother and father.

[7] *See* Allan Bloom, trans., Jean-Jacques Rousseau, *Émile: or, On Education* (New York: Basic Books, 1979). This translation is dedicated by Mr. Bloom, "To the memory of Victor Baras, My Student and Friend." It was anticipated by the Bloom translation, *Politics and the Arts: Rousseau's Letter to M. d'Alembert on the Theater* (Glencoe, Ill.: Free Press, 1960). *Closing* is dedicated by Mr. Bloom, "To My Students."

[8] See Allan David Bloom, *The Political Philosophy of Isocrates* (Ph.D. diss., University of Chicago, 1955).

[9] *See*, on Leo Strauss, Anastaplo, *The Artist as Thinker*, pp. 250–72. *See also* Laurence Berns, "Aristotle and the Moderns on Freedom and Equality," in Kenneth L. Deutsch and Walter Soffer, eds., *The Crisis of Liberal Democracy: A Straussian Perspective* (Albany: State University of New York Press, 1987), p. 148. Mr. Strauss is drawn upon at length in the interpretive essay in the Bloom translation of Plato's *Republic*. *See* note 6 above.

[10] *Closing* was on the *New York Times* best-seller list for almost a year after it first appeared there on April 26, 1987. It reached the top of the list on June 7, 1987, remaining there for ten weeks. See *Publishers Weekly*, July 3, 1987, p. 26. In May 1988 *Closing* appeared on the paperback best-seller list for what promises to be an extended stay. George Plimpton has suggested that *Closing* was pushed to the top of the best-seller list largely because of the introduction that Saul Bellow provided for it. Donna Rifkind, "Literary Logrolling as Art," *Wall Street Journal*, May 24, 1988, p. 26. *See* note 12 below. Compare note 40 below.

[11] *See*, e.g., David Reiff, "The Colonel and the Professor," *Times Literary Supplement*, Sept. 4, 1987, p. 950; Robert Paul Wolff, book review, *Academe*, September–October 1987, p. 64; Martha Nussbaum, "Undemocratic Vistas," *New York Review of Books*, Nov. 5, 1987, p. 20; Jean Bethke Elshtain, "Allan in Wonderland," *Cross Currents*, Winter 1987, p. 477. *See also* Jacob Weisberg, "The Cult of Leo Strauss: An obscure philosopher's Washington disciples," *Newsweek*, Aug. 3, 1987, p. 61; note 29 below. Consider as well Mortimer J. Adler's appearance on William F. Buckley, Jr.'s "Firing Line," #1739, aired on PBS the week of May 27, 1988.

An eminent classical scholar is reported in a *New York Times Magazine* article on Mr. Bloom as having denounced Leo Strauss as "a bloody lunatic." (James Atlas, "Chicago's Grumpy Guru," Jan. 3, 1988, p. 25.) Far more fair, as well as instructive, is the tribute paid to Mr. Strauss by the same classical scholar on another occasion when the auspices were far more favorable. Mr. Strauss could then be remembered by him as "a man of extraordinary mental power with a kind of fantasy of the intellect, creative, almost like a poet. . . . He cared about thoughts and their life and their relations to books and to the world with a white-hot intensity." See Anastaplo, *The Artist as Thinker*, p. 272.

12There is only one reference to Mr. Strauss by name, and that is really a quotation by Mr. Strauss from Winston Churchill to the effect that "the moderns 'built on low but solid ground.'" *Closing*, p. 167. All kinds of other people are acknowledged by Mr. Bloom in his preface, including old students, readers, and typists. Of Saul Bellow, who contributed a most helpful foreword to *Closing*, Mr. Bloom can say, "[He], with his special generosity, entered into my thoughts and encouraged me in paths I had never before taken." *Closing*, p. 23. See note 10 above, note 15 below.

The informed reader expects Mr. Strauss finally to emerge from the survey of political philosophy in Mr. Bloom's long chapter, "From Socrates' *Apology* to Heidegger's *Rektoratsrede*," especially since it concludes with the "study of the problem of Socrates [as] the one thing most needful." *Closing*, p. 310. If anyone emerges here, however, it is Mr. Bloom himself. (Elsewhere it is Woody Allen. See *Closing*, pp. 125, 144–46, 154, 155, 173.) Mr. Strauss's last public lecture at the University of Chicago, on Dec. 1, 1967, was on "The Socratic Question." See Anastaplo, *The Artist as Thinker*, pp. 259–62. The problem of Socrates was repeatedly investigated by Mr. Strauss in his studies of Aristophanes, Plato, and Xenophon.

13Mr. Bloom took his University of Chicago doctorate with the Committee on Social Thought, an interdisciplinary body sponsored by Robert Maynard Hutchins as president of the University. Mr. Bloom began his teaching career at the University of Chicago in the Basic Program of Liberal Education for Adults, founded by Mr. Hutchins, Cyril Houle, and Mortimer J. Adler and rejuvenated by Maurice F. X. Donohue. Compare *Closing*, pp. 54, 70. See note 51 below.

14See, e.g., *University of Chicago Magazine*, Summer 1987, p. 9 ("I'm a Hutchins enthusiast without believing that that was the only way or even perhaps the right way"); *Washington Post*, June 18, 1987, p. C2. See note 51 below. Mr. Bloom can also speak with respect of teachers such as Yves R. Simon (whose essay "Introduction to the Study of Practical Wisdom" may be found in the 1988 volume of *Great Ideas Today*) and institutions such as St. John's College. See, e.g., Eugene Kennedy, "The Scholar Who Made Education a Best Seller," *New York Times, Education Life*, Aug. 2, 1987, p. 36.

15Is there not something Heideggerian, and thus questionable, about such self-assertiveness? The demands of the market might also have been responsible for making so much in *Closing* of the supposed intellectual influences upon Mr. Bloom of celebrities that Mr. Strauss could hardly have taken seriously. See note 12 above, note 51 below.

See, on Martin Heidegger, Anastaplo, *The Artist as Thinker*, pp. 269, 475.

16This may be related to the implicit depreciation of politics in Mr. Bloom's approach. "Never did I think that the university was properly ministerial to the society around it. Rather I thought and think that society is ministerial to the university, and I bless a society that tolerates and supports an eternal childhood for some, a childhood whose playfulness can in turn be a blessing to society." *Closing*, p. 245. Consider, also, *ibid.*, p. 336: "The importance of [his college] years for an American cannot be overestimated. They are civilization's only chance to get to him." Compare *ibid.*, p. 39: "The United States is one of the highest and most extreme achievements of the rational quest for the good life according to nature." See also *ibid.*, p. 97. Compare note 49 below.

A depreciation of the political may be implicit as well in Mr. Bloom's initial response to the Universtiy of Chicago campus: "When I was fifteen years old I saw the University of Chicago for the first time and somehow sensed that I had discovered my life. I had never before seen, or at least had not noticed, buildings that were evidently dedicated to a higher purpose, not to necessity or utility, not merely to shelter or manufacture or trade, but to something that might be an end in itself. The Middle West was not known for the splendor of its houses of worship or its monuments to political glory." *Closing*, p. 243. Thus, it seems, he had not appreciated the majestic aspirations of Midwestern county courthouses or the significance of Civil War and other such monuments across the land. Particularly memorable is the rather insistent Indiana Soldiers' and Sailors' Monument in Mr. Bloom's native Indianapolis. See note 22 below.

17See Anastaplo, *The Artist as Thinker*, p. 259.

18See *Closing*, pp. 66, 285. Compare *ibid.*, pp. 274, 327. Compare, also, Plato, *Apology* 28C-D, *Crito*

44B, *Republic* 516D-E; Anastaplo, *The Constitutionalist; Notes on the First Amendment* (Dallas, Texas: Southern Methodist University Press, 1971), p. 278; Anastaplo, *Human Being and Citizen: Essays on Virtue, Freedom and the Common Good* (Chicago: Swallow Press, 1975), p. 240, n. 32, pp. 242–43, n. 39.

[19] "Aristotle said that man has two peaks, each accompanied by intense pleasure: sexual intercourse and thinking." *Closing*, p. 137. Compare note 9 above.

[20] See *Closing*, pp. 330–31; also, *ibid.*, pp. 110–12, 162–70, 174–77. *See*, as well, *ibid.*, pp. 28, 97, 187. Compare note 9 above.

[21] See *Closing*, pp. 271, 283. Mr. Strauss could speak with passion of "what it means to be a son of the Jewish people—of the *'am 'olam*—to have one's roots deep in the oldest past and to be committed to a future beyond all futures." Anastaplo, *The Artist as Thinker*, p. 271. He could invoke as well, in a time of mourning, "the traditional Jewish formula: 'May God comfort you among the others who mourn for Zion and Jerusalem.'" Ibid., p. 271. Mr. Bloom's uses of religion in *Closing* verge on the sentimental in some instances and on the supersophisticated in others. Neither is the proper response. Compare, however, *Closing*, p. 60.

See, on the relation of revelation to reason, Anastaplo, "Church and State: Explorations," 19 *Loyola University of Chicago Law Journal* 61 (1987), 183–93.

[22] See *Closing*, pp. 302–3. Goethe's text has four stages, not only the three drawn upon here by Mr. Bloom. It is nicely revealing that Mr. Bloom should convert the meditating Faust's "meaning" (or "sense") into "feeling" and that he should omit altogether "force" (or "strength") from Faust's inventory. Thus, it can be said, Mr. Bloom's depreciation of politics is instinctive, so much so as to subvert his usual meticulousness as a translator. *See* note 16 above, notes 42 and 47 below.

[23] See *Closing*, pp. 41, 306, 308. Compare Gisela N. Berns, *Greek Antiquity in Schiller's Wallenstein* (Chapel Hill: University of North Carolina Press, 1985).

[24] "I must reiterate that Rousseau, Kant, Hegel and Nietzsche are thinkers of the very highest order. . . . We must relearn what this means and also that there are others who belong in the same rank." *Closing*, p. 240. *See also ibid.*, pp. 290 ("The great modern philosophers were as much philosophers as were the ancients"), 307–8, 377. Mr. Strauss believed Plato and Aristotle "of the very highest order." Would not those thinkers who misread Plato and Aristotle be of a lower order, including Nietzsche and his predecessors? *See* Anastaplo, "On How Eric Vogelin Has Read Plato and Aristotle," 1986–87 *Independent Journal of Philosophy* (forthcoming).

[25] Mr. Bloom refuses to dull the rhetorical impressiveness of his arguments with qualifications because he, like his stylistic master Rousseau, is more interested in leading his readers to *feel* the power of his positions than in protecting himself in advance from criticism. But unlike his master, Mr. Bloom seems to believe that a people, or life itself, can be significant only in or through the study of books. (There may be something nihilistic about this. *See* the text at note 29 below.) Compare the experience of Sparta, which is not remembered for books.

Eva Brann, of St. John's College, has published a review of *Closing* which may come to be celebrated as the best response to the book. 38 *St. John's Review* 71 (1988). It should have a most salutary effect, not least because of its restraint. Among much else, Miss Brann has this to say:

> The Closing of the American Mind is, I am implying, a *historicist* enterprise or, more fairly, next cousin to it. Since historicism, the notion that the temporal place of a text determines its significance more than does the author's conscious intention and that history through its movements is a real agent, is Mr. Bloom's *bête noir*, this is no small charge. But there is no getting around the fact that the book continually places and positions great names evaluatively from the outside in—of internal philosophical substance it contains very little. Similarly it persistently sums up the spirit of the times and seeks its genealogy in intellectual movements. . . .
> The title itself is revealing. It is, to be sure, not Mr. Bloom's choice. He wanted the euphonious and accurate title "Souls Without Longing" (the French title is "L'Ame désarmée"). But he condoned "The Closing of the American Mind." The "Closing" part is fine: one of the most convincing chapters is the early one in which he shows how openness corrupted, which becomes the lazily tolerant path of least resistance, forecloses passionate doubting, and how the springboard of learning is vigorous prejudice. But "the American Mind" is debased Hegelianism, and a scandal. Americans do, happily, still have certain areas of consensus; nonetheless, they have more than one mind among them. Ibid., pp. 75–6.

Further on Miss Brann makes these judgments:

The text seems to be stuffed with truth that is not the whole truth and not nothing but the truth. Of course it is very hard to hit all the small nails squarely on the head with so large a mallet, yet there are fine and there are coarse ways of epitomizing spheres of thought and trends of opinion. Mr. Bloom's often anonymous and torrential mode of presentation makes it hard to tell whether the trouble is with his accuracy or his perspective. Moreover, he sometimes seems to present an anonymous modern opinion as though it had but to come in contact with the air to self-destruct, while his great moderns, Rousseau and Nietzsche, seem somehow to merit awed admiration for setting us on the road we are condemned for following. Mr. Bloom's relation especially to Rousseau is the mystery of mysteries to me. One of the excellences of his exposition is the continual pointing to Rousseau not just as the uncannily accurate analyst but as the brilliantly effective originator of the corruption-prone side of modernity. (The book neglects to its detriment the complementary side, the reverence-producing splendor of modern science and mathematics). But then why is Mr. Bloom not on record as being at least as repelled as he is fascinated by this "inverse Socrates"?

Ibid., p. 77. Mr. Bloom's considerable use of Tocqueville as a guide to understanding American life may reflect the influence upon Tocqueville of Rousseau. Furthermore, Mr. Bloom has become habituated to seeing American things through European eyes. Miss Brann describes *Closing* as "a tract on the love of the love of wisdom." Ibid., p. 78. The current dispute about "elitism" is touched upon in what Miss Brann has to say about her "conviction that people one by one have in them, besides sound sense, the roots of reflection." Ibid., p. 73. See Jacob Klein, A *Commentary on Plato's Meno* (Chapel Hill: University of North Carolina Press, 1965).

Also instructive are the reservations in Miss Brann's review about the theory of the relation of music to the passions that Mr. Bloom finds in Plato's *Republic*. Ibid., pp. 78–9.

See the text at note 40 below, and the text at note 45 below. See also note 33 below. See, as well, Eva Brann, *Paradoxes of Education in a Republic* (Chicago: University of Chicago Press, 1979).

26 Mr. Strauss's care in writing (but not in preparing indexes for his books) reflected his care in reading. See, e.g., Leo Strauss, *Persecution and the Art of Writing* (Glencoe, Ill.: Free Press, 1952). Too much has been made both by some of Mr. Strauss's students and by some of his critics of his discovery about how a decent deception may have to be resorted to on occasion by the prudent man. See, e.g., Benjamin Barber, "The Philosopher Despot: Allan Bloom's elitist agenda," *Harper's Magazine*, January 1988, p. 61; Richard Rorty, "Straussianism, democracy, and Allan Bloom, I.: That Old-Time Philosophy," *New Republic*, April 4, 1988, p. 28. Compare Matthew 10:16.

27 Carl Van Doren, the historian.

28 See, e.g., Leo Strauss, *Natural Right and History* (Chicago: University of Chicago Press, 1953), p. 1. Compare, e.g., Bloom, *Closing*, pp. 28, 163–64, 187. But see note 16 above.

29 See the reviews of *Closing* by Harry V. Jaffa and Harry Neumann to be published in *Interpretation* (vol. 16, 1988). Compare the friendlier reviews to be published there by William A. Galston, Roger D. Masters, and Will Morrisey. Some of the unfriendly reviews (see, e.g., note 11 above) have been poorly informed, if not simply unfair.

In his discussion of "Nihilism, American Style" (*Closing*, pp. 139f.), Mr. Bloom seems to complain that American nihilism has not gone as far as the European original. The "shallowness" of the United States here may reflect a certain resiliency grounded in a sounder political system than any enjoyed by continental Europeans. See note 25 above.

30 Qualified support for Mr. Bloom here may be found in Strauss, *Natural Right and History*, pp. 1–2.

31 See *Dennis v. United States*, 341 U.S. 494, at 508 (1951). See, on *Dennis*, Anastaplo, *The Constitutionalist*, p. 824.

32 See Anastaplo, *The U S Constitution of 1787: A Commentary* (to be published in 1989 by the Johns Hopkins University Press), Lectures no. 10 and no. 11 (originally published in 18 *Loyola University of Chicago Law Journal* 15 [1986]). Compare the "absolutes" drawn upon in the Declaration of Independence as well as by William Blackstone. See, for the most instructive account of what the United States Supreme Court has done to its intended common-law powers, William W. Crosskey, *Politics and the Constitution in the History of the United States* (Chicago: University of Chicago Press, 1953). See, on Mr. Crosskey as a master teacher, Anastaplo, "Mr. Crosskey, the American Constitution, and the Natures of Things," 15 *Loyola University of Chicago Law Journal* 181 (1983). See also Malcolm P. Sharp, "Crosskey, Anastaplo and Meiklejohn on the United States Constitution," *University of Chicago Law School Record*, Spring 1973, p. 3.

33 Mr. Bloom's attempts to make use of mathematics are not happy ones. See *Closing*, pp. 127, 137. See

also note 25 above. I suspect that he also could have made better use of Freud than he does. *See* note 40 below.

34 *See*, for an extended argument for the abolition of broadcast television in the United States, Anastaplo, "Self-Government at the Mass Media: A Practical Man's Guide," in Harry M. Clor, ed., *The Mass Media and Modern Democracy* (Chicago: Rand McNally College Pub. Co., 1974), p. 161. Key questions remain, such as, Why have we permitted television to do all that it has done to us? What does the ever-expanding medical crusade really minister to in us? *See* Anastaplo, "On Death: One by One, Yet All Together," in *Human Being and Citizen*, p. 214.

35 John Van Doren, "Mr. Bloom, the American Mind, and Paideia," *The Paideia Bulletin*, November–December 1987, p. 1. *See*, on Mr. Hutchins and his efforts to reform liberal education at the University of Chicago in the 1930s, Mortimer J. Adler, *Philosopher at Large* (New York: Macmillan, 1977), p. 343. See also Anastaplo, "Jacob Klein of St. John's College," *The Newsletter*, Politics Department, University of Dallas, Spring 1979, pp. 7–8.

36 *See*, e.g., Anastaplo, "Preliminary Reflections on the Pentagon Papers," *University of Chicago Magazine*, January–February 1972, p. 2, March–April 1972, p. 16 (reprinted in 118 *Congressional Record* 24990 [July 24, 1972]).

37 See *Closing*, pp. 328–29. Organized campus resistance to the draft in the Sixties included among its numbers many students who were personally exempt (that is, women and the better male students). *See*, on opposition to the draft and the earliest important First Amendment case (*Schenck v. United States* [1919]), Anastaplo, *The Constitutionalist*, p. 826.

38 *See*, e.g., letter from Barbara Page, *New York Times Magazine*, Jan. 24, 1988, p. 8. Allan P. Sindler, a former Cornell colleague whom Mr. Bloom has properly praised (*Closing*, p. 23), prepared, in 1969 and 1971, accounts of the 1969 Cornell disturbances which are considerably more balanced than is Mr. Bloom's. (I have read only the manuscript versions of Mr. Sindler's accounts.) *See* notes 39 and 42 below. *See*, for a novel evidently drawing on some Cornell disturbances, Alison Lurie, *The War Between the Tates* (New York: Random House, 1974).

39 Consider how an unfriendly critic can comment upon such different responses:

> Among [Mr. Bloom's] various occasions for nostalgia is the good old Western movie, which people used to watch without a bunch of anti-racist and anti-sexist considerations spoiling their enjoyment. Yet he also recounts an incident that deeply troubled him (and, indeed, seems to have been the point of departure for the book itself): one day he was among a group of professors who were threatened at gunpoint by a group of "revolutionary" students. I share his indignation, of course; yet I cannot help noticing his reluctance to profit from this unique opportunity actually to take part in a Western himself.

Tzvetan Todorov, "The Philosopher and the Everyday," *New Republic*, Sept. 14 & 21, 1987, p. 34.

I have been told, by a thoughtful woman who was a student at Cornell during the 1969 disturbances and who engaged in the marathon meetings among students then, that she and her friends had felt betrayed by those faculty members who resigned their posts and left them to cope with the radical minority on campus. (This woman had herself been raised in an academic family on another university campus.) I myself believed at the time that the Cornell resignations (among which was Professor Sindler's) were a mistake, but it is difficult to judge such maneuvers from a distance. But I also recall that this did not keep me from letting it be known, as chairman of the political science department at Rosary College, that I was willing to do everything I could to help one or more of those who had resigned and who might have been in need of a temporary academic refuge. *See* notes 41 and 42 below.

40 A serious study of Mr. Bloom's book could well begin with his considerable use of the word *longing*. *See*, e.g., *Closing*, pp. 62, 125, 133, 134, 135, 157, 167, 169, 196, 205, 206, 243, 282, 320, 329. *See also* notes 25 and 33 above, note 52 below. (He is correct in pointing out the questionable implications of the use of such terms as *values* and *commitment*. *See*, e.g., *Closing*, pp. 194f. But notice Mr. Strauss's reference to *commitment* in the passage quoted in note 21 above.)

The curious blending in Mr. Bloom's soul of *longing* with *anger* may help explain his success with the national reading (or, at least, book-buying) public; there are in *Closing* the vibrations of one tormented soul that resonate in others. Gifted students can be moved by him, even to the extent of telling him things that they would not tell their other teachers. These may include things that are not quite so but which they sense he somehow wants to hear. They are moved much more by longings than he appreciates.

41 When students want to stop intellectual life on a campus, they usually can do so. We probably do not

want schools that are completely unresponsive to students or that are altogether invulnerable to student activity. This is not to deny that there was periodic gross irresponsibility, if not even a kind of intermittent lunacy, on campuses during the Sixties. But it does not help to be so dogmatic as not to recognize the serious questions that students could raise and that faculties and administrations failed to address properly. One of the sadder aspects of the Sixties was the loss of confidence by faculties in their ability to guide students with respect to controversial matters. *See* Anastaplo, *The Constitutionalist*, p. 409; Anastaplo, *Human Being and Citizen*, p. 263, n. 9; Anastaplo, "The Daring of Moderation: Student Power and *The Melian Dialogue*," 78 *School Review* 451 (August 1970). *See also* note 39 above. Compare Wayne C. Booth, *Now Don't Try to Reason With Me* (Chicago: University of Chicago Press, 1970), pp. 175, 217–23, 225, 243–61.

[42] For one thing, the Cornell students were not acting in concert with, but rather in opposition to, government policy. Nor were they simply the mob that Mr. Bloom condemns: there, as generally elsewhere on campuses, the extreme elements were effectively restrained by the bulk of the student body. Compare the odd recourse by a few of Mr. Bloom's students to passing out to the mob quotations from Plato, a tactic that he finds admirable. See *Closing*, pp. 332–33. *See also* note 39 above.

Mr. Sindler's meticulous accounts of the Cornell disturbances (*see* note 38 above) is far more *political* than Mr. Bloom's recollection. I suspect that any poor judgment and cowardice displayed at Cornell by the administration and all too many faculty had little to do with the corrupting educational theories Mr. Bloom makes so much of in this context. Administrations and faculty laboring under the same educational theories did handle themselves much better elsewhere. *See*, for possible corrections of Mr. Bloom's account (if not also of Mr. Sindler's account), *Cornell Alumni News*, November 1987, pp. 28–31.

The concluding paragraph of Mr. Sindler's 1971 account is instructive (pp. 84 and 85):

> This account of how crisis came to Cornell suggests, I hope, the lengthy evolution and multidimensionality of the campus conflict, and the mix of motives and attitudes—creditable and otherwise—of the major actors. It thus provides but a thin understanding to rest the explanation on the existence and effects of a wobbly and irresolute administration, a divided and unnerved faculty and a confused and exploitable student body. These characterizations are accurate enough, but it was the reasons for the wobbliness, division and confusion in the face of the clearly illegitimate methods of dissent which illuminate Cornell's difficulties and those facing many other campuses around the nation. The malaise of higher education, the declining self-confidence of academic men, the shattered consensus on academic values and the relation of the university to society, the bias of faculty in favor of the political Left, the conversion of white racial guilt and empathy to blacks to a quite different posture of abdicating judgment and "giving blacks what they want," the growing casuistry of liberals in condoning bad means when used by favored groups or on behalf of ends thought good—all these complex themes and more comprise the contextual set of larger reasons necessary to explain Cornell's difficulties in reacting effectively to internal campus threats to fundamental university principles. If liberal administrators and faculty persist in crippling their capacity to respond to these threats because of a self-inflicted paralysis of judgment and will, the verdict of one black Cornellian on the great April crisis may come to apply to higher education generally. "Liberals . . . ," he shrewdly observed, "serv[ed] as liberalism's pallbearers."

Also instructive would be a Sindleresque review of Mr. Bloom's *Closing*. See note 39 above.

[43] The 1954 United States Supreme Court opinion in *Brown v. Board of Education* was an important step toward a humane solution of the problems of race relations in this country, but we still have a way to go. Mike Royko, who can be hardheaded (if not even cynical) about American politics, insists that "racial discrimination . . . is the most destructive and persistent of our domestic problems. Name any of our urban miseries—poverty, crime, unemployment, education, housing—and it boils down to race. Add up the cost, not only in dollars, but in fear and distrust, and the bottom line is race." *Chicago Tribune*, March 23, 1988, sec. 1, p. 3. *See*, for reservations about typical "black studies" programs, Anastaplo, "Race, Law and Civilization," in *Human Being and Citizen*, p. 175.

Be this as it may, a psychic and intellectual prototype for Allan Bloom in various respects is James Baldwin. *See*, e.g., Baldwin, "The Discovery of What It Means to Be an American," in *Nobody Knows My Name: More Notes of a Native Son*. (New York: Delta Books, 1962), p. 3.

[44] It is this material that Mr. Bloom's editors evidently insisted should be moved to the front of the book. One risk of massive editorial revisions is the sloppiness of a poor "fit" between a book's parts by people who do not really know what they are doing.

[45] Compare the end of note 25 above. It is true that music is very important for the young today—but also

for Mr. Bloom himself, if one is to judge from repeated reports in the press of the fabulous library of recordings that he can now own. I doubt, however, that the pleasure he gets from all this music today matches the enjoyment he derived from the performance more than three decades ago of the joyful dirge. "There'll be no room for gloom in Bloom's *Republic*." (The words, and performance at a Basic Program symposium, were by Jason Aronson and Werner Dannhauser. The music was borrowed from *My Fair Lady*. See *Closing*, p. 310, n. 9; note 1 above; note 51 below.)

"Even Secretary of Education William J. Bennett, a Bloom admirer, thinks he is a little harsh on old man rock. 'Bloom has eloquently and forcefully dissected the failures of institutions of higher education and pointed the way toward fundamental reforms. But Bloom and I differ on one important point: rock 'n' roll. I'm for it, though only the old-fashioned kind.'" Deirdre Donahue, "A scholar tries to open our minds," *USA Today*, July 21, 1987, p. 2D.

Some rock music is far worse than Mr. Bloom reports it. And probably all of it suffers from being technically inferior to the great music of old. Be that as it may, the typical teenaged response to *Closing* is suggested by this passage from a review in a high school newspaper: "But to this teenaged rock listener, Professor Bloom's arguments are just too extreme. He writes as if rock corrupts every child in America. His ideas about how rock relates to sex are more vulgar than any video on MTV he criticizes." *U-High Midway* (University of Chicago Laboratory Schools). Sept. 16, 1987, p. 2.

Consider, also, Frances Hannett, "The Haunting Lyric: The Personal and Social Significance of American Popular Songs," 33 *Psychoanalytic Quarterly* 226 (1964). Dr. Hannett suggests,

> The poignant and haunting quality of the lyrics and tunes [of "hit" songs] reveals the prevalence of a depressive mood in American society during the last half century. It seems that the sales appeal of popular songs of this period is not to be found in their sex appeal but rather in their experience of the depressive mood or of correctives for it.

Mr. Bloom is anticipated, in what he says not only about music but also about the epistemological errors responsible for the failings generally of higher education, by Richard M. Weaver, *Ideas Have Consequences* (Chicago: University of Chicago Press, 1948). In Mr. Weaver's day, however, jazz was the *bête noir*, not rock. *See,* on Mr. Weaver, Anastaplo, *The Constitutionalist*, p. 822.

[46]*See,* e.g., Anastaplo, *The Artist as Thinker*, p. 477. "It is an age of pious bullies in America, and far too many people are having far too good a time beating up on the young, the poor, the defeated." Reiff, "The Colonel and the Professor," p. 960.

[47]*See,* e.g., Anastaplo, *The Constitutionalist*, p. 409; "What Is Still Wrong With George Anastaplo? A Sequel to 366 U.S. 82 (1961)," 35 *DePaul Law Review* 551, 595–609, 643–47 (1986). *See also* Ellen W. Schrecker, *No Ivory Tower: McCarthyism and the Universities* (New York: Oxford University Press, 1986), pp. 340–41 (the final paragraph of the book):

> The academy did not fight McCarthyism. It contributed to it. The dismissals, the blacklists, and above all the almost universal acceptance of the legitimacy of what the congressional committees and other official investigators were doing conferred respectability upon the most repressive elements of the anti-Communist crusade. In its collaboration with McCarthyism, the academic community behaved just like every other major institution in American life. Such a discovery is demoralizing, for the nation's colleges and universities have traditionally encouraged higher expectations. Here, if anywhere, there should have been a rational assessment of the nature of American Communism and a refusal to overreact to the demands for its eradication. Here, if anywhere, dissent should have found a sanctuary. Yet it did not. Instead, for almost a decade until the civil rights movement and the Vietnam war inspired a new wave of activism, there was no real challenge to political orthodoxy on the nation's campuses. The academy's enforcement of McCarthyism had silenced an entire generation of radical intellectuals and snuffed out all meaningful opposition to the official version of the Cold War. When, by the late Fifties, the hearings and dismissals tapered off, it was not because they encountered resistance but because they were no longer necessary. All was quiet on the academic front.

See also Harvey Klehr, book review, *Academic Questions*, Spring 1988, p. 82. It should be noticed as well that there have been times and places, since the Fifties, when pro-McCarthy academics have suffered for their opinions. Even so, Mr. Bloom's dismissal of the effects of "McCarthyism" in the universities may be still another indication of his lack of a reliable "feel" for politics. *See* note 22 above. Compare Mr. Bloom's instructive review of I. F. Stone's *The Trial of Socrates* in the *Washington Post*, Feb. 14, 1988.

A much more engaging aspect of Mr. Stone's capacities is provided in Andrew Patner, *I. F. Stone: A Portrait* (New York: Pantheon Books, 1988). *See also,* on "McCarthyism," Harry Kalven, Jr., *A Worthy Tradition* (New York: Harper & Row, 1988).

[48] That is, professors could figure out what was in their interest, or at least what seemed to be in their immediate (however ignoble) interest. *See*, e.g., Anastaplo, *The Constitutionalist*, p. 333; Anastaplo, "A Progress Report," *National Law Journal*, June 18, 1979, p. 33, at note 24 in that text. *See also* note 1 above and the epigraph for this book review.

[49] See *Closing*, pp. 28, 260. *See*, for my discussions of the "clear and present danger" test (including Alexander Meiklejohn's pioneering critique of it), Anastaplo, *The Constitutionalist*, pp. 812, 818. *See also* note 32 above.

[50] It is unfortunate that Mr. Bloom, who does love his country, should lead outsiders to conclude, "The odd thing is that Bloom doesn't seem actually to *like* America. Indeed, when it comes time for him to describe anything about the place, he speaks only in what might be called that new grammatical mood invented by neo-conservatives; the denunciative." Rieff, "The Colonel and the Professor," p. 960. Compare note 16 above.

Mr. Bloom can notice, "A Charles de Gaulle or, for that matter, an Alexander Solzhenitsyn sees the United States as a mere aggregate of individuals, a dumping ground for refuse from other places, devoted to consuming; in short, no culture." *Closing*, p. 187. Such an observation does call for the immediate comment that people such as de Gaulle have again and again depended upon the United States to save them from the political disasters that their supposedly superior cultures have helped produce. See also *Closing*, p. 77.

[51] This was while a dozen of Mr. Strauss's students, including Mr. Bloom, were teaching in the Basic Program of Liberal Education for Adults at the University of Chicago. *See* notes 13 and 15 above. *See*, on the Basic Program, Anastaplo, "What is a Classic?," in *The Artist as Thinker*, p. 284. *See also* Anastaplo, "The Teacher as Learner: On Discussion," *Claremont Review of Books*, Summer 1985, p. 22.

It is reassuring that Mr. Bloom is not, in his critique of higher education, as original as he may seem to many of his readers to be. That is, there are models, experiments, and experiences "out there" for conscientious educators to draw upon in attempting the reforms that have long been needed. Among the things to be considered is, of course, "the old Great Books conviction." See *Closing*, pp. 51, 344. *See also* Harvey C. Mansfield, Jr., "Democracy and the Great Books," *New Republic*, April 4, 1988, p. 33; *Closing*, p. 287.

[52] Another way of putting this is to say that Mr. Bloom's next book should be one that Simon and Schuster would *not* want to publish. No doubt, it is difficult to avoid being trapped by one's phenomenal success, by what the world comes to expect of one, by the honors and lavish rewards it seems to offer. When that happens, the human being can be lost sight of.

The classics do teach us that whoever happens to be elevated by chance is especially vulnerable to being toppled thereby. Such a prospect can be particularly distressing for anyone who is congenitally apprehensive. One's defensiveness then can become so immoderate and provocative as to invite attacks. That is, it very much matters what kind of a soul one develops early in life. *See* the text at note 40 above.

In any event, I have observed in the prologue to this review that we see great success turn into a curse in Sophocles' *Oedipus Tyrannos*. In his *Oedipus at Colonus* we can see that the long-suffering Oedipus, of worldwide fame, virtually became a thing (to be manipulated by others) because of what had happened to him. In his case, however, we can also see that an appalling curse somehow became a blessing.

Mr. Bloom observes that "it is always pleasant to give people gifts that please them." *Closing*, p. 69. Proper pleasure comes from giving people the gifts that should please them. What more can Mr. Bloom do now to please his true friends than to use, and hence preserve, both body and soul as he should?

47

Universities Had No Alternative But to Make Unpopular Decisions

JOHN MARCHAM

Anyone who reads *The Closing of the American Mind* will be vividly aware Prof. Allan Bloom left Cornell in 1969 just after vandals swarmed into the groves of academe.

The 1960s were mean years in America, with clashes over civil rights in the South, riots in the big-city ghettos of the North, the assassinations of the Kennedys and Martin Luther King, and violent protests against the Vietnam War on college campuses.

Professor Bloom resigned days after a student occupation of Willard Straight Hall appeared to break the will of professors and administrators to govern Cornell. He carried away and now conveys to hundreds of thousands of buyers of his book a picture of a university making decisions out of fear.

His most indelible images from the '60s are all from Cornell, which he cites at least fifteen times in his book, nearly every allusion painful and seemingly intended to be so. He also appears to be settling a number of scores with individuals.

As one who has reported Cornell nearly continuously since World War II, I found myself reading his accounts of the period after 1963 with rising wonder and dismay. Several of his more scarifying citations:

● The provost learned a black faculty member threatened the life of a black student and did nothing about it.

● Trustees forced President James Perkins to resign because of bad publicity from a building occupation by armed blacks.

● Black students had a voice in naming black professors.

● Cornell fired an integrationist dean because blacks demanded it.

● The firing emboldened blacks and led administrators to cave in to their subsequent demands.

Page 316: Bloom accuses then-Provost Dale Corson of "cowardice" for not acting when Bloom reported to Corson in March 1969 the case of "a black student whose life was threatened by a black faculty member when the student refused to participate in a demonstration." Bloom says Corson told him that "there was nothing he [Corson] could do to stop such behavior in the black student association . . . the administration had to hear what the blacks wanted

John Marcham was Director of University Relations of Cornell University, 1964–1967, and has been editor of the *Cornell Alumni News* since 1961. Reprinted with permission from *Cornell Alumni News*, November, 1987.

. . . no university could expel black students, or dismiss the faculty members who incited them, presumably because the students at large would not permit it."

Asked for details, Bloom now recalls the faculty member to have been a writer in residence. Notes that Corson kept from the period show he met with Bloom and the proctor who would investigate any such case, March 18. Today no record is available of what happened to the case so it is not known whether the student, Bloom, or the proctor tried, were able to bring, or actually brought charges, either on campus or off. The black writer was not listed as on staff after the spring of 1969.

Whatever Bloom remembers Corson saying, the university did dismiss blacks as well as whites for misconduct at the time, and still does.

Page 315: "The usually passive trustees asked for the resignation of the incumbent [President Perkins] because the national publicity about the guns appeared to be damaging the university's reputation."

The statement is gratuitous. The trustees did not ask Perkins to resign; at a meeting after the Straight occupation, trustees stood and applauded Perkins when he entered the room.

He resigned May 31, three days after receiving a letter from fifteen Law professors who said they were concerned with his ability to maintain freedom of inquiry or expression on campus. After he resigned, Perkins said the letter "hit me hard" but that his main reason for leaving was that he underestimated divisions within the university in the wake of the occupation.

Page 316: " . . . a lavishly funded black studies center was established in the faculty appointments to which the black students were to have a voice."

The Africana center was formed in the spring of 1969 and has never been lavishly supported. The Cornell administration considered and rejected a teacher of African history and culture from New York University. Black students objected and appealed the decision to the campus community without avail. Faculty selection committees for the center have never included students.

Page 95: "Black students . . . demanded the dismissal of the tough-minded, old-style integrationist black woman who was assistant dean of students. In short order the administration complied with this demand."

The person in question was an assistant dean in Arts and Sciences. Prof. Alfred E. Kahn, dean of the college at the time, remembers the case much differently:

"The Black Liberation Front (BLF) demanded a meeting soon after I became dean in the summer of 1969. We had a very intense meeting in my office. I said I was certainly not going to fire her in response to their demands. It was so intense that when they left I called Dale Corson and said he'd better call Safety because I didn't know what they were going to do."

Kahn's associate dean, Robert Scott, says today that the assistant dean's work had not been satisfactory and he had begun dismissal procedures well before the students met with Kahn. The assistant dean herself and a former colleague disagree and back Bloom's contention that she was fired because she was not in the black separatist style of the day.

Kahn says that within a week after he *did* fire the woman, "the *new* head of

BLF paid a visit, called the firing a racist act, and demanded I rehire her. I said, 'You can bet I'm not rehiring her!'" The assistant dean protested the firing and a compromise was reached: she withdrew her protest, the college withdrew its firing, she gave up her job, and entered graduate school.

Page 95: Continuing about the firing of the assistant dean, which Bloom says took place before the event involving the faculty threat to the student, March 1969: "From that moment on, the various conciliatory arrangements with which we are now so familiar came into being . . . permanent quotas in admission, preference in financial assistance, racially motivated hiring of faculty, difficulty in giving blacks failing marks . . ."

The date of the firing is clearly wrong by a year. Professor Kahn fixes it as in January or February 1970, not when described in *Closing.* Thus facts do not support the book's powerful opening argument regarding Cornell that a forced firing was pivotal in encouraging blacks to press demands and faculty and administrators to give in to them. By early 1969, and in most instances well before, administrators had already decided to recruit blacks, grant them special aid, and search for black professors.

The suggestion that every academic shrub uprooted since the mid-1960s should be credited to activists, black or New Left, is demeaning both to the worth of the changes and to those who carried them out.

Bloom joined the government faculty in 1963 and left Cornell to accept a post at the University of Toronto soon after the Straight occupation, so it is not surprising if some of his facts are fuzzy and conclusions in his book are frozen in the partisan terms of that period. At that time, Americans chose up sides and argued passionately over black separatism and how universities should respond to it, and there were plenty of ugly events at Cornell to sustain any number of theories.

He singles out for particular ridicule the program of President Perkins to bring black students to Cornell in large numbers for the first time. It is easy today to forget that when college presidents launched such efforts in the mid-'60s, they were neither required to by federal mandates (none existed at the time) nor driven by student demands (free speech and Vietnam were the issues of the day).

No one denies the university was naive in its early efforts to make a Cornell education available to blacks. Separatism quickly replaced integration as a goal of many black leaders nationally, and large numbers of the new students isolated themselves from the rest of the campus. (Predominantly white universities have since come to agree there is value in allowing students entering from all-black high schools a chance to live apart while they adjust to a radically new setting.)

At first recruiters appeared to look beyond well prepared candidates. Some professors did inflate grades—for blacks, and for all men to help keep them out of the draft for Vietnam.

Despite chaos and controversy, the thousand black students who entered Cornell in the first eight years of the program achieved grades only one notch (C plus versus B minus) below the university average. The bulk of them graduated and most went on to graduate and professional schools and solid jobs. Faculty, administrators and students themselves learned from early mistakes and from 1969 until now have gradually improved the program.

Criticizing affirmative action in higher education, Bloom generalizes, "the university degree of a black student is . . . tainted." This assertion flies in the face of our understanding both that college programs for blacks across the country and at Cornell have improved markedly, and that black students at Cornell today are held to the same academic standards as others.

For a quarter century now, partisans have used college campuses to debate the heated issues of the day—Vietnam, black separatism, the Mideast, South Africa, U.S. foreign and military policy. It has been a short next step to try to force institutions themselves to take positions on these issues, and finally to engage in demonstrations that require action to restore or maintain order.

Eventually most colleges and universities have no alternative but to make unpopular decisions of one sort or another. Dealing with the occupation of Willard Straight Hall in 1969 was Cornell's most difficult.

Black students occupied Willard Straight Hall April 19 and armed themselves. The national press riveted attention on campus. The university administration agreed to let the students leave the next day. When blacks emerged triumphantly brandishing their weapons, the scene was flashed around the world and produced angry reactions.

White students quickly rallied to support a demand that the University Faculty agree to drop the conviction of several blacks for earlier campus disruptions. The Faculty agreed and much of the nation's press and many alumni showered abuse on Cornell for what they saw as capitulation.

A special committee of trustees reported in September 1969 on the seizure and its aftermath: "The decision was made to get the blacks to leave peacefully . . . an agreement that exacted an enormous price from Cornell. Cornell had no bloodshed, no headlines of murder, no substantial property damage, no students hospitalized, and in very short order a campus that was returned to relative peace.

"No one will ever know if this was the right way to settle the disruption . . . men made the decision to place the protection of life above the reputation of the university. They knew that the price to themselves and to Cornell was great—but was it greater than the price of human life?"

Partisans who sought to injure universities by forcing them to make unpopular choices often succeeded. We know. We have worked with alumni throughout this period. All too frequently, in the folders of former students recently deceased, we read letters written in anger ten or more years ago to sever all allegiance with a place they once loved but could no longer believe in.

Many who stayed loyal had children or grandchildren of college age and learned to understand if not to love their questioning of authority, particularly parental authority, and their enthusiasms for drugs, music, and political causes that older people could neither fathom nor abide. Others saw university changes as part of an opening of all U.S. society to women and minorities, to new fields of study and endeavor, and into the world beyond our shores.

Many Americans were driven away from universities by the forces campuses confronted in recent years. Clearly, Allan Bloom is among those most unhappy with the way universities in general and Cornell in particular responded.

Cornell took years to discover more successful, less painful formulas for black admissions, black studies, campus governance, and ways of handling dissent. Today professors expect administrators to handle more of the business of campus life. Students seem ambivalent about university authority. Disruptions still occur.

But Cornell and other universities continue to accept the challenge to deal with change, remain coherent, and try to command the love of traditional supporters, people with the patience to understand the complexity of their task and the way change occurs.

48

The Colonel and the Professor

DAVID RIEFF

> This is the American moment in world history, the one for which we shall forever be judged. Just as in politics the responsibility for the fate of freedom in the world has devolved upon our regime, so the fate of philosophy in the world has devolved upon our universities, and the two are related as they have never been before. The gravity of our given task is great, and it is very much in doubt how the future will judge our stewardship. [Allan Bloom, *The Closing of the American Mind: How higher education has failed democracy and impoverished the souls of today's students.*]

> I also believe that we must guard against a rather perverse side of American life, and that is the attempt to launch vicious attacks and criticism against our elected officials. President Reagan has made enormous contributions and he deserves our respect and admiration. . . . In my opinion, these hearings have caused serious damage to our national interests. Our adversaries laugh at us, and our friends recoil in horror. [Lt Col Oliver North, Statement to the Senate and House Select Committee on Secret Military Assistance to Iran and the Nicaraguan Opposition.]

The régime, a term Professor Bloom rather worryingly chooses to employ in his best-selling book, *The Closing of the American Mind* (reviewed in the *TLS* of July 24), when he means to refer to the government of the United States, has acquired some peculiar defenders recently. In his testimony before the Congressional committee investigating the Iran-Contra fiasco, Lt Col Oliver North expended the best part of his eloquence denouncing the hearings themselves. Not surprisingly, what North meant by democracy turned out to be not much more than a bias in favour of the holding of regular presidential elections; thereafter, the President had the authority to do more or less anything he liked, at least regarding foreign policy. This, as was frequently pointed out to North by his rather plaintive interrogators on the committees, had little to do with democracy, since it held the President to be nothing less than an elected king. North, however, was adamant that the executive branch retained a virtually limitless authority to act any way it liked in the service of the country's interests. While, with an eye on the Grand Jury, he sedulously protested that he had done nothing illegal, North was all too ready to concede that there were times when it was absolutely necessary to do illegal, anti-democratic things (the Colonel favoured the catch-all term "covert activities" but it was a distinction without a difference) if American democracy was to prevail over its enemies. The fact that this way of thinking seemed uncomfortably close to the celebrated remark of an American infantry officer in Vietnam that "we had to destroy the village in order to save it" did not pass entirely unnoticed. But the salient question was not, finally, why a marine Lt

---

This review is reprinted with permission from the *Times Literary Supplement* (September 4, 1987):950, 960.

Colonel should have confused the democratic office of the Presidency with the military title of Commander-in-Chief (indeed, the surprise would have been if a Marine Lt Colonel had entertained any other view), but rather why so many people shared North's notion of democracy as being neither an idea nor a system, but, instead, simply an appellation for the American side, a term as windy and malleable as "the free world".

At the same time, one could not help being struck, throughout North's testimony, by the strange, subterranean heat of the American Right's almost romantic admiration for the Soviets, or, more precisely, for their untrammelled ability to attain their ends. When *their* hostages were seized in Beirut, North and his admirers seemed to be saying regretfully they took effective action (this was a decorous way of saying they could kill people without having to worry about folks carping back home); you wouldn't see *their* embassy in Teheran occupied for 451 days, they just wouldn't have stood for it, and so on. With their excess of scruple and deficit of zeal, their dividedness and their naivety, Americans were failing to get the job done. In a word, they were just too democratic for their own good. In contrast, the Soviets, though doubtless evil, had their act together. The thought was inescapable that North, like so many Washington neo-conservatives, might really have been much happier with a Colonel's commission in the GRU and a dacha in the Crimea. Not for the first time, conservative intellectuals wondered whether, after all, democracy was really compatible with the responsibilities of world power.

To North's defenders, on the committees and off, the Colonel embodied those virtues that as far back as the Romans, have been lauded as "old-fashioned". A Republican Congressman, Rep Henry Hyde of Illinois, explained to North with heavy, sorrowful sarcasm, that the Marine was considered a dangerous person (by liberals) because "you personify the old morality, loyalty, fidelity, honor, and worst of all, obedience. Obedience is out of step with the spirit of the age—[its] *Zeitgeist*—obedience is the opposite of what defines the modern man, which is rebellion." The Colonel stared back gratefully, his eyes glistening under his long lashes, and it was clear that this was indeed the way he pictured himself. The only problem was that, admirable though they might be, none of those virtues Hyde extolled were democratic values. Loyalty, fidelity, honour and obedience are precisely the virtues which give dignity to the military life. In contrast, the defiantly civilian spirit of rebellion that Hyde so excoriated had been the midwife to American democracy—the reason of course for Jefferson's insistence on the people's continuing right to rebellion.

More interesting, perhaps, was the use of the word *Zeitgeist*. Terms like *Zeitgeist* and *Gestalt* are very popular with the American Right these days, which uses them as code words for all the bad news of the modern world (usually seen as having been imported from Europe) that has undermined the nation's resolve, and which, if allowed to continue unchecked, will, in Jean-François Revel's catchphrase, cause the democracies to perish. The explanations for this impending defeat are as various as the village explainers who offer them. In recent years, there has been a proliferation of think tanks and research institutes, amply funded by right-wing philanthropics like the John M. Olin Foundation and conservative tycoons like Joseph Coors and Richard Mellon Scaife. Whatever variations there are in the analysis, however, the Right's view of what has happened seems marked by a debased Spenglerian conception of decline, attributed to such familiar causes as the failure of American will, the naive refusal of Americans to recognize evil in the world (an evil which of course finds its material incarnation in the Soviet Union); the legacy of the 1960s with its antinomian disregard for established authority and its sexual avidity and tolerance, particularly of homosexuality; a cultural relativism which led to an insufficient commitment to Western civilization. In other words, the whole enchilada, as President Nixon's friend, Bebe Rebozo, used to say.

Colonel North was, of course, a comparatively minor figure in this debate. If he was, however briefly, the poster boy of the American Right (North will learn first-hand of the redeeming fickleness of the American public; those "Ollie for President" T-shirts will soon look as dated as hula-hoops), the movement has also acquired, in those last months of Ronald Reagan's second term, something more substantial—a new *livre de chevet* in which the themes North grasped intuitively, but expressed imperfectly, are given an erudite academic voice. Its author is Professor Allan Bloom, and it does not come as an earth-shattering surprise to discover that he is the co-director of the John M. Olin Center for Inquiry into the Theory and Practice of Democracy at the University of Chicago; vulgar Marxists may draw their own conclusions.

Non-American reviewers, including Kenneth Minogue in the *TLS*, have tended to view *The Closing of the American Mind* as a scholarly argument about the fate of higher education in America and a lament over the decline of academic standards. In fact, the book is more disturbing.

Professor Bloom, who studied at Chicago with Leo Strauss and remains in most ways a Straussian, is well known in his profession for having made a defiantly literal translation of Plato's *Republic* (in the accompanying commentary, he attacks Cornford's mildly modernizing translation for aiming to be accessible), translations of Rousseau's *Émile* and of his *Letter to D'Alembert*, and for writing with his fellow Straussian Henry Jaffa a book called *Shakespeare's Politics*. This bibliography already comprises a sort of programme for the reordering of the world under the tutelage of the master teacher. It is not, to put the matter gently, a very democratic or tolerant view. Not surprisingly, in *The Closing of the American Mind*, Bloom attributes the blame for what has gone wrong in America to what he calls its "openness" or tolerance. What has happened he argues, is that the élite universities have been transformed from places in which a few lucky students submitted themselves to teachers, who perform the sacerdotal function of initiating these acolytes into what Bloom genuinely believes are the immutable verities (as opposed to the noble accomplishments) of Western civilization, into places in which no discipline or point of view has priority over any other. The result, according to Bloom, has been a betrayal of the universities' essential, Platonic function (Bloom seems to think that training in science or the professions is not something people really need colleges for, insisting that the only essential function of the university is to civilize the young). Not only has real thought been debased, and the American spirit impoverished, but the triumph of what Bloom takes to be a supine cultural relativism has brought forth what is by now several generations of boorish ignoramuses, interested only in cultivating their sexual appetites, their taste for rock music, their nihilistic "niceness", and their pampered guilt over what their ancestors did to the coloured peoples of the world. Instead of their being "a community that is exemplary for all other communities," Bloom argues that the universities have betrayed their mission, betrayed—shades of Colonel North and Congressman Hyde—the West by giving in to the spirit of rebellion and anarchy.

Colonel North is handsome and speaks with the appealing simplicity of a John Wayne movie. In contrast, Bloom's book has nothing of the Marine's irenic self-assurance; it is the cry of a crank, but also the cry of a man genuinely in pain. None the less, allowing for the vast numerical difference between book buyers and television viewers (much of North's appeal, after all, came from his indisputable telegenic qualities), the success of *The Closing of the American Mind* has been phenomenal. In a period when the best seller list is not only invariably dominated, but also almost exclusively populated, by self-help books, accounts of out-of-body travel and celebrities' memoirs (sometimes, as in the case of Shirley Maclaine's recent memoirs, the three genres are combined). *The Closing of the American Mind* still was able to climb quickly to the top, much to the surprise of its publishers, Simon and Schuster, whose first printing was an extremely modest 5,000 copies. There the book has remained, squatting like an irate penguin, for the last four months. Publishers are baffled; booksellers are baffled; even Professor Bloom in his many recent interviews has seemed somewhat at a loss to account for this extraordinary response.

To be sure, Bloom is not the first American author to strike it rich by insisting in print that the country is going to hell. Americans have long had a peculiar fondness for having their deficiencies pointed out to them, as enterprising Europeans have understood since the days of Mrs Trollope and Dickens; and though Bloom, if he could stand outside the magic circle of his own success, would probably discern in all this hoopla another example of the nation's abiding insecurity, or its masochism, the taste probably has nothing more metaphysically significant about it than the American craving for a bit of rhetorical spice—even when it comes at one's own expense. If North seems somehow far more comfortable with the rules of engagement he supposes obtain over there in the Evil Empire, Bloom, for his part, is eerily reminiscent of all those dyspeptic Europeans forced to earn their livelihoods in an America they couldn't abide. In a sense, just as North uses the word democracy as a kind of brand-name (as in "the Nicaraguan democratic resistance", the Contras), so Bloom cherishes America, but exclusively as an abstract construct (as in his glowing references to "the American moment in world history").

The odd thing is that Bloom doesn't seem actually to *like* America. Indeed, when it comes time for him to describe anything about the place, he speaks only in what might be called that new grammatical mood invented by neo-conservatives: the denunciative. Bloom hates American mores, decries American families, despises American teenagers, and takes no notice of the beauty of the American landscape. This is, to say the least, a peculiar stance for a man who claims to love America (indeed, the paradox has led the political writer Sidney Blumenthal to quip, not entirely ironically, that Bloom seems *anti-American* whether he knows it or not), but in fact it is the hallmark of the neo-conservative Right. The real glories of American culture, which, whether Bloom likes it or not, are Hollywood movies and pop music, come in for the professor's special scorn. Rock music is Bloom's particular *bête noire*, because, as he puts it, "civilization or, to say the same thing, education is the taming or domestication of the soul's raw passions". Bloom's extraordinary assumption (the cornerstone of his book, really) that civilization and education are the same thing, indeed his total identification of civilization with repression, leads to a position which excludes not only compassion but simple humanity. Writing of what he believes is a prototypical middle-class adolescent, Bloom conjures up a beast. The passage is worth quoting at length:

> Picture a thirteen-year-old boy sitting in the living room of his family home doing his math assignment while wearing his Walkman headphones or watching MTV. He enjoys the liberties hard won over centuries by the alliance of philosophic genius and political heroism, consecrated by the blood of martyrs; he is provided with comfort and leisure by the most productive economy ever known to mankind; science has penetrated the secrets of nature in order to provide him with the marvellous lifelike electronic sound and image reproduction he is enjoying. And in what does progress culminate? A pubescent child whose body throbs with orgasmic rhythms; whose feelings are made articulate in hymns to the joys of onanism or the killing of parents; whose ambition is to win fame and wealth in imitating the drag-queen who makes the music.

(The drag queen in question is Mick Jagger, an identification that will probably surprise most heterosexual women between eight and eighty.)

"Nobody except small children", Paul Goodman once wrote, "has a claim to be loved, but there is a way of rejecting someone that accords his right to exist and be himself." Goodman is all but forgotten now, and yet his book on education, *New Reformation*, written towards the end of his life, is a terrific antidote to the hate-filled, self-regarding spleen of *The Closing of the American Mind*. Goodman was as devoted to "high culture" as Bloom claims to be, but the difference was that Goodman never made the mistake of thinking that an educational programme was more important than living people. Where Bloom elevates education, and, worse, erudition, above humanity ("Man may live more truly and fully in reading Plato and Shakespeare than at any other time", he writes toward the end of his book), Goodman understood that there are many kinds of intelligence and many ways of leading a decent life. A genuine conservative (rather than an autocrat), Goodman put the matter well when he wrote that "for green grass and clean rivers, children with bright eyes and good color whatever the color, people safe from being pushed around so they can be themselves—for a few things like these, I find I am pretty ready to think away all other political, economic, and technological advantages".

Bloom, embellishing his map with monsters, would no doubt describe this view as a perfect example of the cultural relativism he so decries. In fact, however, this level-headed, realistic humanity is the essential quality that is as absent from *The Closing of the American Mind* as it is from Colonel North's plans for Nicaragua's future. The thirteen-year-old whom Bloom portrays as subhuman could be any kid who likes to dance; indeed, the most telling aspect of Bloom's own description is its utter abstraction. He has found a type, and has no interest whatever in describing a person; a single, contradictory individual. The strange part is that the apprehension of this kind of truth is something most people everywhere know instinctively and have always known. They didn't learn it from Leo Strauss, or from Professor Bloom, but incidentally, in the course of their one and only lives, the way almost everything of value is best taught and most fully apprehended. It takes a professor of philosophy from the University of Chicago to have forgotten this.

Of course, all of Bloom's work, like that of his mentor Strauss, has been, despite its other merits, a self-described blueprint for excluding people, an exercise in the choosing of an elect. It is fascinating that the books Bloom continually returns to are *The Republic*, and Rousseau's *Émile*, which are themselves brilliant master plans for separating out the philosophers from what Bloom, with characteristic disdain, refers to as "the self-contradictory simulacra of community." The teacher, he wrote in his commentary on *The Republic*, "knows which [students] should be led further and which ones should be kept away from the mysteries". The fact is that Bloom has contempt for the senses, contempt for the profound wisdom of daily experience; contempt for anyone, particularly among his students, who fails to bow before his quasi-sacerdotal authority of teacher. However awful life is, it is better and richer than Bloom seems able to imagine. But then, it is awfully difficult to entertain seriously the arguments about what the good life consists of from a man who can write: "When I was fifteen years old, I saw the University of Chicago for the first time and somehow I sensed I had discovered my life." Nowhere in his often autobiographical book does Bloom mention a lover, a child, a sibling, a friend (as opposed to a disciple or a colleague), or a parent who can measure to his university, or even to the so-called "Great Books program" at the University of Chicago where he received his undergraduate education.

But this should really come as no surprise. It is an age of pious bullies in America, and far too many people are having far too good a time beating up on the young, the poor, the defeated. Colonel North represents the traditional Right's inept attempt to revenge itself for the US defeat in Vietnam, while books like *The Closing of the American Mind* represent an attempt by academics still feverishly angry at the students of the 1960s (the decisive moment for Bloom seems to have been the Black Power movement at Cornell in 1969) to express their detestation. The empire strikes back, indeed. In reality, Colonel North lives in a cartoon world of his own devising in which he can describe a country like the Sultanate of Brunei as part of "the democracies" and a real democracy like Costa Rica as a stumbling block to American policy in Central America; and in which he can talk of wanting to go "one on one with Abu Nidal". (Bet the farm on Abu Nidal.) In the meantime, Nicaraguans on both sides die in a stupid war that the US government chooses to fight by that most cowardly of means, proxy, while, back home, men like Professor Bloom, their paychecks assured by right-wing foundations that have also been so active in supporting the Contras, publish books decent people would be ashamed of having written.

49

Allan in Wonderland

JEAN BETHKE ELSHTAIN

We learned more from a three-minute record than we ever learned in school.
Bruce Springsteen, "No Surrender" (1984)

Confronted with that special phenomenon, a best-seller that has nothing to do with our waistlines, pocketbooks, orgasms, or neuroses—or our titillation at others' waistlines, pocketbooks, orgasms and neuroses—reviewers tend to fall into ponderous prose that signifies their *own* seriousness at taking a serious book seriously. This may help to explain the solemn reception of Bloom's self-important tome. But *The Closing of the American Mind* is also the latest entry in a long line of books that have done well by telling us how to be good and chiding us on the ways we are not. Sinclair Lewis savaged the American middle class who gobbled up his satires with alacrity and now advertise his birthplace with pride. H. L. Mencken made a decent living by dubbing nearly everybody else mentally or morally deficient, including that collective subject, the "boobi Americani." More recently, when Christopher Lasch catalogued our culture of narcissism many of those immersed in the phenomena the book depicted, in an ironic turn Lasch savvily appreciated, ingested his critique along with the latest consumer items. Now it is Allan Bloom's turn. Unlike Lewis and Mencken, he lacks serious wit although he shares Mencken's aesthetic mistrust of democracy. Unlike Lasch, his political motivations do not tend towards a generous renewal of America's dream of democracy. Instead, in a 392-page keen, Bloom recreates a now-gone American academic world in which a few men, those who by *nature* were capable of making the transition from "natural savages" to "knowers," became gentlemen at elite institutions: " . . . Harvard, Yale and Princeton are not what they used to be. . . . There is hardly a Harvard or a Yale man any more." These students were a charming lot just on the brink of "the first flush of maturity," ripe to be inducted into the great secrets of the great books by *bona fide* Knowers like Bloom's mentor, Leo Strauss, and, later, Bloom himself.

This world is nearly lost, or we are in danger of losing it, argues Bloom. Higher mental life in the USA is at stake. No, more: the judgement of America "in world history" forever after. The "fate of philosophy" *is* for Bloom the fate of America, hence the world: "the crisis of the West . . . is identical with a crisis of philosophy."

Never has so much weight been placed on so few books. For those of us who

---

Jean Bethke Elshtain teaches at Amherst College and is the author of *Public Man, Private Woman*. This review is reprinted by permission from *Cross Currents* vol. 37, no. 4 (Winter 1987–88):476–479.

might have supposed that America's future course was more likely to be determined by how we handle foreign relations and negotiations, or the vagaries of our
economy, or racial and regional conflicts and pressures, or the future of families
and neighborhoods, or how we sort out the tension between our celebration of
individualism and our ideals of community, or pursue our ongoing, deeply
fraught engagement with protecting dissent and difference yet sustaining social
order, Bloom offers the startling news that the pervasive influence of Nietzsche
and Heidegger has brought us to near ruin. It has done so by eroding, first, the
great European universities, and second, the great American universities modeled
after the great European ones. Because, for Bloom, the way Harvard or Cornell
or the University of Chicago goes is the way America and the world go, his
fingering of texts as the source of our troubles makes a kind of perverse sense—so
long as the reader remains as hermetically sealed-off as Bloom himself.

Others—most notably Martha Nussbaum and Alexander Nehamas—have
challenged Bloom's reading of the classical texts he reveres as well as the
Nietzschean texts he lambastes (at least insofar as their influence circulates to the
vast majority who are incapable of handling such hot stuff). Robert Paul Wolff
impishly insists that Bloom is really a character created by Saul Bellow, who
contributes a foreword, and *The Closing of the American Mind*, a work of parodic
fiction. David Rieff, writing in the *Times Literary Supplement*, fiercely associates
Bloom with Oliver North as exemplars of a crimped and crabby anti-democratic
ethos at work in the waning days of the Reagan era. My own tack will be
somewhat different. I am troubled by much in Bloom. Although he addresses
issues of great importance to the university, and although he is right that *some*
modes of combatting racism, sexism, and all the rest that have been recently
devised within universities are highly suspect, his responses are sadly deficient.
For all his incessant celebration of the elite of knowers, and the importance of that
elite, Bloom is an ignorant man. He is unlearned in the ways of the wider world,
untutored in subjects on which he makes definitive pronouncements—I have in
mind here not Plato but popular culture—untouched by generosity in his
response to those who, unlike Bloom himself, whether through necessity or
choice, do not date the beginning of their 'real lives' from the moment they
glimpsed the University of Chicago. (Or Harvard Yard or, like Hardy's doomed
Jude, the turrets of Oxford.)

Most offensive is Bloom's patronizing attitude toward American youth. His
prototypical youth is the figment of a mind feeding on lofty notions of itself as one
who shares the *Symposium* with Plato, even as the rest of us go about our grubby,
mind-numbing lives. For Allan Bloom gets to dictate who among us is a "serious
candidate for culture," an honor denied one "naive and good-natured" student
who once posed a question to Bloom about sublimation that charmed Bloom
by its candor but indicated "the lad" was already so far gone in the ways of
American culture he would never, no matter how hard he tried, get to glimpse
"the sublime." Bloom assumes that "young Americans," at an earlier point in
time, arrived at the university as "clean slates unaware of their deeper selves and
the world beyond their superficial experience." Their lives were "spiritually
empty." Whether they came from the city or the country, from devout Christian

or Jewish families, whether they had dedicated high school teachers, wise pastors or priests, devoted mothers or fathers—it mattered not to Bloom. They were ciphers. Arriving at the University, the best of them found their slates being written upon by the best of them: male professors who communed with the distant and the deep and were not afraid, as Plato insists his Guardians must not cavil, of treating human material as blank slates. Their very blankness was, for Bloom, "a large part of the charm of American students."

Alas, the charm is gone. The rose is off for Bloom, replaced by demented beings immersed in the "gutter phenomenon" of rock and roll and having succumbed to its hostility to reason, its barbaric appeal to sexual desire, driven round the bend by gross junk that "has the beat of sexual intercourse." Thankfully, a few "good students" remain to whom Bloom can introduce Mozart (more writing on that blank slate). But the vast majority, having been inducted into barbarism by Mick Jagger, a being "unencumbered by modesty," offer a sorry spectacle indeed compared to, say, "the role . . . Napoleon played in the lives of ordinary young Frenchmen throughout the nineteenth century." Softened up by Jagger, they are easy prey for the pervasive Nietzschean undertow, defenseless against the Heideggerian hit, pummeled unawares by the "influence of Thomas Mann's *Death in Venice* on American consciousness." At this point the reader's mind reels: we are with Allan in Wonderland.

If memory serves, the Port Huron statement of 1962 cites Lincoln and Tocqueville and Jefferson and Dewey on "the public and its problems" but neither Nietzsche nor Heidegger, nor Mann, for that matter, loom on the horizon. The inspiration for Martin Luther King was Jesus Christ and Mahatma Gandhi, not German philosophy. The goad that prodded feminists into action and thought was liberalism not nihilism. But, then, any man who claims that Ravel's 'Bolero' is the only piece of classical music that is commonly known and liked by *them*— yucky youth—because it, like rock, "has the beat of sexual intercourse"—is capable of inventing almost anything. The only evidence of the influence of Ravel's 'Bolero' on anybody, let alone the musical taste of American youth, is the satiric seduction scene in Blake Edward's film, "10," when the luscious but vacuous temptress insists that this piece accompany her tryst with the over-wrought Dudley Moore. My students wouldn't know what I was talking about if I told them the only reason they listened to U-2 sing about the Mothers of the Missing in Argentina or Bruce Springsteen detail the sorrows and beauties of the lives of working-class Americans was because these songs, like 'Bolero,' move to the beat of sexual intercourse.

The pop culture Bloom despises is one of America's great, original contributions, a robust coming together of black gospel and white folk and hillbilly music that springs from the lives and souls of ordinary people. Not Harvard or Yale gentlemen, but human beings celebrating joys and lamenting tragedies, express-ing hopes and confronting fears. To be sure, there's a lot of schlock in pop, and a good deal of its imagery troubles. But the point is to learn to distinguish between the good and the bad. That is difficult to do if you despise your subject matter, as Bloom despises America's young and the wider culture that helps to sustain them—for better and for worse.

Bruce Springsteen, for example, the greatest current rocker, has helped to make hunger and homelessness popular *political* issues. He has articulated the despair of Vietnam Veterans. And Springsteen also understands that music alone cannot change the world but that it does hold forth a promise to make that world "a less lonely place, . . . more than just a place." Arguing against the pop-side of hyper-individualism, the "I got my music, and you got yours," Springsteen extends our sympathy in unsentimental ways. What a contrast to Bloom who sees fascists lurking in every protest, nihilism in each dissent, and barbarism in any popular song. *The Closing of the American Mind* is a disturbing example of what Albert Camus urged us to try to avoid with these words: "We all carry within us our places of exile, our sorrows and our ravages. But our task is not to unleash them on the world: it is to fight them in ourselves and others." Amen.

50

Mr. Bloom's Planet

LOUIS MENAND

Allan Bloom is a man who knows his own mind, and who thinks well of what he finds there. He is therefore in a good position to explain to people who are a little less sure of themselves just what it is that ails them. *The Closing of the American Mind* is that explanation, presented in the style of an unusually articulate, unusually engaging, and unusually long undergraduate lecture. Many people who are no longer undergraduates have declared themselves glad for the instruction. Undergraduates have reason to feel a little less grateful.

For Bloom's book is a critique of the contemporary university, and it begins with a critique of the contemporary student. "Souls artificially constituted by a new kind of education" is the way he describes today's students. Made "nice," but "not particularly moral or noble," by the lack of constraints on their choices, jaded by premature sexual experience, polluted by the "junk food" of rock music ("our greatest corruption"), they "live in a world transformed by man's artifice and believe that all values are relative and determined by the private economic or sexual drives of those who hold them. How are they to recover the primary natural experience?"

The university's way of ministering to these souls is not Bloom's way—for the simple reason that "the primary natural experience" is the kind of phrase most academics tend to regard with, at the least, skepticism. That skepticism is responsible, Bloom argues, for the disciplinary fragmentation, the theoretical incoherence, the intellectual trendiness, and the pedagogical laxness of our elite universities. He's right, but that doesn't mean the skepticism is wrong.

The bulk of *The Closing of the American Mind* is devoted to an extended narrative in which the history of civilization, cast as the story of thinking heads, is shown to lead by logical progression (or regression) to our present condition. The chief brains in the story are those of Socrates, who established philosophy as the queen of the sciences by showing the exercise of reason to be the highest fulfillment of our natures; of Machiavelli, Hobbes, and Locke, who compromised philosophy's standing as an autonomous enterprise by enlisting it in the service of politics; of Rousseau, who further damaged philosophy's prepotence by questioning the value of reason; of Nietzsche, who exacerbated the damage by questioning the value of values; and of Heidegger, who carried the denaturing of philosophy to its conclusion when he endorsed National Socialism in its name.

That he should choose to account for what he regards as our current cultural crisis by means of a story about books indicates succinctly enough the extent of

---

This review is reprinted with permission from the *New Republic* (May 25, 1987):38–41.

Bloom's divergence from conventional thinking. His argument, as he admits, depends on the belief that "the intellect has an effect on history." No doubt it does. The question is, What affects the intellect? This is the question that informs virtually all of modern thought—from Hobbes and Locke, who founded their political philosophies on an epistemology that considered ideas to be the product of sensations received from external objects; to Rousseau; to Marx; to Freud; to the contemporary academic who explains why people think what they think by genetics or by climatology or by the web of "power relations."

Bloom parts company with all these thinkers not because he disagrees with their answers, but because he does not recognize the legitimacy of the question. *Nothing* affects the exercise of true intellect; its subject is nature and its object is the truth. "Nature" cannot be historicized: my idea of what is natural must, if it is rational, be the same as Plato's. And "truth" cannot be relativized: if you believe a thing is good and I believe it is bad, one of us must be wrong. The university, in Bloom's view, should be the place where for four years young people can withdraw from the degenerated culture of modernity and contemplate the true and the good—which are embodied in the classic texts. Bloom wants the academy to be an ivory tower.

The best test of Bloom's project is Bloom's own book. The evidence it offers is not encouraging: it seems that there is far less in heaven and earth than is dreamt of in his philosophy. It is not just that modern society is floated on the corrupted values of a debilitated tradition; it is that its young people can already be declared soul-dead.

When confronting the depredations of contemporary life, Bloom's favorite weapon of analysis is the paradox. It's one of the attractive features of his thought: it cuts issues open economically, it makes us rethink, it annoys—it's Socratic. Thus: the shibboleth "openness"—the refusal to condemn another's views—has closed our minds; having the freedom to choose means being imprisoned by the fads of the day; feminism, by creating conflicting responsibilities for family and career, has led to the oppression of women; affirmative action is responsible for the deterioration of race relations; and so forth.

These arguments are by now old friends. They have been with us since the '60s; they are the starting blocks for neoconservatism and neoliberalism alike. A mind that refuses to admit their cogency is indeed a closed one. But so is a mind that thinks posing the paradox is enough to discredit the position. Having pointed out the familiar ironies of modern life, Bloom feels licensed to condemn the entire worldview that contains them; and it would be interesting to know just how far down this road those who have so unreservedly praised his book (it has been received enthusiastically in France as well) really care to accompany him.

The "openness" young people make such a virtue of is, Bloom explains, the consequence of their "relativism." Coming from a philosopher, this is, to put it kindly, disingenuous. "Relativism" is a philosophical scare word. It is the belief that on any given subject one opinion is as good as any other opinion. No one thinks this—least of all college students. What many people do think, including some college students, is that it is important to show respect for the views of others—particularly those who show little respect for one's own view. People who think this are not relativists, for the obvious reason that they believe that "openness" is the "right" view to hold.

Of course tolerance for the intolerant has an outer limit. It is our official position as a society that the line gets drawn at the point where expression turns into action, where an intolerant attitude becomes an intolerant practice. But Bloom thinks this is much too generous:

> Freedom of thought and freedom of speech were proposed in theory . . . in order to encourage the still voice of reason in a world that had always been dominated by fanaticisms and interests. . . . The authors of *The Federalist* . . . were not particularly concerned with protecting eccentric or mad opinions or lifestyles. Such protection . . . is only an incidental result of the protection of reason, and loses plausibility if reason is rejected.

Emergency powers for the reasonable man: if his sense of logic is offended, the right of others to offend it may be suspended. But it is precisely offensive speech (leaving aside the question of mad lifestyles) that the First Amemdment is designed to protect. Who cares about regulating the reasonable?

Bloom's point about feminism is not that it burdens women with the impossible chore of producing a family while pursuing a career, since this is a practical problem and therefore presumably admits of a practical solution. His point is philosophical: "The women's movement is not founded on nature." Which gives rise to the following bit of cultural history, meant to show the way prior arrangements respected nature's law: "That man is not made to be alone is all very well," Bloom speculates, "but who is made to live with him? This is why men and women hesitated before marriage, and courtship was thought necessary to find out whether the couple was compatible, and perhaps to give them basic training in compatibility." But this makes nonsense of the notion of the natural, since courtship is a historically and culturally specific institution, by no means the universal norm, and the idea that marriage is founded on compatibility or is a response to existential aloneness would have seemed eccentric before the 18th century. This little piece of the argument is emblematic of Bloom's whole critique: the academic in the ivory tower manages, by the exercise of unadulterated reason, to produce a philosophical justification for the status quo ante.

But the most notable feature of the book is its attack on youth and its culture, an attack that shows a spirit that can hardly be called generous and a habit of mind that can hardly be called open:

> Picture a 13-year-old boy sitting in the living room of his family home doing his math assignment while wearing his Walkman headphones or watching MTV. He enjoys the liberties hard won over centuries by the alliance of philosophic genius and political heroism, consecrated by the blood of martyrs; he is provided with comfort and leisure by the most productive economy ever known to mankind; science has penetrated the secrets of nature in order to provide him with the marvelous, lifelike electronic sound and image reproduction he is enjoying. And in what does progress culminate? A pubescent child whose body throbs with orgasmic rhythms; whose feelings are made articulate in hymns to the joys of onanism or the killing of parents; whose ambition is to win fame and wealth in imitating the dragqueen who makes the music. In short, life is made into a non-stop, commercially prepackaged masturbational fantasy.

I suspect that one of the reasons *The Closing of the American Mind* has evoked so much unqualified praise is that it gratifies our wish to think ill of our culture (a wish that is a permanent feature of modernity) without thinking ill of ourselves. It does this by making young people our scapegoats—something that has become a bad cultural habit recently. Their toys, their entertainments, their efforts to make sense of the world are all derided by Bloom. Today's students belong to a demographically powerless generation; they are squeezed between the baby boom and the baby boomers' children. Caught in an older generation's backlash against its own former values, they have been blamed for drugs, for promiscuity, for cultural illiteracy. Now they discover that they are unworthy to sit at the feet of Socrates. They deserve better than this from those who would be their teachers.

TEN

Relativism and the Decline of Public Morality

Can Religion Cure Our Ills?

Paul Gottfried, criticizing Bloom from the Right in chapter 1, points out with interest that Bloom seems to begin an argument for religion but then stops short of advocating it. Gottfried argues that this omission shows that Bloom must secretly agree with Herbert Marcuse, a Marxist atheist, and with Jean-Jacques Rousseau, against revealed religion. And Timothy Fuller, who is *defending* Bloom later in this book, agrees with Gottfried that the similarities between *The Closing of the American Mind* and *One Dimensional Man* are striking.

From the Left, however, William Greider in *Rolling Stone* says that anyone who makes Bloom's argument in favor of the family and morality must be just another dangerous Jerry Falwell–type religious fanatic in disguise. Robert Bellah agrees with Bloom that America is sick, but he seems to fear religion more than the decay of the country, because he supposes religion to be antidemocratic.

However, in this chapter, William R. Marty in "Athens and Jerusalem in *The Closing of the American Mind*: Bloom, Nietzsche, and God," reassures liberals by reminding us that Christianity historically and logically has provided necessary and strong support for the doctrines on which American democracy is founded: the equality of all men, respect for human life, limited government, and the social contract. (Marty could have added that it provided similarly necessary support for modern science, which has developed almost exclusively in Christian or post-Christian countries.) Marty agrees with Nietzsche that the ideology of the "death of God" is a political catastrophe which may yet destroy Western civilization—that only a revival of religion can heal America. Marty's comprehensive essay provides a profound analysis of a perplexing practical question raised by Bloom: are reason and revelation logically opposed? Marty reminds all friends of American democracy that relativism—the only practical alternative to religion for most men—leads to war and cruelty, not to peace and tolerance.

Will Morrisey, in the previous chapter, says that Bloom understood and anticipated everything that his critics from both the Right and the Left would say about religion. The intended audience of the book, says Morrisey, is college professors, and most of them are easy-going atheists who are uncomfortable with any discussion linking morality and religion. Given the intended audience, Bloom agreed to change the title of the book from *Souls Without Longing* to avoid all danger of appearing religious, and felt constrained to refrain from any direct mention of the "R" word.

51

Athens and Jerusalem in *The Closing of the American Mind*

WILLIAM R. MARTY

Allan Bloom has written an extraordinary book. It is written with power and grace, it is filled with playfulness and biting wit and shocks of recognition: " . . . students have powerful images of what a perfect body is and pursue it incessantly. . . . [t]hey no longer have any image of a perfect soul, and hence do not long to have one. They do not even imagine that there is such a thing" (67). Bloom illuminates our situation, and the human condition. He shows us the changes wrought by the changes in our vocabulary: what it means when we replace the understanding that we have souls with the understanding that we are selves; what an emptying it is when we replace good and evil, beautiful and ugly, with values and tastes and lifestyles; what a change there is when we replace the search for nature and truth with the concepts of culture and ethnocentrism; what a decisive difference there is when we look for guidance outside ourselves to nature through reason as opposed to when we look within, to our selves, and ultimately through our selves, to that bottomless basement of the id.

Bloom shows us, too, how we have changed from a natural rights liberalism to a liberalism of relativism and openness. He shows us that the latter's purported openness closes our minds, impoverishes our souls, and eliminates any serious motive for the study of other cultures, other times, other understandings of what is true. It closes our minds to the possibility that there *is* a truth to be found. Bloom has given us, in some respects, a brilliant account of our situation, one demanding a rethinking of our condition, and he gives us materials and tools to use in that rethinking. He puts us deeply in his debt.

Bloom has written, then, an important book, but also a curious and flawed one. He appears to decry the degeneration from a natural-rights based liberalism to an impoverishing liberalism of value relativism and an openness that closes. One expects a vindication of natural rights, indeed of natural right. *It never comes.* We see our regime portrayed as a self-conscious project of modern reason, of philosophy, and we see its gradual degeneration into non-reason. It is a striking picture, and one that poses mysteries: whence come the natural rights and the

William R. Marty is Professor of Political Science at Memphis State University. This essay copyright 1989 by William R. Marty. The author wishes to thank Robert L. Stone for his invitation to write this review, for his careful editing and suggestions, and his great patience in awaiting its completion, and to J. Harvey Lomax for his careful reading and suggestions. Further thanks go to Memphis State University for professional-development-assignment time to explore the wisdom and folly of Christians in politics, a project of which this has become part.

natural right that are the foundation of the American mind and regime? What has happened to natural rights and natural right, and why does Bloom not seriously attempt their vindication?

The key to understanding what is curious and flawed in Bloom's work is given, it seems to me, in one of his penetrating observations about human nature. "Indignation," he says, "is the soul's defense against the wound of doubt about its own; it reorders the cosmos to support the justice of its cause" (71). It is illuminating, then, to observe the place where Bloom seems to become indignant. It is an outburst directed at Nietzsche's student Max Weber, and at Weber's students, when they seem to attribute *everything* of importance to religion.

> *Secularization* is the wonderful mechanism by which religion becomes non-religion. Marxism is secularized Christianity; so is democracy; so is utopianism; so are human rights. Everything connected with valuing must come from religion. One need not investigate anything because Christianity is the necessary and sufficient condition of our history. This makes it impossible to take Hobbes or Locke seriously as causes of that history, because we know that superficial reason cannot found values and that these thinkers were unconsciously transmitting the values of the Protestant ethic. . . . Philosophy's claims are ignored . . . (211)

As this rare eruption by Bloom indicates, it is the tension between religion and philosophy that lies at the heart of his account, as it lies at the heart of the West. And Bloom *does* suffer the "wound of doubt" about his own, for Bloom understands religion to be poetry, a form of irrationality, not a revelation from without but a projection from within, and the greatest modern philosopher, Nietzsche, to whom Bloom is powerfully drawn, has gone over to the enemy, finding nature morally meaningless, reason consequently useless as a guide to how we should live, and nobility to be rescued only, if at all, by the poets, the creators. Not reason, but unreason, must henceforth be our guide. We await some new Moses. And Bloom, the partisan of reason, is forced to admit: " . . . the very existence of man as man, as a noble being, depended on men like him— so he thought. He may not have been right, but his case looks stronger all the time" (51).

Bloom's often profound account suffers from his failure adequately to confront Nietzsche's claim that when God dies, the West must die. This leads to Bloom's failure, first, to recognize how dependent on religion the "values" of the West, and of our founding, are; second, to notice how it is the death of God that destroys the limits on the working out of the principles of freedom and equality, a working out that without those limits leads, as Bloom notes, to an unbridled individualistic selfishness and the creation of the bourgeois man with a trivial existence, a man concerned about the health of his body but not about the true, the noble, and the beautiful, or the state of his soul; and finally, his failure to deal with the ground of rights and right.

Let us turn, first, to the manner in which Bloom's partisanship in the contest between philosophy and religion hides from him a full understanding of the formation of the American mind and regime. We will see that Hobbes and Locke *were* important, as Bloom thinks, but that they did *not* invent rights, rights by nature, human freedom and equality, government by consent or contract theory. Bloom ignores much. He ignores the British parliamentary tradition, the rights of

Englishmen, natural law, the common law, and much else. And in particular, he is at pains to ignore what *no one of the time could ignore,* the intimate relationship between many of these ideas and Calvinist theology and practice.

A Blindness to Religious Foundations

"Rights . . . are new in modernity, not a part of the common-sense language of politics or of classical political philosophy. Hobbes initiated the notion of rights . . ." (165, see also 288). This claim on behalf of Hobbes and philosophy is ill-founded. Rights were well-known in America (and England) prior to Hobbes and Locke. Consider the dates. Hobbes published the *Leviathan* in 1651, *De Cive* in 1642. But Calvinist Massachusetts Bay Colony, to cite one example, recognized and adopted a body of rights and liberties, one including most of what we have in the Bill of Rights, and more; and one including the famous rights to life, liberty, and property, in 1641. Among the "Rites, liberties, and priviledges concerning our Churches, and Civill State to be respectivly impartiallie and inviolably enjoyed and observed . . . for ever" were the following: "No mans life shall be taken away, no mans honour or good name shall be stayned, no mans person shall be arested, restrayned, banished, dismembred, nor any wayes punished, no man shall be deprived of his wife or children, no mans good or estaite shall be taken away from him, nor any way indammaged under Coulor of law, unlesse it be by vertue or equitie of some expresse law. . . ." These "liberties Immunities and priveledges" were "due to every man" from "humanitie, Civilitie, and Christianitie" (cited in Stone 503). Hobbes did not "initiate the notion of rights."

Calvinists also knew and practiced governments by contract and consent, in church and state, before Hobbes and Locke wrote. They found their authorization, or ground, in sacred scripture. God had bound Himself to Adam, Abraham, and Moses in sacred covenants, as He had bound himself to mankind in a new covenant, the covenant of grace, through the "second Adam," Jesus, for the redemption of mankind. Therefore, if "the omnipotent Ruler of the universe freely contracted to limit His rule by following rational procedures and laws, then surely it is incumbant upon man to disallow absolute government over himself in both church and state" (cited in Beitzinger 41).

Was this important? Some thought so, and quite early. In 1603 James I of England, formerly James VI of Scotland, was confronted with a call to reform the Anglican church by adopting the Presbyterian form of church polity. The initial call was to replace church hierarchy and bishops with elected ministers of equal rank. James I responded to these Calvinist proposals for the reform of church polity by exclaiming that they "as well agreeth with Monarchy, as God, and the Divell." He told his Anglican bishops: "If once you were out, and they in place, I knowe what would become of my *Supremacie. No Bishop, no King.*" (Beitzinger 35, Grimes 15) James I recognized that the Calvinist ideas of elections, covenants, and consent in church polity were the foundation for a profound reordering, and he proved himself that rarest of men, an accurate seer. When Calvinists gained control, the head of his successor, Charles I, fell.

James I of England knew in 1603 that there was a connection between

Calvinist theology and destruction of his legitimacy. The Calvinist emphasis upon covenants, upon the right to form both ecclesiastical and civil polity by sacred contracts, upon the right to elect or approve ministers and civil magistrates, and to remove them upon manifest unworthiness, predated Hobbes and Locke. The Pilgrims, Calvinists, made their Mayflower Compact in 1620. The Puritans, Calvinists who stayed within the Anglican church to purify from within, made their "errand into the wilderness" in 1629, ratifying by charter and by internal covenants their governments of church and state. Calvinists helped form the republican mind and establish republican practice. They knew and practiced rights, contracts, and government by consent well before Hobbes and Locke wrote their classic treatises. (Only the elect were involved initially, but Roger Williams was changing that, and others quickly followed, in the 1630s and 1640s, even as both he and John Milton were publishing defenses of religious toleration and freedom of expression—before Hobbes and Locke and their part of the modern project. Of course the Calvinists should have been involved in this move toward religious toleration: they had done much to make it necessary.)

In England, too, the Calvinists knew of these matters—of natural law, and the natural rights consequent to them, of equality of men as men, of governments based on compacts, contracts, and consent—they knew enough to make the revolution that formed the backdrop to the thought and writings of Hobbes and Locke, and those who wish to see if the words and phrases and concepts are there, and are used, need only consult the debates in the General Council of the Parliamentary Army held between October 28 and November 11, 1647 (cited in Mason 8–22).

The Calvinists, it should be mentioned, brought something else with them to America—the understanding that men are sinners. They understood, then, the need for strong governments to compel men to behave. But Calvinists, more than other Christians, drove the logic to its conclusion: as men are sinners, *no one* can be trusted with unrestrained power. John Cotton, for example, taught that it is necessary to limit the power of any man, in any office, secular or divine, whether of kings, princes, and magistrates, or officers of the church, or husband or wife or servant. "Let all the world learn," he said, "to give mortall men no greater power than they are content they shall use, for use it they will. . . ." The problem was human nature. Because "there is a straine in a mans heart that will sometime or other runne out to excesse . . . It is necessary therefore, that all power that is on earth be limited . . ." (Miller and Johnson 212–13).

There is a sobriety in the American founding absent in later revolutions more dominated by Enlightenment and Rousseauistic understandings of human nature. Calvinist understandings helped prepare that sobriety. When Madison wanted to explain and justify the contrivances to prevent tyranny in the American constitution, he did not have to resort to philosophical expositions. He was able to use a language understood by all: "It may be a reflection on human nature, that such devices should be necessary to controul the abuses of government. But what is government itself but the greatest of all reflections on human nature? If men were angels, no government would be necessary. If angels were to govern men, neither external or internal controul on government would be necessary

(Hamilton, Madison, Jay 322). The loss of this understanding has cost millions their lives and freedoms in subsequent revolutions.

The students of Nietzsche were right. Religion did have something to do with the "values" and institutions of the time. And Bloom is wrong. Modern liberal democracy is *not* entirely a product of the Enlightenment (See Bloom 259). That will be even clearer as we proceed.

Locke: A New Ground for Rights and Right?

Calvinists found the ground of rights, right, and obligation in God. Bloom's understanding is that Locke provided a different ground: the state of nature and the law of reason. Let us turn, then, to Locke, and Locke's natural rights theory, which Bloom holds to be absolutely central to an understanding of the American mind and regime, and to an understanding of the formation of the idea of natural rights.

Locke did not alone form the American mind, although he was enthusiastically received. But one must ask which Locke this was. Was the ground of American natural rights doctrine, and natural right, to be found in Bloom's atheist Locke, secret admirer of Hobbes, whose state of nature included the "most important discovery that there was no Garden of Eden," whose man "is on his own," whose "God neither looks after him nor punishes him," to whom "Nature's indifference to justice is a terrible bereavement . . ." (163)? Was this the Locke so enthusiastically received by ministers and political men alike? Was this the Locke so frequently quoted from the pulpit and this the Locke who helped raise a nation against infringements on its people's liberties? Was that in fact the way Locke *wrote* in his *Two Treatises of Government*, in his essays or the reasonableness of Christianity, in his letters on toleration? It was not. Instead, Locke portrays himself as a theist, a believer in God, and indeed the Christian God, and he *hinges* his arguments upon that theism, and makes of it the ground for natural rights.

Take Locke's most famous sentence, the foundation on which he builds his theory of natural rights. It begins: "The state of nature has a law of nature to govern it, which obliges every one: and reason, which is that law, teaches all mankind who will but consult it that, being all equal and independent, no one ought to harm another in his life, health, liberty, or possessions. . . ." (Locke 1952, 5). This is memorable, but one may legitimately inquire, can it stand alone? *Does* reason tell "all mankind who will but consult it" that all men are equal? Did it teach this to Plato, or Aristotle, or Nietzsche? Does it teach this to Allan Bloom, or his readers?

But allow Locke equality. Does the conclusion that one has *no right* to harm another flow, inevitably, by reason, from equality? Hobbes, according to Bloom the Navigator to that "Columbus of the Mind," Locke, did *not* draw the conclusions from equality that Locke here presents. Hobbes, no mean reasoner himself, concludes that from equality of ability stems, by a series of steps, a war of "every man, against every man" (Hobbes 184–85). "And because the condition of Man . . . is a condition of Warre of every one against every one; in which case every one is governed by his own Reason. . . . It followeth, that in such a condition, every man has a Right to every thing; even to one anothers body" (Hobbes 190).

This is *not* the right that Locke derived from natural equality by reason. Oh, it is true that Hobbes would have us sacrifice this right, and all rights except the right to self-preservation, to an absolute sovereign, out of fear, so that the sovereign could create a mortal god, beneath the immortal, but nonexistent, God, to give us an artificial moral order, but it is an *artificial* order, and it obliges out of fear and expediency, not genuine moral obligation. When we no longer fear the sovereign, we do as we please, by *right*. When our neighbor no longer fears the sovereign, he does as *he* pleases, by *right*, even to the use of *our* body. One does not want to depend on the "rights" derived from equality by reason when left alone with a Hobbesian man.

Where then *does* Locke find moral obligation in this foundation of his whole system? Here is how he continues " . . . for men being all the workmanship of one omnipotent and infinitely wise Maker—all the servants of one sovereign master, sent into the world by his order, and about his business—they are his property whose workmanship they are, made to last during his, not one another's pleasure . . ." (Locke 5–6). We are equal, not in our abilities, but as creatures of God. We have no right to harm another, or to harm *even ourselves*, because we are *not* our own property, or another's, but *God's*; and it is *His* business, not our own, that we are about. Without that, we have neither moral purpose nor moral restraint. As Locke put it, in A *Letter on Toleration*, "The taking away of God, even only in thought, dissolves all" (1968 135). And Locke drew the inferences, arguing that atheists should not be tolerated, because "promises, covenants, and oaths, which are the bonds of human society, can have no hold upon an atheist . . ." (1968 135).

Locke writes as a theist. His arguments use, as the final ground, obligations imposed, or permissions granted, or capacities given by God. As John Dunn, a scholar who steeped himself for years in the Lockean manuscripts, published and unpublished, and the diaries, letters, and notes of his life, puts it: "[A]n extremely high proportion of Locke's arguments [depend] for their very intelligibility, let alone plausibility, on a series of theological commitments" (Dunn xi). Locke's *arguments* for natural right, and natural rights, depend on a moral universe, and moral obligations, created by God.

Rights and Right in America

Whence come natural rights in the American revolution? They come, as they came in Locke, from God and the moral universe created by God. In the Declaration of Independence, we were declared to be entitled to independence by "the Laws of Nature and of Nature's God." This was not, to Jefferson at least, the God of orthodox Christianity, but it was the god of a natural theology, and the arguments for natural right stem, again, from God's donation: "We hold these truths to be self-evident, that all men are *created* equal, that they are *endowed by their Creator* with certain unalienable Rights . . ." [emphasis added]. Whence come rights? They come from God, our "Creator," the "Supreme Judge of the world," to Whom the Signers appealed for "the rectitude of our intentions," and on Whom, in the guise of "divine Providence," they relied for protection in this matter in which, in quite unHobbesian manner, they pledged "our Lives, our Fortunes and our sacred Honor." (Rights and right come from God, it may be noted, not from government, and *not from contract and consent*; preservation of them is the very purpose of government and contract and one of the two tests of its legitimacy; and these rights cannot be destroyed by government *or by consent.*)

Let us quickly survey the scene. Alexander Hamilton, in *The Farmer Refuted*, accused Samuel Seabury of sharing Hobbes's view that "Moral obligation . . . is derived from the introduction of civil society; and there is no virtue, but what is purely artificial. . . ." Hamilton called this an "absurd and impious doctrine," and urged that: "Good and wise men, in all ages, have embraced a very dissimilar theory. They have supposed that the deity, from the relations we stand in, to himself and to each other, has constituted an eternal and immutable law, which is, indispensably, *obligatory* upon all mankind. . . ." This Hamilton termed the "law of nature," and upon it depend, he said, "the natural rights of mankind. . . ." (cited in West 17). Right, in this view, derives from God and His moral law, as it does in Locke, St. Thomas, or Cicero.

James Wilson, too, stood with Locke and condemned the Hobbesian views of the foundations of things as "narrow and Hideous," and as "totally repugnant to all human sentiment, and all human experience" (West 17).

John Adams as well held, in 1765, that " . . . liberty must at all hazards be supported. We have a right to it, derived from our Maker" (cited in Peek 13). God again. Adams was later to assess alternatives:

> Is there a possibility that the government of nations may fall into the hands of men who teach the most disconsolate of all creeds, that men are but fireflies and that this *all* is without a father? Is this the way to make man, as man, an object of respect? Or is it to make murder itself as indifferent as shooting a plover . . . as innocent as the swallowing of mites on a morsel of cheese (Peek 193–94)?

So Adams, our most learned founder, on rights without God.

In America, natural rights were defended as endowments from God, as deductions from a moral universe created by God. Even Jefferson, apparently the least religious of the founders until late in life (he wrote Adams, in 1823, that evidences for the existence of God are "irresistible" [Reichley 94]), wrote: "And can the liberties of a nation be thought secure when we have removed their only firm basis, a conviction in the minds of the people that these liberties are the gift of God? That they are not to be violated but with his wrath? Indeed, I tremble for my country when I reflect that God is just" (Mansfield 35).

George Washington said, similarly, in his Farewell Address, "And let us with caution indulge the supposition that morality can be maintained without religion. Whatever may be conceded to the influence of refined education on minds of a peculiar structure, reason and experience both forbid us to expect that national morality can prevail in exclusion of religious principle" (Kaufman 24–25).

What is the ground of rights and right in the American revolution and founding? It is God, and His law, ruling a cosmos, a world and nature of moral order. That was true of the Calvinists. It was true of the public Locke. It was true of the Declaration (that is the substance of what was declared) and the American people. Bloom is silent about this, ignoring thereby the full force of Nietzsche's understanding of the necessary *ground* of a natural right derived from reason. It is true that state-of-nature theory can be a theory of nature *without* God, but that leads to quite different results, and a quite artificial moral order—as Hobbes knew. To the extent that we *have* become Hobbesians, our natural right and rights place fewer and fewer *limits* upon us and we become, as Bloom notes, more concerned with our *selves*, selfish; more mindful perhaps of rights, but of rights without the *limits* imposed by our status as creatures; more concerned, then, with our interests, and less concerned with others, or the common good.

Once, as creatures of God, we were to serve His purposes, not our own, hence our rights had limits. We had no right to abandon our station, hence we had no right to suicide. Others too were His creation, about His business, hence we had no right to harm another—thus we have no "right to privacy" that allows us to destroy the life of an unborn child; no right, for we know not God's purposes, to destroy the handicapped infant; no right to "release the old from suffering," euthanasia. . . .

Right Without God: The British Moralists

The thrust of modern philosophy, culminating in Nietzsche, is that natural rights, and right by nature, depend on God; or, rather, that since God does not exist, that no such rights or right exist *by nature*. Thus David Hume, on principles that make it impossible to know anything as true, including cause and effect, moral truths, the truths of science, or even the truth of his own ideas, was understood to have destroyed the possibility of knowing objective moral truths by reason, and he concluded (without understanding, as Nietzsche did, the abyss into which this plunges us) that: "Reason is, and ought to be, the slave of the passions, and can never pretend to any other office than to serve and obey them" (cited in Hallowell 201).

Hume hoped, of course, that it would please our passions to behave sociably. Self-interest is to be our guide. Still, there are problems. What of the maxim that "honesty is the best policy," a formulation that exactly catches the shift from natural right to enlightened self-interest. The difficulty, of course, is that if it is against one's self-interest in particular cases to be honest, then self-interest as a "moral" guide leads us to be dishonest. Hume, considering the question of the man who considers that "he . . . conducts himself with most wisdom who observes the general rule and takes advantage of all the exceptions," says: "I must confess that, if a man think that this reasoning much requires an answer, it would be a little difficult to find any which will to him appear satisfactory and convincing" (Hallowell 201). Perhaps it is no wonder that Nietzsche viewed the British moralists with such scorn. Decent British gentlemen, brought up as gentlemen, habituated to codes of honor and virtue raised on scaffolding not of *their* making, they could hardly bring themselves to believe that, if ultimately guided by self-interest, or passions, anyone would, well, behave selfishly, or basely. We have rather too much evidence now to the contrary.

Jeremy Bentham carried on this tradition, developing what is perhaps the standard secular ethical system in the English-speaking nations, Utilitarianism.

"Pain and pleasure," he asserts, are our "sovereign masters." "It is for them alone to point out what we ought to do, as well as to determine what we shall do. . . . They govern us in all we do, in all we say, in all we think. . . ." (Hallowell 209). There are, he asserted, " . . . no eternal and immutable rules of right, no Law of Reason, no moral law of Nature, no Natural Justice" (Hallowell 209). As for natural rights, Bentham says: "There are no such things as natural rights, no such things as rights anterior to the establishment of government,—no such things as natural rights opposed to, in contradistinction to, legal . . . *Natural rights* is simply nonsense . . . rhetorical nonsense,—nonsense on stilts" (Hallowell 215).

Bentham rejects, as well, consent and contract theory. "Men obey the laws of government not because they have consented to do so, not because the laws embody principles of justice to which their reason inclines them to render obedience, but because 'the probable mischiefs of obedience are less than the probable mischiefs of resistance'" (Hallowell 215). Law is the expression of a will in the form of a command. No more than that. "To say that the supreme body in a state cannot do something, to say that its acts can be illegal or void, to speak of its exceeding its authority is, Bentham says once again, nonsense and "an abuse of language" (Hallowell 215).

Having erected principles entirely congenial to tyranny and raw will-to-power, Bentham, decent Englishman that he is, would use them to promote "the greatest happiness for the greatest number." But why the strong, or anyone, would prefer the pleasure or happiness of the greatest number to his own if pleasure is the *only* standard is left in necessary obscurity.

John Stuart Mill continued this tradition. "Utility, or the Greatest Happiness Principle, holds that actions are right in proportion as they tend to promote happiness, wrong as they tend to produce the reverse. . . . By happiness is intended pleasure . . . ; by unhappiness, pain. . . ." (Hallowell 219). To avoid conclusions unpleasant to a man who retains remnants of a better code, however, J. S. Mill introduces the idea that not only the quantity of pleasure and pain must be taken into account, but also the quality. Some pleasures, it seems, "are more valuable than others." But, as John Hallowell notes, "to say that one kind of pleasure is in itself more desirable and valuable than another kind is to introduce, surreptitiously it may be, some other standard than that of pleasure to differentiate between them. . . . For it is logically impossible to hold *both* that pleasure is the only thing desirable and that pleasures can differ in quality" (Hallowell 220).

Having modified the pleasure principle by noting that there are some pleasures more worthy than others, Mill gives it another wrench by suggesting that, after all, there are certain "social utilities" "vastly more important, and therefore more *absolute* and imperative, than any others. . . ." These are to be guarded "by a sentiment not only different in degree but also in *kind* . . ." They "are to be distinguished from the milder feeling which attaches to the mere idea of promoting human pleasure or convenience. . . ." The "appropriate name" for these social utilities is "justice." By such means is right restored, and justice returned to its priority over pleasure and pain (Hallowell 223).

By the time he has finished modifying Bentham, J. S. Mill can say: "In the golden rule of Jesus of Nazareth, we read the complete spirit of the ethics of utility. To do as you would be done by, and to love your neighbour as yourself, constitute the ideal perfection of utilitarian morality" (Hallowell 222). Governance by pain and pleasure, it turns out, leads us to the principles of the One who told us to "pick up your cross and follow me"—the One who showed upon the Cross what love may require. If one can believe this, then one is led by utility back to the ethics of Jesus. Nietzsche, a serious man, could not take any of this seriously.

Right Without God: Nietzsche

Whence come natural rights and natural right? They come from God. But God, philosophers tell us, is not. The British moralists were not much troubled by this. The continental philosophers and poets were, and spent a century working out the consequences: Nietzsche, whose powerful project Bloom describes, ending in contradiction and madness; Doestoevsky, insisting, in a series of fevered but brilliant novels, that without God "all is permitted," but nothing finally avails; Weber, dividing his studies between the soul-destroying rationality of the bureaucratic man and the life-affirming, "noncontemptible," irrationalities of the religious man; Camus, tracing out all the consequences of the loss of God in art, literature, morals, and politics, and struggling to rescue meaning, or create it, through will; and Sartre and Heidegger, venturing into the abyss and returning with advice that powerfully condemns their potent philosophical constructions.

Locke said that: "The taking away of God, even only in thought, dissolves all." And Nietzsche, who understood the force of this to the depths of his soul, was nonetheless forced to conclude that "God is dead." It was catastrophe. Reason had won its ancient contest with religion, but that proved a pyrrhic victory, for without God, nature stood bare, stripped of good or evil, nobility or baseness, natural right or natural wrong, purpose or end. And that meant that reason itself was henceforth rendered helpless—*the death of God was the death of reason*—for without meaning and purpose in nature: "the quest begun by Odysseus and continued over three millenia has come to an end . . . there is nothing to seek" (Bloom 143). Nietzsche concluded, in Bloom's words, that: "[v]ictorious rationalism is unable to rule in culture or soul . . . it cannot defend itself theoretically and . . . its human consequences are intolerable" (196). Philosophy, in razing the Temple of God, had felled the House of Reason, and destroyed the Abode of Man.

Without God, Nietzsche believed, reason dies, right dies, the West dies, man dies. The death of God is disaster, not liberation. In consequence, "Nietzsche was ineluctably led to meditation on the coming to be of God—on God-creation—for God is the highest value, on which the others depend" (Bloom 198–89). God is the central necessity, but God is but the projection of some extraordinary man. We must await, then, some new Moses to bring forth new tables of the law. He will not look up, for God is not; or out, to a moral and purposeful nature, for there is no meaning in nature; but he will look within, to his self, and down, to the anarchic and chaotic cauldren of the id, not to reason, but to will, passion, desire, all the obscure and irrational forces swirling within, and somehow, from this, will come the new Commandments, the ground of a new culture, the foundation of a new people.

But there is to Nietzsche's teaching a hard and dark side, and Bloom exposes it. Nietzsche is not an egalitarian. "The rarest of men is the creator, and all other men need and follow him" (Bloom 201). And Nietzsche is not a pacifist. "Since values are not rational and not grounded in the natures of those subject to them, they must be imposed. . . . Rational persuasion cannot make them believed, so struggle is necessary" (Bloom 201). "Nietzsche," Bloom adds, "was a cultural relativist, and he saw what that means—war, great cruelty rather than great compassion" (202). Max Weber, one of the fathers of social science, extended the analysis and concluded that the state is simply "a relation of domination of man by man, founded on legitimate violence—that is, violence that is *considered* to be legitimate" (Bloom 212). And Bloom comments: "Just over the horizon, when Weber wrote, lay Hitler" (213).

Nietzsche was not a fascist, Bloom tells us, but his "project inspired fascist rhetoric, which looked to the revitalization of old cultures or the foundation of new ones . . ." (202). And Bloom points to the social sciences, as well, which adopted Nietzsche's value relativism without ever questioning whether it was "harmonious with democracy" (154). "Social science," Bloom says, has "dealt with Nazism as a psychopathology, a result of authoritarian or other-directed personalities, a case for psychiatrists. . . . Social science denies that thought, especially serious thought, even the very thought at its own root, could have had anything to do with Hitler's success" (154). But, Bloom adds, "Once one plunges into the abyss, there is no assurance whatsoever that equality, democracy or socialism will be found on the other side" (154).

Fascism was no accident to be explained by psychopathology. The ground had been prepared by a great philosopher, Nietzsche, who had denied that reason could govern, and who had conjured up the image of the Overman, hard and cruel, for whom the rest of us are mere clay, to be formed to his purposes; and by Nietzsche's followers, among them founders of the social sciences, who had adopted and spread his understanding that there is no right, there are only "values," no right order, only "cultures"—some knowingly, in deepest distress; more mindlessly, ignorant of what they wrought. The Nazis seized all this, brought the new understandings to bear, and imposed, with the all-too-willing acquiescence of mass and elite alike, their brutal new directions.

With Nietzsche, philosophy had been prepared to await some new Moses, to give meaning again to the universe. And Nietzsche, the philosopher who had announced that philosophy cannot guide, had given some indication of what philosophy, henceforth, could accept. But Nietzsche's anticipations had looked horrifyingly like . . . the Nazis. More interestingly, philosophy's acknowledged representatives in this century, the spawn of Nietzsche, prepared by him, could not distinguish two horrors hardly matched down through the ages from our new Moses. Thus Heidegger, increasingly recognized, according to Bloom, as "the most interesting thinker of our century," (154) was, it appears, a committed Nazi, hoping that in *them* had been found our new culture creators. And then there was

Sartre, *the* Existentialist, "who had all those wonderful experiences of nothingness, the abyss, nausea, commitment without ground—the result of which was, almost without fail, support of the Party line" (219).

Yeats, in a terrible foreboding, had spoken of a "rough beast" slouching toward Bethlehem to be born (Yeats 1582). That beast emerged from its womb at last in the guise of Hitler and Stalin, to be welcomed, in the one form or the other, by Heidegger and Sartre, and by all too many others, as our new Messiah. It was a dreadful culmination to the Age of Reason, but a legitimate one if Nietzsche is right, for if there is no God, no meaning in nature, if there are no natural moral limits, and we are governed by will, and irrational urges from within, then there are no grounds, in reason, for rejecting the Nazis, no foundation but "authenticity" and success for recognizing the emerging culture creators. Nietzsche, perhaps the culmination of the philosophic tradition, whose "case looks stronger all the time" according to Bloom, left no grounds by which to condemn Hitler, the Nazis, the Holocaust, Stalin, and the Terror, except failure to prevail. We taste in the politics of Heidegger and Sartre the fruit of Nietzsche's philosophy—of a nature divorced from God, of a reason without guidance from nature, of action without limits imposed by natural right.

A Reconstruction of Right? Bloom's Response

Is there a way back from the downward path traced by Machiavelli, Hobbes, Rousseau, Nietzsche, and Heidegger? Bloom says that: "A serious argument about what is most profoundly modern leads inevitably to the conclusion that study of the problem of Socrates is the one thing most needful" (310). It seems "imperative to begin all over again, to try to figure out what Plato was talking about, because it might be the best thing available" (310). Let us look, then, at Socrates, as presented by Bloom, to see if we can salvage reason and reconstruct natural right. (We need not worry about natural rights—they are but an invention of modern philosophy, or so Bloom imagines, and are, he says, merely man's fundamental passions for self-preservation and satisfaction of wants—the opposite of the old virtues or religious commandments.) (287–88)

The picture painted by Bloom of Socrates and philosophy proves an unpromising one on which to reconstruct natural right, moral virtue, or the duties of citizenship. Bloom is excused by the fact that he does not appear to be attempting any of those things. Consider Bloom's Socrates.

"The philosopher wants to know things as they are. He loves the truth. That is an intellectual virtue. He does not love to tell the truth. That is a moral virtue. Presumably he would prefer not to practice deception; but if it is a condition of his survival, he has no objection to it" (279). Bloom makes the point again and again. Thus Socrates's defense "cannot be characterized as 'intellectually honest' " (266). Thus, after his condemnation, Socrates tells myths to those who had voted for him. "The tales are not true, but they reinforce the gentleness that kept them from fearing and hence condemning Socrates" (281). To protect themselves, philosophers engage in "a gentle art of deception" (279).

The philosopher will deceive, then, for his life, and to protect philosophy. This is, if not noble, expedient. But Bloom paints a picture that goes beyond the sacrifice of a moral virtue for survival. He indicates, in any number of places, that the practice of moral virtue is not of great concern to the philosopher. Thus the philosopher is characterized as one "sitting around talking about virtue, rather than doing virtuous deeds. . . ." (266). Thus Socrates is summarized as saying that "the greatest good for a human being is talking about—not practicing—virtue . . ." (277). And Bloom adds a gloss: "(unless talking about virtue is practicing it)" (277). Again: "Socrates thought it more important to discuss justice, to try to know what it is, than to engage himself in implementing whatever partial perspective on it happened to be exciting the passions of the day . . ." (314). Noble deeds, Bloom notes, are the specialty of the gentleman, not the philosopher (279).

One reason the philosopher leaves the practice of the moral virtues to the gentleman is that the philosopher scorns the field of moral virtue, the city, and the beneficiaries, the citizens. They are important to him primarily because he must find a way in which to co-exist with them (278–79). This co-existence requires deception, thus Socrates deceives each about what is important to him. He deceives Crito, the family man, into thinking he is a good family man, and he deceives Laches, the soldier, into thinking he is a good soldier. But Thrasymachus, the political man, is not deceived. He "sees the truth about Socrates" (283). He "sees that Socrates does not respect the city" (283).

Far from respecting the city, to Socrates "all societies look pretty much the same from the heights, be they Periclean Athens or Des Moines, Iowa" (293). *All societies.* In the lifetime of many, including Bloom, that would include the genocidal fury and furious will to dominate of Hitler's Germany, the implacable and remorseless terror of Stalin's Russia, and the ideological madness and horror of Pol Pot's Cambodia. One wonders what Bloom's statement can mean. It is certain that Bloom's Socrates peers down from a height most of us cannot scale, a height from which moral distinctions, and human misery, appear very small.

And if all cities look much the same from the heights, the noble deeds of the political man on behalf of the city seem slight, and wasted, as well. The political man " . . . is measured by his success in preserving the people. Those virtues are means to the end of preservation, i.e., the good life is subordinate to and in the service of mere life" (274). The practice of moral virtue to save the people, then, is subordination of "good life" to "mere life"—a chilling view of the dignity and worth of most people. But, by Bloom's account, the citizens of Athens hardly seem to have been Socrates's concern. "The university," Bloom says, "began in spirit from Socrates's contemptuous and insolent distancing of himself from the Athenian people . . ." (311). And, "[T]he theoretical life . . . cannot, at least in its most authentic expression, be, or seriously be understood to be, in the city's service" (274).

The picture Bloom paints of a near indifference to the practice of moral virtue or the performance of noble deeds may seem to be contrasted with what we know of Socrates, who could have escaped his death, but did not; who acted against religious fanaticism (if ineffectively); and who did, after all, behave with honor as a soldier of Athens. Still, it looks different as Bloom paints the picture. Why did Socrates accept death? "[B]ecause he is old, because it is inevitable, and because it costs him almost nothing and *might* be useful to philosophy" (285). As for soldiering, Bloom says that Socrates "distinguished himself as a soldier exclusively in retreats. . . ." (274) Bloom's presentation forces questions: Would Socrates have been reluctant to give up his life earlier, at greater cost to himself? Is there much for which the philosopher is willing to sacrifice his life? Indeed, in this light, Bloom instructively contrasts Achilles' "laments and complaints about why he must die for the Greeks" with Socrates' attitude toward his death. "Anger characterizes Achilles; calculation, Socrates. Whatever sympathy there might be between the two kinds of men is founded, to speak anachronistically, on Achilles' misunderstanding of Socrates" (285). A gulf, it appears, separates the hero (who will die, if angrily, for his people) and the philosopher, (who will die for philosophy, when he is old, when it costs little.) (There are times, reading Bloom, when one thinks one would rather rely, when in danger, on the first passer-by in a pickup than on the whole procession of the greatest philosophers in history.)

The philosopher will deceive. He talks about virtue rather than doing noble deeds. He lacks respect for the city. He contemptuously and insolently distances himself from his fellow citizens. Perhaps we had better examine Bloom's portrait of the philosophic way of life. Let us start with Bloom's reporting of Aristophanes' Socrates, and his assessment of that account, then turn directly to the nature and concerns of the philosopher. We will then be in a position to see whether a return to Socrates, as understood by Bloom, will restore a ground for natural right, moral virtue, or the duties of citizenship.

Aristophanes paints a picture of Socrates that makes him appear ridiculous. But that portrait is, if Bloom is correct, accurate in its essentials. Bloom first reports how the philosopher spends his time. Aristophanes' Socrates is "a grown man who spends his time thinking about gnats' anuses." This stands in marked contrast to the concerns of a gentleman—"war and peace, justice, freedom and glory" (270). Bloom comments: "If science is just for curiosity's sake, *which is what theoretical men believe* [emphasis added], it is nonsense, and immoral nonsense, from the viewpoint of practical men" (270). Science (and science and philosophy are one at the beginning) is "just for curiosity's sake" and not for the sake of the things of the city such as justice and freedom.

Aristophanes' Socrates does not involve himself in the affairs of the city. But his atheism, and its consequence, an undermining of the city's laws and morals, does finally bring him to the attention of the city. The instrument is a father, wishing to escape his obligations to pay the debts of his son. "Socrates's atheism was the right prescription for him," Bloom says, "insofar as it meant that he need not fear Zeus's thunderbolt if he broke the law, if he perjured himself. The law is revealed to be merely manmade, and hence there is no witness to his misdeeds if he can escape the attention of other men" (275).

The father is liberated by Socrates' atheism, in Aristophanes' portrait, from honesty and his debts, but so too is the son liberated . . . from reverence for his father and mother. "This the father cannot stand and returns to his belief in the gods, who it turns out protect the family as well as the city. In a rage he burns down Socrates's school" (275). Bloom judges that: "Aristophanes was prescient. The actual charges against Socrates were corrupting the youth and impiety, with the implication that the latter is the deepest cause of the former. And whatever scholars may say about the injustice of the indictments of Socrates by Aristophanes or Athens, the evidence supports them (275).

Bloom and Aristophanes alike paint a picture of the philosopher as unconcerned with the city, its citizens, and the moral virtues—unconcerned not only with the things of pride (glory and honor) but also unconcerned with freedom, justice, and preservation of the people of the city. The reasons for this appear to be two. First, the philosopher finds no moral order and purpose in nature, hence the laws of the cities are mere conventions. Second, the philosopher is superior to other humans, as is his way of life to other ways of life, hence he is right to focus on philosophy, and bend his efforts almost entirely to the preservation of philosophy and philosophers. In a meaningless world, pursuit of understanding is the only life that is not self-deceptive, and provides what genuine joy and happiness there is. Let us examine this sad tale.

The first accomplishment of the philosophic way of life is to liberate one from fear of the gods. Thales is prototypical. Bloom writes that, "[p]erhaps most important for Thales was seeing that the poetic or mythical accounts of eclipses are false. They are not, as men believed prior to the advent of science, a sign from the gods. Eclipses are beyond the power of the gods. They belong to nature. One need not fear the gods" (270–71). "The theoretical experience," Bloom adds, "is one of liberation . . . freeing the thinker from fear of the gods . . ." and " . . . simultaneously a discovery of the best way of life" (271).

Philosophy liberates a man from fear of the gods. It liberates him, as well, from illusions about his cosmic significance. Philosophy, Bloom says: "is austere and somewhat sad because it takes away many of men's fondest hopes. It certainly does nothing to console men in their sorrows and their unending vulnerability. Instead it points to their unprotectedness and nature's indifference to their individual fates" (273). Philosophers, in this respect, have no special dispensation. "There is no moral order protecting philosophers or ensuring that truth will win out in the long, or the short, run" (279). But only philosophers can face the reality that: "As are the generations of leaves, so are the generations of men,—'a somber lesson that is only compensated for by the intense pleasure accompanying insight. Without that pleasure, which so few have, it would be intolerable" (277).

In a meaningless world, the problem of the philosopher is how to face death. The task of philosophy is defined by Socrates, Bloom says, as "learning how to die" (277). And only philosophers, Bloom believes, face death undeceived. The philosopher scorns alike the "vulgarly courageous" whose courage requires "unfounded beliefs about the noble," and the "religious fanatics," who march into oblivion gaily, believing in a better life after death (285). Instead, as death is final, the philosopher tries to avoid it, which deceives the vulgar into thinking the philosopher is like them, and, when death cannot be avoided, faces it squarely, which deceives gentlemen and the vulgarly courageous into thinking the philosopher, like them, is exercising courage for the sake of the noble (289).

But the philosopher is not like other men:

> Only the philosopher does not need opinions that falsify the significance of things in order to endure them. He alone mixes the reality of death—its inevitability and our

dependence on fortune for what little life we have—into every thought and deed and is thus able to live while honestly seeking perfect clarity. He is thus able to live while in the most fundamental tension with everyone except his own kind. He relates to all the others ironically, i.e., with sympathy and a playful distance. Changing the character of his relationship to them is impossible because the disproportion between him and them is firmly rooted in nature (282).

This unbridgeable gulf "firmly rooted in nature" between the philosopher and all others is a repeated theme of Bloom's. The great modern philosophers "were perfectly conscious of what separates them from all other men, and they knew that the gulf is unbridgeable" (290). Philosophers "always see through such hopes for individual salvation and are hence isolated" (290). "The philosophers in their closets or their academies have entirely different ends than the rest of mankind" (291). Indeed, "the philosophic experience is understood by the philosophers to be what is uniquely human, the very definition of man . . ." (273).

Only the philosopher, if Bloom is correct, can look the ultimate meaninglessness of things squarely in the face without flinching and even with a certain prideful joy. In describing the feelings of Thales when he successfully predicted an eclipse of the sun, Bloom describes the ultimate experience of the philospher:

> satisfaction at having solved a problem; pleasure in using his faculties; fullness of pride, more complete than that of any conqueror, for he surveys and possesses all; certitude drawn from within himself, requiring no authorities; self-sufficiency, not depending, for the fulfillment of what is highest in himself, on other men or opinions or on accidents such as birth or election to power, on anything that can be taken from him; a happiness that has no admixture of illusion or hope but is full of actuality. (270)

What Bloom offers us is not a reconstruction of a moral universe, or natural right, but the life of philosophy, a life available only to a very few. The rest of us, if not mere pawns, are best left with our illusions, or "natural rights" as self-interest, the highest we can reliably reach. The philosopher, in the meanwhile, must defend himself, as he did for nearly 2000 years by forging an alliance with gently deceived gentlemen (277), and as he does now by changing sides, deflating the illusions and pretensions of the gentlemen, and joining the *demos* (288–89). There is no rescue of right or natural moral order to be found in Bloom's Socrates, no answer to the figure who dominates his book: Nietzsche.

Athens and Jerusalem
Nietzsche understood that the death of God is the death of reason, of right, of man. Athens depends, finally, on Jerusalem. Our need for God is desperate, then, but that is not, in itself, an argument that God is. If philosophy has killed God, then it has killed itself, and us. The paradoxical thing is that Bloom, the partisan of reason, who is deadset against the illusions, as he sees them, of religion, gives evidence himself that puts the issue between Athens and Jerusalem back into doubt.

"Philosophy," he writes, "is the rational account of the whole, or of nature" (264). But if reason cannot explain the whole, or nature, then reason points beyond itself, to mystery, and to the possibility that this is, after all, a creation, and that God is. Let us look, then, at some of the difficulties with a purely scientific or materialistic explanation of things that Bloom himself notices.

Descartes, Bloom notes, "had reduced nature to extension, leaving out of it only the ego that observes extension" (177). But that ego is crucial:

> Man is, in everything but his consciousness, part of extension. Yet how he is a man, a unity, what came to be called a *self*, is utterly mysterious. This experienced whole, a combination of extension and ego, seems inexplicable or groundless. Body, or atoms in motion, passions, and reason are some kind of unity, but one that stands outside of the grasp of natural science. (177)

Locke, whose essay on human understanding led to the suspicion that he was not a believer, nevertheless failed at the critical point—the attempt to explain human understanding in purely physical or scientific terms. As Bloom puts it: "Locke appears to have invented the self to provide unity in continuity for the ceaseless temporal succession of sense impressions that would disappear into nothingness if there were no place to hold them" (177). And Bloom comments: "We can know everything in nature except that which knows nature. To the extent that man is a piece of nature, he disappears" (177).

Man is aware, conscious of himself as a self, a unity. There is no explanation for that. Man is also creative, able to act and to choose. And there is no explanation for that. "The faith in God and the belief in miracles are closer to the truth than any scientific explanation, which has to overlook or explain away the creative in man" (199). How can this creativity be explained? How can man rise above the laws of motion or body and think and choose and make and do? Freud has no answer. His psychology "finds causes of creativity that blur the difference between a Raphael and a finger painter. Everything is in that difference, which necessarily escapes our science" (199).

Indeed, Bloom finds Freud paradigmatic for the sciences. "Freud says that men are motivated by desire for sex and power, but he did not apply those motives to explain his own science or his own scientific activity. But if he can be a true scientist, i.e., motivated by love of the truth, so can other men, and his description of their motives is thus mortally flawed" (203–204). "This contradiction runs throughout the natural and social sciences," Bloom says. "They give an account of things that cannot possibly explain the conduct of their practitioners" (204). Bloom gives examples: "The highly ethical economist who speaks only about gain, the public-spirited political scientist who sees only group interest, the physicist who signs petitions in favor of freedom while recognizing only unfreedom—mathematical law governing moved matter—in the universe are symptomatic of the difficulty of providing a self-explanation for science and a ground for the theoretical life . . ." (204). "Biologists," Bloom adds, "cannot even account for consciousness within their science, let alone the unconscious" (199–200). In the end, natural science ends at man. "[I]t ends at that part or aspect of man that is not body, whatever that may be. Scientists as scientists can be grasped only under that aspect, as is the case with politicians, artists and prophets. All that is human, all that is of concern to us, lies outside of natural science" (356).

As Bloom paints the picture, science and, by implication, philosophy, fail to portray a world in which there can be scientists and science, philosophers and philosophy. Naturalism fails by its failure to explain man. Reason points beyond naturalism. It would seem premature, then, if not obscurantist and dogmatic, to consider the issue between Athens and Jerusalem to be settled. On Bloom's evidence, one cannot reasonably be an atheist, though one may be an agnostic.

But Bloom has given us more to think about. In many respects, the great figure in his book is Nietzsche. He sets the problem that must be solved. He is the one who drives us back to Socrates. (And he, one suspects, is the lens through which Bloom's striking understanding of Socrates is filtered.) *Bloom's* Socrates, so concerned with death, so unconcerned with others, hardly seems an answer. So we must look again at Nietzsche.

"God is dead," Nietzsche tells us, but we cannot live without God. We await, then, some new Moses, following "obscure drives" from within, to bring us new tables of the law. These tables come, not from the High and Holy God, but from the soul's basement, the "fathomless and turbulent sea called the id . . ." (178). And we have seen what Nietzsche, peering into the abyss, finds there. He calls forth the Overman, hard and cruel, to form us, mere clay, to his new horizon. He calls forth will, and will to power. He proclaims that "A good war makes sacred almost any cause" (Bloom 220–21). He, though not a fascist, inspires fascist rhetoric, and fascist action. And it is Nietzsche who prepared thinkers of the rank of Heidegger and Sartre to accept Nazis and Stalinists.

Must we accept Nietzsche? Must reason collapse and hang, henceforth, on what spews out from the turbulent chaos of the passions and desires from within? Bloom mocks the idea that we will find good and moderation by plunging within. The new psychology, looking within, assumes selfishness, Bloom tells us; it only distinguishes between good and bad forms. Bloom says:

> For us the most revealing and delightful distinction—because it is so unconscious of its wickedness—is between inner-directed and other-directed, with the former taken to be unqualifiedly good. Of course, we are told, the healthy inner-directed person will *really* care for others. To which I can only respond: If you can believe that, you can believe anything. Rousseau knew much better (178).

And so he did. It is not good that has spewed forth from the basement of the soul, not from Nietzsche, not from all those so concerned with "self-fulfillment," not from the spawn of Nietzsche. We have seen those "rough beasts" slouching toward Bethlehem to be born, our new Messiahs, and they have come forth as Hitler, and Stalin, and Pol Pot. Perhaps we had better look again at the *old* Moses. If *reason* cannot find good and evil in nature, and *will* cannot bring good forth from within, then whence came those images we have had of good and nobility and the noble soul? If not from within, then from without. If not from reason, then from revelation. The tables of the law given us by Moses look not at all like what we have gotten from Nietzsche, Bloom's Socrates, or furious fanaticisms of this age. The self-sacrificial love of Jesus looks not at all like the "honesty is the best policy" enlightened self-interest ethics of utilitarianism or the self-fulfillment ethic of the self-psychologies. It is just possible that Nietzsche was mistaken, that the tables of the law came not from within, but from the High and Holy God.

The issue between Athens and Jerusalem is not settled, and if modern philosophy and the practice of men without God are indications, we must be thankful for that.

Bloom remembers, in a touching way, his grandparents, and their spiritually rich life, though they held lowly jobs and were "ignorant" by "our standards." Then he says something worth consideration.

> I do not believe that my generation, my cousins who have been educated in the American way, all of whom are M.D.s or Ph.D.s, have any comparable learning. When they talk about heaven and earth, the relations between men and women, parents and children, the human condition, I hear nothing but cliches, superficialities, the material of satire. I am not saying anything so trite as that life is fuller when people have myths to live by. I mean rather that a life based on the Book is closer to the truth, that it provides the material for deeper research in and access to the real nature of things (60).

It is misleading to end without noting that, while much of modern philosophic thought has rejected the possibility of discovering objective moral truth by reason, much of the religious community continues to hold that moral truth *is* discoverable by unaided reason or by an innate moral sense. Revelation is not needed, on most issues, for people to know right from wrong. Roman Catholic natural law tradition is an example of this view.

It should be noted, as well, that much of Christianity has not been hostile to reason or philosophy. In this tradition, reason is understood to have been given to man to be used. Whatever reason indisputably proves true, cannot be contrary to truth. In this tradition, it is possible to work out a synthesis of reason and revelation and to delineate the proper spheres of each. The attempt by St. Thomas Aquinas to synthesize Christian revelation and Aristotelian philosophy is the most famous example of this effort.

Further, it should be noted that, while the tension between Athens and Jerusalem is genuine, the interplay has also been fruitful and needed. Nietzsche thought God necessary to reason. But reason is necessary, as well, to revelation, for revelation must be interpreted and applied. The religious have demonstrated, all too often, that furious passions can be unleashed in the name of God. And those passions prove, all too often, to have been in the service of one's own interest, cause, or will, or in the service of narrow and unreasonable interpretations of the faith. Religious passions can ennoble; they can also disfigure and destroy. The worst evils are perversions of the highest goods. Reason, given by God, is necessary to the faith.

In sum, borrowing from Frederick Douglass on quite another issue, neither Athens nor Jerusalem will die out, nor be driven out; but they shall go with us, either as evidence against us [depending on our use of them], or testimony in our favor, throughout our generations (40).

In conclusion, we owe Bloom a great debt for showing us our problems and providing us with tools by which we may grapple with them.

Beitzinger, A. J. 1972. A *History of American Political Thought*. New York: Dodd, Mead and Co.

Bloom, Allan. 1987. *The Closing of the American Mind*. New York: Simon and Schuster.

Douglass, Frederick. 1970. The Destiny of Colored Americans, in Herbert J. Storing, ed. *What Country Have I?* New York: St. Martin's Press. 39–40.

Dunn, John. 1969. *The Political Thought of John Locke.* Cambridge: Cambridge University Press.

Grimes, Alan P. 1960. *American Political Thought.* Rev. ed. New York: Holt, Rinehart and Winston.

Hallowell, John H. 1984. *Main Currents in Modern Political Thought.* New York: University Press of America.

Hamilton, Alexander, James Madison, and John Jay. 1961. *The Federalist Papers.* New York: Mentor/New American Library.

Hobbes, Thomas. 1968. *Leviathan.* C. B. Macpherson, ed. New York: Penguin Books.

Kaufman, Burton Ira. 1969. *Washington's Farewell Address.* Chicago: Quadrangle Books.

Locke, John. 1952. *The Second Treatise of Government.* Thomas Peardon, ed. Indianapolis: Bobbs-Merrill.

Locke, John. 1968. *A Letter on Toleration.* J. W. Gough, ed. Oxford: Clarendon Press.

Mansfield, Harvey C. 1976. *Thomas Jefferson.* In Morton J. Frisch and Richard G. Stevens, eds. *American Political Thought: The Philosophic Dimension of Statesmanship.* Dubuque, Iowa: Kendall/Hunt.

Mason, Alpheus T. 1965. *Free Government in the Making.* 3rd. ed. New York: Oxford University Press.

Miller, Perry and Thomas H. Johnson, eds. 1963. *The Puritans.* 2 vols. rev. ed. New York: Harper and Row.

Neuhaus, Richard John. 1988. The Return of Eugenics. *Commentary.* 85: 15–26.

Peek, George A. 1954. *The Political Writings of John Adams.* Indianapolis: Bobbs-Merrill.

Reichley, A. James. 1985. *Religion in American Public Life.* Washington, D.C.: Brookings Institute.

Stone, Robert L. 1987. Professor Harry V. Jaffa Divides the House: A Respectful Protest and a Defense Brief. *University of Puget Sound Law Review.* 10: 471–505.

West, Thomas G. 1988. Allan Bloom and America. *The Claremont Review.* VI: 1 and 17–20.

Yeats, William Butler. 1968. The Second Coming. *The Norton Anthology of English Literature.* vol. 2. rev. M. H. Abrams, gen. ed. New York: W. W. Norton and Co.

ELEVEN

The University in Democratic Society

What Is Its Proper Role?

Thomas Jefferson founded the University of Virginia because he believed that the purpose of universities in democratic societies is to train good citizens. Bloom, on the contrary, argues in part 3 of *The Closing of the American Mind* that the purpose of America is to provide good universities, the only places where community and friendship can exist in our times (382). But, "What is the . . . university . . . other than a free lunch for philosophy and scientists?" (263).

> This is the American moment in world history, the one for which we shall forever be judged. Just as in politics the responsibility for the fate of freedom in the world has devolved upon our universities, and the two are related as they have never been before. The gravity of our given task is great, and it is very much in doubt how the future will judge our stewardship (382).

And of what does our stewardship consist? "To sum up, there is one simple rule for the university's activity: it need not concern itself with providing its students with experiences that are available in democratic society" (256).

Timothy Fuller, in "The Vocation of the University and the Uses of the Past: Reflections on Bloom and Hirsch," agrees with Bloom. Justice requires that the low be in the service of the high. F. Russell Hittinger, in "Reason and Anti-Reason in the Academy," agrees with Bloom that the question of the role of the university in democratic society is the most important political question today for Americans, because the crisis of the American university *is* the crisis of America, and thereby of the entire West.

Mortimer Adler agrees with Jefferson that the purpose of universities in America is to train good citizens. Adler and Bloom agree that there is no necessary reason why the universities must be the home of philosophy. Very few philosophers have been professors. Therefore, to ask that the university serve society is not to ask that the highest serve the low. And besides, at the time of the Enlightenment, philosophers switched parties from the aristocratic to the democratic, as Bloom admits (288). John Van Doren, writing in the *Paideia Bulletin*, agrees with Bloom that the present defect of schooling at all levels is basically intellectual, but agrees with Jefferson against Bloom on the larger question of whether universities serve democracy or vice versa. "Plato might have acknowledged . . . that in a democracy we are *all* guardians, and so we must all have the education of guardians."

Tom Hayden, in "Our Finest Moment," agrees with Adler and Van Doren that Jefferson's plan for the University of Virginia is the model of the university in democratic society. It is a place where good leaders and good citizens are trained, in an institution that can criticize the mistakes of democracy.

It is noteworthy that Bloom rejects American and German universities as products of the mistaken Enlightenment, which sought to remove Aristotle and the Bible from the curriculum. But Bloom presents no alternative. Walter Nicgorski reminds us that Catholic colleges are more resistant than others to the decay Bloom laments. Bloom admits that, in America, "Catholic universities have always kept some contact with medieval philosophy, and hence, Aristotle" (378). Then J. M. Cameron points out that the English university stands as an alternative to American and German institutions.

Bloom carefully avoids any controversial call for general reform, such as a return of American higher education to Cambridge and Oxford (the architectural models for the University of Chicago and Yale) or even to the University of Virginia. "One cannot hope and should not hope for a general reform. The hope is [merely] that the embers do not die out" (380). "[T]he only serious solution is the one that is almost universally rejected: the good old Great Books approach, in which a liberal education means reading certain recognized classical texts . . ." (344). Martha Nussbaum, in *The New York Review of Books*, argues that to read the great books is undemocratic and un-American because none of them are written by women, and few of them are written by Africans or Asians. According to Gregory B. Smith, Nussbaum reflects the currently fashionable opinion within American colleges. Further evidence of the refurbishing of Western civilization courses can be seen in an article from *The Wall Street Journal* which describes the purge of several great books from the curriculum of Stanford University in December of 1988. Dante's *Inferno* was replaced in the curriculum by *Yo Rigoberta Menchu*, the autobiography of a Marxist female Guatemalan Indian. No wonder that Bill Honig, the Superintendent of Public Instruction for the State of California, in "What Is Right About Bloom?" is alarmed. Honig argues that because there is now so little concern for ethics and the ideas of great men in our schools, we risk cultural suicide.

The conclusion and summary for the debate surrounding *The Closing of the American Mind* is provided by William T. Braithwaite's judicious and imaginative essay, "Mr. Bloom and the Critics: What Could It All Mean?"

52

The Vocation of the University and the Uses of the Past: Reflections on Bloom and Hirsch

TIMOTHY FULLER

The rediscovery of tradition and the search for continuity are well underway. Several generations of progressive education, inspired by pedagogical reflections running from Rousseau to John Dewey, have emphasized the mastery of skills and techniques unsullied by reverence for inherited bodies of learning. The skills were to allow us to create an open, experimental society that would be in a state of continuous and spontaneous improvement. It is now increasingly argued that this was a mistaken approach to educating the young. In devaluing the canon of traditional literature and philosophy in favor of such topics as current events and values clarification, the mistake was amplified by the politicization of curricula: the past was aggressively dismissed not only as outdated (the irony of this accusation was submerged in the earnestness with which it was proclaimed) but also as an actual barrier to liberating ourselves from superstition, racism, sexism, class bias, prejudices of all sorts. At the extreme, such education turned enlightenment into wilful ignorance of the past in revulsion from what was alleged about it so as to be free from its limitations. Sadly, this project has succeeded if the current reports of the expanding ignorance of the young are accurate.

Nevertheless, the new quest for tradition does not necessarily manifest deep feelings much less intimacy with tradition's subleties. On the contrary, we are immersed in a struggle for control of the uses to which the past shall put in which traditional voices may or may not be much heard.

Traditions have come to be seen as conventions which, when viewed from a perspective of proclaimed detachment, seem to many to have arbitrary foundations. Either they need not be the way they are, or else they enjoy transitory, local meaning lacking either perpetual or universal significance. This has led to revolutionary relativism: the effort to relativize the commitment to our intellectual heritage in order to project a future alternative that is putatively superior. This future alternative claims to be superior mostly as it is abstractly imagined to be free of what we currently identify as the defects of what we have been and are. Why this alternative is less arbitrary, whether it could be less vulnerable to the very critique that is employed to justify it, is an embarrassing question. The past

---

Timothy Fuller teaches at Colorado College and is editor of Michael Oakshott's *Essays on Education: The Voice of Liberal Learning* (1989). This essay copyright 1989 by Timothy Fuller.

becomes experimental evidence, at best raw material for designing this improved future.

The revolutionary relativists are countered by the cultural conservatives or counter-revolutionaries. We are engaged in a great academic civil war. There are parties of the right and parties of the left, and a silent majority of teachers and students in the middle-ground who are the prize sought by each side.

We might recall the distinction Hegel made between the practical study of the past and the philosophical study of the past. The practical study of the past is an effort to extract from history moral lessons to guide present actions. According to Hegel, the only lesson to be learned is that we do not ever learn from history what to do; at most, we find convenient evidence to support whatever responses we have already chosen to take to present circumstances. Philosophical history, by contrast, is the effort to contemplate the past as a whole to see if necessary patterns of development come to sight. Such patterns do not tell us what to do. They may only reveal the inescapable parameters within which we must try to act, showing us why the world must be as it is. . . .

This is the common ground of the left and the right such that one notices striking similarities between the cultural criticism of Bloom's *Closing of the American Mind* in the 1980s and Herbert Marcuse's *One-Dimensional Man* in the 1960s. In spite of their obvious political differences, both challenge the superficialities of modern culture; the criticisms of each find common ancestry in Rousseau's remarks in the *Second Discourse* on the artificialities and shallowness of modern, polite society.

To put it another way, we are submerged in a great pluralistic tangle the dimensions of which undoubtedly far exceed what is revealed by reference to a left-right split. Thus, for example, Roger Shattuck of the University of Virginia in a recent paper for the American Council of Learned Societies, follows E.D. Hirsch in urging emphasis on "human continuity," "human greatness," and their portrayal in "masterworks," while admitting that there is no consensus on the list of masterworks. He encourages academic communities to carry on great debates by creating lists and counter-lists of great books in the hope that eventually there will emerge a refurbished "core tradition" in the humanities.[1]

This is the self-conscious *use* of the past for present purposes. E.D. Hirsch's own defense of the great books, in *Cultural Literacy, What Every American Needs to Know*, does not question the Deweyite aspiration to universal, democratic literacy which he calls "cultural literacy." He reaffirms the aspiration to a universal, democratic culture buoyed up by technical prowess, pleading for the use of the great books as resources for making universal participation in the technological society possible. . . .

To Bloom, Hirsch's literacy policy, superficially similar to Bloom's, must be a formidable barrier to the opening of the mind to deep philosophical reflection on the assumptions of contemporary culture. For if Hirsch insists upon the positive contribution to technical civilization that the works of the past can make, Bloom, with greater vehemence and dramatic eloquence, insists on the root and branch opposition of the Bible and traditional philosophy to many of those same assumptions.

For Bloom, the marriage of the great works of the past to modern technology is merely a way to decorate the drab dungeon constructed by modern man in his restless search for the comfortable, safe, unheroic life. Bloom's argument, that the damnation of the great books with faint, utilitarian praise, will not inspire most students, or repair the damage done by the vulgarization of modern schooling, is well founded. In this respect, Bloom is more deeply moved by traditional learning than Hirsch, with due apologies to Hirsch who is certainly not to be faulted for championing traditional learning.

Bloom's reverence is born out of a genuine awe at the power of the classics to challenge all our modern assumptions whenever we permit them to penetrate through the fashionable interpretations we impose upon them. To those who have felt the full impact of traditional thought, Bloom believes, it will be clear how powerful an antidote to modern pretensions it is. But Bloom also believes that the full impact of the experience is so overwhelming that it is fitting only for a few, the philosophers, who have the stamina to live with the knowledge of the frailty of most human claims.

In his thumbnail sketch of the history of political philosophy from Socrates to Heidegger, Bloom asserts that Socratic inquiry was shown from the outset to lead to fundamental, uncompromising skepticism. He believes, not without reason, that a full encounter with the Platonic arguments will elevate the minds of students to a vantage point from which the ordinary goings on will seem puny and mundane, and that this will eventuate in a vocation to pursue the philosophic life as an end in itself.

This is coupled, however, with Bloom's clear commitment to deeply felt moral and political values which he finds necessarily bound to the preservation of Western civilization and, in particular, to the continued strength of America. He ends his book, saying: "This is the American moment in world history, the one for which we shall be forever judged. Just as in politics the responsibility for the fate of freedom in the world devolved upon our regime, so the fate of philosophy in the world has devolved upon our universities, and the two are related as they have never been before. The gravity of our given task is great, and it is very much in doubt how the future will judge our stewardship" (382).

The mighty controversies this has provoked are known to every academic who has not been secluded in research above the Arctic circle. I think those who underrate the importance of this dispute are mistaken. But what I want to emphasize for now is the tension between Bloom's patriotism and his philosophical skepticism. There are two different implications in Bloom's demand for studies that will open up the minds of our pupils.

In one dimension, opening the minds of students means leading them into the treasures of liberal learning—the great art, literature and philosophy of the past. It means seeing beyond mere pragmatism and vocational training. It means, as Michael Oakeshott has said, reflecting on the quality of a life and not on the mere fact of life. It means liberating oneself from preoccupation solely with getting and spending. It means, in other words, what it has usually meant to teachers who have themselves reflected on what they are trying to do, going back to Socrates.

In the other dimension, however, opening the student mind means revealing an awful truth: our only certainty is that our opinions are founded on no certainty whatever. This, Bloom tells us, is so unsettling that only a special sort of person is able to face it, appropriate it to himself and to live the highest, the philosophic life, in consequence. Those who have accused Bloom of simply concealing a tract for neo-conservatism inside his philosohizing, do not realize how extra-political his position is.

Bloom's so-called elitism refers to the life-long secluded pursuit of philosophy, in an attitude of relative detachment from the political world. It is certainly not a political program for installing a ruling class, nor can specific policies be deduced from the philosophic activity Bloom has in mind. We learn this lesson, Bloom tells us, in reflecting on the trial and death of Socrates. The lesson was accepted by virtually all philosophers down to the seventeenth and eighteenth centuries when, in the enthusiasm for the enlightenment project, philosophers began to think they could bring the world into line with themselves and thus end their historic necessity of living on the fringes of political life in order to protect philosophy, and themselves as philosophy's guardians, from Socrates' fate. But the result of this has been to import into ordinary life the "atheistic" experience induced by philosophic inquiry.

What Bloom identifies as the atheism of philosophy is really the generic skepticism of the philosophic method itself when carried on without end as a way of life. Bloom intends no dogmatic theological speculation of an atheistic sort for that would itself be an end to philosophizing; he certainly seems to believe that people could only benefit from relearning to read the Bible regularly.

To put it differently, one can have an allegiance to that civilization and country in which the philosophic life is least likely to be suppressed without relinquishing one's ultimate allegiance to philosophy. From the point of view of ordinary citizens this, to the extent that it becomes a public matter, may seem to be an atheistic—in the sense of unpatriotic—attitude. On the other hand, since we all live today as individuals claiming rights antecedent to government, we might all be said to be incipiently unpatriotic. Locke's doctrine of the right of revolution has certainly had such an implication from the start.

In any event, as Bloom sees it, the infusion of the modern philosophers' revolt into ordinary life has resulted in vulgar hedonism, materialism and value-relativism. The dilution of philosophic vision, often leading to the degradation rather than the elevation of ordinary life, was the result of philosophy forgetting the ancient wisdom on the intractability of the human condition. From this standpoint, the project to enlighten has incurred the opposite of its stated intentions. The relativist habits of mind of contemporary democracies are not infrequently equated with open-mindiness but, as Bloom shows, they often close down serious inquiry by translating every conviction into an irrationally held opinion. Modern academics, who are not true philosophers, have learned just enough to undermine belief in anything, but not enough to search for eternal truths that are more than just subjective preferences, or, at least, to keep quiet about their ignorance in the matter. Instead, they have raised their ignorance of the eternal things to the level of a surrogate eternal truth.

The denouement is in Heidegger's brief allegiance to the Nazis. For, according to Bloom, Heidegger hoped to repair the damage done by the intrusion of modern philosophy into ordinary life by a dramatic fusion of philosophy and life in a regime. This late modern debasement of philosophy was the disastrously mistaken effort to cure the failure of the enlightenment project of modern philosophy—Heidegger's disaster followed from correctly diagnosing the disease while prescribing a remedy that would only make it worse.

This twentieth century catastrophe has taken on an amiable, relaxed, and shallow character in its translation to America. Americans do not explore the further reaches of the world in which God is dead and all things are permitted. Perhaps they haven't yet heard much about them. Perhaps this is America's good fortune, but it *is* a matter of fortune and not conviction that American disenchantment is still primitive.

To Bloom the great books exemplify a specific historical development within Western civilization. The lesson for philosophers is to put as much distance between themselves and the Heidegger of 1933 as possible, but not by opting for relativism. The surest source for understanding this problem well is Plato's Socrates. The same teaching in its popular form is to respect the traditions of constitutional government in the modern liberal tradition, granting to them the respect that their practical achievements demand. The surest sources for understanding this are the documents of the American Founding and their explication in *The Federalist*. The fit between the philosophical and the practical forms of this understanding is tension-ridden, but they can live with each other, and they can be made to form a powerful educational program for the universities.

---

1   Roger Shattuck, "Perplexing Dreams: Is there a Core Tradition in the Humanities?" *American Council of Learned Societies* (April 24, 1987).

53

Reason and Anti-Reason in the Academy

F. RUSSELL HITTINGER

By the time you read this review, most of what is going to be said about Allan Bloom's *The Closing of the American Mind* will have been said. The book has fetched the attention of the media. The nation's major newspapers not only reviewed the book within days of its publication (which is rare, even in the case of most "popular" literature), but have reprinted abridged portions of it—especially from the chapter concerning the effect of rock music upon the intellectual and moral development of students. As I write this review, this Sunday's *Washington Post* and *New York Times* advertise it with the bold stringer: "At last you will know why today's young Americans are 'isolated, self-centered, tolerant of everything and committed to nothing." It's the sort of stringer that gets one on television, which happened quickly for Professor Bloom. Interestingly, it is also the sort of stringer that is apt to engage concerns which cut across the ideological spectrum. To the cultured Left, who are the mandarins of our university system, this sounds like the predictable effect of six years of Reaganism and neoconservative economics. To the cultured Right, the stringer immediately arouses the suspicion that it is indeed an accurate report from the "graves" of academia, where objective truth and disciplined learning have been on the wane for quite some time. There is something in this book for everyone. As an academician who has written a serious book, Professor Bloom has the rare opportunity of an audience outside the classroom.

The book consists of three discussions, which are interwoven throughout. In the first place, Professor Bloom attempts to give a profile of our university students—in general, he says, those who inhabit the best twenty or thirty schools. Concerning the students, who Bloom characterizes as "flat souled," the report is not likely to surprise anyone who has worked in universities for these past two decades. I do not think that anyone would deny that, among our students, sentiments have been divorced from formal education, and that teachers can no longer assume that the students have what Bloom calls an "eros" for learning. That eros has either been flattened out and constrained to a thin utilitarian motive, or it has been seduced by other objects (e.g., the bacchanalian revel of rock music) and rendered unfit for the discipline required for high-level learning. The pathology outlined by Bloom is most apparent to those who teach in the liberal arts (including the theoretical wing of mathematics). The problem is not just that students have jumped ship for business programs or for ersatz majors in quasi-sciences; nor can the problem be blamed simply on the fact that the

F. Russell Hittinger teaches philosophy at Fordham University. He is the author of *Religion as a Good*. This essay is reprinted with permission of the *Intercollegiate Review* (Fall 1987): 61–64.

students are sorely deficient in the knowledge prerequisite for university classes in the liberal arts. All of this, of course, is true. However, the problem spotlighted by Bloom is that students are not *interested*—so much so that one is tempted to say that even a competent demagogue or sophist would be hard pressed to arouse a lively response. In other words, the pathology of the "flat soul" seems to transcend the sum of the parts of the other problems. If nothing else, Professor Blooom has done a good job in conveying both the insight and frustration of teachers.

In the second place, Professor Bloom examines the nature of American institutions, and why they are especially vulnerable to the effects unleashed by the collapse of the Enlightenment. His basic argument is that the university has a deceptively important role to play in American society precisely because our political society was created from the rib of the Enlightenment. America was born when the Enlightenment was at its high tide. Bloom might overstate his case when he says that it is "only in a liberal democracy that the primacy of reason is accepted" (primacy of reason, here, construed in contrast to convention or tradition), he is no doubt correct that the American regime was explicitly founded upon an intellectual consensus that is identifiably of the eighteenth-century Enlightenment. We need not rehearse here all of the intellectual geometry of the "founding" in order to agree with Bloom's main point: "that for modern nations, which have founded themselves on reason in its various uses more than did any nations in the past, a crisis in the university, the home of reason, is perhaps the profoundest crisis they have."

American students, Bloom observes, are unlike their European counterparts, for our students do not have conventions or traditions to fall back upon once reason is disparaged. Nor, significantly, do American students have the same, well-developed literary culture that conveys a tradition of learning, and which is capable of training the sentiments even when the authority of reason is at a low ebb. Bloom's point is well taken. When the French and German intelligentsia capitulated to the irrational currents of romanticism, and scoffed at the scientific and philosophical ideals of the Enlightenment, Europe was thrown into the grip of one ideology after another. Terrible wars ensued. Nevertheless, students had ready access to high caliber literature. While this was not an adequate substitute for the philosophy and science jettisoned after the Enlightenment, it was capable of sustaining *some* sense of high culture. European universities flourished, even amid the rubble of the wars. Our universities seem unable to flourish in the midst of prosperity.

In an American context, when reason is disparaged we are in deep trouble, for we have nothing to fall back upon except the vagaries of popular culture. Paradoxically, Americans, who are generally characterized as intellectually barbaric, are more dependent upon rational symbols and disciplines than their European cousins. In my view, this is the most provocative and constructive contribution of Professor Bloom's book. Again, it cuts across the agenda of either the Left or the Right. But it is the cultural conservatives who will find the lessons suggested by the book most disagreeable. Although it might be true that the "liberal" mandarins of our schools have misjudged and mismanaged the problem, we are all affected by the loss of confidence in rationality occasioned by the collapsed of the Enlightenment. There is nothing constructive to be gained by championing its collapse, or by exploiting its ill effects in favor of some "better guide" than reason. If the Enlightenment was fundamentally misconceived, and if we truly are prepared to say good riddance (i.e., it is not to be corrected, but dismissed altogether), then one has to be prepared to abide by the implications—which, in the case of America, are radical rather than conservative. Once again, Bloom's provocative, yet deceptively simple point is that, whereas the French or the Germans *could* regard the rational symbols of modernity as representing a collective, yet passing, fit of insanity, and then go on to sink back into non- or parational symbols of traditional "French" or "German" culture, Americans enjoy no such luxury. We need universities precisely because America is so directly the product of a rational experiment.

So, in answer to the question of why students are "flat souled," Bloom argues that the crisis of confidence in reason has abandoned them to popular culture, which in America is not even minimally able to form the sentiments required for citizenship, learning, and for all those other good things which could be enjoyed if one were to unplug, for the time being, the earphones connected to the Sony. When reason flees the schools, and in particular the universities, then the dire predictions of the fate of egalitarian democracies will come to pass. As Sheldon Vanauken has pointed out in his recent book *The Glittering Illusion*, few people of the eighteenth and nineteenth centuries really believed that the masses are capable of the kind of rationality required if an egalitarian democracy is to work over the long haul.

Unfortunately, what Bloom never resolves is a question that dawns on the reader rather early in the book: that is, is it not in the very nature of a regime founded by a rational experiment that, short of a utopian realization of its ambitions, the regime is almost bound to collapse? If Bloom is correct, then it seems that we are forced to either accept the popular culture, or to devote ourselves exclusively to the cultivation of a philosophical culture adequate to the rational demands of the founding experiment. We need Mr. Jefferson's yeoman farmers to receive Fulbright scholarships to be trained in something resembling Plato's academy. Furthermore, it is reasonable to ask whether our "founders" ever entertained such a dilemma; or has Bloom, the proficient translator and interpreter of Plato, arranged the terms of the dilemma in such a way that they correspond very closely to the problematic of the *Republic?* This is a question that the reader will have to ask and answer for himself. It is, however, curious that while Bloom clearly outlines the pathologies which ensued once the Enlightenment spent itself, and while he argues strenuously on behalf of America as a distinctively rational experiment (and hence, that there is something fundamentally correct about the founding), the overall drift of the book seems to imply that a liberal democracy of this sort is unable to sustain such an experiment. America can only be America if it recovers a pre-Enlightenment political culture. Perhaps there is a Straussian "key" to unlock this dilemma, or maybe I am reading too much into this aspect of the book.

Finally, it is worth mentioning that one will be disappointed if he looks to this book for specific recommendations regarding educational reform. Bloom's way of translating practical problems into philosophical issues is the strong suit of the book, so I am not prepared to complain about the absence of concrete proposals. There is, however, one matter that can be touched upon in passing. While Professor Bloom expresses some ambivalence about the so-called "great books" approach (i.e., not even great books are capable of overcoming a bad case of flat-soulness), he does recommend the approach. Perhaps it is impious to ask whether the great books method isn't a "conservative" version of the intellectual smorgasbord found everywhere else—albeit, the diet is more substantive. But one wonders whether it is any more conducive to the discipline required if one is to move among and between the differentiated areas of knowledge. After all, one of the great achievements of the Western university system since the high Middle Ages is the differentiation of the sciences and their respective methods. (I should mention that the role played by medievel men in constructing universities which are recognizably similar to our own is never mentioned by Bloom. His analysis skips over the historical period in which universities were first founded.) The specific content and methods appropriate to these areas of knowledge would seem to be as, or more, important than a collection of great books, which only invite the student to carry on a seemingly interminable conversation with "great" minds.

54

Mr. Bloom, the American Mind, and Paideia

JOHN VAN DOREN

One of the best-sellers in the country this year has been Allan Bloom's book, *The Closing of the American Mind*, of which the subtitle is, *How Higher Education Has Failed Democracy and Impoverished the Souls of Today's Students*. Mr. Bloom is as unhappy with schooling in America at the college level as those of us in the Paideia project are with its earlier stages. Is his book not, then, a blow on behalf of Paideia, confirming our view of the educational situation, and implying support of our efforts to improve it?

We can say yes to the first half of this question more readily than we can to the second. Certainly, Mr. Bloom reminds us that the present defect of schooling at all levels is basically intellectual. The jumble of "subjects" into which the curriculum has fallen is part of the problem, as is the reduction of learning to psychological adjustment and job skills, rather than the struggle for truth and an underlying understanding of things. And this reduction has not been at odds with what the universities teach, but in line with it, reflecting the chaos of learning which has overtaken them and the low view of human nature which, at least in the social sciences, they have adopted.

Mr. Bloom recalls this for us in trenchant terms reminiscent of those used half a century ago by Robert M. Hutchins, then the president of the university at which Mr. Bloom teaches (whom he does not mention). For the complaint as to higher education in this country is at least as old as that, though Mr. Bloom does not go very far toward acknowledging the fact, and though few writers on the subject have been as eloquent as he in making the case.

But he is curiously defensive when it comes to speaking of others besides himself who have complained about the state of the academy. He is particularly offended by the students of the '60s who engaged in sit-ins, building barricades, and other distressing behavior inspired by their concern for civil rights and their dislike of the war in Vietnam. Mr. Bloom's prose, in speaking of them, is not so much sharp as strident, and his criticism becomes personal, even nasty, in tone. And that is consistent with what as readers of his book we come to see, which is that he does not think any but his own kind are competent to criticize the educational enterprise. Indeed, he is quick to defend this against the intellectually

John Van Doren is a Fellow, Institute for Philosophical Research Chicago. This review is reprinted with permission from the *Paideia Bulletin*, vol. 3, no. 5 (November–December 1987): 1–2.

unwashed, as it were, who he seems to believe could not, with their bad manners, have been serious.

We are not much surprised, therefore, to realize that for all his talk about democracy, Mr. Bloom is concerned with the education of the few and not with that of the many. It is "the small number who will spend their lives in an effort to be autonomous," and "for whom, especially, liberal education exists," that he cares— the elite of "greatest talents" who are "most likely to take advantage of a liberal education and have the greatest moral and intellectual effect upon the nation." The rest he dismisses as hopelessly content with "relevance" or a brief "enthusiasm" that subsides with the pressures of life, though he is even more scornful of those he perceives as drug-addicted lovers of deafening music, played to the rhythms of their unrestrained sexual indulgence, in which he is, perhaps, a little too interested.

This concern is not the one that those in the Paideia project have, who think that "the best education for the best is the best education for all," as Hutchins once wrote. Bloom can understand very well what Paideia's concern is, but he cannot, or will not, envision it except for those who, like his master, Plato, he thinks deserve the education of guardians, while the rest of us learn civilized pieties. Paideia asserts what Plato might have acknowledged, though he could not conceive any way to achieve it, which is that in a democracy we are *all* guardians, and so we must all have the education of guardians. Thus, Paideia's aim is not the making of rulers, but the teaching of those who are ruled to participate in ruling. It is a pity that Mr. Bloom does not want to make the hard march to this end, as he should. We can only console ourselves at the absence of so likely a companion with the thought that at least he has seen, and has to some extent shown, where the road lies.

55

Our Finest Moment

TOM HAYDEN

NPQ: In *The Closing of the American Mind*, Allan Bloom suggests that the cultural and political movements of the 60's introduced a value relativism which pervades society today.

Do you give any credence to that view of the 60s?

Hayden: I think Bloom is absolutely right in drawing attention to the deficiencies of the moral climate on American campuses. He is right to say that specialization goes too far, that objectivity masks a moral neutralism, that the teaching and counseling of undergraduates is often under-emphasized. But these trends were not the results of the 60s revolt. On the contrary, they were among the very causes of the early student movement.

Granted, Allan Bloom had a life-shattering experience at Cornell when a handful of black students carried shotguns onto the campus. But that incident was a bizarre and isolated chapter in the history of higher education. When Bloom compares the impact of a few armed blacks with the coming of Nazi storm troopers and the fall of the German universities in the 30s, he drifts into unreality.

On the contrary, one can argue that the finest moment of the university was when students and faculty stopped the university's business-as-usual during a time of national crisis. We were spending $30 billion a year on death and destruction; hundreds of Americans per week were coming home in body bags. Professors at Columbia and Berkeley were among the intellectual architects of that war, and to this day I am astounded by the fact that of nearly 1000 academic articles written for leading political science journals during the 60s, only one was about Viet Nam.

It was honorable to protest that situation, and those who did so should be blessed in our history. They are the exact opposite of Nazi storm troopers. They were, on the contrary, calling on us not to be "good Germans." That's what Bloom doesn't understand.

I'll give another example. One week after the Kent State shootings, Kingman Brewster, the president of Yale, led one thousand Yale students to Washington in protest. They spent an entire week involved in the process of lobbying the government to terminate the war. Was that a worthy undertaking by a university leader? Absolutely. Did that damage Yale? Did it morally and intellectually cripple the thousand students who participated? I think not. What would

---

Tom Hayden was a founder of the Students for a Democratic Society (SDS) and a prominent anti-war activist in the 1960s. This interview is reprinted with permission from *New Perspectives Quarterly* vol. 4, no. 4 (Winter 1988):20–25.

Bloom make of that situation? His focus is so confused because he chooses his events so selectively.

If we accept Bloom's Platonic model—the legitimacy of questioning everything—then of course one of the occasional consequences will be rebellious behavior. But far from being a time which gave birth to moral relativism, the 60s introduced morality into an amoral society and a materialistic university. To view the 60s as mindless because many of us followed C. Wright Mills and Albert Camus rather than Allan Bloom's prescriptions is wrong. The 60s were an intellectual and intensely introspective decade.

If there has been an erosion of general education, that erosion comes from turning the university to the specialized uses of society, and Bloom knows that. That omission is another reason why his book is so baffling. He complains that students become economics majors prematurely and they all go to university with fantasies about becoming millionaires. How was that caused by the 60s? Those attitudes obviously result from the drive of the marketplace and the tendency of the university to provide for the immediate professional needs of society.

NPQ: Blooom argues that, in the 60s, thinking stopped with the moral indignation over the Vietnam War and racial injustice. Does Bloom have a point?

Hayden: Of course he has a point, but it's confused because the cloistered community of scholars Bloom describes has not existed for many centuries.

At my university, to be much more accurate about the 60s than Bloom, the Dean of Women was not encouraging reading in Greek tragedy. She was deploying a network of informants who notified parents of the white girls who were seen socializing with black men in the student union. That was the University of Michigan in 1960. That administrative behavior deserved a revolt, and it's not anti-intellectual to revolt against those attitudes.

Let's look at Berkeley at the end of the 60s. Black Panther Eldridge Cleaver wrote a best selling book called *Soul On Ice*. He was then invited by students to give lectures at the University of California. Faculty members agreed to supervise students and give them credit. But the Regents, under the demands of then Governor Reagan, went wild and abolished credit for the course. That action set off a storm of protest: 5000 people marched to the Sproul steps, fires were set, Moses Hall was occupied, there were hundred of arrests, the sheriff's department was brought onto campus.

Admittedly, Cleaver was no academic and his subsequent intellectual meanderings raise serious questions about what many of us saw in him in the first place. But his presence in the lecture hall hardly meant a dilution of the critical function of the university. It is clear that it was intellectually challenging to listen to, and argue with, an articulate voice of a very real struggle that was going on in society. It might have actually benefitted society if the debate had been engaged in the critical atmosphere of the university instead of purged and de-legitimated as if it were unworthy of credit or student involvement.

Those were the sorts of incidents that made students give up on the university as the bastion of free thought. They could have been fascinated with the latest models of cars, but instead, they were willing to grapple with Eldridge Cleaver. What could possibly have been unworthy about that? I argue that it was politically, not intellectually unacceptable, and the primary attack on critical thinking came from Reagan and Meese, who was then in the California governor's office. To blame the students for then reacting in extreme ways, for a tendency to overstate their rhetoric and for trashing the university, is only blaming the victims for being driven to frustration.

Speaking of mindlessness, how should we regard the official claim that the US was in Viet Nam to stop Chinese communism? Speaking of moral relativism, how are we to interpret Edward Teller's views on limited nuclear war? If academic leaders proclaim that the university is doing the best it can, but it can't improve on a black admission rate of 5% or 6%, and they say those things loudly on the edge of the Oakland ghetto, or Morningside Heights, the university will unfortunately reap a whirlwind. And it did.

Furthermore, let's also not forget the 60s are over. We have the most conservative president we have ever had, the most traditional US Secretary of Education we have ever had, the whitest universities elitists could want and the income base of the people attending our universities is safely affluent. But Bloom is still trying to metaphorically annihilate this pathetic handful of blacks with their shotguns. In fact armed blacks are nowhere to be seen and reading the Black Panther Party Newspaper never quite made it into the core curriculum.

NPQ: What about Bloom's view of the university today?

Hayden: I am sympathetic with Bloom's description of the university's treatment of the undergraduate: "The student must navigate among a collection of carnival barkers, each trying to lure him into a particular side show. This undecided student is an embarrassment to most universities because he seems to be saying 'I am a whole human being; help me to form myself and let me develop my real potential,' and he is the one to whom they have nothing to say." I am very touched by that description, but what baffles me is that Bloom doesn't recognize it could have been printed on the back of an SDS membership card in 1962.

The university over the past 30 years is more unchanged than changed. Bloom criticizes the push for "relevance" by 60s students but ignores the fact that the university was, and is, quite "relevant" to the military industrial complex. It is very relevant to agribusiness. It is very relevant to the nuclear arms race. The university has always been involved in all those things.

NPQ: In Bloom's mind, when the current preoccupations of a democratic society become the primary concerns of the university, the university loses the critical detachment necessary to preserve and pass on the core values of Western civilization. Pursuit of knowledge is then eclipsed by the needs of the moment and the opinion of the masses.

Hayden: Bloom has it backwards. This man who makes so much of being able to distinguish between shadow and substance in Plato's cave becomes blind to the fact that the anguished cry of the students in the 60s was not so very different from Bloom's own lament. The editorials I wrote from 1957 to 1961 in the *Michigan Daily* were based on Cardinal Newman's concept of the university; a community of scholars, on the remoteness of the curriculum from the real dilemmas of life, on the failure of the university to stand as a critical institution representing inquiry, on the cowardly silence of the intellectual community in the 50s.

Bloom continuously asserts that higher education has failed democracy, but it seems difficult for him to comprehend that, at least in the United States, higher education is not separate from democracy. It's an institution that is a full participant in our democratic society. It is not Plato's cave. We live in an economy and a culture where ideas are not separate from improving productivity, improving cultural literacy or improving the quality of life.

Higher education is fully integrated into—or contaminated by, depending on how we view it—American society. As a result, as long as we have a US Constitution there will be the possibility of strikes or other disruptive activity any time the component members of an institution are treated like numbers or feel their point of view is not represented.

Let me again use the University of California as a real-life example. One of the three constitutional functions of the University of California is to provide public service. If Bloom wants to eliminate that public function, then his perspective is narrow indeed and his constituency weakened because taxpayers expect a university to perform public service. However, historically, the University of California has tilted toward agribusiness rather than farm labor and toward the nuclear arms race by allowing leaders of the Livermore laboratories which make all our nuclear weapons, to lobby Congress and the White House against arms control treaties. So the question isn't whether the university should be involved in public service but in what public service?

NPQ: Do you agree with Bloom when he takes the question of relativism outside of the university to society?

Hayden: Perhaps the difference between Bloom and myself is that I think there are eternal debates and he thinks there are only eternal truths. There is, for example, an eternal debate about such issues as the death penalty and abortion. If an institution like the Catholic Church can take more than one position on such subjects over 2000 years, how are we to establish universal or permanent truth?

We play with the cards we are dealt. The quest is to achieve personal responsibility—to have a set of values we can live by so when we look back on our lives we won't be ashamed. But in the pursuit of values, it is a natural that we will sometimes change our minds. Bloom would describe that change as degeneration into situational ethics and moral relativism. If that's his view, he is a dogmatist, and there is a difference between pursuing the truth and being a dogmatist because a dogmatist has no need for the pursuit. He seems to view truth as a matter to be handed down. I view it as something to be rediscovered and revised.

The only things that are eternal are the questions that have been posed since the beginning of time, and men and women have answered those questions in different ways. They will continue to do so. On this matter it is not the American mind, but the mind of Allan Bloom that appears closed.

NPQ: Bloom implies there are no classic texts outside of the Western tradition that are superior to our own as acquisitions of civilization. In the name of refuting cultural relativism, Education Secretary William Bennett has made a similar point. Is Tom Hayden's core curriculum that far from Secretary Bennett's or Allan Bloom's?

Hayden: I find myself in agreement with those, including conservatives, who want to return to a core curriculum. In fact, such efforts have already begun in California. I also agree with Bloom that classic philosophy is the highest level of inquiry and knowledge, that philosophy is more important than any other discipline, and that the Great Books should be at the center of any general education.

A core curriculum assumes there are cultural traditions every American should be familiar with because we need a democratic society, not a passive elitist society, and democracy is a discipline and habit that needs to be cultivated. Each generation of students needs to review the arguments that have been made over centuries about the purpose of life, about the role of human beings in public affairs, about why citizenship has value. These are not new ideas. The basic arguments about these propositions are, for example, in Thucydides' *History of The Peloponnesian Wars.* When Thucydides said he was writing a book that would have value for all time, he was correct.

If we were to actually consider the content of a core curriculum, the debate would probably split into several camps: the European oriented, the Pacific oriented, the Third World oriented and those who have become so intellectually numbed by their participation in the specialized university that they would throw up their hands and deny that any core curriculum could be defined.

So we would have a debate on the content of the core curriculum, but we would begin by agreeing that in a democratic society we need a democratic culture that is partly transmitted learning (the Great Books) and partly learned behavior (giving 18-year-olds the vote and participation rights in the university itself). The university's role is to transmit the philosophical questions of the ages and to educate students in the discipline of thinking ethically. If the university doesn't do it, then we are at the whim of television and market forces, which are, inherently, not democratic.

Students who have their input in the debate; society and politicians would have their input too. Ultimately, the faculty would have to make the final judgments and we would assume those judgments will change from time to time. A core curriculum will not be like the Ten Commandments. Agreement would involve a continuing democratic debate.

There would be tremendous struggles over what should be included. Do we want *The Tibetan Book of the Dead* or *The Bahagavad Gita* as part of the core curriculum? That's a fine debate. Let's have that debate. If a person like myself suggests specific content, people may say, "Well, he is trying to impose a Tom Paine left wing agenda." If specific suggestions are made by Secretary Bennett, then people may be afraid he is going to leave out the contributions of minorities. I would argue we shouldn't shrink from the debate. If someone wants to remove Tom Paine from the core curriculum, fine, let's argue it.

There are numerous legitimate issues around the boundaries of a curriculum. For example, in California, the cultures of Mexico and the Pacific are very important. To leave out Carlos Fuentes or Gabriel Garcia Marquez would be a tragedy. To include them means we are not talking about a Western tradition in the European sense that Bennett and Bloom seem to be. But I've seen Bennett's suggestions on what might appear in a core curriculum, and if that is a conservative administration's starting point, it's clear to me we have a common culture in America because, with some revision, I could live with the curriculum. I am also part of that tradition.

56

Faculty Reactions to
The Closing of the American Mind
WALTER NICGORSKI

Is there not a paradox in this stinging critique of our democratic tendencies being so well received and such a good seller? In terms of being noticed (and by and large favorably so) and in terms of sales, Bloom's book has had success unmatched by any serious book about the intellectual life and universities of this nation within my memory. Yet it is a book that makes the most of the weaknesses of recent America, her students and universities and even of the Enlightenment sources that shape her way of life. So sharp is the criticism that one worries that it has slipped at times into caricature or, at the least, overstatement. Perhaps, there is no more of a paradox in Bloom's success than that in evidence in the 1960s and other times when America, especially her media, seemed to indulge her most severe critics. Then and now, one might speculate, it is our very lack of any sort of profound self-understanding that opens us to fascination with those who find us and our institutions dramatically deficient. One might then conclude that Bloom's success goes far to support the argument of his book. Seemingly self-assured, the American mind has closed around certain democratic generalities that produces a flabby tolerance of whatever is put forward and in fact glorifies for the moment (the New Left in the 60s, Bloom now) that which is done with commitment and, in this case, verbal dash.

I prefer to understand Bloom's success in a somewhat different way, believing that it stems in part from uneasy and questing souls beneath the apparently closed public mind. Not only among educators but also among those who attended universities in the last two generations, even among the holders of that degree Bloom finds symptomatic of our disease, the MBA., there is a strong undercurrent that senses that universities should be doing much better at nourishing the deepest and most enduring concerns of the human person and that in tending to such matters well, higher education best serves both human life and liberal democracy. Those puzzled and distressed about our democratic life and the university's role in it are, perhaps, not decisive in any way. But Bloom appears to have written for them, to have sought to articulate the uneasiness and explain the sensed shortcomings. I suspect this is the way Bloom understands his success and how he intended it to be. Bloom sought to reach those, not necessarily engaged in

Walter Nicgorski is a humanities professor at Notre Dame University. He is the editor of *Review of Politics* and coauthor of *An Almost Chosen People The Moral Aspirations of Americans* (1976). These remarks are reprinted with permission from *Programma*, Program of Liberal Studies, Notre Dame University, 1988.

university life, but capable of seeing the problem and well-positioned enough to have some impact on our coping with it.

Bloom seems to understand his own classroom teaching and the mission of the university to have primarily this same audience. It will surprise no one, least of all Bloom, that his concern with this audience draws upon him the charge of "elitism." Bloom does claim that his student "sample" consists of those "students of comparatively high intelligence, materially and spiritually free to do pretty much what they want with the few years of college they are privileged to have—in short, the kind of young persons who populate the twenty or thirty best universities." Speaking of the same group, he adds that "they, above all, most need education, inasmuch as the greatest talents are most difficult to perfect. . . ." It is probably Bloom's own understanding of the limitations of democracy that allows him to see this privileged student pool from the leading universities as those "of the greatest talents." Practicality must have allowed this collapse of two groups that do not clearly overlap. Behind it all, I suspect, is the fact that he has made his peace with "vulgar aristocracy" (as opposed to natural aristocracy) through his interpretation of the classical political philosophers.

Bloom writes that the ancient philosophers "were aristocratic in the vulgar sense, favoring the power of those possessing old wealth, because such men are more likely to grasp the nobility of philosophy as an end itself, if not to understand it. Most simply, they have the money for an education and time to take it seriously." Later Bloom adds, "In antiquity all philosophers had the same practical politics, inasmuch as none believed it feasible or salutary to change relations between rich and poor in a fundamental or permanently progressive way." What Bloom's inferences about the practical politics of the ancients obscure is how the theoretical inquiry of the ancients carries us beyond the alternatives of a politics of the wealth and a politics of the poor. The two great political works of the period, Plato's *Republic* and Aristotle's *Politics*, seek to moderate those extremes, Aristotle explicitly seeking a dominant middle class as a way of opening to natural aristocracy. Might not our circumstances allow a practical politics more directly informed by the work of ancient theory than apparent ancient practice?

But even as this question is put to Bloom one must acknowledge that he serves us all well by challenging the uncritical democratic tendencies that are so dominant. Bloom writes, "Almost no one wants to face the possibility that "bourgeois vulgarity" might really be the nature of the people, always and everywhere. Flattery of the people and incapacity to resist public opinion are the democratic vices, particularly among writers, artists, journalists and anyone else who is dependent on an audience." The one simple rule for universities, he writes, is to provide students with experiences not available in democratic society. Bloom sees the differences between the many and the few, hence the question of the limitations of democracy, as one of the great questions to which thoughtful human beings should ever be returning.

Finally, let me confess that I have reason to distrust my judgment that Bloom overstates the deficiencies of the students and universities of the recent past and present. My experience in higher education has been almost entirely here at

Notre Dame and in the Program of Liberal Studies. And I insist that this confession is no mere flattery of my readers! Bloom himself notes at one point that Catholic higher education has resisted some of the academic folly of the time. And when Bloom notes that "the contents of classic books have become particularly difficult to defend in modern times, and the professors who now teach them do not care to defend them, are not interested in their truth," I know that I am in some one of the Isles of the Blest, here in the PLS. In some ways then, we have reason to lead rather than follow the academic world that surrounds us.

57

Academic Problems and Cosmic Solutions

J. M. CAMERON

Anyone who has worked in the universities of North America, state or private, religious or secular, must necessarily share many of Professor Bloom's concerns. Our undergraduate students are poorly prepared in the humanities. They know little history and have only a sketchy acquaintance with what have hitherto been taken to be the classics of our culture. Indeed, sometimes a sketchy acquaintance would be an excessive estimate; sometimes there is a blank. Experiences that were formerly central episodes of the emotional development of late adolescence and early manhood or womanhood, notably 'falling in love,' are said by Bloom no longer to exist or to exist only in attenuated forms. Sexual initiation takes place in the early teens, so that by the time young men and women enter the university they no longer tremble on the edge of a tremendous and fascinating mystery—the kind of thing they may uncomprehendingly come across in Dante or Shakespeare or the romantic poets—but are sexual beings in accordance with an established routine. They think there are soul-doctors just as there are body-doctors and that felt emotional discomforts are, as they put it. "no big deal," analogous to hangovers or premenstrual cramps.

In part this desolate condition of the undergraduate comes from the disappearance of the old-style bookish home, in which reading was a common occupation and pleasure. Reading was the life of many adolescents fifty or sixty years ago—I speak from my own experience. This produced young women and men who were in one way unimaginably simple by modern standards—we had done very little 'living'—but in another sophisticated and experienced: we had come across all the great poetic and philosophical themes in the books we were ceaselessly concerned with—Shakespeare, the romantic poets, the Bible, the novel—Fielding and Sterne, Jane Austen, Dickens, Thackeray; this meant that we had already learned to understand the great issues of human life through our acquaintance with the symbolic forms given to them in literature. This curious combination of innocence and cultivation meant that we were rewarding students. Of course, we were often stupid and idle and insufferably snobbish in our view of ordinary people who led lives of anxious toil. But I suppose it is the comparative absence today of undergraduate students of this kind that accounts for a part of the sadness of Bloom as he contemplates the university scene.

It seems obvious that we are not going to restore the bookish home as a means of improving the preparation of undergraduates. In any case, we attempt to

J. M. Cameron teaches at the University of Toronto and is the author of *On the Idea of the University* (University of Toronto Press, 1978). This paper was presented at the Canadian Learned Societies Conference, Windsor, Ontario, June 1988, copyright 1988 by J. M. Cameron.

give some kind of higher education to a very high proportion of the population, something never attempted before, and many students, therefore, come from homes in which the notion of a bookish preparation would not be intelligible. There may, nevertheless, be things that can be done about the "rawness" of the undergraduate, though Bloom doesn't go into this problem.

Bloom wants to argue that there are immense deficiencies in the universities as teaching bodies. They are ravaged by relativism and historicism. They are sceptical as to the possibility of establishing truth in any fundamental field of inquiry outside the natural sciences. Freedom means that every view, no matter how absurd or foolish, has a right to be propagated and entertained. We don't see this as clearly as we should, for manifestly the democracy of views doesn't prevail in the natural sciences at the level of higher education. Astrology, flat-earth theory, "creationism," are not in the scientific community given any status on free speech grounds, though they may at the lower levels of education.

Again, Bloom has a deep distrust for many senior members of the university. There are some biting accounts of what he sees to be the moral and intellectual collapse of the faculty at Cornell in the events that culminated in the armed occupation of university premises by militant Black students. I was in England at that period, but I was present at similar if less notorious goings-on at my university and witnessed the orgies of liberal guilt and the pusillanimity of administrators and the refusal of the authorities to proceed against those who broke open private files, published (inaccurately) private correspondence, committed minor assaults, and nightly, during the occupation of an administrative building, imported and consumed illicit substances, brought in from outside by visiting pop and rock groups whose business it was to maintain the right level of frenzy for keeping the occupiers in a resolute frame of mind. When, in the end, they marched out with banners—inscribed with such slogans as "Down with Examinations!" and "Death to the Greek Colonels!"—an eposide ended that had no penal consequences for the organizers of the sit-in or for those who had committed, admittedly, minor crimes. On all this I sympathize with Bloom and agree that these events of twenty years ago—far removed of course, from the younger faculty member today—shed a strange light on academic man in the English-speaking countries. About what seem to be the long-term consequences of these events, notably the presence of student representatives on a variety of committees concerned with such matters as examination results and tenure and the now widespread practice of giving special advantages to visible minorities and women as university entrants and as candidates for senior positions, about these there is still much controversy, and Bloom seems to think they are tainted by their origins. I don't think this follows.

Even if we take—with some qualifications—Bloom's general indictment as having substance—and I have no difficulty over this—two important problems remain. On the one hand, his book is misleading; on the other hand, it is lacking in useful suggestions for reform. These two problems, the misleading and the lack, are, I believe, rooted in the same position: his suggestions that we are grappling with matters that have to be dealt with, as it were, on a cosmic scale and that depend upon a particular interpretation of the philosophical tradition; we have to get Socrates, Plato, Aristotle, Machiavelli, and others *right* in order to understand what has gone wrong with the university project and in order to produce remedies for what is wrong; as to the possibility of there being remedies for our disorders Bloom is sceptical. There is in this book, or so it strikes me, a pervasive twilight-of-the-gods atmosphere. Nietzsche was the prophet of the bad things to come (though he himself no doubt thought these would be good and purifying things to happen). Bloom doesn't have this consolation, though he does think Nietzsche a prophet for the present age.

Now, I think that even if Bloom were right in his exegesis of Socrates *et al.* and in his reverence for a certain view of the philosophical tradition, that of Leo Strauss, it wouldn't follow that this was an indication of *the* way to make the universities better places in England and North America, in France and Germany. I think there are certain imperatives that we can share, no matter what our convictions may be in matter of high doctrine. And to tie university too closely to a certain interpretation of the history of human thought and one on which, to put it mildly, there is much divergence among men and women of good will and good intelligence, this seems to me horribly wrong and would be, if taken seriously, disastrous.

But first I should like to assemble a few passages from Bloom of a kind that illustrate what I have in mind when I accuse him of requiring subscription to a particular philosophical doctrine. I think some of these positions are wrong and implausible for reasons I shall advance; but even if they had a stronger claim on us than I think they have, I think we should still be mistaken in linking the cause of university reform to these philosophical positions. Bloom speaks of . . .

> great questions that must be faced if one is to lead a serious life: reason-revelation, freedom-necessity, democracy-aristocracy, good-evil, body-soul, self-other, city-man, eternity-time, being-nothing. Our condition of doubt makes us aware of alternatives but has not until recently given us the means to resolve our doubt about the primacy of any of the alternatives. A serious life means being fully aware of the alternatives, thinking about them with all the intensity one brings to bear in life and death questions, in full recognition that every choice is a great risk with necessary consequences that are hard to bear. That is what tragic literature is about. It articulates all the noble things men want and perhaps need and shows how unbearable it is when it appears that they cannot coexist harmoniously.(227)

I think there can be no doubt that we are caught up in the rhetoric of such a passage, with its suggestions that life is hard, choices difficult (in two senses—hard to choose wisely and hard to make the decided-upon choice), and that all the opposites symbolized by the formulas enunciated are the stuff of our noblest literary form, that of tragedy. I think this is in part an exercise in the mock heroic, for the opposition mentioned seem to be of different kinds, and not all of them seem to be conflicting alternatives of the required sort. Body-soul, self-other, eternity-time, seem to be speculative distinctions. Of course, they are capable of provoking anxiety; but it is an anxiety over how to make the distinction, what formularies obscure and what illuminate the distinction. There can be no question as to whether they coexist harmoniously. The question is *how* they coexist and, sometimes, what the referring character of a given term is. For example, for Aristotle we talk about the soul by talking about the body, whereas for Plato we talk about the soul by referring to mathematical and other formal operations. But I can't see that any of the quandaries we may find ourselves in as a consequence of reflecting on such analyses are in the least tragic in the sense in which *Antigone* is tragic. The choice whether to believe in God or not, if with Pascal we think in an Augustinian way about this question, may well be a tragic choice, for if we choose God we accuse him of causing the tears of a child and if we reject him suffering is a brute fact which has no rationale. Bloom tells us, rightly, that for Nietzsche conflict was a condition of creativity whereas for us (that is, those of us who live contentedly within the Anglo-American cultural community) conflict is something to be avoided or made unreal by a loose use of the concept of dialectic. Bloom argues that America overcomes that tragic conflict, over belief in God

> in new ways. God was slowly executed here; it took two hundred years, but local theologians tell us He is now dead. His place has been taken by the sacred. Love was put to death by psychologists. Its place has been taken by sex and meaningful relationships . . . . We are learning to 'feel comfortable' with God, love and even death. (230)

All this is very amusing and hits some targets with accuracy. But as characterizing intellectual culture within our universities it is scarcely a caricature. Of course, there are a lot of silly people about and simple reductionist talk always gets into the newspapers and is the staple of popular sophists. After all, Socrates had to endure Thrasymachus. Allan Bloom has to endure Professor X and Doctor Y; but he has other colleagues.

About the University Bloom has some moving and hopeful things to say. He tells us.

> . . . I did see [at the University of Chicago] real thinkers who opened up new worlds for me. The substance of my being has been informed by the books I learned to care for. They accompany me every minute of every day of my life, making me see much more and be much more than I could have seen or been if fortune had not put me into a great university at one of its greatest moments. . . . Never did I think that the university was properly ministerial to the society around it. Rather I thought and think that society is ministerial to the university, and I bless a society that tolerates and supports an eternal childhood for some, a childhood whose playfulness can in turn be a blessing to society. (245)

Bloom holds that this wonderful and beneficient institution is "in its content and its aim . . . the product of the Enlightenment." (256) The Enlightenment is understood in an unusually large sense as the work not only of such eighteenth-century figures as Montesquieu, Diderot and Voltaire but also of Machiavelli, Bacon, Montaigne, Hobbes, Descartes, Spinoza, and Locke. (262) It is a philosophical enterprise and an enterprise of philosophers; and its central theoretical concern is "the relation of mind to society" and Bloom holds this is for "the entire philosophical tradition, ancient and modern" "the most fruitful beginning point for understanding the human situation"; and this is confirmed by the fact that "the first philosophy of which we have a full account begins with the trial and execution of the philosopher" (263). . . .

> The university is always in danger of losing contact with its animating principle, of representing something it no longer possesses. Although it may seem wildly implausible that this group of rare individuals should be the center of what really counts for the university, this was recognized in the universities until only yesterday.

It was, for example, well known in the nineteenth-century German university, which was the last great model for the American university. However bad universities may have been, however extraneous accretions may have weighed them down, there was always a divination that an Aristotle or a Newton was what they were all about (272).

I have said enough, not to do justice to Bloom's rich and provoking book but enough to make it possible to discuss some of the problems that seem to me to arise from his treatment.

First, one or two curious things about the way he sets his scene. There is no suggestion that the University is a medieval invention, and yet this is surely a relevant fact. Rashdall, no friend to clerical obscurantism, wrote that the University is "distinctly a medieval institution—as much so as constitutional kingship, or parliaments, or trial by jury." It wouldn't be hard to explain how in its institutional structure and in its spirit its origins still speak to us. There are several occasions on which Bloom shows himself to be enchanted by one of the great myths of the Enlightenment: that thinkers on the side of the sciences had to fight to free themselves from the oppressive power of religion. Of course, there is something in this; but the whole story of the struggle of natural science to emancipate itself is a complicated one. After all, Galileo's enemies were in the first place his own colleagues who dispensed themselves from the need to look through his telescope at the spots on the moon. Again, his principles of selection—I mean of those names he is always mentioning *honoris causa*, from Aristotle to (with reservations) Max Weber and Freud—seem curious. . . .

The omission of Newman's name from Bloom's roll call of honour is perhaps connected with his ignoring the English university tradition altogether except in singling out Newton for honour. He is concerned only with those universities set up on the later European model. Oxford and Cambridge, closer to the old university tradition going back beyond the Enlightenment, presented an alternative to the European model even after the reforms that began in the middle of the nineteenth century. Perhaps Bloom is worried by the relative absence, outside the natural sciences, of a graduate school, something that worried Flexner. But since much that is forbidding, in Bloom's estimation and that of others, in the present university is its neglect of undergraduate education, and since the very deficiencies of preparation about which Bloom complains have to be remedied at the undergraduate level if they are to be remedied at all, a system much more centered on undergraduate education than is the case in any American or European university deserves some examination. In fact, I think there is a lesson for the university reformer in North America in the English experience.

If I could sum up what is in my view vicious in the practice of undergraduate education in almost all North American universities and colleges I should say the following things. First, there is no leisure; five courses a week, with required reading and writing are too much. Second, the concern with grades and grade averages induces a servile attitude to the grading process. Third, the *modes* of teaching—there are many exceptions to this generalization and Bloom himself is one of the exceptions—are servile. Fourth, serious texts are avoided. Teaching is frequently geared to xeroxed handouts of pp. 345 to 378, say. Fifth, too often the modes of examination are trivial and rely, even when essay-type questions are required, on the regurgitation of lecture material. The system, and especially that part of the system that thinks quantitatively of x credits in some mosiac (sometimes in clashing colors) as constituting a degree, has behind it strong vested interests, including administrators and undergraduates. For them it is of course often very convenient.

But it is a thoroughly bad system, in so far as we are concerned with liberal education and not with something like the disastrous—this is Bloom's characterization, and I agree with it—MBA. I don't think it can soon be displaced in the big universities, but I think it possible to set up something like a liberal arts college within the university on lines close to those of the ancient English universities. And the same thing would be even easier in a big liberal arts college. It is in these colleges that reform or, if not reform, experiment has in fact begun. I don't myself think as well of the Great Books program as does Bloom, but no one who has visited, say, Saint John's in Annapolis can doubt that it is aiming consciously at a nobler kind of undergraduate education than is common.

58

Old Books, New Prejudices, and Perennial Questions

GREGORY B. SMITH

The success of Bloom's book roughly coincided with another event that aroused public interest, the curricular debate at Stanford. The two are connected in substance as well. . . . In the Stanford affair, there is clearly a political debate not far from the surface of this academic discussion. In one way, what one hears is a cry for recognition. It is an assertion that we should not forget those who have been left behind by the American dream. It would be narrow and insensitive to ignore and isolate ourselves from the plight of our fellow human beings. An educated person should be aware of the multitude of accidents that significantly shape our lives for better or worse. Our task is to liberate as many as possible from politically and economically limiting circumstances. No truly free life is possible otherwise. But ultimately the only real way to liberate individuals is through a serious education. Education is what emancipates us from our limiting material circumstances, whether we are formed by the ghetto or middle-class suburbia. . . .

Only the notion that we have a *shared* humanity, despite the many accidents of fate, provides a common ground for friendship and community. This notion aligns itself with the belief that the job of the university is to raise us up to a vision of that shared humanity and the higher community that can sustain us as we inevitably participate in the varied other communities that we cannot simply transcend. In this way we see ourselves linked across the ages with a great chain of humanity, a chain that it is our task to pass unbroken to our children. To sustain that chain we must go out and acquire the brightest and the best faculties and bring to them together with the brightest and best students regardless of race, gender, or class. Those students must then go forth to be an example and a light throughout the rest of the community and in a world where ignorance, prejudice, self-interest, and hate continually reassert themselves despite our noblest efforts.

This view does not hide a political prejudice and no political agenda is implied. In fact it requires that the university be de-politicized. The University represents the one retreat from the political world where, in one somewhat unpoetic phrase, we are concerned with the "authoritative allocation of values," or in an even less elegant formulation, we compete over "who gets what, when,

Gregory B. Smith teaches at Carleton College. This essay © 1988 Gregory B. Smith. The essay as it appears here is a considerably shortened version of the original.

where, and how." If we understand the university correctly, not primarily as a sophisticated trade school where we sell useful skills and information, but as the place where we gain wisdom, insight and understanding into the meaning of being human and happy, we see that it offers a good that can be shared without anyone diminishing their own share. That is the model of the non-political. The university is the model for that preserve within this frenetic modern world where we need not be acquisitive, assertive, and self-interested—where we can base community on friendship rather than coercion, domination, and self-aggrandizement. Our society desperately needs such a center especially at a time when our churches, the other possibility of such a retreat, are in danger of becoming even more politicized than our universities. . . .

Praise of the Great Books in no way discourages the study of other cultures which may indeed deserve even greater coverage than they now have. There have been great civilizations in China, India, Japan, Egypt, Persia, Turkey, in the Inca and Mayan civilizations of the Americas, etc. There is Buddhism, Hinduism, and Islamic religion. These things all deserve to be part of a serious curriculum. And their study will teach the detractors of Western Civilization several valuable lessons. They will learn that all of the above believed in *natural* inequality, not "structural inequality." They will also learn that *only* within Western Civilization does one find the principles that attack and invalidate racism, sexism, and other injustices. That one finds injustice in the West is not an argument against the *principles* of Western Civilization but a sign that many individuals are slaves to their passions, emotions, and prejudices, and impervious to the liberating and emancipating influence of reason.

If its detractors return to Western Civilization with an open mind, they will even find an attack on sexism, classism and other injustices as early as Plato's *Republic*, an argument for complete equality of the sexes and the abolition of private property. The *Republic* also presents an argument that maintains that only Reason entitles one to rule, not race, sex or social class. Taking Western Civilization seriously will also demonstrate that in all non-Western civilizations there is substantial cultural homogeneity. This is precisely because non-Western cultures are "closed." Closure is what binds all culture not influenced by Greek thought and/or the Bible. Only a Westener would feel guilty about being told he or she was ethnocentric—another favorite buzz word along with such other popular "centrisms" as phono-, logo-, and phallo-. If we were to tell a Mayan, pigmy, or aborigine that he is ethnocentric we would be met with incomprehension; "our ways are the way of the universe." Even if one could explain the concept ethnocentrism, the response would be, of course we are ethnocentric, that is what it means to have a culture. However, closure is a vice if one happens to be a proponent of Western Civilization—then one is chided for being insufficiently "open." These are the issues to which the study of the Great Books will alert us. . . .

At this point in history we cannot afford many more generations of superficially educated students—who have dabbled in much and cultivated nothing—who then become immersed in the narrow techniques and expertise necessary to make a living. They will end up alienated and unaware of the truncated nature of their existence, and the world's greatest democracy will drift and founder incapable of achieving an integrated vision of its place between past and future. Whether we like it or not, the spirit of the West now resides in America, and we must rise to the task of giving it a congenial home. Our universities must be that home; unfortunately the politicization of the university has made it something less than a hospitable venue. Bloom has raised for us important questions about the place of the university in our national life, its perennial mission and the task that confronts Americans as the champions of Western civilization. He deserves our thanks for raising these questions.

59

"The Stanford Mind": Two *Wall Street Journal* Editorials

The Stanford Mind

Experience even in the Communist world has stilled the dreams of the 1960s, but at least one place continues to revere them—the ivory foxhole known as the American academy. A good example is Stanford University, which earlier this year caved into political pressure and cashiered its popular "Western Culture" course requirement for freshmen.

Stanford's educators promised to replace it with something better, and now we're learning what they had in mind. The course's eight traditional "tracks"— great works, history, philosophy and so on—will be redesigned to conform with "legislation" Stanford enacted for a new Culture, Ideas and Values (CIV) course. One of this year's "tracks," Europe and the Americas—an experimental prototype that could become permanent next year—certainly gives new meaning to the notion of "Great Books." As the *Chronicle of Higher Education* recently described it, "During this transition year, the term 'Western' is slowly being phased out."

Of the 15 great works previously required, only six remain. The rest have been replaced by lesser known authors. Dante's "Inferno" is out, for example, but "I . . . Rigoberta Menchu" is in. This epic tracks Ms. Menchu's progress from poverty to Guatemalan revolutionary and "the effects on her of feminist and socialist ideologies."

Aquinas and Thomas More are out, but "Their Eyes Were Watching God" by feminist Zora Neale Hurston is in. Ms. Hurston's book offers a critique of the male domination of American society. Locke and Mill go down the memory hole, replaced by such as the U.N. Declaration of Human Rights and Rastafarian poetry.

Virgil, Cicero and Tacitus give way to Frantz Fanon. Mr. Fanon's "The Wretched of the Earth" celebrates violent revolution and is praised on its own book jacket "as a veritable handbook of revolutionary practice and social reorganization." Plato's "Republic" is said to illustrate "anti-assimilationist movements," whatever those are. Martin Luther and Galileo are out, but such timeless notables as Juan Rulfo ("The Burning Plan") and Sandra Cisneros ("The House on Mango Street") are in. And so on.

As for the six classics that survive, both the 20-page CIV course summary (excerpted nearby) and the fall-quarter syllabus suggest they aren't taught like they used to be. Under this autumn's syllabus subject-heading title Conventions of

---

Reprinted with permission from the *Wall Street Journal* (December 22, 1988):A12, cols. 1, 2.

Selfhood, one discovers that Augustine's "Confessions" aren't a rumination on religious faith, but are read to accompany a lecture on "the body and the 'deep' interior self." Two days later the class discusses "multicultural selves in Navaho country." As the students move forward to the section on Making Other Cultural Selves, they will discuss "labor, gender, and self in the Philippine uplands," with readings that day from Genesis and Revelations. The 18-year-old freshmen end their first term at Stanford with seven classes on Forging Revolutionary Selves.

Much of this amounts to an intellectual fashion known as "deconstruction"—reading texts not as inherently worthy but to serve some professor's private agenda. We await the lecture that interprets Marx (still required) through the work of Groucho and Harpo.

Now, we're the first to defend the right of any private university to offer this stuff with a straight face for $18,000 a year. And Stanford isn't apologizing. Charlie Junkerman, assistant dean for undergraduate studies, confirms to us that he told Mike Iwan and Norm Book of the *Stanford Review*, "We . . . think it is a challenging and probing comparative project. We couldn't have had any better people to construct a pilot CIV for us."

But perhaps Mr. Junkerman will forgive those who now snicker at Stanford's earlier high-sounding defense of its course change as encouraging "diversity." The new course is a vindication of those who saw it as a capitulation to political intimidation. CIV's new curricula are "really quite wild," says French professor Robert Cohn, a voice in Stanford's intellectual wilderness. "The choices reflect a blatantly left-wing political agenda."

The new course rides the main hobby-horses of today's political left—race, gender and class. The West is perceived not through the evolution of such ideas as faith and justice, but through the prism of sexism, racism and the faults of its ruling classes. The new course was also supposed to draw upon non-Western cultures, but "Europe and the Americas" still includes mainly Western authors. The difference is that rather than illuminate the West, the replacement authors mainly attack it.

In "The Closing of the American Mind," Allan Bloom describes the political conformity that now prevails throughout the American academy in the name of a fraudulent "diversity." As the West is "phased out" in Palo Alto, it's clear enough what's happening to Stanford's mind.

Stanford Slights The Great Books For Not-So-Greats

Stanford University decided earlier this year to replace its traditional freshman requirement, "Western Culture," with one titled "Culture, Ideas, Values." Preliminary to implementation of the new curriculum, some 50 students this year are taking a course that has been proposed for one of the eight "tracks" to replace the Western Culture curriculum. The following excerpts are taken from Stanford's outline for that course, entitled "Europe and the Americas."

This course has been designed to meet the requirements for the new Area One requirement in Culture, Ideas, Values, which will take effect by 1989–90. The following remarks are intended therefore to make explicit the ways in which this course fulfills the spirit and the letter of the new legislation.

One of the main goals of this course [is to examine] culture in the context of complex relations between master and slave, colonizer and colonized, marginal and dominant, women and men. Indigenous views of Spanish and Christian values will be studied along with critical voices within European and Christian tradition. The negritude movement will be studied as a complex critique of Europe that uses languages and forms adapted from Europe. Contemporary writings by a range of North Americans shows a wide variety of life experience, assumptions, and histories that coexist within this nation.

First quarter: The Spanish debate over indigenous rights raises issues around race as well as religion; readings on European enlightenment include Wollstonecraft on question of gender, and Flora Tristan on question of class. Race, gender and class are all thematized in Chungara de Barrios' autobiography and Anzaldua's poetic essays.

Second quarter: Race is a central focus of materials on the Haitian revolution, and materials from the twentieth century negritude movement which developed in the post-emancipation context of modern "scientific" racism. Gender is a central issue in Jamaica Kincaid's novel "Annie John," a mother-daughter story. Roumain's "Masters of the Dew" plays out a class drama around the conflict between tradionalist peasant culture and modern proletarian consciousness.

Third quarter: Marx and Weber are essential sources on class; Franz Fanon on race; gender, ethnicity and class are central themes in Rulfo, Menchu, Chavez and Anzaldua.

The syllabus includes instances of nearly every form mentioned in this section. A partial list includes:

Poets: Jose Maria Arguedas, Pablo Neruda, Ernesto Cardenal, Audre Lorde, Aime Cesaire.

Drama: Shakespeare, Euripides,

Fiction: Garcia Marquez, Naipaul, Melville, Hurston, Findley, Rulfo, Ferre.

Philosophy and social theory: Aristotle, Rousseau, Weber, Freud, Marx, Fanon, Retamar, Benedict.

History: James, Guaman Poma.

Scientists: A number of social scientists, such as Benedict and Fanon, are included. Other materials can be added if desired, such as readings on 18th century natural history, or late 19th century race science.

Diaries, memoirs, etc.: Columbus, Cabeza de Vaca, Equiano, Lady Nugent, Dyk, Augustine, Menchu, Barrios de Chungara.

Popular culture: Films on popular religion and healing in Peru ("Eduardo the Healer") and the U.S. ("The Holy Ghost People"); folk tale traditions of the trickster.

Painting, sculpture, music: Popular musical traditions in the Caribbean (Reggae lyrics, Rastafarian poetry), U.S. (corrido), Peru (Andean music); Peruvian folk painting *(retablos)*; 16th century iconographic depictions of the Americas.

Buildings, structures, machines: While not explicitly included, these will come up in discussion of plantations and plantation society.

This will be a five unit course. We propose to follow the "Great Works" format, with two lectures a week.

This syllabus was prepared with the support of the Stanford Humanities Center.

[Descriptions of course readings:]

Shakespeare: "The Tempest"; Cesaire: "A Tempest"; "Song of Roland"; Euripides: "Medea." Works of imaginative literature that establish paradigms of the relationship between "European" and "other" will be analyzed, e.g., Euripides' "Medea," whose main character is both "barbarian" and female; the medieval "Song of Roland," which polarizes Christian and pagan (Muslim) stereotypes; Shakespeare's "Tempest," whose figure of Caliban draws on contemporary reports of natives in the recently discovered "New World"; Cesaire's "Une Tempete," and adaptation of the Shakespeare play that uses the Caliban-Prospero encounter as a model, in part, for colonizer/colonized relations.

Melville: "Bartleby, the Scrivener"; Marx: "The Communist Manifesto." Herman Melville's tale of the interplay between callous, uncomprehending bureaucratic-administrative rationality (to use a Weberian idiom) and the resistance of absolute refusal points both toward Weber and Marx. It underscores both the ambiguities of "rational" authority and the force of uncompromising resistance within a modern capitalist context.

Genesis and Revelations; Nora Zeale Hurston: "Their Eyes Were Watching God"; Film: "The Holy Ghost People." The Old Testament selections are discussed in their own right, and as a means of speaking about the distinctive Afro-American religious consciousness exemplified in Zora Neale Hurston's novel of the 1930s. This particular form of religiosity suggests comparisons and contrasts with Weberian themes. "The Holy Ghost People" portrays a southern white "snake handling cult" and suggests parallels and contrasts with Hurston's work.

60

Responses to "The Stanford Mind": Letters to the Editor, *Wall Street Journal*

MICHAEL VANNOY ADAMS, CHARLES JUNKERMAN, AND ALLAN BLOOM

Are the 'Great Books' Constructive?

In your Dec. 22 editorial "The Stanford Mind," which condemns Stanford University's revision of its traditional Great Books curriculum, you say: "Much of this amounts to an intellectual fashion known as 'deconstruction.'" You define deconstruction as "reading texts not as inherently worthy but to serve some professor's private agenda." Any professor who uses any method of reading texts merely as an excuse to serve a private agenda is irresponsible. Some professors misuse deconstruction in this way.

However, contrary to what you imply (and to what many professors on both the political left and right apparently believe), there is no ideological bias inherent in deconstruction. It is an ideologically neutral method of reading texts. These texts may be great books or not-so-great books or "texts" in the sense of any form of discourse. Deconstruction is an impartial method equally congenial (and potentially valuable) to the political left, right and middle—in fact, to anyone with a serious interest in values and in the criticism of values. It is an error to dismiss deconstruction out of sheer ignorance.

In misdefining deconstruction, you inadvertently perpetuate the pervasive confusion that currently exists about the method. Deconstruction is simply a method of reading that exposes to scrutiny the structural oppositions, metaphysical or ideological assumptions, and predominant values implicit in texts. It is a "critical" method in the best sense of the word. A professor of political science might, for example, use deconstruction in a perfectly nonpartisan way to analyze rhetorically the "text" of the recent presidential campaign and the different values of George Bush and Michael Dukakis. Such an analysis might—but need not—involve an examination of the race, gender and class values of the candidates, among other important issues.

MICHAEL VANNOY ADAMS
Associate Provost and Lecturer in
Humanities in the University
New School for Social Research

Reprinted with permission from the *Wall Street Journal*, January 4, January 6, and January 27, 1989.

Stanford's Philosophy Is an Open Book

I found your Dec. 22 editorial "The Stanford Mind" fairly predictable in its application of arguments from Allan Bloom to the recent reform of our Western Culture Program. What was less predictable, and far more disturbing, was the apparent confidence you felt in publicly snickering at writers whose work I can be fairly certain you do not even know. It seems to me that your editorial is another instance of the closed American mind, and a further argument for the necessity of courses like "Europe and the Americas" in our colleges and universities.

Your attack on the "Cultures, Ideas and Values" (CIV) program is misinformed on several counts. For example, when you say that "Dante's 'Inferno' is out, but 'I . . . Rigoberta Menchu' is in," you imply that there was some sort of one-for-one swap, and that, further, Dante is not being taught in the CIV program at Stanford. You must remember that the "Europe and the Americas" course is a pilot for one of at least eight tracks in the CIV program. Other tracks will have emphases different from it, and many of them will teach Dante. You must also recognize that "Europe and the Americas" has an ample representation of canonical "Greats" including Homer, Aeschylus, Euripides, Plato, Aristotle, Augustine, Shakespeare, Voltaire, Rousseau, Marx, Melville and Freud.

But I will not quibble, because your point is, in fact, a categorical one: that all college students should receive a foundation course in the Great Books of the "Western" tradition. By citing Allan Bloom at the close of your piece, the reader is invited to supply arguments from "The Closing of the American Mind" that might be marshaled in defense of your position. Primary among these is Prof. Bloom's contention that there are a certain number of books that are considered (the agentless passive voice is necessary here for obvious reasons) to contain a measure of wisdom unavailable in lesser books, and that these "Great" Books should form the core of a liberal education.

Prof. Bloom's error, I believe, is to misconstrue the nature of the tradition he champions. The truly vital tradition of liberal education has never been to read the same Great Books as one's predecessors, but to continue to ask the greatest questions one can pose. Questions are the beginnings of curricula and satisfactory answers are their destinations. It would be foolish to assume that we ought to ask the same questions as were posed 50 years ago when Robert Hutchins designed the University of Chicago's Great Books Program. But even if we do ask some of the same questions, it does not necessarily follow that we will all turn to the same books in search of our answers.

For example, 50 years ago John Locke seemed indispensable in answering a question like "What is social justice?" In 1989, with a more interdependent world order, a more heterogeneous domestic population, and mass media and communications systems that complicate our definitions of "society" and "individual," it may be that someone like Frantz Fanon, a black Algerian psychoanalyst, will get us closer to the answer we need.

In your editorial, you seem confident in your ability to distinguish between writers who are "Great" and those who are "Not-So-Great." Into this second category, you sneeringly relegate "such timeless notables" as Rigoberta Menchu, Zora Neale Hurston, Sandra Cisneros and Juan Rulfo. On what basis, I wonder, do you dismiss them? Have you read any of them? Can you even place them in their countries of origin? I doubt it. I suspect strongly that it is solely on the basis of their names that you rank them as you do. This apparent inability to consider such writers seriously reveals an insidious prejudice: that people we have never heard of, people with "funny" names, cannot possibly have much of anything worthwhile to say to us. This kind of confident close-mindness is just another piece of evidence that Stanford's curriculum reform is not only necessary but overdue.

Finally, you seem to feel no discomfort in totally disregarding the professors who developed and are now teaching this course. You quote me as saying, "We couldn't have had any better people to construct a pilot CIV for us" without identifying the people involved. Perhaps you don't know who they are. In fact, all three of them have international reputations in their fields, and the combination of disciplines they represent gives them the scholarly scope needed to rethink how culture is taught in our universities: Gregson Davis, Classics and Comparative Literature; Mary Pratt, Spanish and Comparative Literature; and Renato Rosaldo, Anthropology. Any of the universities with which we compare ourselves would envy a team like this. Most of those universities are watching this course with a lot more understanding—and consequent approval—than you were able to muster in your editorial. Maybe this is because they assume that books are to be read and valued for what they have to say, not for the name-recognition of their authors.

CHARLES JUNKERMAN
Assistant Dean of
Undergraduate Studies
Stanford University

Educational Trendiness

Stanford is a trendy place and it responds to trends. Its shameless self-congratulation about this is sufficient to render Stanford ridiculous in the eyes of serious people no matter what their political persuasion.

Charles Junkerman, Stanford University's assistant dean, says in his Jan. 6 letter to the editor: "It would be foolish to assume that we ought to ask the same questions as were posed 50 years ago. . . . For example, 50 years ago John Locke seemed indispensable in answering a question like 'What is social justice?' In 1989, with a more interdependent world order, a more heterogeneous domestic population, and mass media and communications systems that complicate our definitions of 'society,' and 'individual,' it may be that someone like Frantz Fanon, a black Algerian psychoanalyst will get us closer to the answer we need."

This is not an argument. It is the dogmatic and ignorant assertion that we have nothing to learn from old thinkers. Mr. Junkerman *dixit*: There are no permanent human questions. Exactly the same rationalization could be used to replace Pascal with Jerry Falwell, if Stanford happened to be pandering to pressures from Protestant Fundamentalists. Today's questions are the only legitimate questions and today's preferred answers are the only respectable answers. Locke's profound dissenting voice is silenced because "we need" Mr. Fanon's racism and incitement to terrorism, aping as it does, recent German and French writers. Inasmuch as Locke was and is the decisive philosophic source of the Declaration of Independence and the Constitution, we now know what Stanford thinks of the American regime.

Mr. Fanon, on the other hand, is a *demonstrably* inferior and derivative thinker to whom one would pay any attention if he were not the ideologue of currently popular movements, and did not, as a black Algerian, fit Stanford's job description. Stanford students are to be indoctrinated with ephermal ideologies and taught that there can be no intellectual resistance to one's own time and its passions. Stanford has committed itself to the leveling of the distinction between serious and trivial thought, the awareness of which is the essence of liberal education. This total surrender to the present and abandonment of the quest for standards with which to judge it are the very definition of the closing of the American mind, and I could hope for no more stunning confirmation of my thesis.

ALLAN BLOOM

61

What's Right About Bloom?

BILL HONIG

Cultural Suicide

Allan Bloom is correct when he points out in *Closing of the American Mind* that nobody is willing to say, "I think this idea is more important for our way of life than another idea." Bloom challenges us to once again take up the profound task of conveying what Walter Lippmann used to call the "eternal verities."

Like Bloom, I believe the great thinkers of Western civilization had some penetrating, trenchant ideas about what makes us tick and how society should be organized. Classical ideas are so powerful that they apply to all groups of people.

The real question is, how did we get to the point in this country where transmitting our values to the next generation became an illegitimate task? Unless we figure out what values are important and how to teach them, both our civic and ethical traditions are in deep trouble.

But when we talk about values, ethics and civic tradition in America, we find a central paradox: our effort to free individuals and respect pluralism creates a tension with our need to hold, celebrate, and pass on common moral and ethical standards. In the last 20 years, this relationship has become very unbalanced because we have started to conceptualize the individual as completely free from any standard or restriction. This idea of freedom as radical individualism has unfortunately become the stock and trade of the intellectual, the artist, and much of the university leadership in this country. By and large, intellectuals at the research university have become hostile to the idea of common human truths and have abdicated their responsibility to argue for the common good and the continuity of culture. They have instead distanced themselves from the culture and embraced the role of breaking new ground with avant-garde ideas.

Too much of the university today is caught up in the trendy leftist strain of feminism and Third Worldism. For example, some feminists will say we shouldn't read the classics because women didn't write them. Or a University of California committee on general education strongly objects to requiring that American History and democratic tradition be taught to undergraduates, but easily agrees to a proposal to teach all students "global interdependence." In the name of respecting pluralism, intellectuals are reluctant to support the idea of common human truths.

Bill Honig is superintendent of Public Instruction for the State of California, Regent of the University of California, and author of *Last Chance For Our Children: How You Can Help Save Our Schools* (1985). This article is reprinted with permission from *New Perspectives Quarterly* vol. 4, no. 4 (Winter) 1988:36–39.

I have even heard people comment that Abraham Lincoln did not speak as an American, but as a white Protestant male; or that Martin Luther King Jr. spoke only as a black male. One student of Hispanic origin recently remarked, "I can't read Freud because its not my culture." Well, Freud's truths are about more than one culture; they're about how human beings operate. And Lincoln's and King's ideas are the very stuff of our civic tradition.

Radical individualism, reinforced by a university hostile to common human truth, results in young peole who have no ability to make relationships and connect to some broader social purpose. They are steeped in an ethical relativism which prevents them from looking to a standard outside their immediate lives and peer groups for guidance. This state of affairs, in turn, leads to anomie, apathy and even anarchy in our society, and a susceptibility to totalitarian solutions. If there are no standards that are worthwhile, if there are no traditions, if there is no wisdom of the past, that is cultural suicide.

Modernist Dilemmas

Reacting to the fact that "common core values" are neglected in our schools, religious fundamentalist groups have sought to impose the sectarian teaching of Christian dogma. When I first ran for Superintendent of Public Instruction in 1982, I said to the fundamentalists in California, "Look, I agree. Education and curriculum are adrift. There is no purpose to them. They are relativism. I know that down the road we are going to have big fights over narrowing the horizon of choice over which books should be read or not read. Your answer is way too narrow, but at least you are raising the right question."

Similarly, when Allan Bloom calls for narrowing horizons he is in danger of going too far. When he condemns rock music, for example, he goes a little too far because most kids take rock n' roll with a grain of salt—it just goes in one ear and out the other. But Bloom raises the correct concern, echoing Gresham's law that "the easy drives out the hard."

Rock music has a completely different mission than education. Rock is easy, spontaneous, immediate and emotionally unleashing. It is entertainment. Education is hard, long-range, developmental, slow and incremental. Learning virtue isn't a release; it is discipline. But discipline and release are linked. For example, it takes hard, disciplined practice in the basics of playing a musical instrument to get to the point where it is possible to be truly expressive, creative and spontaneous.

To the extent Professor Bloom is making the argument about the easy driving out the hard, I agree with him. I reject the argument of those who say Bloom's critique is just a cover for maintaining the status quo and squelching new ideas and forms of expression. If anything, our whole culture is dynamically oriented to individual expression, change and the new. The hard, not the easy, needs bolstering.

Professor Bloom also goes too far when he suggests that the women's movement has neglected childbearing and childrearing in the pursuit of personal fulfillment. I think the women's movement is one of the exciting revolutions going on in the United States today. Just think, we have doubled our talent pool as women get involved in all kinds of different activity! There are ways that women see things that men just don't see. Women are more grounded. That's helpful.

Nor does Bloom seem to have sympathy for the living, practical question of how women should reconcile individual pursuit of a career with family obligations and biology. More than an issue of feminism per se, this problem is a modernist dilemma. Modernism frees the individual from social obligation. But we are never totally free because moral, economic and biological realities will always bind us. Obviously, we can't have a situation where individuals pay so much attention to their careers that their kids grow up crazy. But people shouldn't live oppressed lives. That's bad too. The very concrete practical problem, which millions are working out in their daily lives, is discovering the mid-point that balances two legitimate poles of tension.

62

Mr. Bloom and His Critics: What Could It All Mean?

WILLIAM T. BRAITHWAITE

By now, two years after publication of Allan Bloom's *The Closing of the American Mind*, its reviewers have wrung it out pretty thoroughly. The notices to date certainly exceed a hundred, sixty-odd of them intelligently selected by Robert L. Stone for this collection. The critics are many, and we can be grateful for that thoughtful ordering of their commentaries by which Mr. Stone presents a substantial cross-section of the sympathetic, the hostile, the in-between, and the few genuinely insightful.

Mr. Bloom's book is well-traveled on America's political, intellectual, and social maps. Reviews have appeared in publications both august and obscure (*The New York Times, U-High Midway*), on the Right and on the Left (*National Review, The Wall Street Journal; The New Republic, The Nation*). It has been noticed abroad (*The Idler,* Toronto). It attracted the attention of the mainstream press (*The Christian Science Monitor, The Washington Post*) and the "alternative" press (*New Perspectives Quarterly, Rolling Stone*). And it was reviewed in scholarly journals, the academic press, and special-interest periodicals (*Interpretation, The Chronicle of Higher Education, The Journal of Negro Education*).

Mr. Bloom and his book are a genuine social phenomenon. Nearly everyone, it seems, had something to say, or at least wanted to say something, about them. Perhaps it is time to begin to reflect on what all this could mean.

We can, first, thank Mr. Bloom for the reminder that philosophy has political consequences. We very much need this reminder in our public discourse just now, dominated as it seems too often to be by that moral relativism Mr. Bloom justly deplores. Thinking, and hence also what the greatest minds have thought, do matter. How we live is affected by how we think we ought to live (however inarticulate those thoughts may sometimes be).

In any regime which aspires to endure, someone has to think about, and to know, the meaning of what people are doing. Mr. Bloom weighs in the balance what is being done in American higher education, and he finds it wanting. Whatever the merits of his particular allegations, his effort at a serious extended argument about the real meaning of education is an act of high citizenship.

The Latin root of "education," *educere*, means to draw out. Education thus means a drawing out of human nature the capacities that are there to be

William T. Braithwaite is Professor, Loyola School of Law, Chicago, and author of "The Legal Profession Today," *The Great Ideas Today* (Encyclopedia Britannica, 1989).

developed. The species is so constituted, however, as to have the capacity for cruelty and viciousness as well as for nobility and self-sacrifice. Education is thus inescapably a moral enterprise. It involves nurture of some capacities and the stifling of others. The choice of which is a political one, fraught with danger if ill-advised.

These things, too, Mr. Bloom's book calls to our attention. In trying to trace out the philosophic ancestry of some of our modern corruptions, he reminds us of the sovereignty of inquiry, reason, and deliberation in human life. He encourages us to consider whether it may have been improvident to abandon the old-fashioned axiom of moral philosophy that thoughts (not "feelings") determine character.

Day in and day out, one meets in the classroom students who have been led to believe that what one thinks really does not, in the end, matter very much. You have your "values," I have mine, and everyone knows values are "subjective." My classroom is in a law school, and I wonder how much law can be learned by students as morally and intellectually handicapped as Mr. Bloom says some are.

Second, then, we can thank Mr. Bloom for the reminder that *education* has political consequences. He is not the first teacher to do this, of course, nor even the first teacher of philosophy to do it. Mortimer Adler has been saying many of the same things for forty years. Mr. Adler's triology, *The Paideia Proposal* (1982), *Paideia Problems and Possibilities* (1983), and *The Paideia Program* (1984) is far more practical in approach and democratic in aspiration than *The Closing of the American Mind*. And other teachers have indicted the preparatory levels of our educational system: Jonathan Kozol, *Death at an Early Age* (1967); John Holt, *The Underachieving School* (1969). But Mr. Bloom's seems to be the voice most heard at the moment, and the lesson does bear repetition.

That philosophy affects education, and education affects our communal (i.e., political) life, should not need as much emphasis as it presently does for us. These relations have been recognized in the West since at least 399 B.C. That was the year Athens condemned and executed Socrates, the father (he himself might say midwife) of Western philosophy, for corrupting the youth and impiety. Mr. Bloom's charge against American higher education is essentially the same as Athens's charge against Socrates.

My angle of vision on *The Closing of the American Mind* is that of a teacher of law. For a decade, I have seen in my classes many signs of the impoverished minds of which Mr. Bloom writes. Some part, at least, of what he said is true in my observation. The period of *his* observations is somewhat longer—his own career, the last thirty years or so. It includes, that is, the students in college since the decade just after World War II.

The older graduates among these students, if they chose law as a career, are now judges, senior partners in law firms, and chairmen of committees in Congress and state legislatures. What should we expect of political and legal institutions moved by men and women who are products of the "higher" education Mr. Bloom indicts?

A major premise of his argument is that the ideas of certain modern philosophers have contributed to a decline in quality of college and university education. He names prominently Heidegger, Nietzsche, Rousseau, Locke, Hobbes, and Machiavelli. Whatever may have been the effect of the ideas of these men on college and university education, some at least have not been without effect in jurisprudence.

The philosophic ancestor of Oliver Wendell Holmes's understanding of the nature and source of law, for example, is Thomas Hobbes's *Leviathan* (1651). Holmes's *The Common Law*, published just a century ago, is one of the half dozen most influential American law books of the last hundred years. It is still recommended reading in some law schools.

Bloom's argument that modern philosophy has contributed to the corruption of higher education is, to some of his reviewers, a controversial thesis. Not less so (and for somewhat the same reasons, I suspect) is Holmes's influence on jurisprudence. Some legal scholars have thought him one of the greatest judges and writers on jurisprudence of the twentieth century. Others have judged him a mischief if not a corrupter.

One salutary result of Mr. Bloom's book could be to provoke more serious public discourse about what importance we should give to education of the young. Every year, over 40,000 of the students whose college preparation he finds so defective enter law school. Three or four years later, they are graduated, enroute to jobs as judges, legislators, and private counsel to business and industry. These are the kind of jobs held by the most influential of the "power elite."

Can the law school education of these young people expect to be any better than what their college education has prepared them for? I cannot think so. If Mr. Bloom is right in substance, are we a people thinking seriously about our future? If our youth have no understanding of the past and no vision of the future, as he alleges, what can we expect them truly to understand, and to do, about the law when they become—as some will—judges, politicians, and civil servants?

American law has not yet recognized teacher malpractice as a tort. Mr. Bloom's book can prompt us to wonder whether the law should. Would it be better to live in a regime, like Socrates's Athens, where corrupting the youth was a capital crime? Whatever Athens's sin against philosophy, it at least regarded education as a serious business, serious enough to kill a man for.

Bibliography

This bibliography contains all of the reviews and essays on Allan Bloom's *The Closing of the American Mind* known to the editor as of April, 1989. Essays reprinted in the present volume are indicated with a single asterisk. Essays printed in the present volume for the first time are indicated with a double asterisk.

1 Stephanie Abarbanel, *Family Circle* (February 23, 1988): 46. 2 Mortimer Adler, interview, Firing Line, Southern Educational Communications Association, May 6, 1988. 3 Mortimer Adler, *Reforming American Education: The Opening of the American Mind* (1989). *4 Henry Allen, *Washington Post* (June 18, 1987, Style Section): C1. *5 George Anastaplo, *Great Ideas Today* (1988):252. *6 George Anastaplo, paper presented under the auspices of the Institute of Human Values, Halifax, Nova Scotia, at the Canadian Learned Societies Conference, Windsor, Ontario, June 10, 1988. 7 Andrew J. Angyal, *Greensboro News and Record* (July 19, 1987). 8 *Antaeus Report* (Winter 1988):1. 9 W. S. Armistead, *Conservative Digest* 14 (April 1988): 25. 10 Leslie Armour, *Library Journal* 112 (May 1, 1987):66. 11 Stanley Aronowitz and Henry A. Giroux, *Harvard Educational Review* 58/2 (May 1988):172. 12 James Atlas, *New York Times Magazine* (January 3, 1988):12. 13 A. J. Ayer, *Sunday Times* [London] (June 28, 1987). 14 Steven Baldner, *Canadian Catholic Review* (November 1987):389. *15 Benjamin Barber, *Harper's Magazine* (January 1988):61. 16 Richard Barbieri, *Independent School* [Boston] (Winter 1988): 69. 17 Hazel Barnes, *American Book Review* 10/1 (March–April 1988):6. *18 Robert N. Bellah, *New Oxford Review* 54/6 (July–August 1987):22. 19 J. Brian Benestad, *Crisis* (September 1987): 26. 20 Ralph Kinney Bennett, *Reader's Digest* 131/786 (October 1987): 81. 21 Paul Berman, *Village Voice* (August 11, 1987):30. 22 Laurence Berns, *Gadfly* [St. John's College, Annapolis] (May 1989). *23 Richard Bernstein, *New York Times* (September 25, 1988):26. 24 Judith H. Best, *History of Education Quarterly* 28 (1988): 177. 25 Charles Rowan Beye, *New England Classical Newsletter* (Fall 1988):30. 26 Milton Birnbaum, *Modern Age* 32/1 (Winter 1988):9. 27 *Black Enterprise* 18 (Summer 1987):17. 28 John Blades, *Chicago Tribune* (September 17, 1987):V, 10. 29 Arnaud de Borchgrave, *New York City Tribune* (March 16,

1988). **30** Leon Botstein, *Bard* (Spring, 1988):41. **31** Ezra Bowen, *Time* 130 (August 17, 1987): 56. ****32** William Braithwaite. ***33** Eva Brann, *St. John's Review* [Annapolis] 38/1 (1988):71. ***34** Jessica Branson, *U-High Midway* [Chicago] 63/1 (September 16, 1988):27. **35** David Brock, *Insight* (May 11, 1987). **36** David Brock, *Washington Times* (May 18, 1987):B-1. **37** Victor Brombert, *New York Times* (May 29, 1988): E-18. **38** F. Bruning, *Macleans* 100 (August 31, 1987): 7. **39** A. S. Bryk, *American Journal of Education* 96 (1988):256. **40** James P. Buchanan, *Chronicle of Higher Education* (September 16, 1987):B-2. ***41** J. M. Cameron, paper presented under the auspices of the Institute of Human Values, Halifax, Nova Scotia, at the Canadian Learned Societies Conference, Windsor, Ontario, June 10, 1988. **42** Warren H. Carroll, *Faith and Reason* (1987):403. **43** *Chicago Maroon* (September 23, 1987):11. **44** Joseph Coates, *Chicago Tribune* (May 1, 1987). **45** David Cole, *Nation* 246 (1988):892. ****46** Christopher Colmo. **47** Francis Cousté, *L'Education Musicale* (May 1987):1. **48** Charles Cox, *Richmond Times-Dispatch* (December 27, 1987):H1. ****49** Steven Crockett. **50** Frederick J. Crosson, *Programma* [Program of Liberal Studies, Notre Dame University] (1988):6. **51** *Daily Telegraph* (January 18, 1988). ***52** Werner J. Dannhauser, *American Spectator* (October 1988):12. **53** Werner J. Dannhauser, *Chronicle of Higher Education* (February 10, 1988). **54** Michel Danthe, *Journal de Genevé, Samedi Littéraire* (May 23, 1987):1. **55** *Denver Post* (October 18, 1987):1-A. **56** Douglas J. Den Uyl, *Reason Papers* 13. **57** Donald J. Devine, *Modern Age* 32/1 (Winter 1988):14. **58** J. W. Donohue, *America* 158 (March 26, 1988):319. ****59** Shadia B. Drury. **60** *Economist* 303/94 (May 16, 1987). **61** Edward Edy, *Cornell Alumni News* (November 1987):25. **62** Jean Bethke Elshtain, *Cross Currents* 37/4 (Winter 1987–1988):476. **63** Ronald L. Emmons, *Chicago Tribune* (October 13, 1987):I, 17. **64** E. M. Epstein, *American Business Law* 25 (1987):361. **65** Edward E. Ericson, Jr., *Reformed Journal* (September 1987):30. **66** B. L. Erven, *American Journal of Agricultural Economics* 69 (1987):1037. **67** J. Escoffie, *Socialist Review* 18 (1988):118. ***68** D'Evelyn, *Christian Science Monitor* (July 3, 1987). **69** James Ewing, *Blade* [Toledo, Ohio] (August 1, 1987). **70** Marion Fay, *San Francisco Chronicle Review* (July 5, 1987):1. **71** H. D. Forbes, *Idler* [Toronto] 17 (May–June 1988):47. ***72** Betty Friedan, *New Perspectives Quarterly* 4/4 (Winter 1988):14. **73** Robert Fulford, *Toronto Star* (July 25, 1987). ****74** Timothy Fuller. **75** Marc Fumaroli, *L'Express* (March 20–26, 1987):158. **76** François Furet, *Le Nouvel Observateur* (April 17–23, 1987):109. **77** Paul Galloway, *Chicago Tribune* (May 1, 1987):1. ***78** William Galston, *Interpretation* 16/1 (Fall 1988):101. **79** F. Gannon, *Harper's* 276 (May 1988):33. **80** David Gates, *Chicago Sun-Times* (May 1, 1987):41. **81** David Gates, *Newsweek* 105 (April 20, 1987): 72. **82** Frédéric Gausson, *Le Monde des Livres* (June 5, 1987). **83** J. P. Gee, *Tesol Quarterly* 22 (1988):201. **84** Lambert Gingras, *Le Presse* (February 6, 1988):J-1. **85** *William Goldstein, *Publishers Weekly* (July 3,

1987):25. **86** I. Goodwin, *Physics Today* 41 (1988):50. **87** Tom Gorman, *Hyde Park Herald* (July 29, 1987): 7. ***88** Paul Gottfried, *Chronicles* 11/9 (September 1987):30. **89** Gerald Graff, *Voice Literary Supplement* (January–February 1989):24. **90** Harvey J. Graff, *Society* 25/1 (November–December 1987):98. **91** Maxine Greene, *Phi Delta Kappan* 69 (June 1988):755. **92** D. L. Gregory, *Duke Law Journal* (1987):1138. ***93** William Greider, *Rolling Stone* (October 8, 1987):39. **94** David Gress, *New Criterion* 5/9 (May 1987):24. **95** K. A. Groskauf, *University of Pennsylvania Law Review* 136 (1988):1263. **96** Todd Gudgel, *Grey City Journal* (May 1, 1987):1. **97** John Hamer, *Seattle Daily Times* (August 13, 1987). **98** Leslie Hanscom, *Newsday Magazine* (September 20, 1987):8. **99** T. L. Haskell, *Journal of American History* 74 (1987):984. **100** Jeffrey Hart, *Policy Review* 42 (Fall 1987):84. **101** Paul Harzem, *Behavior Analyst* 10 (1987):177. ***102** Tom Hayden, *New Perspectives Quarterly* 4/4 (Winter 1988):20. **103** Albert Hayes, *Cedar-Rapids Gazette* (July 5, 1987): 2F. **104** Albert Hayward, *Los Angeles Times Book Review* (May 17, 1987): 1. **105** Michael Heaton, *Plain Dealer* (October 2, 1987). **106** Fred M. Hechinger, *New York Times* (October 6, 1987): 21. **107** Robert A. Herrera, unpublished essay, Department of Philosophy, Seton Hall University (1988). **108** Robert Hilburn, *Calendar/Los Angeles Times* (September 6, 1987):64. ***109** Michael W. Hirschorn, *Chronicle of Higher Education* (May 6, 1987):3. **110** Linda R. Hirshman, *University of Pennsylvania Law Review* 137 (November 1988):177. ***111** F. Russell Hittinger, *Intercollegiate Review* (Fall 1987):61. ***112** Bill Honig, *New Perspectives Quarterly* 4/4 (Winter 1988):36. **113** Sidney Hook, *American Scholar* (Winter 1989):123. **114** R. L. Houbeck, *Serials Librarian* 13 (1987):113. **115** *Insight* (May 11, 1987):8. **116** Russell Jacoby, *New Perspectives Quarterly* 4/4 (Winter 1988):30. **117** Harry V. Jaffa, *Interpretation* 16/1 (Fall 1988):111. **118** Jane Jeffries, *Uncommon Reader* [Henderson, Ky.] (Fall 1987):30. **119** Reed Jolley, *Eternity* (November 1987):46. **120** David Kagan, *Washington Times* (May 25, 1987):6M. **121** Kevin J. Kelley, *Guardian* [N.Y.] (November 4, 1987). **122** Christopher Kelly, unpublished essay, Dartmouth College. **123** Eugene Kennedy, *New York Times*, Education Life (August 2, 1987):XII, 34. **124** Hugh Kenner, *National Review* (October 9, 1987):37. **125** Charles R. Kesler, *American Spectator* 20/8 (August 1987):14. **126** James J. Kilpatrick, *Chicago Sun-Times* (August 23, 1987):13. **127** B. A. Kimball, *American Journal of Education* 96 (1988): 293. **128** Roger Kimball, *New York Times Book Review* (March 1987):7. **128** S. Klingber, *College and Research Libraries* 49 (1988):278. **129** Henry Klingeman, *National Review* (October 9, 1987): 41. **130** Claus Koch, *Die Zeit* 40 (September 25, 1987):68. **131** Alfie Kohn, *Psychology Today* 21 (August 1987):70. **132** Konstantin Kolenda, *Humanist* (September–October 1987). **133** William Kowal, *Congress Monthly* [American Jewish Congress] 55/4 (May–June 1988):10. ***134** William Kristol, *Wall Street Journal* (April 22, 1987):30. **135** Peter Augustine Lawler, *Modern Age* 32/1

(Winter 1988):27. **136** H. A. Lawson, *Quest* 40 (1988):12. **137** Thomas Leahey, *Cont. Psychology* 33 (1988):672. **138** William Lehmann, Jr., *Lutheran Education* (December 11, 1987). **139** Christopher Lehmann-Haupt, *New York Times* (March 23, 1987): 13. **140** Peter Levine, *Antaeus Report* [Ohio Wesleyan University] (November 1987). **141** S. Levy, *Hospital and Health Services* 33 (1988):139. **142** P. Loeb, *Psychology Today* 22 (1988): 59 **143** Loren Lomasky, *Reason* [Cato Institute] (December 1987): 37. **144** R. W. Lovin, *American Journal of Education* 96 (1988): 143. **145** Marjie Lundstrom, *Sunday World-Herald* [Omaha] (November 8, 1987):K, 1. ***146** Jeff Lyon, *Chicago Tribune Magazine* (November 27, 1988):X, 10. **147** John Lyon, *Mod andn Age* 32/1 (Winter 1988):30. **148** P. L. McClaren, *Harvard Educational Review*, 58 (1988):213. **149** Edwin McDowell, *New York Times* (November 17, 1987). **150** Jonathan R. Macey, *Cornell Law Review* 73 (July 1988):1038. **151** Jonathan R. Macey, *George Washington Law Review* 56 (1987):50. **152** John McFarland, *Faculty Association of California Community Colleges Bulletin* (October 1987):4. **153** Larry McGehee, *Fulton Daily Leader* (September 28, 1987):2. **154** Tibor R. Machan, *Georgia Journal* (Summer 1988):39. **155** Bill McLean, *Ann Arbor Scene Magazine* (November 1987):32. **156** William McWhirter, *Time* 132 (October 17, 1988):74. **157** Myron Magnet, *Fortune* 117 (February 1, 1988):86. ***158** Harvey Mansfield, Jr., *New Republic* (April 4, 1988):28. **159** Tycho Manson, *Maclean's* 100/30 (July 27, 1987):45. ***160** John Marcham, *Cornell Alumni News* (November 1987):27. **161** Jan Marejko, *L'Impact* (November 1987). **162** J. R. Martin, *New Republic* 198 (1988):41. **163** Martin Marty, *Context* (May 15, 1987). ****164** William R. Marty. **165** Roger Masters, *Interpretation* 16/1 (Fall 1988):139. **166** Bill Marvel, *Dallas Morning News* (July 10, 1988):F, 1. **167** George Frederic Mau, *Journey Magazine* [Lynchburg, Va.] (May–June 1988):6. ***168** Louis Menand, *New Republic* (May 25, 1987):38. **169** Jack Miles, *Los Angeles Times* (August 30, 1987):15. **170** Olivier Millet, *La Réforme* (January 16, 1988). **171** Kenneth Minoque, *Times Literary Supplement* [London] (July 24, 1987): 786. **172** Lee Mitgang, *Cleveland Plain Dealer* (June 21, 1987): 6-G. **173** Bernard Mitjavile, *Causa* (May–June 1987):38. **174** Thomas Molnar, *Modern Age* 32/1 (Winter 1988):35. **175** Ashley Montagu, *Chicago Sun-Times Bookweek* (April 26, 1987):13. **176** Marion Montgomery, *Modern Age* 32/1 (Winter 1988):39. **177** Geoffrey Moore, *Financial Times* [London] (July 11, 1987). ***178** Will Morrisey, *Interpretation* 16/1 (Fall 1988):145–156. **179** Steven C. Nahrwold, *Elkhart Truth* (1987). **180** V. Nell, *Reading Research Quarterly* 23 (1988):6. **181** Richard John Neuhaus, *Religion and Society Report* 4/9 (September 1987):8. **182** Harry Neumann, *Interpretation* 16/1 (Fall 1988):157. **183** W. R. Newell, letter to *New York Review of Books*, dated October 24, 1987. **184** W. R. Newell, unpublished essay, Department of Political Science, University of Nebraska at Lincoln. **185** *Newsweek* (April 20, 1987): 72. **186** *New Yorker* (July 6,

1987):81. *187 Walter Nicgorski, *Programma* [Program of Liberal Studies, Notre Dame University] (1988): 8. 188 Robert Nielsen, *Influence* (February–March 1988):8. 189 Michael Norman, *New York Times* (March 16, 1988):B6. 190 A. Norton, *University of Chicago Law Review* 55 (1988):458. *191 Martha Nussbaum, *New York Review of Books* 34/17 (November 5, 1987):20. 192 Dennis O'Brien, *Commonweal* 114/13 (July 17, 1987): 422. 193 Dennis O'Brien, *Economist* (May 16, 1987):94. 194 Delia O'Hara, *Chicago Sun-Times* (May 6, 1987). 195 Clifford Orwin, *Interpretation* 16/3 (Spring 1989). 196 George A. Panichas, *Modern Age* 32/1 (Winter 1988):4. 197 Barry Paris, *Carnegie* [Pittsburgh] (October 1, 1987):7. *198 Robert Pattison, *Nation* (May 30, 1987):710. 199 Marcel Peju, *Jeune Afrique* 1381 (June 24, 1987):48. 200 William Phillips, *Partisan Review* 60/1 (Winter 1988):11. 201 Ernest Pinson, *Jackson Sun* [Jackson, Tenn.] (November 8, 1987). 202 Michael Platt, unpublished essay, University of North Texas. *203 John Podhoretz, *National Review* (October 9, 1987):34. 204 Norman Podhoretz, *New York Post* (January 26, 1988). 205 Norman Podhoretz, *Weekend Australian Magazine* (July 4–5, 1987):8. 206 Peter R. Pouncey, *Amherst* 40/2 (Winter 1987):11. 207 Kevin Pritchett and G. C. Rivers, *Dartmouth Review* (June 1, 1988):10. **208 Pamela Proietti. 209 Juan Pedro Quinoncro, *ABC Literario* [Madrid] (April 11, 1987):4. 210 S. K. Reed, *People Weekly* 28 (September 14, 1987):141. 211 Henry Regnery, *Modern Age* 32/1 (Winter 1988):2. 212 *Res Publica* [Warsaw] (January 1988):145. 213 Patrick Reyntiens, *Spectator* (November 14, 1987):41. 214 George Richardson, *St. Louis Post-Dispatch* (June 3, 1987): "You" Section, 1. 215 David Rieff, *Times Literary Supplement* (September 4, 1987): 950. 216 Jeffrey Rodgers, *San Francisco Chronicle Review* (July 5, 1987): 1. 217 D. Roediger, *Monthly Review* 40 (1988):22. *218 Richard Rorty, *New Republic* (April 4, 1988):28. 219 Bernard Rosenberg, *Dissent* 35 (Spring 1988):223. 220 Eric Roussel, *Tribune Médicale* 218 (April 25, 1987):62. 221 Marie-Cécile Royen, *La Cite* (May 2, 1987):18. 222 Claes G. Ryn, *Modern Age* 32/1 (Winter 1988):45. 223 A. P. Sanoff, *U.S. News and World Report* (May 11, 1987, and September 28, 1987) 102:78. 224 Glenn N. Schram, *Christianity Today* 31/17 (November 20, 1987):67. 225 Mary Beth Searles, *Daily Northwestern* (May 1988). 226 Greg Sheridan, *Australian Weekend Magazine* (July 25–26, 1987):1. 227 Robert Skidelsky, *New Society* 84 [U.K.] (April 29, 1988):28. 228 Michael Skube, *News and Observer* [Raleigh] (June 7, 1987):1-D. 229 A. Smith, *Esquire* 108 (December 1987). **230 Gregory B. Smith. 231 Joseph Sobran, *National Review* 39 (April 24, 1987):51. 232 L. R. Sorenson, *Politics and the Life Sciences* 6 (1988):2115. 233 Raphael Sorin, *L'Air du Matin* (May 4, 1987). 234 *Der Spiegel* 10 (March 7, 1988):252. *Der Spiegel* 15 (April 11, 1988):237. 235 S. Frederick Starr, *Washington Post Book World* 17/16 (April 19, 1987):1. 236 Jerry Stockdale, *Davidson Update* (November 1987):10. 237 Chuck Stone, *Capital Times* [Madison] (April 13, 1988). 238

Robert L. Stone, *Essays on* The Closing of the American Mind (Chicago Review Press, 1989). **239** Cushing Strout, *Cornell Alumni News* (November 1987):33. **240** Georges Suffert, *Le Figaro* (March 24, 1987):2. **241** Georges Suffert, *Le Figaro Magazine* 13242 (March 28, 1987):19. **242** Andrew Sullivan, *New Republic* (October 26, 1987). **243** Andrew Sullivan, *Public Interest: Summer Books* (Summer 1987):129. **244** Anne Summers, *Australian Financial Review* (July 17, 1987). **245** Maureen P. Taylor, *Michigan Law Review* 86 (May 1988):1135. **246** William L. Tazewell, *Virginia Pilot and Ledger Star* (May 3, 1987). **247** T. Teachout, *Commentary* 85 (1988):69. **248** Bart Testa, *Toronto Globe Mail* (August 15, 1987). **249** B. Thompson, *Library Journal* 113 (1988):6. **250** Eva M. Thompson, *Modern Age* 32/1 (Winter 1988): 52. **251** William Thorsell, *Report on Business Magazine* [Toronto] (October 2, 1987). **252** Stephen J. Tonser, *Modern Age* 32/1 (Winter 1988):57. **253** Jean-Marie Trimbour, *Le Republicain Lorrain* (April 3, 1987). **254** Hans E. Tuetsch, *Feuilleton Roman* 179 (August 6, 1987):20. ***255** John Van Doren, *Paideia Bulletin* 3/5 (November–December 1987):1. **256** J. P. Vangigch, *Systems Research* 5 (1988):180. **257** Richard Vigilante, *National Review* 39 (October 9, 1987):34. **258** Herbert von Borch, *Feuilleton Roman* (June 21, 1988). **259** Joerg von Uthmann, *Frankfurter Allgemeine Zeitung* (April 1988). **260** Richard C. Walls, *Creem* [Los Angeles] (March 1988):46. **261** J. Walsh, *Science* 237 (1987):1100. **262** Mark Weiner, *Stanford Daily* (April 21, 1988):7. **263** Jacob Weisberg, *Washington Monthly* 19 (September 1987):49. **264** Robert Weisberg, *Stanford Daily* (April 21, 1988):5. **265** C. E. Wells, *University of Chicago Law Review* 55 (1988):363. **266** George F. Will, *Washington Post* (July 30, 1987):A-19. **267** Thomas G. West, *Claremont Review of Books* 6/1 (Spring 1988):1. **268** C. G. Wilbur, *Academe* 74 (1988):6. **269** Ronald J. Willy, unpublished essay, Marquette University. **270** John B. Witchell, *Presbyterian Record* (June 1988):35. **271** Alan Wolfe, *Partisan Review* (January–March 1988):155. **272** Gregory Wolfe, *Hillsdale Review* 8/3 (Fall 1986 [sic]):1. **273** Robert Paul Wolff, *Academe* (September–October 1987):64. **274** Robert Wood, unpublished address to Wesleyan University, Middletown, Conn., September 25, 1987. **275** Edmond Wright, *Contemporary Review* (October 1987):221. ***276** Richard L. Wright, *Journal of Negro Education* 57/1 (Winter 1988):119. **277** D. Wrong, *New York Times Book Review* 93 (April 19, 1988):1. **278** R. V. Young, *Fidelity* (January 1988): 44. ***279** Frank Zappa, *New Perspectives Quarterly* 4/4 (Winter 1988):26. ****280** Michael Zuckert, paper presented at symposium, "The Modern University—from Bologna to Bloom," held at Rhode Island University, March 1988. **281** L. S. Zwerling, *Choice* 25 (Summer 1987):189. **282** L. S. Zwerling, *Choice* 25 (September 1987):189.